D1161485

THE
POST-SOVIET
NATIONS

Studies of the Harriman Institute

Columbia University

THE POST-SOVIET NATIONS

Perspectives on the Demise of the USSR

Alexander J. Motyl, EDITOR

COLUMBIA UNIVERSITY PRESS

New York

Columbia University Press
New York   Oxford
Copyright © 1992 Columbia University Press
All Rights Reserved

Casebound editions of Columbia University Press books are Smyth-sewn
and printed on permanent and durable acid-free paper

Library of Congress Cataloging-in-Publication Data

The Post Soviet nations : perspectives on the demise of the USSR/Alexander
    J. Motyl, editor.
    p. cm.
    Includes bibliographical references and index.
    ISBN 0-231-07894-3
    1. Nationalism—Soviet Union.   2. Soviet Union—Ethnic relations.
3. Minorities—Soviet Union.   4. Soviet Union—Politics and government—
1985–1991.   I. Motyl, Alexander J.
DK33.P65   1992   92–17109
947.085′4—dc20   CIP

Printed in the United States of America
c 10 9 8 7 6 5 4 3 2 1
p 10 9 8 7 6 5 4 3 2 1

LIBRARY
ALMA COLLEGE
ALMA, MICHIGAN

Studies of the Harriman Institute
Columbia University

T HE Harriman Institute, Columbia University, sponsors the Studies of the Harriman Institute in the belief that their publication contributes to scholarly research and public understanding. In this way, the Institute, while not necessarily endorsing their conclusions, is pleased to make available the results of some of the research conducted under its auspices.

Contents

Preface

THIS volume is transitional. And like all transitional things, it partakes of two realities, one that was and one that is about to be. Its appearance is marked by the closing of one era of Soviet politics and the ushering in of another. And just as the Soviet Union could never be the same after perestroika, so, too, Soviet studies must change fundamentally in order to keep up with its elusive subject. This book exemplifies the ongoing transition—and bears witness to all its hopes and problems—that Soviet studies is experiencing as the former Soviet Union attempts its own transition.

The culprit is, of course, Mikhail Sergeevich Gorbachev. His reforms and, mostly, the unintended consequences thereof transformed, if not indeed destroyed, the Soviet totalitarian state. In so doing, they also destroyed traditional Sovietology. For regardless of how the aftermath of perestroika turns out, Sovietology—or is it post-Sovietology?—will be in need of massive restructuring. Assumptions have to be abandoned, answers have to be revised, questions have to be reformulated. Although the outcome of such a professional perestroika is still uncertain, one of the central intellectual foci of a restructured Sovietology is sure to be the post-Soviet nations and their new states, which have asserted themselves as the key actors in the drama that is the USSR's transformation. The message of this book is, thus, simple: bona fide Sovietology ignores what used to be known as the "Soviet nationality question" at its own peril. The practices of the past, when the non-Russians could be ignored as nonissues, will no longer do. Too much has changed in center-periphery relations for the "nationalities" to be consigned to a scholarly ghetto.

Eleven distinguished Sovietologists, whose accumulated professional expertise represents more than two centuries of Sovietology, have accepted the intellectual challenge of overcoming the isolation of the non-Russians by integrating the post-Soviet nations into their areas of interest. Of necessity, their contributions are historical and reflective: historical, because now more than ever current developments in the former USSR can be understood only in the context of the past; and reflective, because the uncertainties of the present can be overcome best by individuals with the expertise and perspective that only many years of scholarly activity can provide.

This volume, then, is an attempt both to close certain lacunae as well as to take the first step on the long and arduous road to creating a Sovietology that is as new as the Soviet Union has already become. As the former periphery becomes central and the former center becomes increasingly peripheral, a multipolar Commonwealth of Independent States—or whatever the entity or entities that ultimately succeed the current system are called—will demand that Soviet studies transform itself into some variant of nationality studies. Although such a transformation, as I suggest in the concluding essay, will necessitate additional conceptual and theoretical restructuring of the profession, an important step toward bridging the intellectual gap between center and periphery will already have been taken by the contributors to this volume. In demonstrating that just as the Soviet parts must be understood with reference to the whole, so, too, the whole must be viewed with reference to its parts, the authors have set an example that cannot be ignored.

They accomplish this task by illustrating how nationality issues suffused all aspects of the formerly Soviet polity, economy, and society. Their topics speak for themselves: Gregory Gleason on the historical development of Sovietology, Walker Connor on nationality policy, Ronald J. Hill on ideology, Neil Harding on legitimation, John N. Hazard on state and law, Mark R. Beissinger on elites, Amy Knight on the political police, Theodore H. Friedgut on participation, Zvi Gitelman on modernization, Richard E. Ericson on economic structure, and Walter D. Connor on class.

As readers will notice, the authors are explicitly *not* concerned with providing new empirical findings on the post-Soviet nations. Rather, their primary goal is to incorporate the nationality dimension into Sovietology and in this manner to contribute to the perestroika of a scholarly pursuit that has largely ignored the "non-Russians" in its fascination with Russia. But the authors attain two other goals as well. First, by integrating the nationality question into the Soviet sytem, they are transforming the post-Soviet nations from ethnographic categories into political actors—a shift very much in keeping with the enhanced political role of those nations during and after perestroika. Whatever slim justification there may have been for focusing largely on non-Russian language and culture in the pre-Gorbachev period has surely disappeared in a time of imperial disintegration and republican independence.

And second, by explicitly exploring the relationship between ethnicity and such classic political science concepts as elites, coercion, participation, political economy, and modernization, the authors are actively facilitating Sovietology's own transformation into a subfield of comparative politics. As the Soviet Union's successor states shed their totalitarian traits and become "normal," Sovietologists will have little choice but to recognize that their foci of interest closely resemble those of other countries and that theory and comparison, which remained foreign to Soviet studies for most of its earlier existence, are consequently imperative.

Effecting a perceptual transformation and facilitating a professional one are a tall agenda for what I have defined as a transitional volume. At this stage of Sovietology's development, however, providing the right answers is less important than asking the right questions and operating with more useful assumptions. This the authors do. And, as readers will surely note, they often provide what are probably the correct answers as well. Most important perhaps, what the authors unquestionably accomplish is to impel readers to reconsider the former Soviet Union—and by extension Sovietology—and, thus, to approach it from the perspective of the intellectual requirements of tomorrow rather than of yesterday.

It is to the authors that I extend my most sincere thanks. Not only are their contributions of the excellence that we have come to expect of them, but also their willingness to embark on so demanding a project is testimony to their adventurous, inquisitive, and imaginative spirits. I also thank Robert Legvold, Director of The W. Averell Harriman Institute for Advanced Study of the Soviet Union, Marshall Shulman, Director emeritus of the Harriman Institute, and Seweryn Bialer, Director of the Research Institute on International Change, for their unflagging support of the Nationality and Siberian Studies Program in general and of this project in particular. Special gratitude is due Kate Wittenberg of Columbia University Press and Charles F. Furtado, Jr., Program Secretary. Finally, I thank the Mellon Foundation, without whose generosity, foresight, and dedication to scholarship neither the Program nor this book would have been possible.

Alexander J. Motyl
New York City
February 1992

THE
POST-SOVIET
NATIONS

1. The "National Factor" and the Logic of Sovietology

Gregory Gleason

I T was fashionable some seventy-five years ago to speak in terms of what was taking place in Russia and its borderlands as the "Great Soviet Experiment." The leaders of the Bolshevik Revolution had taken the reins of power into their hands, but their political control over society was far from consolidated. There was an air of indeterminancy about the whole enterprise. At the same time, there was a passionate confidence among the Bolshevik leaders that they were on the path to a brave new communist future. They paid little heed to the fact that Karl Marx's utopian doctrines, although exhaustively written about and debated, had never been tested in practice. What the Bolsheviks feared most was that the grand experiment would never have a chance, that it would be overwhelmed by hostile foreign powers or subverted by internal opponents even before it got underway.

The Bolsheviks anticipated the establishment of a rationally man- aged society in which man's inhumanity to man would be eliminated, in which economic exploitation would be replaced by cooperative production, in which individual citizens would demand from society only what was needed and would freely give to society all that their abilities would permit. Most important of all, the Bolsheviks foresaw a society in which national discord and enmity would be overcome finally and irrevocably. They expected that the new society would create an unprecedented intellectual cosmopolitanism. A "proletarian internationalist" consciousness would eliminate the ethnic strife that beleaguered so many European societies and that earned the Tsarist empire the derogatory epithet "Prison of Nations." The newly created "socialist man" would find freedom not in cherishing ethnic diversity, but in celebrating his essential commonality with his proletarian coun- terparts, his "comrades."

To many contemporary observers surveying the situation, the uto-

1

pian ideals of the Great Experiment seem less like misguided but well-meaning illusions than tragic and cruel hoaxes.[1] The Soviet experiment would not only fail to eliminate national enmity and strife, but also would itself eventually become the victim of ethnic disputes. By the late 1980s, competing and conflicting nationalist strivings had brought the process of political and economic reform to an impasse. Gorbachev's ambitious perestroika reform program was foundering on the shoals of age-old ethnic animosities while the much-heralded creation of Soviet socialism—"the new historical community of the Soviet people"—was fragmenting into dozens of proud, ambitious, and fearful nations. The "national factor" had become the determining aspect of "post-Soviet" economics, politics, and society.

The contemporary reorganization of the USSR and the political realignments that are sure to follow will no doubt reshape the political maps of Europe, Asia, and the Middle East. Developments in the former USSR, accordingly, are of the utmost importance not just to Sovietologists but also to the entire world. In times of peace, a political reorganization of this scale is without precedent. Uncertainties abound; the past is surely prologue. It is doubtful that we can comprehend the changes awaiting us without clearly understanding the role of the national factor in bringing about the end of the Soviet Union. The present volume represents the results of a research project directed by Alexander Motyl under the auspices of Columbia University's W. Averell Harriman Institute for Advanced Study of the Soviet Union. The goal of the project—and of this volume—is to illuminate the processes of change in the USSR through a systematic analysis of the main thematic determinants of the national factor in the Soviet Union.

If the reorganization of the USSR offers practical challenges to citizens and policymakers, it also offers social scientists an exceptionally rich laboratory for testing basic theories of political change and development. Societies within the former USSR have returned to the most fundamental questions of political, economic, and social theory: Who governs? How should property be defined? How should wealth be distributed? How should social burdens be shared? The present situation is perhaps as close as civilization may come to what theorists call an "initial condition." My purpose in this introductory essay is twofold. First, I offer an explanation of why the field of comparative communist studies has emphasized the particular features of political development in the USSR that are reflected in the nationality themes explored in this volume. Second, I analyze some of the inherent capabilities and limitations of Sovietology as we seek to adapt the research tools and methods of social science to the demands of the changing contemporary circumstance.

Beyond Nationalism and Back Again

The irony of the nationalist resurgence in the USSR is that, according to Marxist-Leninist ideology, the solution to the "national question" was supposed to be the most important and enduring contribution of the establishment of a socialist order.[2] Karl Marx reasoned that nationalism was a passing phenomenon logically tied to another passing phenomenon, capitalism. Just as capitalism would be transcended, nationalism—and perhaps even ethnic identity itself—was destined to disappear into what Marx called "the waste heap of history." Marx claimed that the nation was a product of economic relations fostered by capitalism. When capitalism was replaced by socialism, the nation-state would wither and disappear as well. Declaring in his *Communist Manifesto* that "national differences were losing their significance" and that the "working man has no country," Marx urged the workers to hasten the downfall of the bourgeois governments of Europe and to abandon the feelings of national loyalty that gave legitimacy to those governments."[3] He might just as well have insisted that the "working man has no nation; that the Polish worker is not a Pole, that the Lithuanian laborer is not a Lithuanian, that the Turkic 'rabotnik' is not a Turk." In Marx's thinking, communism would represent a new historical stage that would carry society far beyond nationalism.

Marx's concepts were mainly theoretical. Vladimir Lenin, the founding father of the Soviet state, brought these ideas into practice.[4] Like Marx, Lenin looked forward to a world where nations—that is, the cultural communities of individuals who saw themselves as a common closely knit and naturally related group such as Poles, Germans, Tatars, Russians, and so on—did not matter. And like Marx, Lenin thought that nationalism would disappear in the new socialist order. But unlike Marx, Lenin succeeded in bringing the theoretical doctrines of Marxism into practice in the real world. To achieve his practical goals, Lenin was forced to make theoretical compromises. Although the theoretical Lenin had always been an opponent of federal arrangements, the practical Lenin, once he found himself in power, saw that the Bolshevik experiment faced overpowering odds unless he could garner the support of nationalist leaders in the borderlands of the crumbled Tsarist empire. Hence, in the early days of Soviet power, Lenin made a "tactical compromise" that gave official sanction to the idea of "national-statehood" in exchange for political support. Some observers locate the source of the contemporary travail of the Soviet state in the structural consequences of this "Leninist compromise." As Dias Valeev vividly expressed it, "the incompatibilities among groups, formalized in the [Soviet] Constitutional structure, were land mines buried in the 1920s at the very foundation of our government. Now they have begun to explode."[5]

The Soviet Union that Mikhail Gorbachev inherited nearly seven decades after Lenin's compromise contained within it all the contradictory pressures that the original Leninist bargain was designed to resolve. Gorbachev set out on an ambitious effort to rehabilitate Soviet socialism by reorganizing the Soviet administrative system, to breathe life into the moribund economy, and to revivify the indolent socialist worker. Gorbachev's program, however, failed rather spectacularly to achieve its economic objectives. The reform's meager success gave new meaning to the ancient dictum that the "only thing more difficult than revolution is reform." In successive stages of perestroika, the economic reforms fell short of their goals.[6] As they did, Gorbachev turned to increasingly more bold measures. In this step-wise, escalating fashion, the reform grew into a revolution.

Even as the efforts at economic reform proceeded, Gorbachev found himself faced with swelling pressures to reorganize the political and economic structures to accommodate the ethnic and social diversity of the Soviet Union. Harkening back to the Constitutional guarantees dating from the Leninist compromise, the most influential of the nationalist groups began to claim the rights granted to them by virtue of their status as "Soviet republics." In the fall of 1988, the Estonian republic declared "sovereignty," claiming control over the land and assets located on its territory. Other republics soon followed suit. By the end of 1990, each of the fifteen republics of the USSR had claimed sovereignty. Nationalist ferment swept the Union of Soviet Socialist Republics into the final phase of the "Great Experiment."

Once the process of disintegration began, it accelerated quickly. A "war of laws" between central and republican officials ensued. In an ascending spiral of local assertiveness, the republics began insisting on new prerogatives and new guarantees from the central Soviet government. In desperate political maneuvering to circumvent the dismemberment of the USSR, Gorbachev proposed the creation of a reorganized structure that he called a "renewed Union." A country-wide referendum was held in March 1991 to determine whether the Union should be retained in its then current form. Following the referendum, a decentralized plan for the establishment of a "Union of Soviet Sovereign States" was announced. But on the eve of the signing of the "Union Treaty," the abortive August coup of 1991 sent debilitating shock waves through the shaky political structure. At this critical juncture, the meager remaining moral authority of the central government collapsed. Gorbachev's Moscow government was restored to legal authority only by a voluntary agreement of the leaders of the republican governments. In the aftermath of the coup, political coalitions frantically regrouped under the banner of nationalist movements.

Following the August coup, the ethnically based republics replaced the "center" as the linchpin of the Soviet system. With the withdrawal of the Baltic states, Georgia, and Ukraine from the Union, the USSR, in a certain sense, ceased to exist. The "Hammer and Sickle period" of Soviet socialism—with its insistence on the common political consciousness of the "working class" regardless of national or ethnic background—came to an end. In its stead, the idea of ethnically based national unity re-arose as the basic legitimizing force of the successor states. The original meaning of the Latin concept of the state as a *"res publica"*—a "thing of the people"—replaced the communist party as the leading and guiding force in the societies of the USSR. It appeared that the great clash of "isms" yielded a new situation; nationalism would now rule in the wake of communism. The Soviet Union had attempted to go beyond nationalism to communism. With the collapse of communism, nationalism was back again.

The patchwork of ethnographic and administrative structures made the development of traditional constituencies problematic and the formation of effective new coalitions difficult. The republics that chose to remain in the Union emerged as the basic political constituents of the new system. Since their legitimacy was supplied by the Leninist compromise that granted them recognition in terms of "national statehood," the federal principle itself became not the solution to problems but the very source of difficulties.[7] Since the titular national groups of republican status owed their claim to legitimacy to the principle of national self-determination, their political dominance within the Union was challenged by other national minority groups who had equally legitimate but frequently contrary claims. Some ethnic and national communities that had been virtually eliminated by the homogenizing effects of decades of Marxist-Leninist assimilationism now rebounded to life with even more vitality than they had possessed before the Revolution. Some groups that did not even exist as national entities before the Bolshevik Revolution now claimed that the principle of national self-determination guaranteed them the right to political independence. Amid these conflicting nationalist claims and the resulting political tug-of-war, only one conclusion was widely accepted: nationalism had vanquished communism.

One "National Question" or Many?

The conclusion that we may be tempted to draw from the sequence of events in the USSR is that something called "nationalism" has replaced communism. There is a sense that now that we have a word—even better, an "ism"—to explain what has happened in the USSR, we can draw into clear comprehension the processes of transformation in the former East Bloc and the USSR. Furthermore, there is an expectation that since all the stable, democratic governments of the developed world passed through nationalist revolutions, the nationalist revolutions in the USSR represent a difficult but necessary stage in the natural transformation of these countries toward the essentially European forms assumed to be their final destination. The progression seems clear: diversity, nationalism, national self-determination, democracy, and human freedom.

As psychologically reassuring as this interpretation might be, it would be a great mistake to place the societies of the USSR on such a presumed continuum of political development. In the first place, even though social scientists are often accused of failing to think historically, only someone in the grip of complete historical amnesia could fail to appreciate that the nationalist strivings in the USSR possess as much potential for harm as for good. Moreover, from the point of view of explaining the past and being able to anticipate the future, it is important to note that nationalism is not a single cause. Nationalism is not an "ism" as such. It is not an integrated set of propositions about the nature, values, and processes of society in the way that, for instance, communism, socialism, or capitalism are.[8] Nationalism, in its historical development, emerged as a confluence of many factors. It represents an aspiration for two separate and not always compatible freedoms, one collective, the other individual. In its collective aspect, nationalism represents a yearning for a cultural community—a nation—itself to be free from the domination of other states or nations. In its individual aspect nationalism is the yearning of the individual for the freedom to be a member of the nation of his or her choice. But to point to "nationalism" as the cause of any particular event is to mask a vast complexity of causal relationships. We are ill-prepared to understand the Soviet collapse or to comprehend what will follow if we do not appreciate the diversity of forces that brought this situation about.

There were many different roots of the nationalist resurgence in the USSR. The nationalist resurgence, to begin with, is a consequence of a series of specific shortcomings of Soviet-style socialism. The economic theory behind Soviet-style socialism made three key assumptions.[9] First, it was assumed that a centrally organized, rationally managed economy could be designed to satisfy human needs. Second, it was assumed that individual rewards could be disassociated from social contribution. And third, it was assumed that the transformation of virtually all private property into public, commonly held property would eliminate the psychology of human acquisitiveness. On all three counts, these assumptions proved unwarranted. The centrally planned economy produced not rationally managed prosperity but only the bureaucratic allocation of scarcity. Second, the idealistic assumption of voluntary collectivism simply failed to take into account prevailing tendencies of human psychology and the dilemmas of collective action. In theory, this utopian assumption made for interesting Marxist philosophizing, but in the real world of the Soviet administrative system it resulted in the society-wide institutionalization of opportunistic behavior and free-rider problems.[10] And finally, the assumption of the possibility of holding all property in common only led back to a truth that has been well understood at least since the classics, namely that "that property which is common to the greatest number has the least care bestowed upon it."[11]

On the level of more practical affairs, the Soviet collapse represents a failure of particular public policy instruments of the Soviet system. It indicates, for instance, a failure of coalition politics. It marks a failure of reliance upon distant rather than local political and economic control. It reflects a failure of the Soviet effort at constructing a

regionally specialized and integrated economy with consciously designed trade complementarity and economies of scale. It means the
failure of assimilationist policies that, paradoxically, reinforced national identification even as they perpetuated and exacerbated racial
discrimination. And it marks the failure of the presumption of ideological omniscience that undergirded a one-party system.

The Soviet collapse also represents a step in the process of decolonization. And, as typical liberation politics, the process of decolonization engages natural mechanisms of response to what is essentially
foreign domination. Traditional Marxist explanations of "national liberation" stressed that class-based identification would overcome national identification. But on this count, the nineteenth-century roots of
Marxist theory are clearly apparent. Marxists failed to take into account
the pace of technological change and the socio-occupational restructuring that followed. In the modern world, classes have grown amor-
phous. Class-based politics, accordingly, have grown ambiguous. In
large industrial societies, the traditional socio-economically defined
classes were fragmented by cross-cutting cleavages. Since class-based
groupings ceased to unite interests, these groupings, as "a matter of
strategic efficacy," tended to disaggregate.[12] Under these circumstances, nationalist identity became the principal vehicle of political
mobilization.

Such an explanation offers insight into why so many of the nationalist movements in the USSR and Eastern Europe have former communist leaders at their forefront. Ambitious political leaders grew to
appreciate that appeals to proletarian unity had lost their power but
that the banner of national unity had grown even more popular than
it was before the communist period. Thus, while for many years there
was an impressive display of uniformity and singularity of opinion
among the communist leaders in countries of Eastern Europe, with the
sudden revolutionary political changes of 1989 a full spectrum of
political views emerged among these leaders almost instantaneously.
Some former leaders joined the "far right," while others joined the "far
left."

How do we explain these sudden conversions? Psychology tells us
that human beings do not so easily change their most fundamental
values and their deepest political convictions. This is especially true in
revolutionary times when high levels of uncertainty require that one's
instincts rather than calculations of interests serve as one's moral
compass. Participation of communists in the nationalist movements

might be explained by asserting that there had been "crypto-nationalists" lurking among the members of the communist party *apparat* all along. To some extent this is undoubtedly true. But how are we to explain the existence of the "crypto-centralists," that is those nationalists who still hold to the old order, *sans* ideology, even more than they apparently did before the collapse?[13]

One explanation of the crypto-centralist phenomenon is that an explicitly "Eurocentric" understanding of nationalism may have hindered our ability to comprehend the real nature of the many different kinds of coalitions a nationalist movement may conceal.[14] For example, many Western scholars and analysts, reasoning that the logical extrapolation of a nationalist movement was a separatist movement, naturally anticipated the rise of powerful "pan-Turkic nationalist" sentiment in the Central Asian republics.[15] Pan-Turkic sentiment appeared to have been fueled by the spread of Islamic fundamentalism in Iran, particularly after the Soviet invasion of Afghanistan in 1979. Indeed, the most often repeated explanation in the Western world for that Soviet military adventure was the purported fear in Moscow of nationalist contagion seeping across the USSR's southern border.[16] Using the conventional "models" of nationalism, it seemed quite plausible to explain the Soviet invasion and occupation of Afghanistan in terms of presumptions that Muslim fraternal unity linked the different groups of Central Asia against Moscow.

Events during the period of perestroika provided compelling evidence against this hypothesis, however. The contestation among groups within Central Asia was greater than that between Central Asia and Moscow. At the first Congress of People's Deputies in 1989, the Central Asian delegates became notorious for being the most "centrist." When Muscovites voted a bare minimum of support for the continuation of the USSR in the national referendum on the union in March 1991, voters in the key Central Asian republic of Uzbekistan voted virtually unanimously in favor of retention of the union.[17] The erosion of Moscow's party unity, central economic control, and the emergence of an anti-Moscow coalition among Central Asia's native groups quickly transformed the political landscape in Central Asia in ways not expected by those of us who thought in terms of the "nationalism versus communism" formula.

What these reflections suggest is that nationalism is not to be understood as a single development in the USSR and its neighbor-lands. The nationalist resurgence is a complex phenomenon involving the specific failures of the Soviet system, the social complexity of modern societies, and the political coalitions that formed during the Soviet period. Most important, the view that there was not simply one "national question" in the USSR also implies that there will not be one form of "nationalist resolution" to the problems inherited from the past. The trajectories of the national minorities of the former Soviet state are apt to be quite different.

In sum, there is not one "national question" in Russia and its neighborlands. There are many national questions. If, in the future, the various national communities of the region can be expected to assume political and economic structures that are less influenced by Marxist ideology and more influenced by local particularities, how capable will Sovietology be in providing insight into the unique features of these societies? Of course, the answer to this question lies in the robustness of our analytical methods. But to appreciate the methods that Sovietologists have used in the past, we should reflect briefly on the history of Sovietology—a field whose peculiar methods and interests emerged as products of unique circumstances.

The Roots of Sovietology

Only in a very limited sense was the Bolshevik Revolution successful in producing a qualitatively new society. But precisely to the extent that it was successful, the intellectual community of the Western world was not well-suited to understanding that new society. For the American intellectual of the time, John Reed's moving account of the Revolution and the ideas behind it, *Ten Days that Shook the World*, described a world that was as mysterious as it was dramatic. True, America did have a Russian emigré community that dated from before the revolutionary period. But by and large these people had left the travail of the old world with the intent of abandoning their old identity and assuming a new world identity as quickly as possible. They contributed little to building an American awareness of Russia. At the time of the Revolution, Russian language courses were offered at only a handful of American universities. What information existed about the eastern world of the Tsars was mainly of travelogue variety.

The emigrés that fled the Russian Revolution were of a different sort than their predecessors. Often people who had been forced for reasons of personal safety to leave their homeland, virtually all of them had suffered the loss of family, position, and property. Quite naturally, these emigrés were rarely favorably disposed to the Revolution's goals, let alone its means. It was this group that became the chief source of insight into the emerging eastern world during the 1920s.

Intellectual preparation in North America was also not up to the tasks of bringing the Soviet experiment into focus. The field of political science was still in its infancy, concerned mainly with questions of formal structure of governments and parliaments. The field of comparative economic systems had not yet been invented. Scholars' access to data on the Soviet Union was extremely limited, confined mainly to newspaper accounts or to what the Soviet foreign ministry distributed as part of its public relations campaigns. Moreover, in the 1920s and 1930s, a mood of isolationism discouraged much serious public reflection on foreign events, particularly in far-off Russia. The U.S. government's analytical capacity was based on the efforts of only a handful of specialists.[18]

By the late interwar period a few solitary figures with field experience and keen insight into the USSR began to emerge. Scholars such as Leonard Schapiro and Bertram Wolfe brought a sophisticated intellectual perspective, as well as their first-hand insight into the workings of the Soviet system, to bear on the Western academic community's approach to the USSR. But it was World War II that worked the most profound change in the way that Western scholars approached the Soviet system.[19] As a result of the war, America discovered a need for an analytical capacity to understand the intentions and capabilities of its adversaries. The Office of Strategic Services (OSS) established during the early years of the war was charged with analytical work that focused on the Third Reich but also considered the countries of Eastern Europe and, to some extent, the USSR. The specific methods developed in these years relied heavily on the analysis of written materials. These materials were limited in quantity and were instrumental in intent. A technique called "propaganda analysis" was worked out by the OSS analysts. The technique stressed the ability to "read between the lines" to discern the hidden agendas of the Nazi wartime broadcasts and news reports. A large cadre of talented emigrés and second-generation Americans with language capabilities was recruited into this work.

Sovietology as a field of study came into existence only in the late-1940s, following very closely in the shadow of the world war. Although the emergence of "two rival camps"—socialism and capitalism—had long before been proclaimed in Bolshevik rhetoric, in fact the great divide between East and West in practical terms came about only after the USSR's acquisition of the nuclear weapon. With that change, the USSR became a "superpower." In a practical sense, the U.S. defined the "West" with the policy of containment, the Marshall Plan, the Baruch Plan, and later with NSC-68, the U.S. government staff paper that articulated the basic principles of America's posture in the Cold War. Stalin was happy to play along with this game, for it offered him a rationale to consolidate his control over his own country and the countries of Eastern Europe.

In the late 1940s, America felt a need to further develop a capability to see into the society that was emerging as its rival. Private foundations stepped forward with support for the establishment of such institutions as the Russian Institute at Columbia University and the Russian Research Center at Harvard University. A generation of skilled area specialists who had cut their teeth in the OSS was drawn into the academy. Such talents as Vera Dunham, Barrington Moore, and Herbert Marcuse turned their attention to the scholarly interpretation of the Soviet enterprise.[20] These scholars brought with them an intimate knowledge of the cultures and histories of the peoples they studied. They also brought with them the methodologies they had helped devise in the days of wartime propaganda analysis. Under these circumstances, the art of "Kremlinology" developed. Scholarly attention turned toward the interpretation of Soviet political symbology through such means as scrupulous contextual analysis or the evaluation of hidden meanings in leaders' statements. The proficient Kremlinologist was someone who could tell you who was who, who was in Stalin's favor, and who stood next to whom on the dais at the May Day Parade. A good Kremlinologist could explain how the official ideology of the Soviet state, Marxism-Leninism, acted as a roadmap to guide the calculations of those in the Kremlin. Perhaps the best example of the methods and style of this period is represented in exegetical exercises like Nathan Leites's *The Operational Code of the Politburo*.

The Kremlinological approach prevailed in the field throughout the early 1950s. But with the USSR's launch of *Sputnik* in 1957, the Western world was shocked into a recognition that the USSR was on a new and palpably threatening course of development. Fearing the loss of American supremacy in science and technology, the U.S. Congress adopted a major educational package to revitalize academia and to prevent America from falling behind its rival. The National Defense Education Act primarily focused on efforts to improve America's research in basic science. But the NDEA also channeled support through Area Study Centers that it created at universities all around the United States. At the same time, a changing political environment made it possible for American scholars to begin conducting field research in the USSR with the official sanction of the Soviet government.[21] In the late 1960s academic exchange agreements were expanded and, on the American side, placed under one umbrella organization, the International Research and Exchanges Board. Similar educational and scientific exchanges were established on a bilateral basis between Canada and the USSR, England and the USSR, and France and the USSR.

The *détente* initiatives of the period between 1971 and 1973 included additional agreements on trade, technical exchanges, and cultural exchanges, further increasing opportunities for direct academic contact. As a result of these new opportunities, a new generation of scholars began to emerge. These were individuals who had been trained by the Kremlinologists but who were themselves emphasizing approaches that were the product of the behavioral revolution in social science.[22] During this period, the number of American students enrolled in Soviet area courses rose substantially.

By the mid-1970s, the great expectations of the early *détente* gave way to more pessimistic views of the Soviet Union's prospects for enduring change. Much of the intellectual excitement in the field waned. Younger scholars began to think of Sovietology as a backward and underdeveloped field that had been, in a word that was prominent in those days, "ghettoized." Many beginning graduate students were discouraged from concentrating on the USSR by advisers who scoffed at the idea that there even was such a thing as a Soviet-type economy or Soviet political system. The economies of the socialist East bloc countries, it was fashionable to observe, were neither socialist nor economies. Opportunities for field research during this period nevertheless remained at a high level. Large numbers of Canadian, American, and British linguists, historians, political scientists, and economists took advantage of the opportunity to conduct long-term research in the USSR.

With the increase in superpower tensions in the early 1980s following the Soviet invasion of Afghanistan, a new cycle of higher funding for Sovietology began as the U.S. Congress provided increased support for graduate and post-doctoral research and a number of private foundations sought to strengthen the field.[23] By this time the generation schooled in Kremlinological methods had given way to one more directly influenced by broad-gauged methodological approaches.[24] The scholars schooled in the Kremlinological method were already writing their memoirs. The mid-generation scholars were methodologically a more esoteric group. A new generation of "post-behavioral revolution" scholars was entering its productive years, trying to devise methodological approaches appropriate to a Soviet Union that had irreversibly broken with the old paradigm.

Sovietology and the Study of Nationality Relations

This sketch of the development of the Sovietological community suggests that Sovietology was very much a product of its times and not a product of the larger traditions of social science theory building. It is for this reason, critics assert, that Sovietology failed to anticipate the full implications of ethnic diversity within the USSR. Sovietology's concerns, its methods, the political orientation and training of its practitioners, critics charge, produced a systematic bias ill-suited to explaining, let alone predicting, the nationalist revolutions in the USSR.

Sovietology, say the critics, failed in four key respects. First, the inordinate emphasis on the implications of the fusion of the party and state in the Soviet Union produced a "state-centric" view of the entire society. This emphasis on the Soviet central government obscured a clear comprehension of the wider sociopolitical linkages in the system and, consequently, distorted the clear perception of the national factor. Second, Sovietology exaggerated the role of ideology to the extent of discouraging empirical research design. Sovietology, consequently, contributed little to social science theory building other than the totalitarian model. Third, the critics say, Sovietology was guided by a political agenda closely tied to the foreign policy purposes of Western governments. The field, accordingly, was given to exaggerating both the moral failures and the material prowess of Soviet society. Finally, critics claim that, from its inception, the field of Sovietology amounted essentially to "Russian studies," not Soviet studies.

It is undeniably true that the logic of Sovietology begins with the premise of the prominence of the state. Complete nationalization of the means of industrial production during the 1920s and the collectivization of agriculture carried out in the late 1920s and early 1930s put virtually all the resources of the society in the hands of the state. In the process, political and economic control over the society was fused. During the 1930s this process was extended in fits and starts to what might be called the social-psychological sphere of the society. Social pluralism was replaced by social monism. The response of the most significant early Western scholarship was to describe this concentration of power in the state in terms of the "totalitarian syndrome."[25] For decades, this model served as a departure point for virtually all research on the USSR, even research that was critical of the model.

Sovietology's peculiar conception of the role of the state set researchers off in directions quite unlike that of their colleagues working in other geographical areas.[26] Latin Americanists were debating issues of the role of the state, the interplay of the "autonomous state" with social movements, or the role of elites or land tenure patterns in strengthening the state. But the emphasis was on the interaction between state and society.[27] Meanwhile, Africanists were analyzing the minimal capacities and limited horizons of Africa's "soft states." Asianists were divided into separate groups. One group, emphasizing Japan, conceived of the state primarily as an agent of mobilization and a catalyst of change.[28] The other group, emphasizing China, comprehended the contemporary state as the product of modern ideas set in the context of ancient cultural traditions.[29] Europeanists were concerned with interest formation and the impact on the state of structural differentiation within societies.[30] Americanists saw the role of the state as basically a question of federal relations. In the approaches of all of these fields, the relationship between state and society was a subject of question. For Sovietologists, in contrast, the state's primacy was a given. Since power is a zero-sum commodity, if the state were strong, the national groups could not be.

It is also true that Sovietology was the least empirical of the various branches of area studies research. The dominance of the state in Sovietological research was undergirded by the fact that the Soviet state had not only a claim to power by virtue of its capacity, but also a theoretical rationale for its primacy, namely, Marxist-Leninist ideology. The ideology insisted that nationalism could not long continue to be a force. Consequently, Soviet policymakers expended great efforts to assure that what was projected in the official ideology was realized in life. Soviet nationality policy was essentially anti-nationality policy. For Sovietologists, then, precisely to the extent that the ideology continued to have relevance for Soviet policymakers, nationalism could not.

The dominance of the state also restricted the amount of information that was available to Western students of the USSR.[31] Statistics—in the original meaning of the term, "state mathematics"—were carefully controlled by the Soviet state. Western scholars had little direct insight into public preferences provided by survey research. Opinion polls played little role in the USSR since workers' consciousness was supposed to be a function of party activities, not the other way around. Central newspapers were carefully censored. Those newspapers relatively less restricted by the censors were not available. Newspapers of the local (*oblast* and *raion*) levels, for instance, were not permitted to cross Soviet frontiers. In the absence of hard data, most research on nationality questions ended up exploring little more than Soviet ethnographic discussions.

It is also true that the emphasis on ideology and the lack of empirical orientation limited Sovietology's contribution to the larger movements in social science. Sovietology's critics contend that the field is responsible for only one invention, the totalitarian model: a construct that proved useless to researchers in other fields with the possible exception of Chinese and Albanian studies. This criticism has to be taken seriously not because it points to an attitude of laxity on the part of Sovietologists but, just the opposite, because it suggests how different the nature of the work is from that done by Europeanists. Sovietologists were required to be not only analysts and theorists, but journalists as well. They were required to collect their own raw data, analyze it, decide on research strategies and then, in some sense, test their hypotheses. Sovietologists were often accused by colleagues in other fields of writing little more than "slow journalism." Sovietologists often found themselves dominated by descriptive work, trying to get the story right rather than to explain what it meant. Efforts to apply models such as interest group theory met with mixed success.

A third criticism of Sovietology is that, because of its background, its Kremlinological roots, its close connection with funding sources in Bonn, London, Paris, or Washington, the field developed an agenda that was either dictated by the policy community or, at minimum, closely paralleled that of the policy community. The basic institutions of the Sovietological community, in other words, were interwoven with the purposes of Western governments in a way that suggested the academic counterpart of a conflict of interest. The confluence of institutional interests that President Eisenhower labeled the "military-industrial complex" and that subsequent scholars have referred to as the institutions of the "national security state" acted to limit the scope of research questions that were of interest to Sovietologists.[32]

In response to this criticism it is important to note that, while government support for research on the USSR always played a greater role than it did, for instance, in research on the African countries, it is not clear that this support played any direct role in shaping the research agendas or the values of academic researchers. As the foregoing historical survey suggests, distinct generations of Sovietologists had very different backgrounds. These historical factors shaped the field's research interests more than conformance to institutional interests. To be sure, it is difficult for an individual to be involved in a superpower rivalry on the scale of the Cold War without experiencing a psychological propensity to dehumanize the opponent. But even if this criticism were true, it would suggest that scholars would have been more attuned to nationality problems, since presumably they would constitute one of the exploitable "weaknesses" of the Soviet system.

A fourth criticism of Sovietology was that it was really never Soviet studies to begin with; it was Russian studies. "At best, mainstream Sovietology is the study not of the Soviet Union but of specific areas of Russia," charged Alexander Motyl, "At worst, it is Kremlinology writ large."[33] There are two prominent interpretations of Motyl's critique. The first interpretation is that Sovietology saw the USSR only through the traditional "Moscow-centric" view and was therefore incapable of predicting the collapse of Soviet communism. A second interpretation of Sovietology is that Western analysts tended to see all the problems in the USSR from the Russian perspective and were therefore insensitive to the internal dynamics of the nationality regions.

It seems to me that those who hold to the first interpretation are mistaken. The charge that Sovietologists failed to anticipate the nationalist revolution is patently wrong. The articles in this volume provide ample testimony to the fact that the approaches of leading scholars have long emphasized the role of national relations in the USSR. In works such as Richard Pipes's *The Formation of the USSR*, the compromises and conflicts of the early Soviet nationality problem were masterfully chronicled. The work of writers such as John Armstrong, Robert Conquest, Teresa Rakowska-Harmstone, and Ann Sheehy prodded those Sovietologists who were working on other issues to remain mindful of the nationality question's continuing relevance. Particularly after the census returns of 1959 were published, revealing large population increases among some national groups, leading Sovietologists understood that national identity would be of increasing importance. Demographic shifts encouraged investigation of the implications of population for nationality relations.[34] Scholars such as Jeremy Azrael, John Dunlop, Darrell Hammer, Roman Szporluk, and Alexander Yanov devoted attention to the roots and implications of these problems, particularly with respect to the Russian majority's relations with minorities.[35] Although the coverage was not uniform, a good deal of work was done on some of the more obscure minority areas.[36]

The Soviet nationalist resurgence of the mid-1980s was more rapid and more influential than many expected, but it was seen by most specialists as an "inevitable" development rather than a surprising one. By the time Solzhenitsyn's article "How Are We To Reconstruct Russia?" appeared, with its argument for the reorganization of Russia in the form of a pan-Slavic state, the suggestion was taken seriously by Western Sovietologists. It was not dismissed as preposterous as his similar suggestion was two decades earlier.[37]

The second interpretation of Motyl's critique is, in my view, a correct one. This interpretation asserts that Western analysts tended to be insufficiently sensitive to the local determinants of change. There are many reasons why some Western, and particularly American, researchers underemphasized the importance of national minority groups in the USSR.[38] America is a melting pot. American conceptual approaches are basically integrationist. Although on a rhetorical level Americans maintain support for Woodrow Wilson's principle of "national self-determination," American policymakers have always been reluctant to act on this principle. For instance, when in the late 1960s Biafra attempted secession from Nigeria imploring American assistance, the U.S. government looked the other way without a moment's hesitation. Americans have simply not been well-disposed toward viewing nationality relations as more than "family matters." Moreover, the history of American political development since the nineteenth century has been a history of centralization. Americans naturally expected that other large countries would follow a similar evolution.

But arguing that a cultural vantage point influenced a pattern is more of an excuse than an explanation. From a methodological point of view, the more important criticism is that Sovietology did not do an adequate job of seeing what was taking place on the ground in the

USSR because it did not do an adequate job of equipping researchers with the tools needed to conduct the research. As James Critchlow observed, Sovietologists were too often "hypnotized by the symmetry of the all-Union and republican institutional structures into assuming that politics in the republics was merely a reflection of what was decreed by Moscow."[39] Critchlow's criticism points to a shortcoming in research methods and skills rather than a systemic failing of Sovietology as such. Despite their emphasis on the state, the approaches of the early generation of scholars such as Towster and Fainsod clearly stressed what Fainsod called the "facade of totalitarianism."[40] To see the real story behind the facade, Fainsod maintained, the researcher had to penetrate to the local level. Even the theorists of totalitarianism emphasized that although the state was powerful on the surface, the fact that it relied upon terror and coercion to induce popular compliance concealed an essential weakness, a weakness that could be appreciated only by clearly understanding processes at the local level. The writers of the interest-group approach and the school of institutional pluralism further emphasized the fissures in the system.[41] Writers in the first wave of the behavioralist reinterpretations such as Brian Silver stressed the importance of multinationality.[42] By the 1980s, scholars were describing and analyzing the extensive prerogatives of local officials, the process of "local power accretion," and the "local revolution" taking place in the Soviet system.[43] What the Sovietological community lacked—and still lacks—is a cadre of specialists who combine social science methodological skills with local area specialist skills.

The National Factor in Post-Communist Studies

In the past few years the situation in Russia and its neighborlands has changed very rapidly. The analytical ability to comprehend the internal dynamics of these processes of change is clearly as important as were the Kremlinological methods of four decades ago. But no clear method or comprehensive concept for understanding the profusion of national trajectories has yet emerged. Will Sovietology be replaced by nationality studies? Will Sovietology as a discipline be abandoned in favor of conventional disciplinary approaches? Researchers studying the European, North American, and Pacific rim countries, in which data are plentiful and access virtually unimpeded, make their contributions by pushing the frontiers of knowledge forward in narrowly defined fields of specialization. Can we expect a similar evolution for Sovietology?

Such an evolution might very well be the optimal course for the future development of Sovietology, but it is one unlikely to be taken, primarily because individual researchers work within the context of institutions that shape their behavior by structuring their incentives. For greater specialization to take place on a widespread scale, institutions would have to change accordingly. What are the prospects that this might happen?

There are essentially three types of institutions that have played a role in shaping the Sovietological community: the branches of the government analytical community; the "free-standing" research institutes; and the academic community. In the Sovietological sphere, the task of U.S. government agencies has always been to provide an analytical product directly to policymakers, not to shape public opinion or to provide information for the academic community. Not all Western governments have observed such a strict separation between government purposes and public purposes. Germany, for instance, has a system of institutes (*Stiftungen*) financed by the government but with sufficient operational autonomy for them to serve broadly defined public purposes as well as producing a product for policymakers. In contrast, the assumption in the U.S. that it is not the function of government to shape public opinion but to respond to it has limited the role that government analytical capabilities have played in shaping the direction of Sovietological research.[44]

A second category of institutions includes free-standing research institutions such as the Hudson Institute in Indianapolis, the Center for Strategic and International Studies in Washington D.C., and the Kennan Institute for Advanced Russian Studies, a branch of the Smithsonian Institution's Wilson Center for International Scholars. In addition to these research institutions, there are coordinating organizations such as the National Council on Soviet and East European Research, the International Research and Exchanges Board, and the Joint Committee on Soviet Studies of the Social Science Research Council. Particularly in recent years, these institutions played the leading role in shaping Sovietology. But the vitality of these institutions draws heavily from the academic community through their research grant programs for scholars. The permanent research staffs of these organizations are modest in size. The exception to this rule is the research staff of Radio Liberty and the newly created Research Institute of Radio Free Europe/

Radio Liberty. Radio Liberty's staff has long been a leader in the field of nationality studies.

A third category of institutions is the academic community. Following the passage of the National Defense Education Act in the U.S., a network of research institutes developed attached to universities. These include the Russian Research Center of Harvard University, Columbia University's Harriman Institute for Advanced Study of the Soviet Union, the joint UC Berkeley-Stanford Program on Soviet Behavior, Stanford University's Hoover Institution on War, Revolution and Peace, the UCLA-RAND Joint Program on Soviet Behavior, and Duke University's East-West Center on Trade, Investment and Communications. In addition, most of North America's major universities have research centers, such as the University of Toronto, the University of Washington, the University of Texas, the University of Illinois at Champaign-Urbana, and a score of others. There is also a small number of research institutes that are devoted to particular nationality groups such as Indiana University's Uralic-Altaic Center, Harvard University's Ukrainian Research Institute, and the University of Alberta's Canadian Institute of Ukrainian Studies.

The great bulk of fundamental research takes place under the auspices of these institutes. The continuing problem the academic community has in looking at the nationality picture is a consequence of the disciplinary divisions of colleges and universities. It is a simple problem easily explained by the rational-actor model. One need only consider the individual researcher's incentive structure. At academic research institutions professional advancement—indeed, professional preservation—depends upon the production of conventional scholarship within a discipline. Interdisciplinary journals such as *Soviet Studies, Russian Review,* and *Slavic Review* were the principal instruments of publishing research results. High-visibility journals such as *World Politics* sometimes featured Sovietological articles, but usually only those of interest to a wider readership. The refereed specialist journals in the disciplines are intensely competitive, sometimes with article acceptance rates of one in ten. These journals rarely have area specialists playing pivotal roles in the referee process. The leading economics, political science, and sociology journals tend to publish only theoretical work. Consequently, publishing purely descriptive material in the disciplinary journals is virtually impossible.

All major universities have research centers or committees devoted to Soviet studies, whether defined as Soviet, Slavic, or Russian studies.

But in virtually all cases professors' appointments are within the disciplinary departments. The internal decision-making process in anthropology, economics, geography, history, political science, and sociology departments relies basically on peer review. Peers generally view a scholar's work not on its brilliance in what they find to be a compact and impenetrable sub-speciality (e.g., Tuvinian economics) but by his or her contribution to the larger discipline. An economics faculty will typically be made up of ten to twenty people who specialize in things like mathematical models, savings rates, divorce, air traffic control, the restaurant industry, and so on. They often do not know much about the "Tuva republic" and, frequently enough, don't care to. Since these are the people who make the hiring, tenure, and promotion decisions, a competence in general economics always wins out over the ability to conduct the detailed study of the economics of a small and remote "national group" buried someplace in the USSR. Labor-intensive work in exotic languages and cultures is considered an avocation, and a foolhardy one at that. In other words, once out of graduate school, scholars tend to gravitate toward the mainstream. If they are comparativists, they tend to choose something big like "comparative price theory" or "Russia and Eastern Europe." They emphasize the extremely narrow niche of "non-Russian Sovietology" at their professional peril.

The basic problem of Sovietology as it comes to grips with the national factor is that the government agencies do not contribute directly to the field, the free-standing research institutions often rely upon academic researchers, and academic researchers only focus on extremely narrow specializations at the expense of their careers. At the same time, if the ranks of "post-Soviet Sovietologists" are filled with generalists, few will be capable of monitoring the low-level dynamics of change. What is the solution to this dilemma? When the problem is viewed in this way, three points seem particularly important. The first concerns the academic environment, the second concerns outlets for information in the field, and the third concerns the focus of Sovietological research.

With respect to the academic community, it is important to note that the best way to solve the problem of the "rational faculty member" is not to struggle vainly against the system of peer review. Rather, it is to continue to emphasize programs that will integrate research efforts and increase the incentives for selective specialization. Research institutes will need to stimulate team projects on particular research areas. The key shortcoming in the field is the lack of expertise in vernacular languages. As James Critchlow, for years an insider in policymaking continue ignoring the very existence" of information about autonomous political life within the non-Russian republics.[45] But it is futile to expect any one individual to acquire all the research skills necessary to command vernacular languages, Russian, and the methods of an advanced discipline. The natural sciences use collaborative research teams of specialists to solve the problem of integrating disciplines. The social sciences would benefit from adopting this model.

Substantial strides have already been made in solving the problem of outlets for specialized research. For many years research was sustained by less illustrious but critically important journals such as *Nationalities Papers* and the enormously useful *Radio Liberty Research Bulletin* (which was later renamed *Report on the USSR*). In the early 1980s the situation began to change with the creation of journals like *Central Asian Survey* and later, in 1990, the *Journal of Soviet Nationalities*. Still, the outlets for timely and important descriptive information on nationalities problems in the USSR remain limited.

Will the expansion of these institutional bases solve the problem of undercoverage of the national minorities? Certainly as the Soviet Union changes and the art of Kremlinology recedes into the background, the focus of Sovietology will broaden. As it does, some caveats regarding the focus of Sovietology should be borne in mind. First, if it is to understand the "national factor," Sovietology will need to be more mindful of concepts. There has been a Soviet nationality problem in the USSR, but there have not been any "Soviet nationalities." We need to begin thinking and talking in terms that do justice to the national diversity of the region. Second, the vernacular languages will need greater attention, but Russian-language expertise will continue to be a requirement for research. As Ronald Hill ironically notes in his contribution to this volume, the Russian language may now really become the *lingua franca* of the successor states. Third and finally, we need to unlearn some of the "bad habits" of Kremlinology. As every Sovietologist has discovered since glasnost appeared, it is no longer possible to cut out every interesting newspaper article from *Izvestiia*.

The National Factor, Soviet Dénouement, and the Future

At the time of the Russian Revolution of 1917, the Bolshevik leaders insisted that their great experiment represented a unique development in human civilization. They expected that their proposed society would usher in a new stage in world history. Today, after several decades of reflection on the Soviet experiment, many observers would agree that the social, economic, and political institutions of the Soviet period were indeed unique. But uniqueness of design is hardly a sufficient criterion for successful social and political institutions. By and large, observers of the experiment fall into four categories. The "historians" stress that political terror, decades of police-state repression, and the forced inculcation of an official ideology could not be expected to leave a benign legacy in any society. The "economists" stress that utopian communism ran counter to the laws of nature. Such a collectivist society with a centrally planned allocation of scarcity could only lead to free-rider problems and economic opportunism on a vast scale. The "politicists" aver that the historical record shows clearly that once the millennial phase of revolutionary ardor is exhausted, only the devices of a personalistic totalitarian dictatorship could manage to keep communist doctrine alive. In its "post-heroic phase," communism has never been successful in motivating people in the absence of a Tito, Stalin, Mao, or Fidel. Finally, the "nationalists" emphasize that the political and social structures of the Soviet period resulted in an "unnatural political community," one that could be expected, eventually, to unravel under the fissiparous forces of nationalist feelings.

The fact that the "Leninist tactical compromise" served as the cornerstone of the Soviet state clearly attests that nationalism played a pivotal role at the beginning of "the Great Soviet experiment." Just as surely, nationalism played a key role in the *dénouement* of the Soviet experiment. Pretensions and illusions of a Soviet multinational fraternity have now been abandoned. The "Hammer and Sickle period" of Soviet socialism is past. But the end of "hammer and sickle socialism" scarcely means that the area's inter-ethnic problems are solved. Such questions as relations between regional minorities and majorities, inter-ethnic language disputes, issues of "post-Soviet" political realignment, and the creation of structures for new commercial relationships all cry out for new solutions. If anything, the legacy of the Soviet period will make finding solutions to these problems more difficult. In virtually all of the Soviet neighborland regions, for instance, the Russian-speaking population, previously in the majority, now finds itself having swiftly acquired the status of a minority group. As some disgruntled former colonizers complain, they now find themselves, true to the Hegelian metaphor, in a situation in which the Master has become the Slave.

Under the prevailing conditions, crafting formulas that make it possible for the neighbors on the Eurasian continent to live together peaceably will not be easy. It is fortunate that the lessons of the authoritarian past remain so fixed in people's minds. Many people now agree that the only possible path to permanent solutions will be forms of voluntary compromise. And democratic institutions, whatever else their strengths and weaknesses, are above all forums for seeking such voluntary compromises. The contributions to the present volume offer a composite picture of the various aspects of the national factor that will shape this bargaining process. If the new "democratic experiment" in the USSR is to succeed in Russia and its neighborlands, the national factor will surely play a decisive role.

NOTES

1. Boris Yeltsin, for example, explained to an international television audience that the "tragic Soviet experiment" should have been conducted in a smaller country. See "Tragicheskii eksperiment kommunizma luchshe by provesti v malen'koi strane," *Izvestiia,* September 6, 1991, p. 1.

2. For a comprehensive treatment of national relations and Marxist theory, see Walker Connor, *The National Question in Marxist-Leninist Theory and Strategy* (Princeton: Princeton University Press, 1984).

3. Karl Marx and Friedrich Engels, *Ausgewählte Werke,* Vol. 1 (Berlin: Dietz Verlag, 1981), p. 435.

4. Lenin's works have been published in several editions in a number of languages. The authoritative, though still incomplete, Russian language edition is V. I. Lenin, *Polnoe sobranie sochinenii* (Moscow: Izdatel'stvo Politicheskoi Literatury, 1960–1965).

5. Dias Valeev, *Druzhba narodov* no. 11 (1989):181–182.

6. An analysis of the political economy of reform at an early point in the perestroika process may be found in Timothy J. Colton, *The Dilemma of Reform in the Soviet Union* (New York: Council on Foreign Relations, 1986). Also see Anders Aslund, *Gorbachev's Struggle for Economic Reform,* revised ed. (Ithaca: Cornell University Press, 1991); Jeremy Azrael, "Restructuring and the Polarization of Soviet Politics," Rand Report, N-3143, Rand Corporation, Santa Monica, CA (1990).

7. An early statement of this argument may be found in Teresa Rakowska-Harmstone, "The Dialectics of Nationalism," *Problems of Communism* 23(3) (May-June, 1974):1–22.

8. In fact, capitalism does not fit in this category very well either. It is interesting to note that "capitalism" is not a term used by Adam Smith or

David Ricardo. The term originally carried the meaning of a perjorative epithet along the lines of "plutocracy."

9. Adam Przeworski, "The "East" Becomes the 'South'? The "Autumn of the People" and the Future of Eastern Europe," *PS: Political Science and Politics* 24(1) (March 1991):20–24, at 22.

10. According to the theory of collective action, in a collectivist society a "rational" individual could be expected to rely on the efforts of others. "Rational" (that is, value maximizing) individuals in an egalitarian collectivist society will recognize that their contributions (that is, the products of their labors) as well as their benefits (that is, the amount that they withdraw from society) will be divided by the total number of individuals in the society. Since little proportionality exists between contribution and withdrawal, "rational" individuals will have an incentive to contribute less than the average contributor and withdraw more than the average beneficiary. Since each rational individual faces the same payoffs, the overall effect will be to ratchet the productivity of the society downward as each individual calculates how to maximize the withdrawal of benefits in the midst of this declining productivity. Moreover, the gloomy prognostication that follows from this model does not take into account the pernicious effects of social institutions that emerge when individuals find that, regardless of the level of their sacrifice, the level of benefit is directly related to personal access to those in a position of distributive authority. See Mancur Olson, *The Logic of Collective Action* (Cambridge: Harvard University Press, 1965). Also see Alexander J. Motyl, *Sovietology, Rationality and Nationality: Coming to Grips with Nationalism in the USSR* (New York: Columbia University Press, 1990), especially chapter 2.

11. Aristotle, *Politics* book 2, chapter 3.

12. Nathan Glazer and Daniel P. Moynihan, *Ethnicity: Theory and Experience* (Cambridge: Harvard University Press, 1975), p. 9.

13. For example, a discussion of how Islom Karimov, President of Uzbekistan, supported the GKChP (State Committee on the Extraordinary Situation—the August "putsch" committee), can be found in Valerii Vyzhutovich, "Ottseplennyi vagon," *Izvestiia,* September 13, 1991, p. 3.

14. The great influence of Hans Kohn and those who followed in his footsteps may have ironically had the unfortunate effect of encouraging many researchers to conceive of the general processes of nationalism in terms of the unique experiences of East European varieties of nationalism. See Hans Kohn, *The Idea of Nationalism: A Study in its Origins and Background* (New York: Macmillan, 1944).

15. See Alexandre Bennigsen, "Several Nations or One People? Ethnic Consciousness among Soviet Central Asians," *Survey* 24(3) (1979):51–64. Also see Alexandre Bennigsen and S. Enders Wimbush, *Muslims of the Soviet Empire* (Bloomington: Indiana University Press, 1986).

16. For a critical assessment of this thesis, see Martha Brill Olcott, "Soviet Islam and World Revolution," *World Politics* 34 (July 1982):487–504.

17. The referendum on the Soviet federal principle was held on March 17 in most of the USSR. In Uzbekistan, 9,830,782 ballots were counted. 9,196,848 voted in favor. Thus only about 6 percent of the votes were in favor of withdrawal from the union. The referendum returns were reported in *Sovet Ozbekistoni*, March 21, 1991.

18. The western world has grown accustomed to the size and scale of the national security community of the postwar period. A vivid account of the much more modest size of the capabilities of the American analytical capacity before the war can be found in George F. Kennan, *Memoirs* (Boston: Little, Brown, 1967).

19. For a vivid account of this period, see John Hazard, *Reflections of a Pioneering Sovietologist* (New York: Oceana Publications, 1984).

20. Vera Dunham, *In Stalin's Time* (Cambridge: Cambridge University Press, 1976); Barrington Moore, *Terror and Progress USSR* (Cambridge: Harvard University Press, 1954): Herbert Marcuse, *Soviet Marxism* (New York: Columbia University Press, 1958).

21. One of the first products of the early exchanges may be found in Jeremy Azrael, *Managerial Power and Soviet Politics* (Cambridge: Harvard University Press, 1966).

22. See Frederic J. Fleron, *Communist Studies and the Social Sciences* (Chicago: Rand McNally, 1969); Roger Kanet, *The Behavioral Revolution in Communist Studies* (New York: Free Press, 1971); Jerry F. Hough, *The Soviet Union and Social Science Theory* (Cambridge: Harvard University Press, 1977).

23. In an effort to improve the quality of research on the USSR and Eastern Europe, in the mid-1980s the U.S. Congress began allocating funds authorized by the "Soviet and East European Research and Training Act of 1983." This funding played an important role in revitalizing the field as the National Defense Education Act had some three decades earlier.

24. An excellent introductory, retrospective bibliography on communist studies may be found in Stephen White and Daniel Nelson, eds., *Communist Politics: A Reader* (New York: New York University Press, 1984).

25. According to its original and most influential statement by Carl Friedrich and Zbigniew Brzezinski, the totalitarian syndrome was said to be distinguished by six features: an official ideology, binding on all members of the society; a single mass party typically led by one man; a system of terroristic police control; a near-monopoly of control by the state of all means of mass communication; a near-monopoly by the state of all means of effective armed combat; and central control and direction of the entire economy. Friedrich later argued that territorial expansionism and control over the courts were additional distinguishing features. See Carl J. Friedrich and Zbigniew K. Brzezinski, *Totalitarian Dictatorship and Autocracy* 2nd ed. (Cambridge: Harvard University Press, 1965).

26. See Theda Skocpol, "Bringing the State Back In," *Items* Vol. 36, Nos. 1/2 (June 1982), pp. 1–8.

27. See, for instance, Peter B. Evans, Dietrich Rueschemeyer, and Theda Skocpol, eds, *Bringing the State Back In* (Cambridge: Cambridge University Press, 1985); Ruth Berins Collier and David Collier, *Shaping the Political Arena* (Princeton: Princeton University Press, 1991); Guillermo O'Donnel and Philippe C. Schmitter, *Transitions from Authoritarian Rule* (Baltimore: The Johns Hopkins University Press, 1986); Alfred Stepan, *The State and Society* (Princeton University Press, 1978).

28. See, for example, Taketsuga Tsurutani, *Political Change in Japan: Response to Postindustrial Challenge* (New York: McKay, 1977).

29. See Lucian W. Pye, *Asian Power and Politics: The Cultural Dimensions of Authority* (Cambridge: Harvard University Press, 1985).

30. Martin Carnoy, *The State and Political Theory* (Princeton: Princeton University Press, 1984); Suzanne Berger, *Organizing Interests in Western Europe: Pluralism, Corporatism, and the Transformation of Politics* (Cambridge: Cambridge University Press, 1981).

31. Prior to the advent of glasnost, research on nationality issues was arcane, formulaic, and generally irrelevant. This situation changed dramatically, particularly in 1988. After this point, Soviet research and writing on nationality issues may still have lacked theoretical sophistication, but they hardly lacked candor. For a survey of nationality issues from Soviet perspectives, see Martha B. Olcott, ed, *The Soviet Multinational State: Readings and Documents* (Armonk, NY: M. E. Sharpe, 1990).

32. See Daniel Yergin, *Shattered Peace: The Origins of the Cold War and the National Security State* (Cambridge: Harvard University Press, 1976).

33. Alexander J. Motyl, " 'Sovietology in One Country' or Comparative Nationality Studies?" *Slavic Review* Vol. 48(1) (Spring 1989):83–88, at 84.

34. See, for instance, Robert A. Lewis, Richard H. Rowland and Ralph Clem, *Nationality and Population Change in Russia and the USSR* (New York: Praeger, 1976); Robert A. Lewis and Richard H. Rowland, *Population Redistribution in the USSR* (New York: Praeger, 1979).

35. See, for instance, Jeremy Azrael, *Soviet Nationality Policies and Practices* (New York: Praeger, 1978); Robert Conquest, *Soviet Nationalities Policy in Practice* (London: Bodley Head, 1967); John Dunlop, *The Faces of Russian Nationalism* (Princeton: Princeton University Press, 1983); Darrell Hammer, *Russian Nationalism and Soviet Politics* (Boulder: Westview Press, 1989): Teresa Rakowska-Harmstone, *Russia and Nationalism in Central Asia: The Case of Tadzhikistan* (Baltimore: Johns Hopkins University Press, 1970); Roman Szporluk, *Communism and Nationalism: Karl Marx versus Friedrich List* (New York: Oxford University Press, 1988); Alexander Yanov, *The Russian New Right* (Berkeley: University of California, 1978).

36. For instance, on Ukraine, see John A. Armstrong, *Ukrainian Nationalism* (Littleton, CO: Ukrainian Academic Press, 1980); Bohdan Krawchenko, *Social Change and National Consciousness in Twentieth-Century Ukraine* (New

York: St. Martin's Press, 1985); Borys Lewytzkyj, *Politics and Society in Soviet Ukraine, 1953–1980* (Edmonton: Canadian Institute of Ukrainian Studies, 1984); James Mace, *Communism and the Dilemmas of National Liberation: National Communism in Soviet Ukraine, 1918–1933* (Cambridge: Harvard University Press, 1983); Alexander J. Motyl, *The Turn to the Right: The Ideological Origins and Development of Ukrainian Nationalism, 1919–1929* (Boulder, CO: East European Monographs, 1989).

37. See Aleksandr I. Solzhenitsyn, "Kak nam obustroit' Rossiiu? Posil'nye soobrazheniia," *Literaturnaia gazeta,* September 18, 1990. An earlier statement of this thesis appeared in Aleksandr I. Solzhenitsyn, *Letter to the Soviet Leaders* (New York: Harper and Row, 1974).

38. It may be significant that European scholars were less convinced of the durability of the omnicompetent state in the USSR. Perhaps for this reason, scholars trained in the European humanistic tradition tended to see the nationalities problem as much more important than many American scholars trained in "value free" social science methodologies. See for instance, Robert Conquest, *The Nation Killers: The Soviet Deportation of Nationalities* (London: Macmillan, 1970).

39. James Critchlow, "Nationality Studies: Where Did They Go Wrong?" *Journal of Soviet Nationalities* 1(3) (Fall 1990):23–32, at p. 30.

40. Merle Fainsod, *How Russia is Ruled,* rev. ed. (Cambridge: Harvard University Press, 1965).

41. Gordon H. Skilling and Franklyn Griffiths, eds., *Interest Groups in Soviet Politics* (Princeton: Princeton University Press, 1971).

42. Brian Silver, "Social Mobilization and the Russification of Soviet Nationalities," *American Political Science Review* 68(1) (March 1974):45–66.

43. See Donna Bahry, *Outside Moscow: Power, Politics, and Budgetary Policy in the Soviet Republics* (New York: Columbia University Press, 1987); Daniel N. Nelson, "Dilemmas of Local Politics in Communist States," *Journal of Politics* Vol. 41 (1979):23–54; Joel C. Moses, "Regionalism in Soviet Politics: Continuity as a Source of Change, 1953–1982" *Soviet Studies* 37(2) (1985):184–211; and Michael E. Urban and Russell B. Reed, "Regionalism in a Systems Perspective: Explaining Elite Circulation in a Soviet Republic" *Slavic Review* 48(3) (1989):431.

44. Perhaps the most direct influence the U.S. government had on the Sovietological community was through siphoning off much of the field's most talented young researchers by virtue of the career advancement opportunities for foreign poicy analysts in the U.S. government.

45. James Critchlow, "Nationality Studies: Where Did They Go Wrong?" *Journal of Soviet Nationalities* 1(3) (Fall 1990):23–32, at p. 30.

2. Soviet Policies Toward the Non-Russian Peoples in Theoretic and Historic Perspective: What Gorbachev Inherited

Walker Connor

ARTICLE 70 of the 1977 Soviet Constitution defined the USSR as "an integral federal multinational state." While some 90 percent of all contemporary countries are also multinational, there are few states so ethnically complex. The 1989 Soviet census listed more than 100 national groups. Although some of these groups were numerically quite small, consisting of a few thousand members, several were impressively large. Twenty-two of the national groups numbered more than 1,000,000 people. From a comparative perspective, this means that there were twenty-two peoples in the USSR, each of whom outnumbered the total population of nearly forty (approximately 25 percent) of today's independent countries. Moreover, the Ukrainian community, the largest national minority in the Soviet Union (surpassed only by the Great Russians), exceeded 44 million in membership. Only twenty independent countries (less than 15 percent of the total) can claim so large a number of people. There were more Ukrainians living within the Soviet Union than there are people within such important countries as Argentina, Canada, Poland, the Republic of South Africa, Spain, or Yugoslavia. Furthermore, the next largest national group, the Uzbeks, numbered 17 million, a figure nearly twice the number of Swedes within Sweden and more than three times the number of Norwegians within Norway, Jews within Israel, or Irish within Ireland.

The Leninist Legacy

It was the official contention of Stalin and his successors that Lenin had bequeathed to the Soviet Union *the* formula for managing and ultimately eradicating ethnic heterogeneity. Thus, the 1986 Program of the CPSU asserted: "The Party has resolved and will continue to resolve [all issues involving the relations among the country's national groups] on the basis of the tested principles of Lenin's nationalities policy."

Seven decades after the October Revolution, the Soviet authorities were thus insisting that they remained steadfast in their commitment to "Lenin's nationalities policy." A charge of violating that policy was tantamount to a charge of apostasy.[1] Yet despite such proclamations of undeviating fidelity, Soviet policy clearly underwent marked shifts over the last seventy years, sometimes seeming to favor a pluralistic approach (most conspicuously the postrevolutionary period of "indigenization" [korenizatsiia]), while other times tacking in the direction of acculturation and assimilation (most glaringly from 1934 to 1953). Cloaking such different approaches under the single rubric of Leninist nationality policy was possible because of the dialectical approach to nations and nationalism that Lenin espoused and also because of the paucity of policy guidelines he bequeathed.

Lenin's dialectical formula for taming nationalism in a postrevolutionary situation was a reflection of his perception of nationalism as the outgrowth of past discrimination. He was well aware of the strong nationalist sentiments pervading the Armenian, Lithuanian, Ukrainian, and other minority peoples, but he felt that this was due to their historic second-class treatment within Tsarist Russia, an empire to which he referred as "the prison of nations." Lenin was convinced that this legacy of hostility and distrust must be expurgated by a period of the strictest national equality. And thus the dialectic: permitting, indeed encouraging for a time the national language and other overt characteristics of the various national groups would lead the groups toward fusion. In 1930, Stalin would acknowledge that to the unenlightened it might appear "self-contradictory" that "we who are in favor of the fusion of national cultures in the future into one common culture (both in form and content), with a single, common language, are at the same time in favor of the blossoming of national culture at the present time;" but he added, "Whoever has failed to understand this dialectical character of historical processes is lost to Marxism."[2]

Lenin felt that the greatest care must be taken to ensure that the non-Russian communities did not perceive sovietization as a continuation of Great Russian chauvinism in a new guise. Encouraging the national language and other cultural characteristics of the various peoples would make clear that a new era in the relations among nations had been entered. And as suspicions and distrust dissipated, nationalism would correspondingly diminish and a natural coming together, a rapprochement of the nations, would proceed until a final merger or fusion took place.

Lenin was far more interested in the message than the medium. He construed language and traditional forms of music, dance, drama, etc. as simply the conduits of the messages that would be shaped by the Communist Party. Concerned lest national distrust and animosity lessen the receptivity of the masses to the party's messages, Lenin reasoned that the party's directives would not be resisted as the orders of an alien (Russian) regime if they came dressed in the local tongue and other appropriate national attire. National accouterment was thus to be pressed into the service of sovietization. In 1928, Stalin would christen this entire approach "national in form, socialist in content."[3]

Lenin therefore bequeathed the broad outline of a plan for achieving assimilation via the seemingly divergent path of encouraging aspects of national uniqueness (what came to be known in the Soviet lexicon as "the flourishing of nations"). However, beyond insisting that coercion be avoided as counterproductive, Lenin did not provide his heirs with any policy guidelines. He did make clear that pluralism, although to be encouraged for a time, had no intrinsic value beyond serving as a transitional step leading to a higher stage at which national differences would have withered away. Thus said Lenin: "The proletariat supports everything which contributes to the elimination of national differences [and it] welcomes any and every assimilation of nationalities—with the exception of those carried out by force or on the basis of privilege."[4] Lenin therefore condoned policies to promote assimilation, while proffering only a single guideline, namely, avoid coercion.

Lenin's anticipated timetable for the dialectical process of flourishing and rapprochement to complete itself was equally nonspecific. His inspiration was the *Communist Manifesto*'s dictum that under capitalism "national differences and antagonisms are daily more and more vanishing" and that the victory of socialism "will cause them to vanish still faster." He therefore saw the process as historically determined and inevitable, and so the exact moment at which the process culminated was of no greater concern to him than it had been to Marx and Engels. Following the October Revolution, he had made a passing reference to the likelihood that "national and state differences . . . will continue to exist for a very, very long time even after the dictatorship of the proletariat had been established on a world scale."[5] But these words were penned during the euphoric days when the worldwide revolution was believed at hand. His "very, very long time" might therefore be construed as a half-century or several centuries.

The important point is that Lenin's dialectical scheme—unaccompanied as it was by specific policy recommendations and a timetable for its completion—although described as a formula for solving the national question, proved to be no formula at all. Those who were in favor of vastly accelerating the assimilation process, those who favored the indefinite perpetuation of national flourishing, and those who held one of the myriad positions between these two extremes were all able to quote Leninist scripture. As noted, Soviet policy, despite declared obeisance to Leninist national policy, was marked by considerable vacillations on the continuum between pluralism and assimilation.

The cornerstone of Lenin's national policy was therefore a period of vigorous national equality as a means of overcoming the suspicions of the past and setting the stage for the natural coming together of peoples. "All nations are equal" was a much publicized slogan from the time of the Revolution until the abjuration of Marxist-Leninism as the state's official creed. Thus, the preamble of the 1977 Soviet Constitution spoke of "the equality in law and in fact of all nations and ethnic groups" while the 1986 Program of the CPSU (Part One) described the USSR as a society in which "national inequality has been eliminated and the actual and legal equality and friendship and fraternity of all nations and ethnic groups have been asserted."

The policy of national equality had three dimensions: (1) economic equality, (2) cultural equality, by which was meant the right of each nation to preserve its particular culture, most notably its language, and (3) political equality. As evidence that political equality was practiced, the Soviets could point to commonplace constitutional and statutory prohibitions against discrimination on the basis of national ancestry or race. But a far more unique manifestation of ostensible national equality was reflected in the political subdivision of the Soviet Union. As of 1990, some fifty peoples of the Soviet Union had an administrative unit named after them. Fourteen non-Russian peoples enjoyed the highest administrative unit—a Soviet Socialist Republic—a unit constitutionally declared to be sovereign and to possess the right to secede from the Union. Stretched out below these SSRs in a descending order of officially ascribed importance were a series of twenty Autonomous Soviet Socialist Republics, eight Autonomous Regions (*Oblasti*), and ten Autonomous Areas (*Okrugi*). The propaganda value of this structure was enormous, for, as noted, 90 percent of all countries today are multinational. And multinational states the world over have been increasingly experiencing ethnically inspired unrest, as discontented minorities demand either greater autonomy or actual independence.[6] A perception of a country as a cluster of ethnically delineated, autonomous or sovereign units is therefore one with great appeal to national minorities everywhere.

Non-Theoretic Dimensions of Policy

There was a wide discrepancy between official declarations concerning the attainment of national equality within the Soviet Union and the degree to which economic, cultural, and political equality were in fact achieved, or even pursued.[7]

ECONOMIC EQUALITY

Not surprisingly, economic equality among the nations was never even approximated. Considering that the Soviet Union covered one-sixth of the globe's land area, and varied intensely from region to region with regard to climate, soils, topography, ease of access, and natural resources, it could hardly be otherwise. As noted elsewhere:

> The geographic distribution of ethnonational groups into distinctive homelands is sufficient in itself to assure the existence of economic discrepancies among groups. There is what might be termed a "law" of uneven, regional economic development. Though the unevenness is apparent when we contrast huge areas such as continents, most, if not all states also reflect economic differentials between regions. This is true of ethnically homogeneous and heterogeneous states alike; Germany, as well as France, illustrates notable sectional differences. Among the contributing factors are regional variations in such categories as (1) topography (ease of transportation), (2) climate, (3) soils, (4) availability of natural resources and raw materials, (5) population density, (6) the current technological capabilities of the local populace, (7) distance from potential markets, (8) the comparative advantage of local industry with regard to (a) age of plant and equipment and (b) margin of profit, and (9) the enduring effect of earlier decisions regarding investments and the locating of support industries and facilities (the infrastructure).[8]

The aggregate impact of such factors in the case of the Soviet Union was enormous. It would be unrealistic to have expected those responsible for planning to approve the expenditure of untold sums of scarce investment capital in an attempt to bring Tajikistan or Turkmenistan up to the level of a Latvia. That we are not faced here with a simple matter of favoring the Great Russians is illustrated by the fact that the inhabitants of the Armenian, Estonian, Georgian, Latvian, and Lithuanian SSRs enjoyed a higher per capita income than did the inhabitants of the Russian Soviet Federated Socialist Republic. Faced with limited resources and the need to consider the security interests and the economic wellbeing and growth of the country as a whole, economic planners adopted the standard of comparative return. The highest priority in allocating investments and in locating industries was given to strategic considerations; and the second most important consideration was economic rationalization, in terms of the presence of raw materials, support industries, markets, infrastructure, and the like.[9] But while perfectly understandable and rational, these yardsticks had nothing to do with national equality.

This is not to deny that living standards improved substantially in the Asian sector of the country during the seventy years of Soviet rule. The point, however, is that discrepancies between regions remained massive. In 1970, for example, the per capita product of the wealthiest SSR was more than two and one-third times that of the poorest.[10] Moreover, upon reaching the stage of "developed socialism," which was heralded by the 1977 Constitution, the heretofore ostensible goal of achieving economic equality among regions was scrapped. What had been practice now became public policy as well; "the need to ensure the utmost efficiency of the whole economy" became the public standard for "distributing the productive forces and investments."[11]

CULTURAL EQUALITY

The central issue of culture policy was the status of the non-Russian languages. In the years immediately following the Revolution, the thrust was definitely in the direction of encouraging the various national languages. Peoples who had never had a written language were provided one. Non-Russian language schools flourished and were made available even to non-Russian communities living outside of their homelands. But all of this began to change during the 1930s. Only Russian-language schools were permitted to operate everywhere. Non-

Russian-language schools were largely restricted to the appropriate ethnically delineated administrative unit. In 1938, the study of Russian was made compulsory in all schools. In 1958–59, the introduction of the "voluntary principle," which permitted parents living within their eponymous administrative unit to send their children to Russian-language schools, additionally undermined the non-Russian schools.[12] Furthermore, most non-Russian peoples witnessed a progressive lessening in the number of years of education offered in their own language. For example, for peoples possessing an autonomous republic or region, the number of possible years of education in their language was, on the average, halved between 1958 and 1972, from the already quite low figure of 5.2 years to 2.7 years.[13]

Those fourteen peoples with a Union Republic fared much better. They could conceivably complete both primary and secondary education in their own language. However, it became evident during the 1970s that union republic status was not to offer permanent immunity from pressure to attend Russian-language schools. The authorities had been applying what might be termed "the nine-to-five rule," for the Baltic peoples (Estonians, Latvians, and Lithuanians) and two of the Transcaucasian peoples (the Armenians and Georgians) were treated preferentially in matters touching on language choice. For example, while the number of indigenous language schools in the republics of these five peoples remained sufficient to meet the demand of those who desired to attend them, elsewhere the number became inadequate. This shortage of indigenous language schools was also reflected in the comparative number of primary and secondary school texts available in the languages of the titular peoples. Among the nine less favored peoples, the proportion of texts per native speaker of the local language was only 35 percent of the corresponding number for those in a republic declaring Russian as their primary language. In sum, data suggest that in nine of the union republics an increasing number of titular people were unable to find a local language school nearby.

The prevalence of Russian as the language of instruction increased with the level of education. At the university level it approached a near monopoly within some republics. At this level, the number of Russian-language textbooks per individual who claimed Russian as his/her primary tongue was more than ten times the corresponding figure for those who claimed the indigenous language as their primary tongue. And this disproportion would have been far greater if limited to the nine less favored union peoples. Moreover, the competitive examinations for entrance to institutes of higher learning were customarily given in Russian, thereby providing a distinct incentive for indigenes to send their children to the Russian-language schools at the primary and secondary levels. Russian thus became the language of success within a majority of the union republics.

There were also pressures upon the five more favored titular peoples. The pre-1978 constitutions of Armenia and Georgia (as well as Azerbaijan) had each declared the respective indigenous language to be the official state language of the republic. But new constitutions, which were drafted in 1978 to reflect the attainment of "developed socialism," replaced the formerly preeminent status of the local language by a phrase holding out only "the possibility of using the native language." The implications of this change did not go unheeded. Unanticipated protest demonstrations in the Georgian capital induced the authorities to order a most unusual retreat. The old phraseology was reinserted into all three constitutions, but the long-term intent of the authorities to upgrade Russian relative to the local languages had been made clear.

POLITICAL EQUALITY

The discrepancy between reality and the theory of political equality, symbolized in the system of ostensibly sovereign and autonomous administrative units, was also substantial. Given the highly centralized administrative system of the USSR and the hierarchical Communist Party, this could hardly have been otherwise. But through their cadre policy and their internal migration policies, the authorities further undermined whatever theoretic latitude the units purportedly possessed for self-rule.

Cadre Policy   As a blueprint for nurturing Marxism within a single, integrated multinational structure, Leninist national policy would seemingly mandate that the visible central organs of authority reflect the ethnonational complexity of the entire population, while the more localized visible power-structures reflect the unique national coloration of the immediately surrounding populace. In particular, one would expect that the visible elite within an ethnically delineated autonomous unit would be composed of members of the titular group. To do otherwise would risk undermining the very raison d'être of such administrative units, namely, to convince each national group that it had its own, truly autonomous political organization. Despite periodic shifts in the degree to which cadres were drawn from the local populace, however, the Soviet leadership remained opposed to the nationalization of cadres per se. Under what was termed "the exchange of cadres" (but what proved to be an essentially one-way supply of key personnel from Moscow), the center resolutely maintained its representatives in all republics. Thus, the 1961 Party Program of the CPSU announced that "the growing scale of communist construction calls for the continuous exchange of trained personnel among nations." And the policy was reaffirmed in the 1986 Program: "it is essential . . . to develop the interrepublican exchange of worker and specialist cadres."[14]

The cutting edge of such a cadre policy was somewhat blunted by the practice of assigning members of the local national group to positions of great visibility and little power. For example, after the demise of Stalin the Soviets followed the practice of appointing a member of the local national group to the most prestigious office in each union republic, namely, the party's first secretaryship. However, the second secretary, *in whom was placed primary responsibility for monitoring cadre policy on the local scene,* was regularly a non-indigene (usually Russian), whose primary loyalty to the center was further ensured by limiting the duration of his assignment in the locale.

The primacy of the state's dominant ethnic element was most apparent in the agencies responsible for internal security. The dominant group was customarily disproportionately represented in the upper echelons of the military; combined with the practice of assigning minority personnel serving in the military outside of their homelands, this procedure minimized any danger of the homeland serving as a focus for a secessionist movement. In the case of the Soviet Union, one study indicated that all of the commanders-in-chief of the country's military districts were Russian.[15] And another study found that 98 percent of all military members of the Supreme Soviet were of Slavic, principally Russian, background.[16] Similar considerations helped determine the national composition of the secret police. The head of the KGB for each of the union republics was customarily a Russian.[17]

In post-Brezhnev years, the trend was toward an increase in the number of local cadres holding showcase positions. But real power remained concentrated in nonindigenous hands, and those cadres who had been drawn from the local national group were periodically warned of the hazards of activities that could be construed as a manifestation of "local nationalism," "bourgeois nationalism," or "national deviation" by the numerous cases of prominent local leaders who were purged on such charges.

Ethnic Dilution Policy   While the guiding principle for granting autonomy to compact national groups should be "one people, one autonomous unit," gerrymandering and population redistribution produced a very different situation. Even as originally drawn, the borders of the autonomous units within the Soviet Union did not approximate ethnic distributions. In nine of twenty-seven union and autonomous republics whose name in each case implied the predominance of a single national group, the titular group did not in fact even account for a majority of the population. In no case did the proportion of the titular people reach 90 percent, and the median proportion it represented was less than two-thirds.[18] The theory of Leninist national policy to the contrary, most peoples, including those purportedly assigned their own unit, thus found themselves sharing an antonomous unit with large numbers of aliens.

Almost equally injurious to the principle of one nation, one autonomous unit were the large numbers of people left outside of the unit bearing their designation. In three of the twenty-seven previously mentioned cases, *a majority of the group's members remained outside.* In half of the cases, less than 80 percent of the membership resided within the confines of the unit bearing their national name.

Subsequent redistribution of population within the Soviet Union further undermined the principle of ethnonational autonomy. Particularly pronounced was the impact of migrations by the state's dominant group. Since 1917, there had been a dramatic influx of Russians into all nontraditionally Russian homelands. As of 1979, Russians accounted for more than 7 percent of the population of each of the union republics other than Armenia. The range was from 2.3 percent in the case of Armenia to 40.8 percent in the case of Kazakhstan, with a mean of 16.7 percent and a median of 12.3 percent.

The penetration by Russians had been even more dramatic with regard to the autonomous republics within the Russian Soviet Federated Socialist Republic. In 1979, the percent of Russians within these sixteen republics ranged from 11.6 percent to 72.0 percent, with a mean of 44.7 percent and a median of 43.3 percent. In six of the sixteen autonomous republics, the Russians constituted an absolute majority, and, in four others, they were the largest single ethnic group.

The overall impact of gerrymandering and population redistribution upon the ethnic homogeneity of the republics had therefore been enormous. By the time Gorbachev came to power, the titular group in a union republic typically accounted for less than two-thirds of the republic's population. In no case did it account for 90 percent of the entire population, and in two cases it failed to account for a majority. Again, even more striking was the case of the autonomous republics within the RSFSR. *In only four of the sixteen cases did a single non-Russian people account for a majority of the population.*

This ethnic dilution of the republics did, of course, lessen their potential for becoming the foci of ethnically inspired demands for greater independence. Recent demographic developments therefore became a matter of growing concern to the authorities. Russian migration out of the RSFSR had been continuing, but the percentage of the population represented by Russians had been shrinking within a majority of the union republics.

There are two principal factors that accounted for this seeming anomaly. The major factor involved differential fertility rates. Although the rates among the non-European peoples dropped during the 1970s, they remained far in excess of those for the Russian and other European peoples. (Only in the six westernmost union republics did the percentage of Russians increase during the decade.) In a figurative sense, the authorities had been running out of Russians. The second factor had been a growing tendency for members of non-Russian ethnic groups either to remain stationary within their republic or, in the case of those outside it, to emigrate to it. In the two decades between 1959 and 1979, the percentage of the nation living outside of its union republic decreased for ten of the fourteen titular peoples and remained essentially static for two others.

In addition to increasing the risk of the union republics becoming foci for nationalist sentiment, the growing ethnic concentration in these units was troubling to the authorities because it was antithetical to the process of the merging of nations. A series of Soviet studies had unanimously concurred that residence within one's homeland-republic exerts a most dampening influence upon acculturation and assimilation.[19] As the individual with primary responsibility for approving these studies concluded: "On the whole, peoples living within their own Union or Autonomous Republics as a rule steadfastly preserve their mother tongue and their sense of national identity."[20]

Given, then, these recent trends (plus the desire to transfer labor from the worker-surplus Asian republics to the worker-short eastern RSFSR), the authorities unsurprisingly demonstrated avid interest in inducing emigration by non-Russian indigenes. In effect, such emigres would do double duty: their departure would automatically raise the percentage of nonindigenes within their native republic and their arrival would lower the homogeneity of their newly adopted union republic. Encouraging such a migratory pattern was particularly pronounced following the Twenty-Sixth Party Congress in 1981.[21]

Retrospect and Prospect

To place recent events in perspective it is necessary to trace the major vacillations in Soviet national policy. As earlier noted, the 1920s and early 1930s were a period of official encouragement for national flourishing on the part of the non-Russian peoples. However, a major aspect of Stalin's purges in the 1930s was the rooting out of all manifestations of nationalism. Charges of "nationalist deviation," "bourgeois nationalism," "separatism," and "antistate activity" became common. Cadres were "denationalized"; histories were rewritten to extol the virtues of the Great Russians and the debt owed to them by the non-Russian peoples; the use of the Russian language was promoted in all social endeavors; attempts were made to bring scripts, grammars, and vocabularies of non-Russian languages into the greatest possible harmony with Russian; the citizenry was regularly warned against nationalist deviations; and officials spoke increasingly of the new supranational Soviet man who had evolved. In short, the trend became lopsidedly in favor of assimilation.[22]

Following Stalin's death, Lavrentii Beria attempted to enlist the resentment engendered by these policies in his drive for power. Under his influence, the CPSU's Central Committee resolved in 1953 "to end the mutilation of Soviet nationality policy," and purges and self-criticism for "abuses of Leninist nationality policy" took place within the upper reaches of the republican wings of the Party. Nikita Khrushchev, in turn, successfully used this very policy change to undermine Beria within the Politburo, by stressing, in his words, that it would "aggravate nationalist tensions between Russians and non-Russians, as well as between the central leadership in Moscow and the local leadership in the Republics."[23] However, the party was publicly committed to rectifying Stalin's extreme assimilationist stance, which precluded too rapid a return to pro-assimilationist measures, so that the first years of the Khrushchev era were marked by a gradual increase in the number of indigenous cadres within the republics, the making of membership in the titular nation a criterion for certain positions (most dramatically the first secretaryship of the republican wing of the party), and a lessening of public pressure to adopt the Russian language. A hint of Khrushchev's true inclinations with regard to the national question was offered in his famous 1956 denunciation of Stalin and Stalinism at the Party's Twentieth Congress. Although he acidly criticized Stalin for the forcible dispersion during World War II of a number of national groups outside of their traditional homelands and although he had the Congress go on record as unambiguously committed to national flourishing, Khrushchev also emphasized that "We must affirm that the Party had fought a serious fight against Trotskyites, rightists and bourgeois nationalists."[24] The remaining years of Khrushchev's tenure reflected a determination to accelerate the merging process. In 1957, the role of the republics in economic planning and management was downgraded. In 1958, the "voluntary" principle with regard to attending either national or Russian-language schools was instituted. During 1959, a spate of non-Russian leaders were purged for "nationalist deviations." The Party Program of 1961 noted that "the boundaries between the Union Republics of the U.S.S.R. are increasingly losing their former significance," and it prophesied that "the nations will draw closer together until complete unity is achieved." Consonant with this prediction, strong pressures were placed upon non-Russian writers to publish in Russian, as part of a program to hasten acculturation and assimilation.[25]

Khrushchev's eclipse signalled a move away from this rapid assimilation model. The republics were reinvested with their previous economic prerogatives and talk of the "complete unity" of nations was shelved in favor of a more equitable balance of drawing together and flourishing. The shift was noticeable in the contrasting tones of Khrushchev's 1961 speech to the Party's Twenty-Third Congress and Brezhnev's 1966 speech to the Twenty-Fourth Congress. Khrushchev had said:

> We come across people, of course, who deplore the gradual obliteration of national distinctions. We reply to them: Communists will not conserve and perpetuate national distinctions.

In a far more conciliatory vein, Brezhnev stated:

In solving any problem, whether it be of political, economic, or cultural development of our country, the Party will show solicitude for the interests and national differences of each people.[26]

Brezhnev's early years were also characterized by a more empirical approach to the national question. In 1966–1967, a leading Soviet journal printed a series of scholarly articles reflecting a broad spectrum of opinion on the national question. Authors included some who were in favor of much more rapid assimilation and those in favor of intense foot dragging in that direction. Moreover, a decision was made to permit and to publish at least some of the findings of a series of sociological studies documenting intergroup attitudes. In 1969 a Scientific Council on National Problems was created. And in 1972, official acknowledgment that there were indeed problems traceable to the country's ethnic heterogeneity came from the highest source. Heretofore the official position had been that the national question had been solved. The 1961 Party Program, for example, had unequivocally stated that "the Party has solved one of the most complex of problems, which has plagued mankind for ages and remains acute in the world of capitalism today—the problem of relations among nations." But in his 1972 speech to commemorate the fiftieth anniversary of the founding of the Soviet Union, Brezhnev, after bowing in the direction of past party pronouncements by noting that "we have every reason to say that the nationalities question, in the form in which it came down to us from the past, has been resolved completely, resolved definitively and irrevocably," went on to suggest that the question was in fact far from being resolved "completely," "definitively," and "irrevocably."

> As I have already said, we have completely resolved the nationalities question in those aspects that we inherited from the prerevolutionary past. But nationality relations even in a society of mature socialism are a reality that is constantly developing and putting forth new problems and tasks. The Party constantly keeps these questions in its field of vision and resolves them in good time in the interests of the whole country and of each individual republic, in the interests of communist construction.
>
> It should not be forgotten that nationalistic prejudices and exaggerated or distorted manifestations of national feelings are extremely tenacious phenomena that are deeply imbedded in the psychology of people with insufficient political maturity. These prejudices continue to exist even in conditions in which objective preconditions for any antagonism in relations between nations have long since ceased to exist.[27]

This public admission that national antagonisms were still prevalent after a half-century of the Soviet experiment represented a striking volte-face from the prior "the national question has been solved" position and was evidently undertaken because the disadvantages of continued denial of a set of serious problems were considered greater than the perils of admission. The successful search for remedies required acknowledgment of the disease. The admission of national antagonisms gave ex post facto official endorsement to those empirical studies already underway and legitimized at a stroke all future research in a field that was taboo to scholarship so long as officialdom maintained that the national question had been solved.

Acknowledging the existence of a serious problem also justified a speeding-up of the assimilation process. In the same 1972 speech, after quoting Lenin, the General Secretary called for a marshaling of forces to this end:

> Lenin spoke out very clearly on this score: "The proletariat cannot support any reinforcement of nationalism—on the contrary, it supports everything that helps to obliterate national distinctions and to remove national barriers, everything that makes the ties between nationalities closer and closer" (Complete Collected Works 24:133).
>
> In resolving questions of the country's further development along the path outlined by Lenin, the Party attaches great importance to the continuous systematic and thorough cultivation of a spirit of internationalism and Soviet patriotism in all citizens of the Soviet Union. For us, these two concepts constitute an inseparable whole. Needless to say, they are being cultivated in the working people by Soviet life itself, by all our reality. But conscious efforts by the Party and all workers on the political and ideological front are also necessary here. Our work in this area is a highly important part of the general cause of the construction of communism.

Consonant with this injunction, the remainder of Brezhnev's rule was marked by a policy of more rapid acculturation and assimilation. A recharged militancy against national deviations became apparent. The number of trials for nationalist proclivities rose, and several non-Russians were removed from high-level posts in their home republics. Editorials, articles, and a new law on industrial associations made evident that the powers of the republics were once more to be curtailed.

The new (1977) Constitution reflected this same *Zeitgeist*. Whereas the 1961 Party Program had committed the Party to actively promote assimilation, the Constitution now formally committed the state to the same cause: "The state helps enhance the social homogeneity of society, namely . . . the all-round development and drawing together of all the nations and nationalities of the USSR." The Constitution also failed to empower the union republics to maintain their own armed forces, a right technically (but never substantively) enjoyed under the 1936 Constitution; and in his report on the new Constitution to the Supreme Soviet, Brezhnev acknowledged that further restrictions on the republics, and even the total eradication of the republics, had been considered but rejected on the ground that such reforms were premature. Further, "the right [to] instruction in schools being conducted in the native language" contained in the 1936 Constitution was reduced to "the possibility to attend a school where teaching is in the native language."[28]

In the years between adoption of the new Constitution and Brezhnev's death in 1982, the emphasis upon the fusing of peoples accelerated. An all-union meeting in Tashkent in 1979 endorsed a series of proposals to intensify the teaching of Russian beginning with nursery schools. The Twenty-Sixth Party Congress in 1981 called for still greater efforts to spread the adoption of the Russian language. Moreover, even more rapid strides toward assimilation were in prospect: A piece in *Pravda* on April 9, 1982 proclaimed that "the processes of the consistent rapprochement and all-around cooperation among all Soviet peoples . . . are intensified in the mature socialist society" that had been ushered in by the 1977 Constitution. And a piece written by the editor-in-chief of *Kommunist,* practically on the eve of Brezhnev's death, warned that Lenin's dictum that "the goal of socialism is not only . . . the convergence of nations, but also their merging . . . does not permit any misinterpretations."[29]

The short tenures of Yuri Andropov (16 months) and Konstantin Chernenko (13 months) indicated no deviation from the commitment to accelerated fusion. Perhaps to underline that this commitment was now so universally and uncompromisingly accepted by the Party hierarchy that crown-changing would no longer be accompanied by policy vacillations and retreats (as had occurred following the demise of Stalin and the ouster of Khrushchev), Chernenko, only a few weeks after Brezhnev's death, reasserted the party's commitment to the fusion of nations and hinted strongly at the coming eradication of the republics.

At the present historical stage and in the future the USSR represents the optimum state form for the cohesion of Soviet nations and ethnic groups in order to attain our program goals. At the same time, we do not regard the established national state structures as something fixed and immutable.[30]

And, upon taking power, Andropov also expressed his dedication to the fusion of nations:

> Comrades, in summing up what has been accomplished, we naturally, give most of our attention to what still remains to be done. Our end goal is clear. It, to quote Lenin, "is not only to bring the nations closer together but to fuse them." The party is well aware that the road to this goal is a long one. On no account must there be either any forestalling of events or any holding back of processes that have already matured.[31]

This paper makes no attempt to trace or analyze developments with regard to the Soviet national question following Gorbachev's appointment as General Secretary of the Communist Party in March of 1985. His early policies, if anything, appeared to be more committed than those of his immediate predecessor to promoting the fusion of peoples. Amazingly, given the ethnonational eruptions that were soon to sweep over the entire country, the 1986 Communist Party Program proclaimed: "The nationalities question inherited from the past has been successfully solved in the Soviet Union." The following year—1987—Gorbachev endorsed glasnost and perestroika, thereby unintentionally unpenning ethnonational animosities and aspirations that would be reflected in large-scale bloodletting and demands for independence. At this writing, the independence of Estonia, Latvia, and Lithuania have been recognized, and an undetailed outline for a loose confederative structure to govern relations among the other former union republics has emerged. It is evident, however, that the national question has hardly run its full course in the region. Several non-Baltic peoples have also indicated their desire for total separation. And, even if all the fifteen republics were independent, there would remain interrepublic problems caused by irredentist situations and inter- and intrarepublic problems caused by the ethnic heterogeneity of the units. The seventy year legacy of Soviet national policy will be felt long after the passing of the Soviet Union.

NOTES

1. For example, propaganda tirades exchanged between the Soviet Union and China during the late 1960s and 1970s were liberally spiced with charges

and countercharges that the other party was violating Lenin's legacy on the national question. Thus a 1972 article by a Soviet author charged that even though, in matters of minorities policy, "the Soviet experience of the formation and development of the USSR was literally before China's eyes . . . China did not proceed along a Leninist path." (A. Voropayev, "According to the Formulas of the Emperors, Great-Han Chauvinism in Action," FBIS, March 31, 1972.) An editorial in the *Peking Review* (17 [July 19, 1974]:18–19) retorted: "Brezhnev and his ilk shamelessly try their utmost to describe what they call 'national rapprochement' as 'the Leninist policy on nationalities' and the continued development along the road chartered by Lenin. . . . It has nothing in common with the Leninist policy on nationalities; it is an utter betrayal of Leninism." The campaign of mutual vilification continued into the 1980s. One 1981 Soviet work, for example, charged that "the leaders of China long ago retreated from the Marxist-Leninist solution of the nationalities question." M. Ya. Sushanlo et al, *Against Maoist Falsifications of the History of Kirghiziya* (Frunze, Kirghizistan: n.p., 1981), p. 136.

2. Joseph Stalin, *Deviations on the National Question,* June 27, 1930.

3. The slogan became commonplace following Stalin's *Remarks to the Peoples of the East* (1925): "Proletarian culture does not cancel national culture, but lends it content. National culture, on the other hand, does not cancel proletarian culture, but lends it form." Stalin's terminology was apparently inspired by the *Communist Manifesto:* "Though not in substance, yet in form, the struggle . . . is at first a national struggle."

4. Cited in Alfred Low, *Lenin on the Question of Nationality* (New York: Bookman Associates, 1950), pp. 115–16 and Bertram Wolfe, *Three Who Made a Revolution,* rev. ed. (New York: Dell, 1965), p. 589.

5. Lenin, *Left-Wing Communism, an Infantile Disorder* (1920).

6. Among the many works documenting this global development are Donald Horowitz, *Ethnic Groups in Conflict* (Berkeley: University of California Press, 1985); Harold Isaacs, *The Idols of the Tribe* (New York: Harper and Row, 1975); and Anthony Smith, *The Ethnic Revival* (Cambridge: Cambridge University Press, 1981). For pertinent works by the present author, see Walker Connor, "Self-Determination: The New Phase," *World Politics* 20 (October 1967):30–53; "Nation-Building or Nation-Destroying?" *World Politics* 24 (April 1972):319–355; "The Politics of Ethnonationalism," *Journal of International Affairs* 27(1) (1973):1–21; and "A Nation Is a Nation, Is a State, Is an Ethnic Group, Is a . . . ," *Ethnic and Racial Studies* 1 (October 1978), pp. 377–400.

7. For a more detailed treatment of this discrepancy, see Walker Connor, *The National Question in Marxist-Leninist Theory and Strategy* (Princeton: Princeton University Press, 1984), Chapter 9.

8. Walker Connor, "Eco- or Ethno-Nationalism?" *Ethnic and Racial Studies,* 7 (July 1984):342–359.

9. See Robert Lewis, Richard Rowland, and Ralph Clem, *Nationality and Population Change in Russia and the USSR* (New York: Praeger, 1976), pp. 116ff.

10. By contrast, the 1970 discrepancy in the case of the poorest and wealthiest states of the United States was 1.9. times. (Data on the Soviet Union derived from Table A.15 in Zev Katz [ed.], *Handbook of Major Soviet Nationalities* [New York: Free Press, 1975], p. 452; and on the United States from U.S. Bureau of the Census, *Statistical Abstract of the United States 1986,* 106th ed. [Washington, D.C.: U.S. Government Printing Office, 1985]. For a survey of six analyses, each of which documents sharp regional economic disparities within the Soviet Union, see Ralph Clem, "The Ethnic Dimension of the Soviet Union" in Jerry Pankhurst and Michael Sacks, eds., *Contemporary Soviet Society* (New York: Praeger, 1980).

11. M. Khalmukhamedov, "Soviet Society: Complete Equity of Nations," *International Affairs* (Moscow), March 1978, p. 29.

12. For a discussion of the nonvoluntary aspects of this "voluntary principle," see Connor, *The National Question,* pp. 256–257, 261, and 480.

13. This trend was approvingly noted in a Soviet editorial as early as 1963: "The use of the Russian language as the medium of instruction is at the present time a growing tendency in the development of the national schools of our country. In the Russian SFSR the process of the voluntary changeover of national schools to the Russian language of instruction from a certain class upwards in accordance with the desire of the parents is even now proceeding very actively in most Autonomous Republics, autonomous Regions and National Areas. At present in the schools of thirty-six nationalities of the Russian SFSR instruction is conducted in Russian from the V, IV, III, II, or I class upwards." (Cited in Ivan Dzyuba, *Internationalism or Russification?* [New York: Pathfinder Press, 1968], p. 178.)

14. The close association that the authorities perceived between cadre exchange and overall national policy was suggested in an article in *Pravda,* July 16, 1971, which reminded readers that the "interrepublic exchange of cadres" remained a key element in the "coming together" of the Soviet nations.

15. Teresa Rakowska-Harmstone, "The Study of Ethnic Politics in the USSR." Paper prepared for the national symposium, "The National Problem in the USSR and Eastern Europe under Brezhnev and Kosygin," University of Detroit, October 3–4, 1975.

16. Ellen Jones, "Minorities in the Soviet Armed Forces," *Comparative Strategy,* 3 (No. 4, 1982), pp. 306–307. The author adds: "A similar pattern emerges from a name analysis of 73 key MOD [Ministry of Defense] officials."

17. Dina Spechler, "Russia and the Russians," in Zev Katz ed., *Handbook of Major Soviet Nationalities,* p. 11.

18. In addition, there were three autonomous republics whose ethnic

heterogeneity was at least suggested by their official designations, each of which contained the names of two ethnic groups. The title of yet another autonomous republic made no mention of any ethnonational group; its highly heterogeneous population was grouped under the name of the region, Dagestan.

19. For a convenient summary of several of these studies, see Brian Silver, "Inventory of Propositions Drawn from Soviet Empirical Studies on the Attitudes of Soviet Nationalities." Paper prepared for the AAASS Nationalities Project Workshop, Banff, Canada, September 1974.

20. Yulian Bromley, *Soviet Ethnography: Main Trends* (Moscow: USSR Academy of Sciences, 1976), p. 119.

21. See Connor, *The National Question*, pp. 316ff.

22. *Ibid.*, p. 397.

23. Nikita Khrushchev, *Khrushchev Remembers* (Boston: Little Brown, 1970), p. 330.

24. For the entire speech, see Henry Christman ed., *Communism in Action: A Documentary History* (New York: Bantam Books, 1969), pp. 158–228.

25. For some remarkable candor concerning this campaign of the early 1960s by both victims and perpetrators, see the *New York Times*, January 29, 1967.

26. Both citations can be found in Connor, *The National Question*, p. 400.

27. *The Current Digest of the Soviet Press* 24 (5):6.

28. As earlier noted, this same wording was soon to be injected into the constitutions of the three Transcaucasian union republics in an abortive attempt to deprive the local languages of their official status.

29. Richard Ivanovich Kosolapov, "Class and National Relations at the Stage of Mature Socialism," *JPRS* 82853, February 11, 1983.

30. Konstantin Chernenko, "60 Years of the Peoples' Fraternal Friendship," *Problemy Mira i Sotsializma* (December 1982):13–14.

31. Yuri Andropov, "Sixty Years of the USSR," *FBIS* (December 21, 1982).

3. Ideology and the Making of a Nationalities Policy

Ronald J. Hill

THIS chapter seeks to clarify the nature of Marxist-Leninist ideology and how it affected the Soviet leaders' approach to the problem of ethnicity. It is suggested not only that by relying on certain ideological views successive generations of leaders failed to address the issues effectively, but also that any government would be faced by the nationality problem, whose complexity makes a simple solution impossible to attain. It thus helps to explain the failure of the communist regime to resolve the issue, despite its claims to the contrary, and also points to the continuing salience of the issue in the post-communist successor systems.

A number of Western specialists have for years been predicting the rise of the nationalist tide,[1] and twenty—or even ten—years ago that meant going out on a limb: very few people seriously considered that it could grow into the major political problem of today, and the very possibility was denied by representatives of Soviet power. Today, no one could ignore the nationality issue.

The Soviet leaders themselves appeared perplexed by it, since it is not readily explicable in terms of their values and assumptions. For years, the official line was that the national question had been solved—although it was unclear precisely what was meant by "solved." And the resurgent sentiments that have now taken on great political salience are something that the official thinking inherited from the past could not adequately account for. A central feature of the traditional Soviet system is that it did not simply strive to find solutions and policies that "worked,"—i.e., relieved the problem at which they were targeted. It was not a system based essentially on pragmatism. On the contrary, the party claimed a special understanding of society, and it had a specific goal toward which it was supposedly "guiding" the human race. For all the clear evidence that the ruling party had lost its vigor in promoting the ideology, Marxism-Leninism was not rejected by the country's rulers, and each generation of new leaders felt duty-bound to reaffirm its commitment to inherited values.[2] Although following the dramatic events of August 1991 the Communist Party and its ideology of Marxism-Leninism have ceased to be the dominant force in the society, it is still important to understand it if we are to appreciate recent history and some of the problems that remain in the post-communist era.

What is the nature of the ideology?[3] This is a notoriously elusive concept, but ideologies are commonly identified as "action-related 'systems' of ideas" concerning "the nature of the distribution of political power . . . normative arguments to espouse a program of reform or reaction, [which] demand action, not just observation and analysis."[4] For a number of years, under the influence of the "totalitarian" model of Soviet politics, Western commentators and students of Soviet politics had a rather static view of "Marxism-Leninism," the official ideology imposed on Soviet society by the Communist Party. It was seen as an essentially unchanging body of doctrine that inspired the leaders, prescribed certain courses of action, and was used dogmatically to justify Communist Party rule.

A great deal in Soviet political rhetoric encouraged such a view of "ideology." It was, first of all, a far more clearly recognizable body of scriptures than the equivalent ruling ideas of other societies.[5] It was based on the works of certain identified historical figures, whose corpus of writings was cited to support philosophical, economic, and political arguments. Moreover, certain claims about it permitted its use by the party to justify its own political monopoly. Let us consider briefly some of the underlying features of this ideology.

The Nature of the Ideology

Philosophically, it adopted the assumptions of the age in which it was created: the nineteenth century, the age of science and rapidly developing industrial technology, following and expanding on the understandings attained in the age of reason and enlightenment. The expansion of physics, chemistry and biology, and the creation of new subdivisions—optics, magnetism and electricity, zoology, botany, bacteriology, astronomy and the like—led to the invention of the "scientist" (first coined in 1840),[6] and the optimistic notion that through observation and reasoning it was possible for Mankind to know everything. "Science" was presented as an approach that could lead the human race to Truth, and offered Man—traditionally seen as the pinnacle of creation, and now the pinnacle of evolution—the possibility of controlling Nature for their own benefit. Such a view was still to be found in Soviet philosophical works until very recently:

"The very structure of science . . . is being reshaped and integrated around one central problem—the problem of man as the highest stage of development of matter. For it is in man himself that mechanical, physical, chemical, biological and social laws are combined in the most advantageous synthesis."[7]

Moreover, when applied in the form of technology, science *worked,* and its attainments were wondrous to behold: it allowed for the elimination of disease, the reduction in death levels (particularly those associated with sepsis, childbirth, and childhood ailments), the general improvement in health and welfare, the creation of material wealth, the possibility of easy and comfortable travel, and of communication by telegraph across continents and under the oceans of the world. Moreover, in response to Malthus's pessimistic arguments, the invention of fertilizers and pesticides, and the development of breed in techniques based on an understanding of genetic principles, offered food in variety and quantities to solve the problems of the feeding the world's peoples.

The ideology of science and technology—"scientism"—took firm root in the nineteenth century, and the founding fathers of Marxism-Leninism were undoubtedly influenced by its values: witness their references to the work of other scholars, and their frequent use of analogies drawn from the natural world. Their assertion was that they had devised methods for analyzing human society comparable with— and complementary to—those devised with such brilliant success to understand and control the natural world. Indeed, they were quite self-conscious about this, as Engels famously asserted at Marx's graveside, comparing his achievement with that of Darwin: "As Darwin discovered the law of evolution in organic nature, so Marx discovered the law of evolution in human history."[8] In short, Marxism was seen even by its founders as the *science* of society, possessing a number of key concepts—particularly *class*—which its authors and their followers believed could be used to understand society. It differed from past approaches in that it supposedly rested on firm conceptual and methodological foundations, rather than on the misapplied faith of religion or the misconceived musings of philosophers. In an age in which "science" and "technology" offered such rich hopes, the claim to scientific status was a powerful—or impudent—one for the founders of Marxism to make. Moreover, as Ulam argues, this view is also compatible with the dominant views of early liberalism: it, too, held that the application of reason through science and education would lead to material wellbeing and spiritual liberation. Such an assertion has had a lasting impact, and until the last represented the official thinking of the CPSU and its leaders, however threadbare it appeared.[9]

When Marxism in Russia became "Marxism-Leninism" under Stalin, it retained its aura of "science," and has indeed been known alternatively as "Scientific Communism" and "Scientific Socialism" in the writings of Soviet ideologists such as V. G. Afanas'ev.[10] A recent edition of the semi-official *Short Political Dictionary* continued to identify Marxism-Leninism as "the ideology of the working class, the genuinely scientific ideology of social development."[11] Even such ostensibly rational and liberal reformist thinkers as G. Kh. Shakhnazarov, who became an aide to Mikhail Gorbachev, have written of Marxism-Leninism as "a universal scientific theory, which is constantly developing and being enriched by the experience of the workers' struggle for socialism in the whole world."[12] Such a statement concords with the Marxist view of the relationship among science, ideology, and class interests. This is a philosophical problem of considerable complexity;[13] from the purely *political* viewpoint, however, in which support must be won on the basis of whatever assertions may be useful, simpler—even "vulgar"—notions of "science" are adequate. In an age when the Soviet Union has landed rockets on distant planets and reached other attainments palpably associated with "science," Marxism-Leninism's claim to scientific status was reinforced. In June 1989, Mikhail Gorbachev still spoke of socialism as having become a science.[14]

More significant, there was a further claim, with tremendous political impact: that the Communist Party had a special relationship with the ideology and that this relationship mandated its rule. The party's monopoly of political power was traditionally justified not by the assertion that its leaders were more competent than any competitors, nor even that the party's policies were more likely to produce desirable results (such as increased wealth and enhanced wellbeing)—both of these typical arguments of political parties in competitive democratic systems—but rather that the leaders and their policies were *scientifically correct,* because they had been derived from this ideology. This "scientific" ideology supposedly gave the party "an understanding of the historical perspective," helped it to "determine the lines of socioeconomic and political development for years ahead" and "correctly to find its orientation in international development," and permitted it to "avoid errors and subjective decisions."[15] That claim of "scientific correctness" implied, of course, that other philosophies and ideologies were objectively *incorrect,* and that policies different from those adopted by the Communist Party likewise were unscientific and incorrect. In this way, the ideology supported the claims of Communist Party infallibility—what Gorbachev referred to at the Twenty-Seventh Congress in 1986 as the party's infallibility complex (which, incidentally, already indicated a somewhat different approach to the ideology—a point referred to below).[16]

Apart from its supposed status as a science in the nineteenth-century understanding of the term, Marxist-Leninist ideology is also exceptionally broad-ranging. The founding fathers—Marx, Engels, and Lenin—and their disciples have taken a wide interest in the affairs of human society, believing them to be systematically interrelated and interactive. The erudition of the original thinkers is impressive, and their search for a unified theory (which led, for example, to the comparison between the development of human society and the growth of plants, with revolutions as the "nodal points" between spurts of growth) is, again, quite in keeping with the spirit of the times. The quest for eternal truths may lately have been undermined by the twentieth-century stress on the relativity of knowledge, but the striving for theoretical simplicity and elegance remains a characteristic of scientific endeavor: the currently fashionable "chaos theory" stresses the similarity of patterns across systems.[17]

Marxism-Leninism and Nationality

Given the founding fathers' wide intellectual concerns, they had things to say about the nationality question. Their specific writings on nationality issues have been analyzed by other scholars, including, for example, Walker Connor, in his massive study of *The National Question in Marxist-Leninist Theory and Strategy.*[18] It has been pointed out that

Marx, Engels, and Lenin shared the common view of the day (perhaps under the influence of Darwinism and evolutionary theory) that some nations were superior to, or more advanced than, others: those "without a history" and "small relics of peoples," which were evidently not to be taken seriously as nations, since they were allegedly no longer capable of leading a national existence and should be incorporated into larger nations.[19] The interest shown by the founding fathers in, say, Ireland was not in the Irish nation *per se,* but primarily in the context of their analysis of *imperialism,* famously identified by Lenin as "the highest stage of capitalism." Some writers have discerned pro-Germanic sentiments in the writings of Marx and Engels, and others observe that Lenin held many of the Russians' assumptions about themselves as the leaders of the Slavs and superior to many of the smaller nations of the Empire: Lenin's interest in the fates of these was, again, principally in their value in helping to bring down the autocracy—not a misplaced interest, in the event.[20] (Lenin was also, in his later years, concerned that the Great Russians should not maintain their chauvinistic attitudes toward the smaller nations and nationalities; such concern was to little avail, given the growing dominance of Stalin, whose views on this question differed markedly from those of his political master.)[21]

The principal point is that, for the founders of the ideology, the concept of nationhood was of at best incidental significance. For *nationalists* it is the nation that constitutes the prime division of the human race—nations being succinctly defined by Rupert Emerson as "the largest community which, when the chips are down, effectively commands men's loyalty."[22] For nationalists, therefore, the nation is a natural phenomenon, to which individuals belong and to which they give their allegiance, which inspires them, and which enjoys an existence apart from the individuals or groups that compose it. Marxists' "scientific" perspective identifies quite different basic groups in society. Out of their materialist assessment of human existence, they identify economic production as the fundamental human activity, and derive a related view of the structure of society. An opposition of interests between those who owned and gained benefit from the means of production and those who worked the means of production without owning them led to the perception that these antagonistic groups—to whom the concept "class" was applied—were the most fundamental division within human society. As Academician Maxim Kin expressed it in 1982, "Marxism-Leninism regards the *socio-historical and socio-*

class community as the most important one among the communities covered by the term 'people.' "[23] This analysis was supported by further assessment of the impact of capitalist industry in breaking down the barriers between one nation and another by standardizing patterns of life according to the demands of industrial production. By the time of Lenin's development of these ideas, particularly in his theory of imperialism, the process of the internationalization of capitalism had gone still further—and the process has continued to this day, particularly outside the communist-ruled world.

Certain Austrian Marxists toward the end of the nineteenth century expressed the view that nations were the natural formations of human society, that they were worth preserving, and that, far from disappearing with the spread of democracy and socialism, they would grow in importance.[24] But such views were decisively rebuffed by the Russian Communists, guided by Stalin, whose own views eventually came to dominate Soviet thinking. Lenin, remaining staunchly internationalist to the end, firmly accepted the idea that the workers have no fatherland. And even in the 1980s, Soviet writers still referred to the nation as "an inevitable product of the bourgeois period," and asserted that capitalism, "Having created the nation, . . . then established specific relations between the nations, relations of mistrust, enmity and oppression."[25]

The Marxist contradistinction between class and nation is not, however, a neutral scientific proposition, a description of tendencies in human society. Their division of society into classes has an obvious normative content: they believed that human beings *ought* to behave in their own economic interests. Hence, their slogan "Workers of all countries, unite!" Hence, likewise, Lenin's call for the European proletariat to turn World War I into an international civil war of workers against the bourgeoisie: this is by no means a simple statement of his expectations. But is it not incontrovertibly clear, as Connor asserts, that Marx, Engels or Lenin believed that the human race would automatically give its allegiance in that way to those groups.[26] The experience of the workers in World War I must have shattered any illusions on that score for Lenin: Marx and Engels were, of course, safely dead by that time. Nevertheless, it remains a respectable position to adopt, to say that workers *should* recognize their true interests and act upon them, and even to go further and suggest that they should be educated to do so. But it is manifestly incorrect to suggest that is their natural reaction: indeed, given Marxism-Leninism's conviction that the bourgeoisie exploits and distorts such allegiances, to say what the natural propensity would be can only be an assertion.

Lenin acknowledged the power of national allegiance at least to the extent that he was prepared to make use of loyalty to the nation in the cause of the revolution, even if, as a good Marxist, he believed that in the long run the nation as a concept would become irrelevant. Hence, exploiting national grievances as a political tactic in the long-term strategy for attaining and securing workers' power was an important part of the Leninist legacy, and as such it, too, is a part of the ideological heritage. The notion of offering (even *guaranteeing*) self-determination of the peoples was a key policy for attaining and holding on to political power by the Bolsheviks. But by the same token, the long-term goal of eliminating national antagonisms, and ultimately creating a unified human race, remained the central element in the ideology. Such an aspiration has remained part of the communists' rhetoric.

One difficulty, however, in approaching the ideology in this way is—as is well known—that Lenin said different things on many subjects in different circumstances at different times, so that the general implications for policymaking are not unambiguous. Indeed, Pipes admirably demonstrates not only the differences of opinion between Lenin and his colleagues over this issue, but also Lenin's ability to change his mind when the circumstances of opposition to his plans obliged him to do so.[27] In fact, Lenin's views on the nationality question evolved, and were still evolving when he ceased active work— as, indeed, they had to be, given his disillusionment at the outcome of World War I, his frustration at the continuing manifestations of Russian chauvinism by many party and state bureaucrats, and his anger at the repressive attitudes and shameless behavior of some colleagues (notably Ordzhonikidze) in the affair of the Georgian communist opposition of 1921–24. To his theoretical appreciation of the precedence of economic and class factors over the cultural dimension of human existence, augmented by a political awareness of the opportunities for exploiting certain grievances, was added a very practical task: that of governing a country of enormous ethnic, linguistic, and cultural variety, with traditions and animosities going back in some cases over many generations, even centuries, and with economic and social structural features intertwined with these other "secondary" factors. If the

Leninist legacy in this respect is incomplete, this is partly because of the founding father's inability to complete the development of his ideas on a subject where reality impinged in ways for which theory had not adequately prepared him.

In the event, Stalin, whose expertise on this issue Lenin had relied on until at least after the Civil War, dominated the whole political system after Lenin's death, and his Great Russian chauvinistic solution became official policy that has lasted until the Gorbachev era, when its potentially fatal weaknesses were acknowledged to a certain extent.[28] A part of that inheritance is Stalin's famous definition of the nation as a "historically evolved, stable community arising on the foundation of a common language, territory, economic life and psychological makeup, manifested in a common culture"—a definition that was repeated almost verbatim as late as 1982, and was never repudiated or significantly modified. Moreover, the 1982 author stresses the point that "the common economic life is the determining factor in the formation and development of a nation [and] all the other attributes of a nation—the same language and territory, and the distinctiveness of culture, consciousness and psychology—do not stamp a definite social community by themselves (although each of these features is obligatory to a nation), but merely when combined with the community of economic life."[29] Even Marxist critics have pointed out the inadequacies of this definition, including its complete omission of reference to a belief among the members of a given community that they do, in fact, constitute a nation—unless that is subsumed under reference to the common or distinctive "psychology" or "psychological makeup." More recent Soviet writers include national consciousness in their definition.[30]

But "ideology" is not simply the ideas of Marx, Engels, and Lenin, supplemented by Stalin's accretions: it develops and is enriched by new formulations and concepts, enshrined in seminal documents such as state constitutions and party programs. The "classical" analyses were thus taken further in the Khrushchev era, with authoritative new statements in the 1961 CPSU program. There, in the "all-people's state," the supposed harmonious development of all Soviet nationalities was extolled as their "flourishing" (*rastsvet*); they were described as undergoing the process of "drawing together" (*sblizhenie*); and this was said to be a step on the way to their complete merging (*sliianie*). Eventually, indeed, as part of the creation of the classless communist society, it was expected that "the obliteration of all national distinctions, [including] language distinctions," would occur, although this would take significantly longer than the obliteration of class distinctions. Presumably that meant long after the classless society of "communism" had been attained. Nevertheless, language specialists such as Iu. D. Desheriev in the 1960s and 1970s rejected notions of the merging of languages, and devised projections of the viability of languages—the principal form in which national distinctions are expressed—mainly on the basis of the size of the community that uses them. Moreover, while urging a single "national" language to be neither possible nor necessary,[31] the use of Russian as the *lingua franca* was vital in the multiethnic Soviet society;[32] prominent non-Russians were enlisted to promote that cause.[33] Even so, one language expert felt moved to speculate on how a universal language might arise,[34] and the question of the complete merging of nations was discussed by other writers.[35] Moreover, the 1961 Party Program repeated the Stalinist formula concerning culture: "national in form, socialist in content," while looking forward to "the formation of a future single worldwide [*obshchechelovecheskoi:* literally, "common to Mankind"] culture of communist society."[36]

These are grandiose visions, indeed, yet these and other formulations of that time concur with the traditional view that national distinctions ultimately yield to economic and social forces. Some Soviet scholars even devised models that projected the stages of this development.[37] It should be remembered that when the Party Program was adopted the Soviet Union was said to have entered the phase of the "full-scale construction of communism," hence the urgency and excitement at the prospects for national integration.

In the Brezhnev era of the 1960s and 1970s, complacency overcame serious attention to policy in this as in other areas. Both policy and propaganda tended to reflect ideology by playing down national distinctions, masking Russian dominance, and declaring that the nationalities problem had been solved. By the 1960s, it was being proclaimed that the many peoples of the USSR lived together harmoniously in a fraternal family of peoples, and by the early 1970s, when the concept of "developed socialism" was being promulgated to depict the stage of development reached under Leonid Brezhnev, "the first internation socialist community" was said to exist.[38]

Moreover, evidence could be adduced to support the notion that the ethnic question was not of great political salience. There was much interregional migration, involving the creation of multiethnic new towns and cities; more than forty of the smaller nations had received a great boost to their identity by the provision of a written form of their languages; there was a fair amount of ethnic intermarriage; and so far as could be judged, ethnic animosities—some of them going back for decades, even centuries—surfaced only very rarely, and were given virtually no publicity. As a recent commentator admitted, nationalistic manifestations in Abkhazia and Northern Ossetia were unknown to the general public.[39] Meanwhile, bilingualism with Russian was being pushed as the official policy in non-Russian areas, and in this field as in others the regime presented the position in self-congratulatory terms. The "solution" of the nationalities question within the USSR was even extended to other countries of the "socialist commonwealth," linked by ideological, political, economic, cultural, educational, and scientific ties, supposedly leading to "a new, socialist [communist] civilization" as "an important stage in the emergence of the future worldwide sociocultural community of people."[40] Such extravagant claims are now proven to have been quite worthless.

Brezhnev's immediate successors, Andropov and Chernenko, added little to the ideological formulations in this particular field, apart from two crucial acknowledgments, one general, one specific. First, Andropov hinted that, for all its supposed reliance on the "scientific" ideology, the party possessed no ready recipes for all situations—indeed, the ideology needed constant refinement;[41] and in the nationalities field, Chernenko (speaking while Andropov was in office) stated that all was not well on the nationalities front, even though the problem had been in the main solved. As Chernenko expressed it, the question "had not been completely removed from the agenda."[42] This carefully phrased and modest reformulation of an ideological position opened the way for more substantial questioning later. With the arrival of Gorbachev and his policies of glasnost and perestroika, the political marketplace was opened to bids from a variety of social forces, and a challenging of traditional policy and assumptions and subsequent reexamination of the standard formulae were permitted. Problems in the area of interethnic relations were subjected to critical (if largely conventional) scrutiny, and earlier complacent analyses sharply criticized,[43] as the self-awareness of national groups surfaced, with consequences that are now very much to the fore and appear to be leading to the inexorable destruction of the state and its system.

Ideology and Nationality Policy

As has been seen, ideological statements can be differentiated from policy, and ideology proves an uncertain guide: it may even be confusing. For example, the question of definition of nationality has led, as a recent commentator pointed out,[44] to markedly wide divergences in the actual number of recognized ethnic groups—only some of which qualify as "nations" or even "nationalities" under the official definition. Yet that issue has certain policy implications: "scientific" it may be, but there is certainly no simple, direct relationship between the values enshrined in the ideology and the policies chosen to implement them. As Archie Brown recently observed: "although Soviet Marxism-Leninism makes some doctrinal claims or policy options more difficult than others to justify within the terms of the ideology, that ideology can be quite flexible if the Party leadership wishes it to be. . . . There are few policy options that are actually ruled out by Marxism-Leninism, although it is an ideology that makes it more difficult to defend some than others."[45]

What ideology may do is supply a number of basic values, such as the abhorrence of chauvinism; but what it certainly has never done, in this field as in any other, is provide a blueprint; nor did it guarantee implementation of its own precepts. In practical politics, judgments have always had to be made about how to deal with particular nationality issues as they arose. For instance, from a Marxist-Leninist (or even plain Leninist) point of view, at what stage is it appropriate and at what stage inappropriate to encourage national self-determination? What are the limits? What exactly is "national self-determination"? Does it necessarily mean independence? By what mechanisms is the question to be decided by a nation? In the course of history is a nation permitted to change its collective mind? And, when applying these questions to the former Russian Empire, is it possible to devise a policy that will treat all nations and nationalities equally and fairly? Is "equal" the same thing as "fair"? And who is to be the judge of equality and fairness? As Connor aptly puts it, a "congenital problem in the pursuit of national equality [is] the difficulty, if not the impossibility, of discovering a universally acceptable formula to achieve equality between unequals."[46] These are some of the questions that arise in approaching the nationality question, and they have to be balanced against priorities in other areas of responsibility. In the course of such an interaction, the ideology itself may be modified, as the authoritative statements of successive leaders bear witness.

In terms of policymaking, Connor's formulation represents an excellent expression of the *general problem* of nationality in the Soviet Union. How can any government treat equally entities that are patently not equal? Can the ethnic question even be effectively managed, let alone "solved," within the former Soviet Union, or within all its constituent parts, now that the union has disintegrated? One of the great difficulties facing Gorbachev (and his predecessors and indeed successors) in confronting different nationalisms stems from precisely this: a policy that may be appropriate in, say, Estonia might not work in Azerbaijan or Turkmenia, since the circumstances—of culture and tradition, of economic development, of geopolitics—are quite different in the various cases. Moreover, the dismemberment of the Soviet Union into its constituent republics will not make the problem disappear: the question is not simply that of a decaying empire, as it is sometimes presented.[47] Solzhenitsyn's statement of September 1990 suggesting precisely the dismemberment of the union into its existing constituent republics is less than convincing on that score.[48]

It is clear, in fact, that there are numerous specific nationality issues that need to be addressed in quite different ways, and the most glaring oversimplification is to see "the nationality question" as consisting solely, or even primarily, or relations between the Russians and the rest. For example, the recent murderous conflicts between Azeris and Armenians over the status of Nagorno Karabakh can be blamed on the Russian-dominated Soviet government in the 1920s, which imposed a particular carve-up of territory; but the issue of proximate concern is a clash between two cultures, in neither of which the Russians, as such, have an obvious stake. In the clashes between Abkhazians and Ossetians and the Georgians over the status of the Georgian language in the Georgian republic, the Russians were called upon to protect the minority's cultural rights against the encroachments of the Georgian nationalists. Similar conflicts have been reported in Moldova (formerly known as Moldavia), where the Gagauz do not relish the imposition of "Moldavian" (Romanian) as the official language to the detriment of their own native culture (which has already suffered with the imposition of Russian), and of their opportunities for social mobility.[49] Elsewhere in the multinational, multicultural former Soviet Union, the potential for cultural and political domination by "intermediate" national groups is vast. Seen thus, the question has both vertical and horizontal dimensions.[50]

That is but one facet of the range of problems that face any policy-makers in devising nationality policy.[51] Another is that this policy is intertwined with demographic, religious, migration, education, cultural and other policy areas, so the task of managing national relations becomes a single component in a complex web of decisionmaking. Its salience will fluctuate, as will perceptions of its relative importance; from both the political and the analytical perspectives, therefore, it is unreal to think in terms of a single "nationality policy" in isolation.[52] A final complication is the tendency, derived from the structure of the state, to equate "nationality" with "republic,"[53] so that "nationality policy" became policy applied toward different republics in terms of cultural, economic, regional, taxation, investment and other relevant policies. In effect, the ethnic dimension became enmeshed in the practicalities of day-to-day government. In any case, for any given policy pertaining to nationality questions, there could be perhaps several explanations, not all of which are clearly attributable to ideological influences. Interpretation thus becomes ambiguous, even when ideological motivation can be identified.

For example, the hierarchy of nationalities and languages identified by Soviet scholars and politicians, in which the Russians and their language occupy the leading position, is quite compatible with the social Darwinism of Marxist thinking; it also accords with traditional Russian feelings of superiority, and gives rise to expressions of chauvinism. The promotion of Russian as the language of interethnic communication, and bilingualism based on Russian as the second language (for all but the Russians), is also a response to the practical need for the citizens of a state to be able to communicate with one another. By contrast, the promotion of the languages of some forty of the less numerous peoples, giving them an alphabet and developing literary forms of the language, had the effect of sustaining separateness where assimilation might have taken place: it cut across the quasi-Darwinian natural evolution—but it was entirely consonant with Leninist warnings against Russian chauvinism. Policy in this area may, indeed, have appeared contradictory: however, it can be seen as a response to specific problems, and an attempt to attain a specific goal with manifest ideological content—demonstrating that under "socialism" the cultures of all nations flourish.

The notion of "proletarian internationalism," likewise, in which nationally the Russians and internationally the Soviet Union played the "leading" role, was both a response to the original clarion call to workers of all countries to unite, and also a reflection of geopolitical and historical reality. It was in the cities of Russia, after all, that the first Marxist-inspired revolution took place: by the same token, of course, that facilitated the perpetuation of Russia's and Russians' traditional aspirations toward a global role. Moreover, from the viewpoint of modern theories of political development and nation-building, the values formally embraced by "proletarian internationalism"—mutual tolerance and collaboration for the common good, under the leadership of the more "advanced" nations—would have to be pursued by practically any regime that inherited such a diversity of national groups. The problem parallels that of tribalism in many new African states.[54] The only alternative would be to permit the breakup of the union, as happened in Pakistan in 1971, and as might have happened in Nigeria in the late 1960s. Yet very few governments (more probably, none), whatever their ideological color, would embrace that as deliberate policy. That is why the breakup of the Soviet Union was accompanied by political struggle between the center and national territorial units.

Thirdly, the subordination of national interests to class interests in the rationale for various policies—alternatively expressed, the faith that the common development of material wealth for all will permit ethnically based antagonisms to be overcome—clearly reflects the mode of thought of the particular ideology. This approach justified the policies of industrialization and urbanization in the peripheral areas, the allocation of cadres from the center to direct the development, the encouragement of migration of skilled workers (primarily Russians) into the "backward" areas, official approval of ethnically mixed marriages, and so forth. It could be further justified in terms of the "leading" nation assisting its brethren to attain the benefits of modernization. It was also, however, a set of policies that entrenched a strongly centralist ethos, and moreover it promoted Russian (or more broadly Slav) notions of superiority, leading to chauvinism, and condemned members of other ethnic groups to a sense of inferiority, exacerbating resentments and tensions, rather than overcoming them.

The point is that in many policy areas it is not clear whether the motivation was directly ideological, or simply pragmatic or political and merely rationalized in ideological terms. Economic development (which certainly was ideologically motivated) requires education for the uneducated, and a healthy workforce, which in turn implies improvements in housing, sanitation, safety and so forth, particularly for those relatively undeveloped areas where much development has been targeted. At the same time, socialist principles imply giving "backward" peoples the chance to take advantage of what modern civilization offers by way of opportunities for self- and collective development and expression.[55] Principles[56] of equality, enunciated in the ideology and expressed in such documents as the Constitution, require at least the appearance of equal treatment of all citizens, regardless of nationality.[56] Yet, the very policy of industrial expansion in the nonindustrialized areas has a differential impact on the various nationalities: some will gain from the welfare and investment policies required by industrialization, while their traditional culture will be undermined and even destroyed unless specific protective measures are also taken. Other nations, however, will be required to supply both the funding (through taxation) and the skills to oversee the modernization: this places them in a position of authority and even domination over the indigenous peoples, in what may appear to be a colonial situation. Moreover, the very need to hold everything together—the most basic requirement of any political system[57]—requires lines of efficient command and communication in a vast and disparate land: those may be most effectively provided by the careful central allocation of trusted administrators, whether of the principal nation or controlled by forms of discipline such as "democratic centralism."

In short, the practical application of the ideology not only reinforced certain natural needs but also cut across certain other ideological values. It is hardly surprising, therefore, that Soviet nationalities *policy* appeared at times confused, contradictory, and even hypocritical. And, in those circumstances, it is equally unsurprising that it has been variously interpreted. For instance, the notion that Russian somehow deserves to be the language of interethnic communication because "the great Russian people played the vanguard role in emancipating the peoples of the USSR from tsardom, from the oppression of tsarist and local enslavers and gave fraternal assistance in the political, economic and cultural development of the national republics"[58] was not greeted with universal acclaim by the peoples who were required to express their undying gratitude in an alien tongue. Nevertheless, the assertion that those who speak only the language of one of the smaller northern tribes are restricted in their opportunities for geographic and social mobility[59] is undoubtedly true; so is the proposition that those whose linguistic facilities are thus limited can be less easily accommodated in an advancing, science-based, technologically oriented economy—or at least their role will be minor:[60] both they and their rulers need them to have access to a major language.

Finally, the sheer impractibility of running central government in all the languages spoken by the population imposes its own logic: a *lingua franca* is imperative. It need not, of course, be Russian: indeed, given the manifest disadvantages of such a choice (despite the advantages enumerated by some commentators)[61] and given the widespread teaching of English as the principal "foreign" language in the education system, a form of English could become the "language of interethnic communication," as it is officially within India and between, say, educated Nigerians and Indians. That would have the additional advantage of opening the former USSR to the influence of Western scientific literature and culture—and, if publication in the language were deployed more widely, a more effective means of influencing the largely English-speaking outside world. It is, of course, quite easy for a complacent Briton or American to talk in such terms, and such a choice as official policy is highly unlikely, if only for reasons of Russian self-esteem: it would signal once again the victory of the West and the dominance of English-language culture, already preparing to feed the country with American carryouts and entertain it with American and Australian soap operas. Official policy may need to bow to popular usage, however, in twenty years time. Finally, although sophisticated analysis suggests that it is possible to devise a language regime that is both efficient and fair,[62] the sheer complexity of the Soviet situation renders the search for such a solution immensely difficult.

The Failure of Nationality Policy

As to the effects of these policies and the accompanying propaganda, they have clearly not created the intended sense of community and internationalism that had been declared.[63] Indeed, as events during 1980 and 1990 in the Baltic republics in particular demonstrated, it led to a buildup of grievances against the migrants that has been reflected in new discriminatory regulations. The values of "proletarian internationalism"—"the unshakable fraternal solidarity of working people," as it has also been called[64]—enshrined in official statements have manifestly not been internalized by the populations or even the communist elites of the major nationalities. Substantially, therefore, by the end of the 1980s the Soviet handling of the nationalities question had recognizably failed.

Tensions in Policymaking

The fact is that the policymakers have been confronted with a number of tensions, some induced by the values of the ideology itself, which the ideology is not capable of resolving. They needed to demonstrate that the various national groups did indeed prosper and live happily side by side, and were not being dominated by Great Russian chauvinism. That implied the "flourishing" of nations: removing any sense of grievance, and permitting the nationalities to develop their potential alongside one another. But that may have conflicted with other goals by creating and reinforcing a sense of national identity that otherwise might have withered.

The need to avoid charges of forced assimilation promoted the perpetuation of national identity. But that also opened the prospects for ethnic discrimination—not only by Russians but also by anyone who became aware of ethnic identity, and among the masses rather than the elite. Aleksei Kosygin may have said accurately on Canadian television that some of his best friends were Jews; but discrimination against Jews was (and still may be) perpetrated by a housing list manager in Odessa, a hotel receptionist in Kiev, or a waiter in Kishinev. It will require arduous effort to eradicate xenophobic and similar prejudices that often go back many generations, and that glasnost and democratization have given a fresh airing.

A different question arises over the peoples of remote areas, which stood at a low level of economic development when the Bolsheviks assumed responsibility for them. The policy options here were akin to those facing the (usually Westernized) leaders of many emerging Third World nations today. The first option is to force them to modernize—which means abandoning their traditional way of life, normally by imposing alien administrative systems, an alien educational system, and the like, and probably on the basis of educational materials and personnel, administrators and managers brought in from outside, most likely educating, training, and administering through a foreign language. Such a strategic decision affecting a whole community is inevitably taken by the political elite, and imposed on a more or less unwilling populace, who cannot be effectively consulted on the matter. It changes their identity irrevocably, and distinctions that enhance the variety within the whole of human society are lost. That was, of course, the gist of Marx's comments on the standardizing effect of international capitalism: in fact, as Ulam argues, of industrialization.[65]

The stark alternative is to insist on preserving the traditional identity, at the risk of leaving the ethnic group to languish in poverty and a primitive lifestyle, cut off from the benefits of modern technology and world civilization.

For a leadership caught on the horns of such a dilemma, Marxism-Leninism provides some guidelines. Materialism leads inevitable toward policies of development: industrialization, with all that it entails, is deemed to be *per se* a good thing. Yet it bears the attendant risks that those to whom modernization is brought will ungratefully rebel, as a result of the sense of self-awareness combined with loss of identity that modernization promotes. The rebellion may simply take the form of demands for effective input into the process whereby decisions that affect them are made: such aspirations can probably be met by modification of the political structures, accompanied by affirmative action policies, such as have been called for at the official level for a number of years.[66]

Current Concerns: Does Ideology Matter?

Even so, there is a further dilemma in handling some of the smaller and more remote nationalities. Of the people of the former Soviet Union, the Ukrainians, the Baltic peoples, the Georgians, the Armenians, and a number of large and medium-sized ethnic groups can doubtless exist as independent states (indeed, some of them have in the past), even as "socialist" states if that is their choice. Whether that is indeed their aspiration (rather than simply that of certain vocal groups among their populations) is being tested in the wake of the collapse of communist rule in the putsch of August 1991.

Yet, even with territorial adjustments, including the dismantling of the whole edifice built on the ruins of the Tsarist empire, the nationality problem will not be "solved." The prospect of independence or even autonomy does not realistically exist for many of the smaller groups, numbering in some cases only a few hundred members. For these, some form of close involvement with a larger nation is inevitable, and in many (but certainly not all) cases that large nation is the Russians. Inevitably, over the medium term, at least, a degree of assimilation will take place, leading eventually to disappearance. This has happened, e.g., to the cultural identity (as opposed to the geographic identity) of Cornwall within England and the United Kingdom. That prospect is, of course, quite in keeping with the views of the founding fathers of Marxism-Leninism on such ethnic groups, and population census figures suggest that it has indeed been occurring over the past several decades.[67]

Since Gorbachev came to office in the mid-1980s, the nationality issue has been addressed with an uncommon urgency, prompted by rapidly developing events on the ground. The anti-Russian riots in Alma-Ata (Kazakhstan) in December 1986 were but the first in a catalog of incidents ostensibly related to interethnic concerns. Gorbachev's rather bland comments on the question to the Twenty-Seventh Party Congress, in February 1986, swiftly gave way to far more urgent appeals for calm and for national harmony. In self-critical style, some of the country's leading specialists were obliged to reexamine the history of the regime's treatment of the issue, as a means of redirecting the course of policy and thereby, perhaps, avoiding catastrophe.

The late Yulian Bromlei, for example, in an article published in January 1989, catalogued past errors, including the damage done by the indifferent bureaucratic approach to national and cultural interests, the promotion of idealized versions of how various nationalities became associated with Russia, and the sheer ignorance of ethnic processes resulting from the failure to collect or to publish appropriate statistics. He also pointed out aspects of regional and national policy that had been overlooked: for instance, the responsibility of multinational territorial units, he indicated in a comment of great relevance for post-communist regimes based on former Soviet republics, is to foster the perpetuation and development of all the ethnic groups on their territory, and not simply that of the titular or the largest nationality (which may not be identical). He suggested that nationality-based district and village soviets, such as existed until the early 1930s, might be resurrected. The status and rights of national minorities might be given constitutional definition, as might the formal status of the local languages and of Russian (as the *lingua franca*)—an area where language policy intersects with nationality policy: in this connection, he suggested studying foreign experience. And, in general, he quoted approvingly the then Politburo member A. N. Yakovlev's call for an acknowledgment of the validity of the variety that exists in society, rather than trying to standardize everything in bureaucratic fashion. The discourse increasingly concentrated on *practical* measures, rather than slogans or ideological statements.[68] Due reference to Lenin may have continued, but the need was now seen as "the elaboration of constructive decisions."[69]

Measures adopted included a revamping of the highest representative bodies of the state—the USSR Supreme Soviet and the newly created Congress of People's Deputies—to establish a forum for far more genuine interest articulation, including that by representatives of the national territorial units; and, in July 1990, a restructuring of the Communist Party's Politburo to include *ex officio* the first secretaries of the union republics.[70] The Communist Party, moreover, in September 1989, devoted a special Central Committee Plenum to the nationalities, which adopted as policy the renegotiation of the treaty of union and a variety of additional measures to devolve authority from the center, and to serve and protect the interests of national minorities— including those minute groups in remote areas for which the ideology's founding fathers had little but contempt.[71] A significant measure of devolution within the party was also contemplated: by the time such ideas were reiterated at the Twenty-Eighty Congress less than ten months later, however, the parties in the three Baltic republics had declared their independence of Moscow, and only the Estonian party sent a delegation to the Congress. In fact, the Communist Party gave increasing signs of paralysis, of intellectual and moral bankruptcy, offering no leadership, direction, consolidation, or coordination to the processes of policymaking and governing Soviet society.[72] Its last vestiges of credibility—already threadbare—evaporated in the three days of August 19–21, 1991, when a failed traditional communist coup led to the destruction of communist power and accelerated the breakup of the union.

To some extent the new organs of state power—the Congress of People's Deputies and the Supreme Soviet—showed signs of willingness to tackle specific problems, such as those concerning the Volga Germans, the Crimean Tatars, the Meskhetian Turks, and other dispossessed and deported minorities.[73] But increasingly, the initiative came from below, with individual ethnic communities making demands, setting the agenda, and using the newly established democratic process to resolve issues regardless of the wishes of the center. In all this, ideology played an apparently minor role, if it figured at all,[74] with events moving so rapidly that policy appeared to limp behind the aspirations of at least some sections of the population. The center's measures proved to be—to use a classic cliché—too little, too late to save the Union and may even fail to preserve the peace.

The impending arrival of "communism," greeted rapturously in 1961, under which national distinctions would become irrelevant, focused attention on the future. It gave way to the complacent depiction of a "developed socialist society," focusing fradulently on past achievements that had left allegedly no unresolved problems. Under Gorbachev, that concept was in turn replaced by "developing socialism" and even "self-renewing socialism"—ideological developments that directed attention much more to the present, with problems that demanded urgent practical solution. In fact, even the attainment of socialism became a rare phrase in the political lexicon, and was unlikely to feature prominently. What were once basic tenets of the traditional ideology were abandoned in the economy, in political practices and structures, and in many areas of policy, including that of interethnic relations. The advent of "communism" was abandoned; the focus on current problems lent pressing significance to creating a new *modus vivendi*. The integrity of the system—indeed, the very viability of this multiethnic society—was at stake, and practical measures were far more urgent than quotations from long-dead thinkers who never envisaged this as a significant or lasting problem.

Conclusions

If Marxism-Leninism is conceived of as a scientific analysis of human propensities to respond in particular ways to different problems, it is quite wrong in its understanding of the relative significance of *nation* and *class* as a focus of loyalty. If, on the other hand, it is seen as an aspiration to overcome some of the divisions among human beings and unite them in the endeavor of enriching their common existence, it is a noble but perhaps misguided ideal. If it is seen as setting out rules for handling the nationality issue within individual societies (or even on the global level), it seems to fail abysmally. In this area, as in others, the Soviet leaders had to make up the rules as they went along, and in so doing they were of necessity interpreting, reinterpreting and therefore modifying the ideology; many of their subjects totally disregarded it. It is not clear whether or not Marxism-Leninism is infinitely flexible, or whether it imposes limits as to what it can accommodate. Recent history suggests that it was treated as if it was only of limited flexibility. In the area of national relations and probably most others, the politicians were forced by circumstances to abandon it as totally inadequate to serve their purposes.

NOTES

1. Hélène Carrère d'Encausse, for example, was one of the more noteworthy exponents of the idea that national distinctions could lead to the break-up of the Soviet system, in her best-selling book published over a decade ago: *Decline of an Empire: The Soviet Socialist Republics in Revolt* (New York: Harper, 1979; originally published in French as *L'Empire Éclaté*, Paris, 1978). The Soviet dissident Andrei Amalrik, in his *Will the Soviet Union Survive Until 1984?* (London: Allen Lane, 1970), also suggested that at a time of crisis the nationalities could revolt; even earlier, in his preface to Vyacheslav Chornovil, *The Chornovil Papers* (New York: McGraw-Hill, 1968), itself an eloquent plea for just treatment for Ukrainians, Zbigniew Brzezinski expressed the view that the nationality issue could become politically more significant for the Soviet Union than the race question had been in the United States (p. vii).

2. As late as June 1990, Mikhail Gorbachev reaffirmed his identity as a "communist" shortly before a visit to the United States: see his interview, "I Am an Optimist," *Time,* June 4, 1990, pp. 13, 17.

3. Apart from my general study of the history and philosophy of science, I am particularly indebted in this context to the insights of Adam Ulam, *The Unfinished Revolution: An Essay on the Sources of Influence of Marxism and Communism* (New York: Vintage Books, 1964) and other historians of ideas. I am also indebted to the contributors to a conference on Soviet ideology held in May 1985, papers from which were published under the editorship of Stephen White and Alex Pravda, under the title *Ideology and Soviet Politics* (London: Macmillan, 1988).

4. These elements of definition are adapted from Carl J. Friedrich and Zbigniew K. Brzezinski, *Totalitarian Dictatorship and Autocracy,* 2d ed. (New

York: Praeger, 1966), p. 88, and Alan R. Ball, *Modern Politics and Government,* 2d ed. (London: Macmillan, 1977), p. 244.

5. Hence the distinction drawn between Soviet ideology and American political beliefs: see Zbigniew K. Brzezinski and Samuel P. Huntington, *Political Power: USA/USSR* (Harmondsworth: Penguin, 1977), ch. 1.

6. According to the *Oxford English Dictionary.*

7. G. Volkov, *Man and the Scientific and Technical Revolution* (Moscow: Progress, 1975), p. 137.

8. Quoted in Ulam, *Unfinished Revolution,* p. 12.

9. By the time the Party held its XXVIII Congress in July 1990, it was clear that Soviet society enjoyed a plurality of ideologies, among which Marxism-Leninism appeared almost completely discredited in the public mind (see below).

10. See, for example, his *Fundamentals of Scientific Communism* (Moscow: Progress, 1977; also G. N. Volkov ed., *The Basics of Marxist-Leninist Theory* (Moscow: Progress, 1979), Part 1.

11. *Kratkii politicheskii slovar'*, 6th ed. (Moscow: Politizdat, 1989), p. 183.

12. G. Kh. Shakhnazarov, *Sotsialisticheskaia demokratiia: nekotorye voprosy teorii* (Moscow: Politizdat, 1972), p. 95. Such forms of expression may, however, have been the price for being allowed to publish under Brezhnev.

13. As argued, for example, in Jorge Larrain, *The Concept of Ideology* (London: Hutchinson, 1979).

14. Speech to closing session of the Congress of People's Deputies, *Pravda,* June 10, 1989, p. 2.

15. The words are Leonid Brezhnev's speaking at the Twenty-Fourth CPSU Congress in 1971): *XXIV s"ezd Kommunisticheskoi partii Sovetskogo Soiuza: Stenograficheskii otchet* (Moscow: Politizdat, 1971), 1, p. 127.

16. *XXVII s"ezd Kommunisticheskoi partii Sovetskogo Soyuza: Stenograficheskii otchet* (Moscow: Politizdat, 1986), 1, p. 101. More recently Gorbachev stressed that the party "does not lay claim to infallibility and to absolute truth," but must "self-critically analyze its every step": *Pravda,* June 10, 1989, p. 2.

17. See James Gleick, *Chaos: Making a New Science* (London: Heinemann, 1988).

18. Walker Connor, *The National Question in Marxist-Leninist Theory and Strategy* (Princeton: Princeton University Press, 1984).

19. Engels, quoted in Richard Pipes, *The Formation of the Soviet Union: Communism and Nationalism, 1917–1923,* revised edition (New York: Atheneum, 1974; originally Cambridge: Harvard University Press, 1954), p. 21.

20. See Pipes, *Formation, passim.*

21. See Pipes, *Formation,* ch. 6.

22. Quoted in Connor, *Nationality Question,* p. 39, n. 11.

23. Maxim Kim, "The Soviet People, a New Historical Community," in

Socialism: Nations and National Relations (Moscow: "Social Sciences Today" Editorial Board, 1982, p. 82 (original emphasis); compare G. Ie. Glezerman: "There is no doubt that the class factor merits priority in the revolutionary transformation of the world": see his Classes and Nations (Moscow: Progress, 1979), p. 8; and, in the Gorbachev era, an editorial in Kommunist firmly stated that "Nothing can revoke the significance of the class approach—this ABC of Marxism": "Dialektika novogo myshleniia" (The Dialectics of New Thinking), Kommunist, 1987, no. 18, p. 9.

24. Notably Karl Renner and Otto Bauer: see Pipes, Formation, pp. 38–9.

25. Volkov et al., Basics, p. 215.

26. See Connor, Nationalities Question, ch. 1.

27. Pipes, Formation, passim.

28. For example, Stalin's policy toward the small nationalities had been identified as plainly assimilationist: see M. Guboglo, "Natsional'nye gruppy v SSSR," Kommunist, no. 10 (1989):53–58 (at p. 54). The author (whose surname suggests him to be of possibly Gagauz nationality) cites the official silence in Soviet Moldavia about the existence of Gagauz and Bulgarian minorities, who were referred to until the beginning of perestroika as Moldavian (moldavskie = pertaining to Moldavia, rather than moldovane = ethnically Moldavian), while Gagauz primary schoolchildren were obliged to receive instruction in Russian. Similar considerations applied to minorities in other republics, such as Kurds and Azeris in Armenia, Poles in Lithuania and Latvia, Belorussians in Estonia, Uzbeks in Kazakhstan, etc. (ibid.).

29. Victor Shevtsov, The State and Nations in the USSR (Moscow: Progress, 1982), p. 7. The original definition appears in Stalin's 1913 pamphlet, Marksizm i natsional'nyi vopros (Marxism and the National Question), reprinted in I. Stalin, Sochineniia: Tom 2, 1097–1913 (Moscow: OGIZ, 1946), pp. 290–367, at p. 296. Shevtsov's contribution is, in part, an attempt to debunk what he terms (p. 13) "Bourgeois ideologists' inclination to make a fetish of the ethnic aspects of a nation, which they represent, in contrast to the social factors, as pivotal in the life of a nation."

30. See, for example, Horace B. Davis, Toward a Marxist Theory of Nationalism (New York: Monthly Review Press, 1978), p. 71; Davis is also far less dogmatic than Soviet commentators have been in his acceptance of Lenin's evolving views on the question. Glezerman (Classes and Nations, pp. 18–19) accepts the significance of national consciousness, as shaped by "the impact of the daily conditions of life," as does M. Kulichenko, in Nations and Social Progress (Moscow: Progress, 1984), pp. 52–53.

31. See, for example, Iu. D. Desheriev, Zakonomernosti razvitiia i vzaimodeistviia iazykov v Sovetskom obshchestve (Moscow: Nauka, 1966), pp. 20 and passim; Iu. D. Desheriev and I. F. Protchenko, Razvitie iazykov narodov SSSR v Sovetskuiu epokhu (Moscow: Prosveshchenie, 1968), p. 121.

32. Desheriev and Protchenko, Razvitie iazykov, pp. 118–19.

33. For example, the Uzbek novelist and party leader (and friend of Leonid Brezhnev), Sharaf Rashidov, in his article, "Dal'neishee sblizhenie i vsestoronnii rastsvet sotsialisticheskikh natsii" *Voprosy filosofii*, no. 2 (1960):30; he also makes the point that the dialect of Tashkent (the republic's capital city) formed the basis of literary version of the Uzbek language: quoted in Desherliev and Protchenko, *Razvitie iazykov*, p. 102.

34. E. Svadost, *Kak vozniknet vseobshchii iazyk?* (Moscow: Nauka, 1968); Svadost is regarded as somewhat idiosyncratic by Soviet specialists on these matters.

35. See, for example, M. M. Suzhikov, *Razvitie i sblizhenie sovetskikh natsii* (Development and Drawing Together of Soviet Nations) (Alma-Ata: Nauka, 1978), notably the conclusion, pp. 226–30.

36. An English version of the text of the Third Party Program of 1961 is to be found in Grey Hodnett ed., *Resolutions and Decisions of the Communist Party of the Soviet Union: Volume 4: The Khrushchev Years, 1953–1964* (Toronto and Buffalo: University of Toronto Press, 1974), pp. 167–264; the section dealing with national relations appears on pp. 242–45; for the Russian version of this section, see "Programma Kommunisticheskoi Partii Sovetskogo Soiuza," reprinted in *Kommunisticheskaia partiia Sovetskogo Soiuza v rezoliutsiiakh i resheniiakh s"ezdov, konferentsii i plenumov TsK* 8 (Moscow: Politizdat, 1972), pp. 282–85. As late as 1978, another specialist, M. I. Kulichenko, was still inspired by the Party Program in looking forward to the eventual creation of an "worldwide culture, single in form and content": see his contribution to Iu. D. Desheriev ed., *Natsional'nyi iazyk i nastional'naia kul'tura* (Moscow: Nauka, 1978), p. 11. See also M. Mchedlov, "K voprosu o stanovlenii kommunisticheckoi tsivilizatsii," (On the Formation of Communist Civilization), *Kommunist*, no. 14 (1976):32–43.

37. For example, M. I. Kulichenko, *Natsional'nye otnosheniia v SSSR i tendentsii ikh razvitiia* (Moscow: 1972), cited in Suzhikov, *Razvitie i sblizhenie*, pp. 228–30.

38. Volkov ed., *Basics*, p. 217; Kulichenko, *Nations and Social Progress*, pp. 172–81.

39. Yu. V. Bromlei, "Natsional'nye problemy v usloviiakh perestroiki," (National Problems in Conditions of Perestroika), *Voprosy istorii*, no. 1 (1989):27.

40. Yu. Bromley, *Ethnic Processes* (Moscow: "Social Sciences Today" Editorial Board, 1983), pp. 123–25; Bromley cites Mchedlov, "K voprosu" pp. 35–36.

41. In a speech to his first Central Committee Plenum after taking office in November 1982, Andropov admitted: "In general, in the economy there are many urgent tasks. I, of course, have no ready-made prescriptions for resolving them": *Kommunist*, no. 17 (1982):16; see also Andropov's important article, "Uchenie Karla Marksa i nekotorye voprosy sotsialisticheskogo stoitel'stva v SSSR" (The Teaching of Karl Marx and Certain Questions of

Socialist Construction in the USSR), *Kommunist,* no. 3 (1983):9–23: there he pointed out (p. 22) that Marxism is not a dogma, but a "living guide to action" which needs constant development as society evolves. Gorbachev later gave prominence to this theme, entitling a section of his book on perestroika, "We have no ready-made prescriptions": see M. S. Gorbachev, *Perestroika i novoe myshlenie dlia nashei strany i dlia vsego mira* (Moscow: Politizdat, 1988), pp. 62–72; in the English edition, pp. 65–74, the reference is to "formulas," rather than prescriptions.

42. *Pravda,* June 15, 1983, p. 3. The identical phrase was used in the first major statement on the national question of the Gorbachev era: see "Internatsionalistskaia sut' sotsializma" (The Internationalist Essence of Socialism), *Kommunist,* no. 13 (1987):3–13 (at p. 4).

43. Notably in the editorial in the Party's theoretical journal *Kommunist,* "Internatsionalistskaia sut' sotsializma." This article expanded on remarks made by Gorbachev at the Central Committee plenum of January 1987, in the wake of the disturbances in Alma-Ata in the previous month (*Pravda,* January 28, 1987).

44. Yu. V. Bromlei, "Natsional'nye problemy," p. 25; estimates have varied between about 60 and 800 ethnic groups!

45. Archie Brown, "Ideology and Political Culture," in Seweryn Bialer ed., *Politics, Society, and Nationality Inside Gorbachev's Russia* (Boulder, CO: Westview, 1988), pp. 16, 29.

46. Connor, *National Question,* p. 485.

47. See, for example, Bohdan Nahaylo and Victor Swoboda, *Soviet Disunion: A History of the Nationalities Problem in the USSR* (London: Hamish Hamilton, 1990), ch. 17, "Crisis in the Empire." These authors refer (p. 354) to "the imperial relationship between the Russians and the non-Russians," and later (p. 357) identify "the main issue" as "the future of the Soviet empire and of the relationship between the Russians and non-Russians." In our view, the issues are substantially more complex.

48. See A. I. Solzhenitsyn, "Kak nam obustroit' Rossiiu? Posil'nye soobrazheniia," supplement to *Literaturnaia gazeta,* September 18, 1990, p. 1. Solzhenitsyn does, however, point out (p. 3) that even a Russia shorn of most of its associated republics would still be a multinational entity. His position in 1990 appears a little less dismissive of the minor nationalities than his stance of 1973: compare Aleksandr I. Solzhenitsyn, *Letter to the Soviet Leaders* (New York: Harper, 1974), p. 31.

49. On this question, see Vladimir Socor, "Gagauz in Moldavia Demand Separate Republic," *Radio Liberty Report on the USSR* 2(36) (September 7, 1990):8–13, esp. pp. 9–10.

50. Nahaylo and Swoboda, *Soviet Disunion,* p. 354.

51. Some of these issues are discussed in Rasma Karklins, *Ethnic Relations*

in the USSR: The Perspective from Below (Boston and London: Allen & Unwin, 1986).

52. See the contributions to Henry R. Huttenbach, ed., *Soviet Nationalities Policies: Ruling Ethnic Groups in the USSR* (London: Mansell, 1990), Part I (essays by Gregory Gleason, Edward Allworth, John N. Hazard and Michael Rywkin). This notwithstanding the constant reference to "the CPSU's Leninist nationalities policy."

53. Or, as one Soviet commentator put it, "The forms of national autonomy should not be confused with administrative-territorial division, as sometimes is allowed to happen": see Iu. D. Desheriev, *Zakonomernosti razvitiia i vzaimodeistviia iazykov v Sovetskom obshchestve* (Moscow: Nauka, 1966), p. 56.

54. See Peter Calvocoressi, *Independent Africa and the World* (London: Longman, 1975, p. 25).

55. L. L. Rybakovskii, *Migratsiia naseleniia: prognozy, faktory, politika* (Moscow: Nauka, 1987), p. 165.

56. Thus, it has been argued that the application of demographic policy differentiated along regional or ethnic lines would infringe constitutional principles: ibid.

57. Blondel, for example, has identified maintenance of the society through the peaceful resolution of conflict as the most fundamental goal of political systems: see Jean Blondel, *An Introduction to Comparative Government* (London: Weidenfeld & Nicolson, 1969), pp. 6–11.

58. Desheriev and Protchenko, *Razvitie iazykov*, p. 119.

59. Ibid., p. 121.

60. A counterargument would point to the rapid expansion of high-technology industry in Asian countries such as Singapore and South Korea, where modern technology has enabled relatively unskilled an uneducated populations to manufacture sophisticated products. Nevertheless, the point still holds: it is not indigenous but Japanese technology and creative expertise that dominate the lives and work patterns of the workforce (as, increasingly, they do in other parts of the world).

61. For example Desheriev and Protchenko: *Razvitie iazykov*, p. 119.

62. Jonathan Pool, "The Official Language Problem," *American Political Science Review* 85(2) (June 1991):495–514.

63. See, for example, Volkov, *Basics*, pp. 218–20; also Yulian Bromley and Mikhail Kulichenko, "The National and the International in the Formation and Development of Socialist Society," in *Socialism: Nations and National Relations*, pp. 54–55.

64. Shevtsov, *State and Nations*, p. 6; see also Afanas'ev, *Fundamentals*, pp. 247–48; Suzhikov ed., *Razvitie i sblizhenie*, Chapter 2.

65. Ulam, *Unfinished Revolution*, p. 44.

66. At the Twenty-Sixth Party Congress, for example, Brezhnev noted the

right of nations to be adequately represented in their party and government organs, and a similar point was made on the sixtieth anniversary of the founding of the USSR by Andropov, who added a warning against approaching the question by means of quotas: see *Pravda,* February 24, 1981 (Brezhnev), and December 22, 1982 (Andropov).

67. For a succinct discussion of this issue, see Jerry G. Pankhurst and Michael Paul Sacks eds., *Contemporary Soviet Society: Sociological Perspectives* (New York: Praeger, 1980, pp. 47–53.

68. Bromlei, "Natsional'nye problemy," p. 41. The lack of statistics in another area of relevance to nationality policy—migration—is deplored in Rybakovskii, *Migratsiia naseleniia,* pp. 4, 17.

69. Bromlei, "Natsional'nye problemy," p. 41.

70. Since the spring of 1990 these included, for the first time, a representative of the party in the Russian republic, which hitherto had not possessed a distinct Party organization.

71. The point was amplified by Guboglo, "Natsionalnye gruppy."

72. Peter Frank, "The End of Perestroika," *The World Today* 46(5) (May 1990):88.

73. See *Pravda,* June 25, 1989, p. 2

74. Alexander Motyl has suggested that by early 1989 ideology had been "silenced"; it was "barren" and "an embarrassment," indeed had "lost its ideological . . . character": see his contribution, "The End of Ideology?" in Henry R. Huttenbach and Alexander J. Motyl eds., *The Soviet Nationalities and Gorbachev* (special issue of *Nationalities Papers* 17(1), Spring 1989):17–21,31.

4. Legitimations, Nationalities and the Deep Structure of Ideology

Neil Harding

S UCCESSFUL ideologies are, by definition, resilient. They adapt over time to changing circumstances, they alter their hierarchy of objectives, seek new constituencies, and manage in one way or another to turn apparent setbacks into victories. For the greater part of the century communism proved itself the most successful of the contemporary political ideologies in virtually all these respects. It burst upon a stunned world in 1917, capturing and consolidating power in the world's largest country, promising a radical transformation of all social political and economic relations. By the end of the Second World War it had transformed the backward and notoriously diverse nations constituting the USSR into an industrialized superpower, had spread its power deep into the European heartland and was on the brink of assuming control of China. All the efforts of its opponents to contain it militarily, blockade it economically, isolate it diplomatically, and assault it theoretically proved to no avail.

They seemed in retrospect to have bolstered its cohesion and confirmed its ideological postulates. The now evident accelerating collapse of communism had little to do with these external assaults; on the contrary it gathered momentum with the progress of detente and the relaxation of superpower rivalry. We may well conclude that the prolonged Cold War actually served to arrest the process of ideological decomposition and to postpone the consequent legitimation crisis that is now so plainly evident throughout the communist world. The Beijing gerontocracy calls out its loyal troops to put down its own people in a bloodbath that outraged the civilized world. Yugoslavia is rent with ethnic dissension, economic chaos, and civil war, even in East Germany old style Stalinism retreated under popular pressure and demands for democracy, while in Poland and Hungary communism as a distinctive ideology and structure of power abruptly disappeared.

Within the former Soviet Union itself the Baltic republics successfully challenged the authority and legitimacy of the center, as did Ukraine. Ethnic and religious tensions between Armenians and Azerbaijanis have again erupted in violence and death. An empire has crumbled.

The old values that bound people and nations have abruptly foundered. The Soviet Union is at the point of transition from its old (and now discredited) mode of legitimation to a new one. The crisis lies in the fracturing of the deep structure of ideology that hitherto grounded political authority and the real power relations of Soviet society. Its precepts and its promises were not only discredited in the eyes of its own subjects but also were openly and trenchantly criticized by Party leaders and intellectuals who were supposed to have been its guardians. The power holders recognize that they can no longer rule in the old way and the people refuse to be so ruled. The old unanimity on unifying principles and the nature of the common social goal has, with astonishing rapidity, been cast aside. Everything is now up for renegotiation: the nature of socialism, property relations, center-periphery relations, political structure and Constitution, individual and group rights. Politics has re-emerged to center stage and the whole discussion of the management of public affairs has become an essentially contested discourse with an ever-broadening range of participants. Among the key participants to the debate are, of course, the minority nationalities. The emergent *political* principle of popular sovereignty gives them immeasurably more room for articulation and organization than the cramped confines of the old *economic* mode of legitimation that has so effectively, and for so long, incorporated them into a "common" productive endeavor over which they had little control and whose benefits they enjoyed only on the express condition that their ethnic and national aspirations were suppressed. It is a sign of the times that now the prime condition of success for the national political elites is that they appear as strident champions of particularistic national claims.

Marxism is, on the face of it, an unlikely basis from which to derive satisfactory principles for the grounding of political authority, not only because it envisaged no permanent role for the State but also, and more basically, because it rejected the autonomy of politics. In the Marxist canon, politics drew up the battle lines for the decisive clashes of the class war. It was part of the prerevolutionary process of refining, articulating, and organizing classes in and for themselves. It was therefore an arrest in the development of a truly human consciousness whose essential precondition was the ending of class (and all other) divisions. It followed that after the Bolshevik revolution no provision was made for politics; its leaders were all agreed that the time for debating in parliamentary talking shops was over, and the time for action to transform material reality and with it humanity itself had arrived. Through works rather than words were socialists to be known. This, in its turn, rested on an assumption that socialism itself, its substantive content and the goals it was to pursue, was not a disputed concept.

The problem was that in the early years of Soviet power there was a heated debate both within the top leadership and among its supporters and detractors as to the nature of the socialist project. Bukharin, Lenin, Trotsky, the Democratic Centralists, the Workers' Opposition, the Mensheviks, and the SRs all had their differing perspectives and priorities that threatened, after the end of the civil war, to surface once again in open debate and to break the fragile hold that the Bolsheviks had secured over most of the Imperial domains. The Bolsheviks knew that they could not win a political debate based on democratic precepts of universal suffrage, popular sovereignty, and free access to the media of communication. Their constituency had been severely depleted in the civil war. The proletariat had been declassed, the urban centers depopulated, industry was at a virtual standstill, and even the surviving trade unions were thoroughly alienated. In March 1920 Lenin reminded the Tenth Party Congress that the Communists were but a drop in the great ocean of the people. Their urban base had collapsed and their rural organization was vestigial and thoroughly ineffective. There could be no question, in this situation, of securing a popular mandate through free, open, and contested elections.

But if the regime could not be grounded in terms of democratic or popular sovereignty, to what principles could it appeal to secure and bind people to its authority? By the end of 1920 the Party theoreticians had already arrived at a model for legitimating state power that was unique in the history of social thought. It was also tightly cohesive and immensely successful in maintaining the integrity of the greatest territorial area with the most complex ethnic, national, and religious differences of any state in history. Too much has been made of the wholesale use or threat of naked coercion and terror in forging and sustaining unity in what many believe to be an unnatural political unit with the size and national diversity of the Soviet Union. Too little attention has been paid to the unifying principles (in which many from idealism or self-interest believed) in the name of which this coercion was utilized.

It was only at the point when the leadership itself came to question those unifying principles that its own will to utilize coercion, to defend its own prerogatives and those of the State, finally began to crumble. This I take to be the central and most crucial feature of the current crisis of contemporary communism. The old economic mode of legitimation has finally been discredited. It no longer serves to bind allegiances nor to justify extensive use of force. Appeal is therefore made to alternative and incompatible precepts of democracy and popular sovereignty—or a properly political mode of legitimation. But then immediately there reemerges the expressly political debate foreclosed in the early 1920s about the nature of socialism, the objects of the Union, the rights of the individual and of Union Republics vis-à-vis the central state. Politics, in short, reemerges as a contested discourse that gives short shrift to those believing that status, position, and possession of a special sort of knowledge warrant their pronouncements. By its very nature popular sovereignty must be impatient with privileged and protected constituencies that isolate themselves from its sway, plural voting (unless good reason supports it) and all public decision-making or administration that is not answerable to it. It is also becoming increasingly clear, and could readily have been predicted, that in its purview and pretensions it is bound only by its own self-imposed constraints. Since the present Soviet specifications of socialism, with its derivative constitutional, legal, social, and economic entailments, was in no meaningful sense a product of democratic deliberation it follows that popular sovereignty could not bind itself to it. If it had done so it would evidently have renounced its own sovereignty and emasculated and discredited itself. Either its will is to prevail in the State or the will of the Party is to prevail. The situation of effective dual power in which the new mode of legitimation enjoyed an overwhelming moral superiority yet found itself confronted on all sides with real power relationships that stemmed directly from the old discredited economic mode of legitimation could not last long.

We should be clear that what is at stake here is not an academic exercise in abstracted political theory. On the contrary what is eventually at issue is the question of power at every level of social economic and political life. Let us be a little more concrete and explore these very real and practical implications of the rival schema of legitimation within the former Soviet Union—how they beget structures of power and patterns of domination and subordination.

The mode of legitimation that worked tolerably well up to the early 1970s was explicitly economic in its justifying rationale, its means of operation, and its means of reproduction. It survived as long as it was plausible to project its economic results as satisfactory and as long as it was possible successfully to exclude a political alternative to it. Its axiomatic starting point is the assertion that as a mode of production socialism is superior to all others. It claims to replace the anarchic planlessness of capitalism with conscious and planned allocation of all the material and human resources available to society so that, for the first time in history, all the impediments to optimizing the articulation of social production are removed. In order to accomplish this, however, it evidently followed that the State (the agency of planning) would have to fully control, and therefore own, the material elements of the productive process: land, factories and machinery, communications, and capital reserves. It would also have to have exclusive control over labor resources and therefore each successive Soviet Constitution guaranteed the State's exclusive right to allocate to each and all the measure of labor. But the State is also a universal distributive mechanism that claims to be more just and equitable than any of its competitors. Here too the State claims exclusive jurisdiction in allocating to each and all the measure of consumption. And the precept upon which the allocation of rewards and status is based is that they should be proportional to productive endeavor. As one contributes to the common productive goals of society so one is to receive. "From each according to his work" was the principle of distributive justice definitive of Soviet-style socialism.

Behind this set of legitimizing principles there lies, of course, a great baggage of more or less intelligible ontological, epistemological, and historical argumentation and assertion that constitutes what might be termed the deep structure of ideology. Since power dispositions within this unique state form (particularly the role of the Party and the salience of planning) eventually derived their authority from it we need briefly to rehearse some of its principal contentions. We begin with the proposition (upon which a great deal hangs) that humans are by nature tool-making and productive beings drawn into relations with others by the necessity of material survival. Humans enter society, therefore, in their capacity as laboring beings and the object of their association with others is to maximize their material satisfaction. Society is here conceived of as essentially a web of productive relationships striving toward optimal articulation. The history of society is the tale of consecutive modes of economic organization striving to overcome the impediments they inherit (as well as those they themselves produce) to the realization of this goal.

If we were to write a conventional social contract account of the grounding of obligation in the Soviet State it would go as follows: Humans are creatures of extensive needs but limited productive capacity. On entering society they renounce their productive autonomy in return for the benefits that accrue from a consciously planned and coordinated social system of production. This social system of production must have a well-elaborated division of labor and this presumes authoritative allocation of function. Individuals therefore accept that this task must be assumed by the most authoritative and inclusive agency of society—the State.

We should, at this point, note that the State accepts individuals not as the bearers of preexistent or inalienable rights, nor as the bearers of distinctive national consciousness, but exclusively as the bearers of labor power. It is, as the Constitution insists, a state that expresses the will and interests of "the *toilers* of all nations and nationalities of the country." It is, at least in theory, blind to the national or ethnic origin of its subjects—that is a matter of irrelevance to the fulfillment of its goals and therefore to its conditions of membership.

It was, on the basis of economic determinism, optimistically expected that experience of a common productive system would generate a common consciousness that would, for instance, require all who participated (and especially those aspiring to positions of power and influence) to be at home in the culture and discipline of modern industry and proficient in its *lingua franca* (which could only be Russian). It would require rapid mobility of labor and substantial migrations of large groups of people, a common educational system, and patterns of socialization that ensured that the ethos and goals of the whole community were absorbed and internalized. The mode of production was to be the great melting pot that would refine the separate nationalities into new material—the historically new community of the Soviet people consolidated in an All-People's State. In return for individuals ceding to the State their erstwhile property rights and direction of their own labor the State promises to reward them in proportion to their contribution to the productive goals of the whole organism. The State is, again, the authoritative allocator of the benefits that are to accrue to each. It further promises that the material benefit derived will continually improve relative both to internal and international standards.

It is the Plan that articulates the optimal disposition of human and material resources available to society and expresses its common productive goals. But society as a whole cannot itself formulate or implement these goals. Their formulation must rest with those who have a deep and "scientific" understanding of the dialectics of social and economic life, understand the laws that govern their development, and have a prescient awareness of the stage of social and economic development that is striving to be realized. These assertions rest, in their turn, upon a materialist metaphysic that declares the world is material reality and wholly knowable because matter is neither capricious nor arbitrary in its make-up. In its behavior it conforms to predictable law-governed patterns of regularity that it is the business of scientists to explore and reveal. Their principal methodological aid in this enterprise is materialistic dialectics that enjoins the necessity of studying the parts in relation to the whole and its developmental change through the clash of antagonistic forces locked within it.

It is, of course, the Party that jealously preserves its exclusive claim to the guardianship and development of dialectical reasoning. It is the metaphysical foundation of its claim to anticipate the future and therefore to lead both society and state and to control, in particular, the formulation of the Plan. According to the primitive positivism that informs this view of science there is but one optimal resolution of any scientific problem—one solution or program that best fits the situation. The status of the Party as the repository of appropriate scientific expertise in the planning function would therefore be impugned if different groupings within it or outside it were permitted to offer rival programs. Science would be reduced to conjecture and disputation. It would thereby lose its quality as science which (according to this superannuated view) must speak with surety and singleness and voice. The metaphysic from which the Party derives its authority therefore demands that Communists be so organized as to ensure that programs, plans, and decisions are authoritatively arrived at and then obligatory. Above all *public* disputation must be ruled out.

The organizational structure and procedural style of Communist deliberations now follows: the accountability of lower Party organs to higher ones, the effective sovereignty of one officer—the General Secretary of the Party—whose office warrants his discourse and places it beyond the bounds of criticism. The procedural style was likewise always impersonal, authoritative, and above all, unanimous.

When, after the Stalin revolution, the Soviet State actually did become the exclusive owner and ubiquitous disposer and allocator of all resources and rewards, it became uniquely capable of reproducing, at all levels, the real power relations that sustained it. It was therefore, at least until the advent of Gorbachev, extremely effective in marginalizing the so-called national question.

If in theory it is the Plan that expresses the fusion of private and corporate interests and fuses individual, social, and state purposes into an indissoluble whole, in practice it obliges individuals to work collectives, work collectives to ministries, Union Republic ministries to Federal ministries, and all to the guidance of the Communist Party. At every stage there is a power relationship. There are disposers and allocators of scarce and highly valued resources and they, above all, have direct material and status interests in preserving their powers and authority and therefore in ensuring that the principles that sustain them are learnt and observed (or, at the barest minimum, are not openly flouted). This was, for fairly obvious reasons, no very difficult task so long as the regime was able to ensure that (a) the volume of patronage, investment resources, welfare provision, goods, services, promotions, wages, etc. available to those it licensed to allocate them continued to grow and *therefore* that (b) the extent of individual, group, ethnic, and national expectations and aspirations could broadly be accommodated or at least dampened down to containable levels. The regime's ability to manage these two necessary conditions for the reproduction of its own power structures was, in turn, intimately bound to the third: that its own agents—especially those at the apex of the system—should themselves in their actions and pronouncements be seen to repose unquestioned faith in the unifying principles that sustained the whole.

It was (and still is) largely within and through what is called the social division of labor—the aggregated work and production processes—that individuals, groups, and national communities are socialized into accepting the values and modes of public activity that sustain the patterns of domination and subordination in Soviet society as a whole. The power to grant or withhold investment resources that central ministries disposed of vis-à-vis the individual Union Republics or particular enterprises was the same power that enterprise managements disposed of vis-à-vis their individual workers. Access to these highly valued and necessarily scarce goods (investment funds and credit in the one case, promotion, housing, schooling, pensions, etc. on the other) was controlled either directly by Party or State cadres or by work collectives or trade unions in which their voices predominated. At the minimum ritualized, but nonetheless significant, tokens of assent to the unifying principles were enjoined upon all who sought access to these goods.

For those within the educational and social elites of minority nationalities seeking access to responsible positions (or the *Nomenklatura* listings) that carried with them exclusive access to the broadest range of special provision (strictly graduated according to status) much more was required. As Party membership was virtually obligatory with all the organizational discipline and universalist metaphysic that went with it, aspirants as a condition of access to power and its attendant privileges, had to be versed in the unifying principles that cemented the whole, be seen to be active in their propagation and severe in putting down all separatist claims that threatened its integrity. Their primary affiliation unambiguously had to be to the historically new community of the Soviet peoples. Before all else they had to be Soviet patriots. The price of preferment and the continued enjoyment of very scarce and highly valued goods (closed shops, foreign currency and foreign travel, cars, dachas, closed clinics and sanatoria, etc.) was incorporation, denial of particularity, and enthusiastic endorsement of the principles and practices that confirmed the Union. As everywhere self-interest proved the most potent prop to the common interest.

Within this system, therefore, prudence, habituation and material interest (and observing the fate of those who refuse to signify) combined to incorporate individuals, groups, and nationalities into the common productive association. They also combined to produce patterns of outward activity that were system-sustaining. All were locked into a structure of complicit legitimation. However much one is inclined to rebel or criticize, one is obliged by prudence (the desire to benefit) to assent. To obtain requires signifying, and each signification and resultant benefit incorporates the individual and simultaneously confirms the existing structures of power. The same precepts bound to the same practices were used to incorporate national elite groups and the ethnic intelligentsia. Advancement was always within the power of the center to bestow or withhold. What the State gave so it could take away. Advancement, or even retention of privilege, was always conditional on signifying in the appropriate manner—on the debilitating daily erosion of the persona that Havel calls living within the lie. Advancement here was national or self-debilitation and was always an augmentation of the central state's power.

Individuals both in theory and in practice were made to feel their powerlessness, ineffectiveness as autonomous producers, and reliance upon a social work process that was consciously directed and therefore required authoritative allocation of function. by the same tokens the major national groupings loosely associated with "their own" Union Republics had to signify both in theory and in practice their assent to an All-Union social division of labor that ostensibly sought, in the specialization of its parts, the optimal articulation of the whole. Economic autarchy and self-sufficiency was a quality of the whole productive organism and of it alone. Its constituent territorial regions were, according to the whole integrative logic of the planning mechanism, therefore best developed according to those specialized areas of production that climate, topology, natural resources, indigenous skills and, above all, the needs that the whole All-Union economy commended.

As with individuals, so with the national groupings: there are costs and benefits that attach to incorporation into so vast and all-embracing a social division of labor and their balance will be different in each particular case. For some there was the blight of "imperialist" agricultural or industrialist monoculture, for others the expansion of diverse industries at the cost of inward labor migration and the dilution of ethnic particularity exacerbated by the absorption of native elites. In all cases there was the trauma of rapid adaptation and disruption of established social practices to meet the demands of this peculiar form of modernity. But to offset these costs there undoubtedly were, at least for many nationalities, very considerable advantages, particularly for those elite groups that might in other circumstances have featured so prominently as the bearers and creators of national consciousness. In the Southern and in the Eastern Republics postwar advances in welfare provision, standards of living, access to education, and promotional prospects—even if unevenly spread—were nonetheless impressive— at least until the beginning of the economic downturn of the 1970s and 1980s. Tensions could be contained so long as there was a general perception of consistent advance and economic expansion could absorb the aspirations of national elites.

We need not here go into the difficulties that confront all social contract theories. We know that they are fictional rather than factual or historical statements and so the absence of cases of explicit consent does not invalidate their logic. It need not be demonstrated that individuals or national groupings positively choose to join a particular regime or give their explicit assent to the operative principles that sustain it. The very fact of living under its laws and enjoying the benefits it confers—what is commonly known as tacit consent—suffices to oblige. The function of the social contract is, nonetheless, an important one. It establishes the aims of the association, the benefits that accrue to contracting parties, and the duties incumbent upon them. The sting in the tail of all such theories (even Hobbes's) is that if the regime reneges on its obligations and fails to deliver the promises made, it forfeits the allegiance of its subjects. The degree of vulnerability of the State in this regard is a function of the extensiveness of the promises it makes. Old Hobbes wisely limited the benefits proferred by Leviathan to the minimal ones of preventing civil strife and providing defense against external aggression. The Soviet State, by contrast, made promises more extravagant than any in history and, to worsen its plight, it unwisely made them amenable to statistical compilation and comparative reference.

The claim that socialism conceived of as an integrated mode of production is superior to all competitors in productivity and equity of distribution is, like many such claims in the Marxist tradition, rather ambiguous. Are we to interpret it as a statement of present fact or of latent potential? This is not an insubstantial interpretive problem for if it is presented as a statement of potential—that an economy of this sort has the immanent capacity to outperform competitors—the fact that it does not presently do so need not be damning. Countervailing and distorting factors might be invoked to explain apparent failings: disastrous starting point, foreign subversion, internal wreckers, the ravages of invasion and war, insufficient experience in articulating the whole planning mechanism, etc. With each decade of repetition, however, these extenuating circumstances lost their plausibility, particularly when it could be demonstrated that competitor regimes had suffered similarly but prospered more rapidly.

The frailty of establishing an economically grounded claim to legitimacy is that it explicitly invites comparison with competitors in areas of activity that readily lend themselves to quantification. Figures on growth rates, productivity, consumption patterns, relative living standards, and so on, can, of course, be massaged and indices of comparison and their baselines judiciously selected. But there are limits even to the proverbial mendacity of statistics. Government control of the appropriate data, the media of communication, and of access to foreign publications or foreign travel, can help to insulate the population from external comparators and exaggerate internal successes. But this can be counterproductive in that broad sections of the population tend to believe the very inverse of what they are told and create for themselves widely extravagant conceptions of Western opulence. The gap between promise and performance is thereby widened in the public mind and disaffection grows.

In all regimes, of course, economic performance is probably the single most important factor in popular assessments of a government's competence. In democratic regimes *governments* succeed or fail at the polls largely on the basis of public perception of their ability to manage the economy. In the Soviet Union, however, *the State itself* was threatened when widespread perception of consistent and chronic failure of the economy was allowed public expression. When this tide of popular discontent was taken up by the most prominent Party and State leaders (as in the Gorbachev period) the hollowness of the State's claims to authority became apparent. The emperor stands revealed. Gorbachev's repeated attacks on the shortcomings of the planning mechanisms, on the graft and corruption that it harbored, on the lack of commitment and initiative that ran through the whole system were, no doubt, refreshing in their frankness and vital to the process of regenerating an economic system that was obviously in decline. They were also necessary to the political task of replacing a discredited and corrupt elite with energetic and able reformers. For these reasons Gorbachev's domestic policies were originally greeted with sympathy and approval. What was not reflected upon was the enormously destabilizing impact all this had upon the legitimacy of the regime—its claim to rule. Admission of gross and persistent errors in the management of the economy and questioning whether centralized planning were any longer possible or desirable finally brought down the very foundations of the State. Acute and fundamental questions presented themselves not only theoretically but also in the demands and protestations of millions of people (especially among the national minorities) roused to a new-found sense of political potency precisely by the crumbling of the old edifice of power.

If it was openly and frankly conceded by the leadership that the economic system was radically flawed and badly administered then what became of the Party's exclusive claim to prescient knowledge and ability precisely in these spheres? In the light of the admitted failure how could it justify its constitutionally guaranteed position as "the guiding and directing force of Soviet society, the core of its political system and of all state and social organizations"? Nor did the deeper Marxist metaphysic that informs this grandiose role escape unscathed. What price now the assertion that dialectical expertise (the Party's preserve) reveals the hidden mechanisms of objective social and economic development? What now becomes of the implicit social contract enjoining forbearance on the part of individuals, groups, and national communities in return for sharing the bounty of conscious collective labor articulated and optimized through the Plan? If the Planners (the paradigmatic personnel of Soviet socialism) had failed socialism what credence could be given to the "scientific" world view upon which the whole project was said to rest?

The crisis of contemporary communism was the bankruptcy of its purely economic mode of legitimation. The old unifying principles that formed its core were discredited. They no longer served to bind or to oblige. Legitimation crisis here was, quite literally, failure to produce the goods.

By the 1970s the Soviet State was clearly unable to fulfill its part of the social contract. Expectations could neither be met nor dampened down. There was, moreover, widespread cynicism about the actual operation of the system of distributive justice. In the Brezhnev years the operation of the principle of socialism "from each according to his ability to each according to his work" seemed to be honored more in the breach than the implementation. Spectacular cases of cronyism, corruption and graft, conspicuous consumption on a provocative scale, the emergence of a decadent *jeunesse dorée,* and the inertia of the leadership, all combined to discredit the system in the popular mind. Its legitimacy ebbed away in proportion as the volume of resources available to central allocators diminished and as the popular perception of distributive abuse grew.

It was, however, with the coming to power of Mikhail Gorbachev that the crisis of legitimation really began to threaten the integrity of the State. The promise of the social contract—that in return for the forbearance of individuals and national groups in pressing their particular claim their material benefits would rapidly grow—had not been honored. The claim that the Soviet mode of production was demonstrably more efficient and dynamic, or more responsive to consumer needs than the capitalist West, now became not only insulting but risible. Witness the persistent shortages of basic foodstuffs, services, consumer durables, cultural and recreational facilities, inadequate housing and declining standards of public health. Gorbachev's policy of glasnost authorized the very public exposure of these abuses and shortcomings and he added his own voice to the chorus of complaints about the inadequacies of planning and the abuses of the past. His motives were, no doubt, mixed. In part he needed a rapprochement with the people and recognized the Party's need to make apology and admit to error. He was sufficiently sensitive as a politician to have realized that a grievance voiced and acknowledged as legitimate is, by that fact, a little less keenly felt. Glasnost in this respect acted as a sort of safety valve to prevent the build-up of an explosive head of steam.

The former Soviet leader also had instrumental purposes that were served—to dislodge in the swiftest possible time those who had either brought the Party into disrepute or who stood against his plans for restructuring. Gorbachev had, for a variety of motives, licensed and authorized open discussion and public debate on a whole range of fundamental questions whose implications threatened the very foundations of the State and the authority of the Party. The enormities of the Stalin period were acknowledged, the forcible annexations of the Baltic Republics were the subject of official enquiry and were undone; relations between center and periphery, the nature and status of differing forms of property holding, the right to strike, the virtues of directive central planning compared to those of the market, the balance between State, cooperative, and individual enterprise—all these fundamental issues were up for renegotiation and reinterpretation in the developing new system. The very licensing of this debate was of enormous significance. The Party acknowledged that it did not have a monopoly of appropriate expertise in the management of public affairs. It acknowledged that there *was* no archimedean point of objective, scientific, and therefore indisputable truth in these matters. It swept the whole monist metaphysic that sustained the exclusive jurisdictions of Party and State to one side. There can therefore be no epistemological defense against pluralism and a thoroughly relativist conception of truth. To grant this is however to grant the legitimacy of a plurality of voices and articulate groups within society.

The rapid changes in these crucial areas were signalled in Gorbachev's own public vocabulary. "Humanism" displaced "materialism," "pluralism" replaced "monism," "parliamentarianism" lost its "bourgeois" prefix and "social democracy" ceased to be the enemy. As the discredited metaphysic crumbled so alternative groundings of political obligation had to be formulated and it was clear from the outset that these could not simply be grafted on to the old ones as Gorbachev had so desperately hoped.

The March 1989 elections were the first really significant evidence of a decisive shift in legitimating principle. Of course the Party (via a three-tier voting system) assured itself a majority in the new Congress of People's Deputies, but this was not the significant point. What was significant was that, for the first time in Soviet history, the precept of popular sovereignty exercised through the free selection of candidates competing for votes on the basis of differing platforms was accepted and implemented. Adroitly Gorbachev immediately moved to have himself elected as first president of this new State body that claimed its mandate, in part at least, from the democratically expressed will of the people. He sat at the apex of two latently opposed structures of power that grounded themselves in fundamentally antagonistic principle and practical implications.

In the entire history of the Soviet Union the State, through its economic and subordinate educational and propaganda agencies, took upon itself the task of creating the new Soviet nation. Now, of course, the resurgent nations of the Soviet Union set themselves the task of creating states and the logic of the democratic process stood strongly in their favor. In the March 1989 elections the people had their first real task of power. They not only toppled many of the mighty from their high seats and humiliated the Party, but also began to realize that it was now they who could set the political agenda. Popular sovereignty cannot for long be cramped and confined. Its goals, the histories it creates, the constituencies it mobilizes, and the representatives it chooses cannot, definitionally, be fore-ordained. The spectacular successes of the Popular Fronts in Latvia, Lithuania, and Estonia demonstrated the rapidity with which political constituencies were made to coincide with expressly national ones. The price of success in appealing for the popular vote in all three Republics was unambiguous endorsement of a nationalist stance. All the impedimenta of nation states in the making made their appearance: the flags and insignia, the vernacular as the obligatory vehicle for politics, the revival of national days and a calendar of martyrs and, especially, the rewriting and recasting of history.

The mythology of a benign and voluntary fusion of peoples in the founding of the transnational Union was, by many, seen, not only as a travesty of the historical facts but also as a deep affront to the pride of many of its constituent nationalities. History lies deep in nationalist politics and looms large even in electoral politics. The recovery (or invention) of an authentic and particular history, veneration of its martyrs, and solemn remembrance of its defeats and past triumphs is always part of the apparatus of modern ideologies in marking off a constituency. It is well under way among many of the former Soviet nationalities. So long as the movement for democracy continues and increases in scope this revisionist reconstruction of histories will play an increasingly prominent role in mobilizing national groupings around distinctive political programs.

All hegemonic structures of power are complex. The more successful and enduring of such political structures have an intricate web of institutional arrangements, patterns of socialization, and allocation of rewards that are bound together by the belief system that ground the whole regime. In the Soviet Union, as other chapters of this book demonstrate, the dominant Russian Party/State successfully deployed the Army, the Russian language, the legal and constitutional systems, the *nomenklatura,* education, and the media of communication to promote cohesion and a sense of common purpose. More negatively, these institutions were used to deny public space to all rival formulations of what should form the public agenda. This chapter, like that of Richard Ericson has, for the most part, been concerned with the manner in which economics has not merely been used to bolster cohesion but has been constitutive of the grounding principles from which all the other institutions of Soviet society derived their authority. My argument is that the consonance of grounding principles with institutional prerogatives and real power and patronage structures proved extraordinarily effective in sustaining the integrity of the Soviet Union for the seventy-odd years of its history. There was an impressive monism to the system—its interlocking structures of power effectively managed the national question, marginalized it, fostered a conception of the common good in terms of which separation was seen as treasonous. The happy and harmonious condominium of all the Soviet people was not merely a Constitutional fiction, it was an obligatory article of faith in all public discourse—the whole metaphysic, from which the integrity of the systems of power derived, demanded it. Those systems of power had as their goal and object the positive role of transcending all particularisms. The Union had to be expressly and actively anti-national. It was the last grand and perverse attempt to realize the universal goals of the Enlightenment, to create a *human* society.

To ascetic and rootless intellectuals such grand projects might have had some genuine appeal. Certainly in war-ravaged Europe of 1917 it seemed plausible, even honorable, to believe that the nation states that had brought such death into the world had had their day. But to ordinary people in ordinary times the badge of universal humanity as an identifier is none at all. Identities distinguish and are therefore distinctive. And democracy itself is borne out of the distinctiveness of constituencies within modern society. Its ideologies in part reflect but also create those constituencies and it is entirely obvious that, for good and ill, national constituencies have become the principal beneficiaries of the process of democratization begun several years ago in the former Soviet Union. The centrifugal nationalisms re-created by this process swiftly wreaked their revenge by dissolving the state power of the mutual oppressor. They drummed the old Union off the stage of history in the last days of 1991. Whether, having profited from and adroitly used the democratization process for their own purposes, these potentially conflicting nationalisms have the will, or even the capacity, to sustain democracy, is a large and threatening question. The omens, it must be said, are not auspicious.

5. Managing Nationalism: State, Law and the National Question in the USSR

John N. Hazard

O N September 2, 1991[1] another marker was placed in the seventy-year search for a legal formula that would have met both the Leninist commitment to "class" as the cement holding Soviet multi-national society together and the often strident demands of the former Russian Empire's non-Russian subjects for recognition of some measure of autonomy.

Lenin had recognized early the political difficulty of reconciling his Marxist-inspired political philosophy and the pressures coming from ethnic regions within what had been the Empire. The state structure established in the first constitution[2] after the revolution reflected Lenin's effort to satisfy both the Marxist ideologues and the ethnic political realists of the time. To respond to the ideologues he carried forward from the experience of the revolutionary years a state institution recognizing only one foundation for the new state: the working class. His legislature was to be called a "Congress of Soviets," but to accommodate the realists he provided in his constitution that "regions with a distinct mode of living and national composition shall enter the Russian Socialist Federated Soviet Republic on a federal basis."[3] Then he added that citizens would have freedom from discrimination on grounds of race or nationality.[4] Institutionally, he created within the Council of People's Commissars a Commissariat of Nationalities, under J. V. Stalin's direction. It was directed to develop policies to meet national aspirations within the parameters of a class-based government.[5] The revolution itself had already nullified one of the inflammatory provisions of the Tsarist Basic Law,[6] which mandated the Russian language in all state offices. After 1917 non-Russian citizens could use their native language in their state-related activities.

The Heritage of Imperial Structures

In more dramatic recognition of ethnic aspirations Lenin began to dismember the Empire. While he held within the boundaries of the new RSFSR the peoples dwelling within the heartland of Siberia and Central Asia, he released, sometimes under pressure of military defeats, the borderlands. Bonds to Great Russians were severed in varying degrees, reflecting what had been their historical status within the Empire.

Although Article 1 of the Empire's Basic Law of 1906[7] had declared that "The Russian State is unified and indivisible," there had evidently been varying degrees of perception of an autonomous status among some peoples, judging by academic attempts to disabuse Imperial subjects of such thoughts. Professor N. M. Korkunov in his standard textbook[8] used in the Imperial University in St. Petersburg thought it necessary to explain that in spite of traditional titles of various regions and popular local conceptions the inhabitants of no region were legally qualified to claim autonomy.

Korkunov's first and most notorious special case was the Grand Duchy of Finland. Its status had been sufficiently controversial to stimulate the drafters of the Basic Law to insert an Article 2 that read, "The Grand Duchy of Finland, which constitutes an indivisible part of the Russian State is administered in its domestic affairs by special institutions on the basis of special legislation." Finland was indeed a special case, historically. It had been taken from Sweden and annexed to the Empire by Alexander I on March 20, 1809. Korkunov argued that the territory had become no different from any other province of the Empire because conquest had destroyed the Duchy. The authority of Sweden had been replaced by the authority of Russia. To be sure, as he noted, the new Finland had special legislation, a special administration, a special court structure, and a parliament. This all limited in some degree the Tsar's power, but his authority was clearly manifest in his "long title" where he was denominated "Grand Duke of Finland." To Korkunov this designation must be read in context, for it stood alongside the titles of "Tsar of Astrakhan and Siberia" from which no conceivable claim of autonomy for such regions could be supported. In spite of the Empire's rejection of Finnish aspirations, they seem to have been nurtured among the Finns to such an extent that Lenin sensed he had to cope with them in some special manner.

The second region that concerned Korkunov was Ukraine. He portrayed a history which could, perhaps, give his students the impression that Ukraine had a claim to autonomy. Ukraine had been joined with Russia in 1654 in a "personal union," in which the Ukrainian State retained its Hetman, who had the right to carry on international relations independently of the Tsar. To refute claims of autonomy because of this history, Korkunov argued that the Hetman had been made subordinate to the Tsar of Russia as a vassal and not as a chief of State equal to Russia. Proof, so Korkunov thought, of this status was the fact that the Tsar was both "King" of Russia and "King" of what was then called "Little Russia." In spite of Korkunov's teaching, the Ukrainians sensed that they deserved special treatment, and Lenin had to face Ukrainian pressures even among his Communists.

The "Asiatic Principalities" had passed through even more varied historical experiences with independence. In Georgia there had been three sovereign Tsars. One had been brought under the "protection" of the Russian Tsar in 1556, after having been induced to "request" it. Another received "protection" in 1605, and the third in 1652. The protectorates were ended by Alexander I on ascending the throne, and all of Georgia was annexed by Manifesto of April 18, 1801. Curiously, the Tsar is said to have had doubts about the wisdom of annexation. He asked his State Council for its view, and having received assurance that annexation was in Russia's interest, he reaffirmed annexation in a Manifesto of September 12 of the same year, declaring that in spite of his desire to permit Georgia to remain independent, he was forced by circumstances to preserve the Principality of Georgia for Russia.

In Central Asia the Tsar's expressed reluctance to annex foreign territory may have caused him to choose a looser form of linkage for two Islamic Principalities. Khiva and Bukhara were declared "protectorates" as the Georgian Tsars had been declared in earlier centuries, but their Emirs were in treaty relations with the Russians. Khiva had enjoyed a loose relationship with Russia since the sixteenth century, but in 1873 the Tsar, provoked by frequent raids on the Russian steppes, occupied the nation. The Emir was forced to sign a treaty recognizing himself as "the humble servant of the Emperor of all the Russias," and ceding to the Tsar the rights of navigation on the rivers, free trade, and ownership of property.

Bukhara signed a treaty with the Tsar on September 28, 1873, under which the Emir established an embassy in the Russian Imperial City of Tashkent, and a Russian Embassy was established in Bukhara. Under the treaty Russian citizens were given the right of navigation, trade, and ownership of real property on equal terms with Bukhara subjects and also the right of transit without payment of customs duties. Lenin inherited these principalities after his Red Army drove out the Emirs, but the heritage of independence, or semi-independence, seems to have required installation of governments differing from those modeled totally upon the RSFSR structure.

The remaining region with which Lenin had to cope was that of the three Baltic peoples. Their contemporary historians claim that they had enjoyed "more or less full autonomy throughout centuries."[9] Their relationship to the Empire differed in historical origin. Estonia and northern Latvia were ceded to Russia in 1721 at the end of the Great Northern War with Sweden, but the Treaty of Nystad established a "Baltic autonomy" which each Russian Tsar on ascending the throne reconfirmed until 1881, when Alexander III refused to make the usual proclamation. The Tsars then restructured what had been centuries earlier a part of the medieval German empire, later passing through periods of considerable independence as Church States before falling under Swedish and Polish domination. In practice Estonia and Latvia, according to historians, continued to be "quite non-Russian republics of the nobility" until the final quarter of the nineteenth century. At that time they were incorporated as "guberniias" within the Empire, and Russian was made the language of instruction in public education.

Lithuania, on the other hand, had enjoyed a very long period of statehood in Medieval times, exerting influence from Novgorod and Pskov in the north to the Black Sea in the south. Russia had invaded twice and had then remained in occupation from 1795 to 1915. During that period the Tsars followed what has been characterized as an intensive policy of Russification, leading eventually to abolition of Lithuanian schools, prohibition of publication in the Latin alphabet, and occupation of tracts of land by Russian colonists. Russia withdrew only when pushed out of much of the land by the Imperial German Army in 1915. Those parts left unoccupied by the Germans petitioned the Russian Provisional Government of 1917 to permit formation of a democratic republic, but the demands were not met, leaving Lithuania in suspense until the Bolshevik revolution.

Lenin Copes with Nationalist Aspirations

Lenin knew the potential for discontent stimulated by the historical experiences of the non-Russian subjects of the Empire. Indeed, he had played upon this discontent in preaching "self-determination" in hopes of weakening the Tsar. One of his earliest acts after gaining power was to issue on November 15, 1917 (n.s.) a declaration that all of the nations of Russia had the right to self-determination, "including independence and the formation of sovereign governments."[10] Nevertheless, as he soon demonstrated, he was unwilling to relinquish territories where people were powerful enough to resist incorporation within his new RSFSR.

To accommodate his policy to realities of the situation, he often had to retreat. The Baltic regions' history presents ample proof of his problems. He first stimulated the formation of Communist-led governments like his own in the RSFSR. Estonia, Latvia, and Lithuania were recognized as Soviet-type republics on December 22–24, 1918.[11] There was, evidently, an expectation that these peoples could be kept within the new family of Communist dominated regions, for the Red Army marched in as the Imperial German armies retreated, but the Communists were unable to hold the line against nationalists. Partisan activity, combined with some help from remnants of the German armies still hoping to handicap Russia, became effective blocks to Lenin's plans. Lenin was forced to sign peace treaties with the new regimes: with Estonia on February 2, Lithuania on July 12, and Latvia on August 11, 1920.[12] In the treaties Soviet Russia renounced all claims on the Baltic countries, but Soviet troops were slow to clear the countries.

Finally, the three Baltic countries declared their independence under circumstances, said by an historian to have been unique in history: both the German and Russian Empires who had been their overlords for long periods had collapsed and local forces were able to establish themselves and maintain independence. Not until 1940, when the disruption in Eastern Europe at the outset of World War II again made it possible for Soviet diplomacy, backed by troops, to regain these regions for Stalin's USSR was Baltic independence suppressed, but the aspirations of the people remained, as became evident in 1987, when Gorbachev's glasnost policy served to renew these aspirations.

Lenin seems not to have thought of fighting in Finland. Indeed he treated Finland with care, signing a decree on December 31, 1917[13] stating that, in reply to the request of the Finnish government for recognition of independence, the Council of People's Commissars of the RSFSR had agreed, in full conformity with the right of nations to self-determination, to recognize the state independence of the Finnish Republic and to create a commission to develop practical measures for the separation.

The same willingness to release a region was not evidenced in the case of Ukraine. A Manifesto of December 17, 1917[14] was sent to the "Ukrainian People," declaring that its Rada government, which had been installed as the Imperial German armies retreated, was "double dealing, talking nationalism but following a bourgeois policy," thus preventing the All-Russian Congress of Soviets from recognizing it as representing the toiling and exploited masses of the Ukrainian Republic. Evidently sensing that some explanation of why Ukraine was not Finland was required, the authors of the Manifesto stated that although the Finnish bourgeois republic still remained bourgeois, no step would be taken to limit its national rights and the national independence of the Finnish people.

Outsiders might conclude that Lenin considered Ukraine as necessary to Russian economic and political survival, and that he had confidence that Ukrainian Communists could hold it against the nationalist bourgeoisie. This was suggested by a greeting sent on December 16, 1917[15] to the "Workers' and Peasants' Rada" governing in the Ukrainian city of Kharkiv. In that greeting, the Russian Council of People's Commissars hailed their fellows as a "true national Soviet authority in Ukraine to which would be transferred all of the land, factories, mills and banks of Ukraine." Lenin had his foothold in the Ukrainian East. He would have to expand that foothold to cover all of Ukraine.

In each region where Communists were successful in establishing a Soviet Socialist Republic of the Great Russian type, drafters were set to work to incorporate Lenin's political principles in their own words. During the spring and summer of 1919 constitutions were adopted in the Ukrainian and Belorussian Soviet Socialist Republics as sovereign states. In 1921 a similar type of constitution was adopted in the Azerbaijan Soviet Socialist Republic, and in 1922 similar-type constitutions were introduced in the Armenian and Georgian Soviet Socialist Republics.[16] All were sovereign states outside the boundaries of the RSFSR.

The model in all of these constitutions was Lenin's: a parliament structured on a single economic class, a Central Executive Committee to legislate during the long intervals between Congress meetings, and a Council of People's Commissars to administer state affairs. None of the constitutions faced what had been the burning issue of language under the Tsars. Perhaps drafters felt that it was self-evident that self-determination included the right of peoples to use their own language, although the Ukrainians evidenced their past history of pogroms against minorities. Their constitution listed two goals: destruction of the Tsarist system of dividing society into formal classes (*sosloviia*) and destruction of national oppression and national discord.[17] An indication that independence was not a goal was placed in the declaration stating the republic's firm determination to enter a United International Socialist Soviet Republic as soon as conditions made possible its coming into being.

Ethnic issues emerged in the Belorussian constitution in a provision for recognition of equal rights for all citizens regardless of racial or national affiliation. It continued to declare it a violation of the Republic's constitution to establish or to permit the existence of any privileges or advantages based on status or to oppress national minorities or to limit their equal rights.[18]

The constitutions in the Transcaucasus similarly sought protection of minorities: Azerbaijan in a Basic Law of May 19, 1921 recognized equal rights for citizens regardless of religion, race, or national affiliation and forbade oppression of national minorities or limitation of their rights.[19] Armenia in a Basic Law of 1922 guaranteed that "all toiling peoples regardless of nationality and creed have equal rights,"[20] and Georgia in a Basic Law of 1922 introduced an article on language, stating that Georgian was the state language, but adding that national minorities are guaranteed the right to free development and use of their native language in both their national-cultural and general state institutions.[21] A following article forbade, as in Armenia, any oppression of national minorities or limitation of their equal rights.

Complex Problems in Central Asia

Because of the varied history of relations between Russia and Central Asian communities under the Tsars development of a Soviet-style government took a variety of forms. The two Principalities that had not been in the Empire but only allied by treaty to the Tsars, Khiva and Bukhara, remained geographically intact, but other Central Asian regions, which had been incorporated outright in the Empire in 1867 under a Governor General of Turkestan (whose seat was in Tashkent), moved through a route patterned on Lenin's model for the RSFSR.[22]

A Turkestan Soviet Socialist Republic was proclaimed by the RSFSR government on April 11, 1921 to incorporate the five provinces of the former Turkestan (Semirechensk, Syr-Daria, Fergana, Samarkand, and Transcaspia) and a neighboring section of the RSFSR.[23] The advance to full sovereignty like that of the Transcaucasian Republics was to be delayed, however, for the RSFSR reserved to itself exclusive competence for the conduct of foreign and military affairs and foreign trade. Further, conformity to the RSFSR's industrial and agricultural plans was required and several economic Commissariats (railways, posts and telegraph, finance) were subordinated to the RSFSR's Commissariats of the same names.

This subordination to the RSFSR indicated that the title of the Republic as a fully empowered sovereign state did not classify a republic. Here was a governmental form within the RSFSR that seems, in hindsight, to have become a prototype for the "autonomization" Stalin, and perhaps Lenin at the time, favored as a cultural solution for all former minority peoples of the Empire to their demands for self-determination.[24]

Khiva and Bukhara were not so speedily introduced to the model of the other Republics. Because of their historical experience as nomadic, nonindustrial regions, Lenin chose a form excluding the word "socialist" from their titles. They became under their constitutions of July 1922 "Soviet People's Republics." Khiva became Khorezm, but Bukhara was left with its ancient name. Khorezm's constitution defined it as "a free soviet society without differences based on nationality and religion."[25] Because of its variety of ethnic groups, its constitution authorized regions distinguished by their cultural way of life and nationality to combine in a single province of like-minded persons and to set up their own national provincial soviet.[26] Each nation within the republic was authorized to open native-language schools,[27] and privileges and advantages based on birth, race, tribe or national affiliation were declared violations of the Basic Law.[28]

In a dramatic statement explaining policy the Khorezm constitution declared, "For centuries, Domuds, Uzbeks, Karakalpaks, Kirgiz and other nationalities have spilled each others' blood. Hereafter, once and for all they are now recognized as equal citizens, brothers in blood. This hostility is extirpated from memory, and an end to this historical mistake is proclaimed."[29]

Bukhara's Basic Law was in like vein.[30] Education was to be conducted in the maternal language in all state-supported schools.[31] In private schools, which were permitted to each nationality, education either individually or collectively was also permitted in a maternal language so long as general state regulations on education were observed. Privileges and advantages based on sex, race, religion, nationality or social positions were abolished once and for all, whether for individuals or groups.[32]

The Seceded States Return to Lenin

Within a few years Lenin brought the seceded states back into the fold, being helped by Communists in each of them. In addition to this Communist leadership, reunion was also compelled by economic necessity: the former regions of the Russian economic unity found it difficult to develop alone, and as small units their leaderships feared recurrences of intervention from the West.

The centripetal forces of economic and military necessity were reflected in law as links were re-created with Great Russians. The Ukrainian government proposed exchanging raw materials with the Russians on January 26, 1919[33] and in May issued a decree directing that military operations be carried out with other republics.[34] By January, 1920[35] economic pressures were felt, as evidenced by a decree extending to Ukraine the RSFSR laws on transport, posts, telegraph, military organization, production, labor, and social insurance. Belorussians went even further, uniting the administrative commissariats with those of the RSFSR, and sending delegates to Moscow to attend meetings of its Congress of Soviets.[36] The Azerbaijan government took the same step in April 1920.[37]

The Russians responded in 1920 and 1921 with conclusion of a series of treaties on economic and governmental questions requiring united action. Commissariats of military and naval affairs, foreign trade, finance, labor and communications, posts and telegraph, and nationalized industry were merged.[38]

Pacifying Nationalist Strife in the Transcaucasus

The experience in Central Asia with creating union as a means of pacifying nationalist strife seems to have proved attractive to Lenin as a model for the Transcaucasus, where similar strife had raged for long periods. Here were Armenians, Georgians, and Azerbaijanis of totally different lineage, cultures, and national religions, each of whom had been created as nationally oriented independent states after their liberation by the Red Army from opponents of Bolshevism, both domestic and foreign. Although Lenin proceeded to support independence for each on a model copied from Ukraine and Belorussia, he must have asked himself whether he had taken the correct road to stop the strife.

Some clue that he was changing his mind is presented by the record of steps taken by the three Transcaucasian peoples through their governments on December 13, 1922. One united republic was formed as a federation of the three previously independent states to be called the Transcaucasian Soviet Federated Socialist Republic.[39] This was not the first attempt at union, for to meet Turkish pressures during World War I the three principal national parties had united to resist the Turks, but the effort had failed.[40] Their Transcaucasian Federative Republic fell apart as the Turkish and German troops advanced, and when the Bolsheviks seized Baku, the Georgians seceded from the federation to appeal to the Germans for protection against the Turks as the lesser evil, and in November proclaimed Georgian independence, followed by the Armenians and the Azerbaijanis two days later. But their declarations did not save them: The Bolsheviks advanced and after months of confusion and transfers of power from Communists to opponents and back again, Georgia, which was the last to yield to the Bolsheviks, was conquered in the spring of 1921. The Transcaucasus was now subject to Communist Party rule. The Party planned, presumably under Stalin's guidance, a future which would re-create union of the Transcaucasian peoples.

The record suggests that Lenin had little to do with this new union. It appears to have been the brainchild of Stalin. Perhaps because he was a Georgian, Lenin had entrusted him in 1912 with the task of drafting a policy on nationalism.[41] Again, in 1917, Stalin was placed in charge of the Commissariat of Nationalities formed within the RSFSR government to guide policy.[42] Although Lenin seems to have supervised national minority policy, his illness of 1922 immobilized him, and Stalin was left with great authority. In consequence, the constitution drafted to structure a new Transcaucasian Federation may be presumed to represent his plan, and not Lenin's for the region. He seems to have concluded that forced union would reduce age-old strife between peoples, for his preamble stated that during the period of resistance to Communists "the bourgeois landlord rightist parties of Azerbaijan, Georgia and Armenia had stimulated national hatred and discord among the masses." Soviet authority was credited with bringing peace and brotherly existence to the region.

The federation was explained as meeting the need to establish concord and planning in restoration of the economy and defense against external and internal enemies.[43] In constitutional structure the three structurally independent republics were to retain their separate identities but in the framework of a federation. Once this step had been taken, Stalin moved fast toward his broader plan, a bringing together of all peoples of the former Russian Empire into a unit, for which the Transcaucasian Federation may have been the forerunner.

"Autonomization" Within the RSFSR

What Stalin might have succeeded in creating remains speculative although recently published documents provide facts on which one can base a thesis. They suggest that policy was changed in midstream from a program of amalgamation of the ethnic republics into the RSFSR, a program dubbed "autonomization," to a program calling for creation of a new entity that would signify to these minorities their acceptance as equal partners of the Great Russians.

The steps taken were these: formation of a commission to prepare, for the next plenary meeting of the Party's Central Committee, a policy paper on mutual relations between the RSFSR and the independent republics that would then be enacted as law; issuance by the committee of its report stating, "It is recognized as expedient to conclude a treaty between the soviet republics of Ukraine, Belorussia, Azerbaijan, Georgia, Armenia and the RSFSR on entry into the RSFSR community [*sostav*], leaving open to Bukhara, Khorezm, and the Far Eastern Republic[44] the decision to conclude treaties on custom affairs, foreign trade, foreign and military affairs, etc."[45] It was planned to make the decrees of the RSFSR's central government binding upon the central institutions of the aforementioned republics.

Within two days, the scheme seems to have been threatened by a letter Lenin wrote to his Politburo colleague, L. B. Kamenev: "You have most likely received from Stalin the resolution of the committee on the entry of the independent republics into the RSFSR. If you have not received it, get it from the secretariat and please read it immediately."[46] Then Lenin reported that he had spoken with Sokolnikov and with Stalin and the Georgian Mdivani, characterized by Lenin as "a Communist, suspected of being for independence." After saying that he thought the matter extremely important, and that Stalin was trying somewhat to hurry the matter, he asked Kamenev to think seriously about the matter and that Zinoviev do so too. Lenin added that Stalin had already agreed to replace in the proposed resolution the words "enter into" the RSFSR with the words "formal union together with the RSFSR in a union of a soviet republics of Europe and Asia."

The purpose of his proposal was clear, Lenin explained. "We recognize ourselves as equal in rights to the Ukrainian SSR and the others, and together and on equal terms with them, we shall enter into a new union, a federation, the 'Union of Soviet Republics of Europe and Asia.'" He added, "It is important that we not give nourishment to those who want independence, but construct a new story (*etazh*), a federation of *equal* republics. The delayed revelation of Lenin's intervention into the planning for the new state, which was evidently being guided by Stalin, came only after Stalin's death, at which time a new edition of the historical documents relating to formation of the USSR was published. Lenin's diary for December 30, 1922[47] appeared in 1957 with a footnote saying that Lenin had addressed a letter to the Politburo on September 27, 1922 [one day after his letter to Kamenev, JNH] criticizing severely the preparatory committee's draft and proposing a different solution to the question, namely a new state structure, a Union of Soviet Republics. The footnote adds that a new draft was prepared by the committee and approved by the plenum of the Party's Central Committee in October 1922 and put before the December 30 Congress, which took the decision to form the USSR.

The pages of Lenin's diary reveal that his illness had delayed his study of the question of union, for he said, "I, so it seems, stand seriously guilty before the workers of Russia for not intervening sufficiently energetically and sharply enough in the notorious question of autonomization. . . . When this question emerged during this summer,

I was ill, and in the autumn I placed extensive hope on my recovery and also on the opportunity which the October and December plenums would give me to intervene in this question . . . but I could not be present at either and so the matter passed me almost completely by."

Lenin then revealed that he had spoken with his security chief, Felix Dzerzhinsky, and with Zinoviev, and had expressed his apprehensions. Dzerzhinsky had told him that Ordzhonikidze was threatening force. This led him to write, "if Ordzhonikidze could go to the extreme of applying physical force, then one could imagine what a morass we have fallen into. 'Autonomization' is clearly incorrect and inopportune." Lenin's final notation explains why Stalin prevented publication of the diary during his lifetime, for Lenin wrote, "I think that the haste and administrative-type enthusiasm of Stalin and also his bitterness against the notorious 'social nationalism' has on this point played the fatal role. Bitterness generally plays in politics the basest role."

Can one conclude that Lenin and Stalin in mid-1922 were at odds on how to deal with the nationality question? The record of 1917 shows that Lenin gave thought to incorporation of the border peoples within the RSFSR, although with a limited "autonomy" for each minority; that Stalin had adopted Lenin's formula as his own and had continued to put it into effect by degrees starting with the three peoples of the Transcaucasus; that Stalin had led his committee in this direction while Lenin was ill; that when Lenin heard from his security chief what was afoot and that his comrade in arms, Ordzhonikidze, was thinking of using force to prevent unification with the RSFSR, he decided to intervene and had ordered that the draft substitute for "autonomization" a new federal structure. His proposal was followed by the drafting committee and approved by the Party's Central Committee plenum, and a few days later by a Congress of representatives of Ukraine, Belorussia, the RSFSR and the Transcaucasian Federation.

If this reading is correct, Lenin had changed his mind on the nationality question under the pressure of events. He had hoped to reconstitute the frontiers of the Russian Empire, although the content of the political system would be different. The minorities would have cultural autonomy but the center would conduct foreign policy, military affairs, and the economy. To wean the minorities away from their fear of continuing Russification, they would be granted "independence" for a time while their Communist parties and the evident difficulty of developing their economies and protecting themselves from hostile forces brought home to them the desirability of realliance with the Great Russians. When a new consciousness that "class," not Russia, was the cementing force, had been formulated in people's minds, the national question would have been solved.

Events transpired to prove to Lenin that his plan was premature at the least, and perhaps impractical at any time. Minority peoples might become Communist-oriented, but they did not develop a faith in the Great Russians. Even Ordzhonikidze threatened revolt. A new partnership of legal equals had to be devised. Yet not all minority peoples needed to be included among the equal partners. For some of the less developed and weaker ones, "autonomization" was still a sound policy. This was the case for Central Asia and for Siberia.

"Autonomization" Ends in Central Asia

After Lenin's death in January 1924 evidence of adoption of a new policy for Central Asia began to emerge. The Central Executive Committee of the RSFSR, which had jurisdiction over the "autonomous" republics of the region, published a decision in October 1924 to approve a resolution of the Central Executive Committee of the Turkestan Autonomous Soviet Socialist Republic declaring that seven years of a gigantic revolutionary struggle had ended victoriously with creation of a new working class society; a new USSR had been brought into being as a powerful home for the cohabitation of equal peoples of all Soviet republics (all remnants of national inequality and slavery had been rooted out); broad cultural and economic development now made it possible to meet the wishes of the working and peasant masses to separate out from the Turkestan ASSR the Uzbek, Turkmen, and Kirgiz peoples as Soviet Socialist Republics; and the Kara-Kirgiz people were to be structured as an autonomous province within the RSFSR,[48] and the Tajik people as an Autonomous Socialist Soviet Republic within the Uzbek Union Republic.[49]

Thirteen days later the USSR's Central Executive Committee published its decision to act upon the request of the parliament of Bukhara and of the Central Executive Committee of the People's Republic of Khorezm to be united with their fellow tribesmen inhabiting the Turkestan ASSR and to admit the newly established states as Union Republics of the USSR. The decision then confirmed the December 4,

1924 decision of the Turkestan ASSR and of the RSFSR to divide the Turkestan SSR into its component parts in accordance with the principle of self-determination of nations.[50] Territorial adjustments were made: the Uzbek SSR would be composed of the provinces of Tashkent, Samarkand, Fergana, Kashkadaria, Zeravshan, Surkhandaria and Khorezm, and the Tajik ASSR.[51]

The remaining provinces of what had been the Turkestan ASSR issued three days later a declaration proclaiming the formation of a new Turkmen SSR to comprise the provinces of Polotoratsk, Merv, Kerki, Lenin, and Tashauz. The official languages would be Turkmen and Russian. On the same day in a second decision the new republic's Congress of Soviets declared its intention to enter the USSR.[52] The USSR's Congress of Soviets on May 13, 1925 accepted both the Turkmen and Uzbek Republics as members of the USSR, amending the constitution to include them and to add their deputies to the Congress in equal number with those of the other Union Republics.[53] Within months after these amendments came into force, the original republics of the USSR amended their constitutions to conform to the change.[54]

The partition of the Central Asian republics to give voice to their minorities seems not to have solved all problems, for the USSR's Congress of Soviets adopted a resolution on the day of admission of the new republics emphasizing the importance of vitalizing local soviets, to increase public participation in their work, to broaden their competence, and to force them to obey centrally issued laws. The resolution ended with a section on "National Minorities," saying that new measures were necessary in order to protect them. It called upon the Central Executive Committee of the USSR "to seat in all elected soviet organs representatives of national minorities and to form separate soviets using the language of these minorities and to organize schools and law courts in the native languages, etc."[55]

Plans for a Second Federal Constitution Emerge

By 1935 Communist leaders seem to have sensed a need for review of federal structures, for the USSR's Congress of Soviets ordered its Central Executive Committee to form a constitutional committee to revise the text to "democratize further the electoral system," so as to replace indirect, open, and weighted elections by direct, secret, and equal elections.[56] Peasants were to be brought up to equality with workers. To the surprise of observers the committee brought forth a completely new structure,[57] commonly believed to have been mandated by Stalin himself.

The new structure eliminated the Congress of Soviets and moved its bicameral Central Executive Committee into the position of supreme legislator, thus enhancing the position, on paper at least, of the nationalities and their chamber of nationalities. Stalin used the occasion to state a criterion for elevation from Autonomous Republic status to Union Republic status. Both developments reveal new thinking on national minorities.

To abolish the Congress of Soviets and elevate the former Central Executive Committee required an ideological reversal of Lenin's emphasis upon "class" as the only basis for legislating the Soviet order. Under the draft, ethnic minorities would be placed in the same status as the people as a whole in the legislative process. Not only would the large ethnic groups be at the top in the state structure, but the lesser ethnic groups would also be among them, for the principle of representation of these lesser groups was continued, since autonomous republics and provinces and national groups were given descending numbers of deputies in the Chamber of Nationalities alongside the full delegations from the Union Republics.[58]

The second notable feature of the reform was less dramatic structurally but remarkable politically. Stalin disclosed a new criterion for advancement from the status of an Autonomous Soviet Socialist Republic to the status of a full member of the federation.[59] He declared that no people could be advanced unless it was geographically situated on a border. His explanation was that Union Republics were granted by the constitution the right to secede from the federation, and this right could be meaningful only if the republic were on a border. If a republic were totally surrounded by sister republics, it could not effectively exercise its independent rights. It would be landlocked.

Stalin professed not to be opposed to advancement of an ethnically defined people to equality constitutionally with the Great Russians, but only to be concerned with assuring that secession not be exercised to the detriment of territorial unity of the Soviet state. He wanted no pockets of bourgeois society within the borders of the USSR. He seems to have assumed that secession would be exercised only to revert to a capitalist economy.

In practice, this geographical criterion required that the Bashkir and

Tatar peoples had to remain as Autonomous Republics, while the three peoples of the Transcaucasian Republic—the Armenians, the Azerbaijanis, and the Georgians—could be released from their bond in the Transcaucasian Federation and admitted to the USSR as Union Republics, as could the Kazakh and Kirgiz peoples of Central Asia. With these elevations the Union became a federation of eleven equal partners, all of which had a constitutional right of secession.

Much of the community of scholars outside the USSR thought this criterion of border location a mask for other motives, as Stalin had on several occasions in his career indicated that the Communist Party would oppose any move to secede from the USSR, yet it became the explanation for rejection of Union Republic status for some numerous, developed, ethnic minorities, for decades to follow.

The outsider cannot but wonder whether Stalin's criterion of border location was a means of concealing his reversion at a late date to his position of "autonomization" of ethnic groups which had troubled Lenin in 1922. He had already elevated so many peoples to Union Republic status that one may wonder why he felt it desirable to put a cap on the process in 1936. He was closing the doors after most of the large minority peoples had been advanced, but history gave him another occasion to demonstrate his thinking. The occasion was expansion of the Soviet state on the eve of World War II.

Territorial Acquisitions in 1939–40

Whatever Stalin's real motives for establishing the border criterion for Union Republic status, he had an opportunity to apply it as he pushed outward the USSR's frontiers in 1939–40. He moved into the eastern regions of Czechoslovakia and Poland in agreement with Adolf Hitler in 1939, attaching these regions to the Ukrainian SSR. He evidently expected Bessarabia and Finland to be absorbed in short order. Finland was first on his list. The Finns resisted, but were defeated in the field, losing in the peace treaty the region close to Leningrad and the northern part of Karelia. Stalin was ready for annexation of this territory, for he had already advanced the Karelo-Finnish Autonomous SSR to Union Republic status so that the new land could be joined to its neighbor and admitted to the USSR on March 31, 1940.[60]

The Moldavian Autonomous SSR was elevated to Union Republic

status on August 2, 1940 when it was joined to the former Romanian province of Bessarabia.[61] Bukovina, which was taken from Romania, and the former Polish province of L'viv were added to the Ukrainian SSR.[62] The formerly sovereign Baltic states of Lithuania, Latvia, and Estonia were brought within the USSR on August 3, August 5, and August 6, respectively, after political and military measures had prepared the way.[63] The USSR constitution was amended to bring the number of Union Republics to sixteen.[64] Evidence that the Karelo-Finnish advancement in status was related to the expectation that Finland would be conquered and dominated by Communists who would join the territory to the USSR was provided after Stalin died. In 1958 the Karelo-Finnish SSR was placed in the category of Autonomous Republics, with the explanation that its economic and cultural base was "closely linked" with that of the RSFSR, and this was reason to return it to the RSFSR in Autonomous Republic status.[65] Stalin's heirs seem to have sensed that it was time to recognize that economic rationality had priority over structuring the state to attract neighboring peoples who had demonstrated that they would and could resist expansion of Soviet power.

A Play for Votes in the United Nations

Two wartime constitutional amendments of 1944 appear to indicate that Stalin was prepared to relax the bonds of federation, almost to the point of re-creating the USSR as a confederation. The first amendment authorized the Union Republics to conduct foreign relations and to establish their own armies.[66] In both cases the federal authorities retained supervisory power, but Stalin was emboldened by his wartime successes to demand from his wartime allies at the Dumbarton Oaks conference on establishment of a United Nations seats for his Union Republics in the new world organization.

Roosevelt and Churchill resisted Stalin's play for votes, but finally agreed to a compromise. The Ukrainian and Belorussian Republics would be seated in the United Nations on the ground that their populations had suffered most from wartime devastation. Stalin accepted the compromise, yet he did not withdraw from the other republics their right to create Ministries of Foreign Affairs. They had, however, no right to establish Permanent Missions in New York.

This amendment expanding Union Republic competence was patently a maneuver to gain votes in the United Nations, and it was accepted as such by the world's analysts; but events proved decades later that it had influenced some citizens of the USSR. When a demonstration erupted in the Kazakh SSR on December 17–18, 1988 as a protest against what was perceived to be a move toward Russification, reporters stated that some placards demanded a seat in the United Nations. Soviet newsmen limited reports, however, to accounts of killings and subsequent criminal trials.[67]

The second amendment of concern to republics was placed in the constitution in 1957. It replaced the provision in the constitution of 1936 establishing the federal legislature's competence to enact codes of law. By the 1924 constitution the federal government's competence was limited to legislating fundamental principles binding upon all republic drafters who had authorization to prepare for enactment by the republic legislature the code to be applied in court. The authorization of 1936 was never used to enact all-union codes, probably because the disruption of World War II was too severe to permit thought on what the codes should contain. Be that as it may, a 1957 amendment[68] restored the 1924 rule, thus continuing the practice of the war years, thus giving at least the appearance that Stalin's penchant for centralization was not shared by his heirs, at least at that time.

A Trend toward "Convergence"

As the years passed, Stalin's heirs seem to have given increasing priority to economic unity over nationalistic diversity. Not only was the Karelo-Finnish status reversed in the interest of economic rationality, but also the Central Asian Republics were grouped by Nikita Khrushchev in a single economic region. Their constitutional status remained unchanged, but their economies were coordinated through a Central Asian Regional Economic Council. There was even talk of regional economic groupings in the Transcaucasian region and in the Baltic region. No such groupings occurred, however, as Khrushchev was dismissed in 1964 before his plans bore fruit.

During Khrushchev's tenure as Secretary General of the Party, Soviet ideologues began to speak of a forthcoming convergence (*sblizhenie*) of cultures that would cause citizens to think in terms of being

"Soviet men" rather than ethnics. One political scientist even stated at a world meeting that the future of the Chamber of Nationalities was being discussed. While such suggestions were threatening to ethnics, nothing took the form of law; but the idea did not die. Brezhnev's successor as Secretary General, Yu. V. Andropov, raised the matter of convergence of cultures at the Sixtieth anniversary of the founding of the USSR. In his 1983 speech he summarized policy on nationalities as based upon: "the completely voluntary union of free peoples guaranteeing maximum stability for the federation of socialist republics; the complete equality of all nations and nationalities and a constant line of policy designed to eliminate their legal but also their actual inequality; the free development of each republic and each nationality within the fraternal union of all; the continuous cultivation of an internationalist consciousness and a steady course aimed at the convergence of all of our country's nations and nationalities . . ."[69] Two paragraphs later he repeated the theme: "the comprehensive development of the socialist nations of our country is logically leading to their increasing convergence." Then he praised the Russian language as a factor "in bringing closer together all of its nations and nationalities; in making accessible to them the riches of world civilization."

Andropov's homage to the Russian language as a factor stimulating convergence of peoples and opening the gates to world culture must be read with an eye on guarantees made in constitutions of the various Union Republics when revised in 1978 following promulgation of the federal constitution of 1977. In all of these constitutions the right of nations to use their national languages was recognized.[70] By the end of 1978 the pressure for convergence of cultures, which had evidently influenced Khrushchev and his colleagues in the mid-1960's, at that time causing discussion of the desirability of eliminating the Chamber of Nationalities from the bicameral Supreme Soviet as well as removing from the Union Republic constitutions guarantees that indigenous languages would be the "state languages," had spent itself. The transition in attitudes was, however, to cause serious disorders in the Transcaucasian republics, where drafters attempted to place in the new constitutions words comparable to those of Article 36 of the federal constitution, which guaranteed only "the possibility to use the native language." Serious riots in the Georgian Republic induced the drafters to reinsert in the three constitutions of the Transcaucasian republics the guarantee of "state language."[71]

The Russian Republic's constitution of 1978 did not depart from the federal constitution's Article 36, however, even though it had within it sixteen Autonomous Republics, five Autonomous Provinces, and ten Autonomous Districts, each with its distinctive language. Its Article 34 adhered to the federal model, guaranteeing only the "possibility to use one's native language." Evidently, the small ethnic groups represented by the formations within the Republic saw no opportunity similar to that in the Transcaucasian Union Republics to press for recognition of their languages as "state languages." Perhaps such protests seemed unnecessary, for it was common knowledge in the USSR that the Russian language was ignored in many regions, so much that Army officers would complain that one-fifth of the recruits could not understand commands in Russian.

Use of a native language in court was guaranteed in the 1977 federal constitution by its Article 159, and interpreters for those who cannot use the court's language, whatever it might be, were guaranteed. Personal experiences in Soviet courtrooms in non-Russian speaking Republics had indicated that Russian was the generally used language until recently, when the rising tide of nationalism swept the native language into the courtroom, although with recognition of the right to interpretation for those who needed it.

To an outsider the contrast between the status of the ethnic formations below the level of the Union Republic—whether Autonomous Republic, Autonomous Province or Autonomous District—was minimal. To be sure only the Autonomous Republics were entitled to call its legislature a "Supreme Soviet," and its executive a "Council of Ministers." The lesser ethnic formations promulgated ordinances through their "Soviets," as did Provinces and Districts in which there was no recognition of the existence of an ethnic culture different from that of the Republic in which they were situated.

Further, all three ethnic formations applied the law codes of the Union Republic of which they were a part. Local enactments had to conform to the various criminal, civil, labor, family, and procedural codes enacted by the Union Republic. Even these Union Republic codes were similar in all but detail, since they in turn had to conform to the federal "Fundamentals," enacted by the Supreme Soviet of the USSR. It is possible that this double layer of legislation might have been abandoned in favor of enactment of federal codes had the USSR survived in the restructuring of the Union planned for August 20, 1991, but with rejection of the proposed "Union" treaty that possibility did not eventuate.[72]

From Andropov's Nationality Policy to Gorbachev's

Andropov's expectation that convergence of cultures was soon to be achieved seems in retrospect the conclusion of an ideologist who knew nothing of the storm brewing among the non-Russian peoples of the federation. His expressed faith in the triumph of the Leninist doctrine that "class" loyalty must replace ethnic loyalty was to be proven ill founded within months of his anniversary speech.

Gorbachev, on inheriting Andropov's mantle, after a brief interlude during which the ailing K. Y. Chernenko was the Party's Secretary General, faced a daunting task. He declared it necessary to rebuild social and political structures within the confines of the 1977 Constitution.[73] Because of this Constitution, which foreign analysts thought a product of Brezhnev's desire to freeze for his successors an economic and political structure he called "developed socialism," Gorbachev met resistance to innovation from conservatives habituated to structures created by Stalin and continued by Brezhnev.

Although a case might have been made for advancement of large Autonomous Republics, such as those of the Tatars and Bashkirs, to Union Republic status, without upsetting the 1977 constitutional structures of the Supreme Soviet's chambers, no case was made publicly for such an advancement. Outsiders who had thought absurd Stalin's requirement that the Republic be on a frontier so that it might secede to become capitalist were even more convinced of this absurdity after World War II. Following the postwar expansion of the socialist camp there were few Union Republics that did not border on a "fraternal socialist state."

Evidently, the trend toward convergence of cultures and homogenization of peoples in a novel society and culture, where the Russian language would be a lingua franca, had put an end to Tatar and Bashkir aspirations. Indeed, a prominent Soviet constitutionalist said in a lecture in Australia at the time that creating new Union Republics would be retrogressive.

Glasnost Opens the Door to Change

A look back from the 1990s suggests that Gorbachev's decision to introduce a policy of glasnost, with its emphasis upon public discussion of social and political currents emerging within the country, opened the door to expression of long suppressed grievances by discontented ethnically defined groups. Perhaps Gorbachev's aim was only to shake up bureaucrats governing the economy without imagination, but his appeal to authorities in various Republics to expose errors of the past so as to rebuild productivity on the basis of facts and not on ideological conceptions of a model "socialist" economy started a landslide.

The leaders of the three Baltic Republics, perhaps because their tutelage by the central authorities had been shorter than had been the case with the heartland, responded with demands for economic autonomy. Even the Communist leaders of these Republics came to side with the "National Fronts," which sprang up in all three Republics and soon demanded independence. Arguments were made that independence was logical since the peoples of the Republics had been forced against their will into the USSR following Stalin's 1939 pact with Hitler.

Unrest among the national minorities spread well beyond the Baltic. In Central Asia citizens learned as a result of revelations of widespread corruption how much they had been abused not only by their own governments but also by collaborators from Moscow. The Party Secretary of the Kazakh Republic was dismissed and replaced by a Russian, causing riots. Then followed a dispute between Armenians and Azeris over administration by Azerbaijan of a territory populated primarily by Armenians. The presidium of the federal Supreme Soviet responded with a resolution of March 23, 1988 denouncing pressures brought to bear upon state organs to solve what the press called "complex-territorial questions" and demanding that nationalistic extremist manifestations be set aside.[74]

The resolution was soon followed by the naming of a special committee of deputies of the Chamber of Nationalities to study the matter,[75] and finally by the assumption by the federal government of direct rule of the region.[76]

Restatement of Policy and Constitutional Amendment

Gorbachev's call of a Communist Party Conference in July 1988, opened to discussion national minority policy. The result was adoption of a resolution calling for "enhancement of the role of the Soviets of People's Deputies and above all of the Council of Nationalities and its standing committees."[77] There was to be an examination of the desirability of forming a special state agency to deal with the affairs of nationalities and national relations. But, this new emphasis was to be balanced with enhancement of the role of the federal government. "Party organizations and Communists of all nationalities" were called upon to be the cementing force, "the soul of the socialist union of peoples, and the active transmitters of internationalism."

No mention was made of rapprochement, of convergence, of which Andropov had spoken in 1983. No reference was made to the Russian language's preeminence: it was to be but a means of communication between nations, whose languages were "to be developed without restriction." The Communist Party was, evidently, to be reinvigorated as the counterweight to renascent Republic power.

Legal measures soon were enacted to implement Party policy.[78] They re-created Lenin's state structures of 1922–23: a 1,250 person Congress at the top; a smaller Supreme Soviet in bicameral form below the Congress, and a Council of Ministers made responsible to the Supreme Soviet to administer the state. The deputies to the Congress were to be elected directly by the people to fill two thirds of the seats, but the remaining one third was to be chosen by organizations. Supreme Soviet deputies were to be chosen by Congress deputies from their own number rather than being elected directly as they had been since the 1936 constitution. Supreme Soviet deputies were to be rotated in numbers up to 20 percent in each year of the Congress's five year mandate.

National formations were to be seated in both the Congress and its derivative Supreme Soviet in fixed numbers established for each formation, in accordance with their status as Union Republics, Autonomous Republics, Autonomous Provinces, or Autonomous Districts.[79]

The Constitutional amendments of 1988 made no change in Article 74, which provided that in the event of discrepancy between a law of the USSR and law of a Union Republic, the federal law prevailed. This provision was tested by the Estonian Republic's Supreme Soviet just prior to the 1988 Constitutional amendments when the Estonians sought to require that federal law be registered before enforcement in the Republic. The presidium of the USSR Supreme Soviet declared the Estonian provision unconstitutional.[80] Subsequently, several republics took the same position, including the Russian Republic. The resolution of the conflict of competence was postponed until a later date.

Although evidently attempting to retain federal supremacy, the federal Supreme Soviet enacted a law on November 27, 1989, not long before restructuring the state agencies, granting the Baltic Republics "within the framework of USSR laws" the right to enact legislation restructuring their social and economic systems.[81] This law, limited at the time to the Baltic region, became later a model for all regions and deserves detailed attention as an indication of the extent to which central policy makers were willing to compromise with Republics as they demanded not autonomy, but independence.

Under the Baltic law the Republics were granted the right to administer the land and other natural resources within the boundaries of the Republics; to regulate the activity of all economic administrative and producing entities on their territory (presumably those subject to central authority); to manage their finances and banks, except local institutions of the USSR State Bank; to tax their populations for the benefit of the Republic; to establish their own Republic budget determining income and expenditures; to set rates of wage payments and pensions; to set fixed prices; to manage their foreign economic activity; to administer state stocks of natural resources, and to create a financial market utilizing rubles and foreign currencies on a mutually advantageous basis.

This grant of economic autonomy was limited; the federal government reserved for itself many important rights. Facilities used by the Armed Forces, trunk petroleum and gas pipelines were regarded as federal property, as was the transportation and power network. The ruble remained the currency for inter-republic settlements. Republics were obliged to perform contracts in inter-republic trade, and the State Economic Plan remained mandatory so long as a market economy was not introduced. This concession proved to be inadequate to calm the Lithuanian Supreme Soviet, which formally declared its independence. Gorbachev responded by shutting the gas pipeline for two months, opening it only when the Republic's Supreme Soviet agreed to suspend the declaration of independence for 100 days.

When the Baltic law was extended to other Republics by law of April 10, 1990,[82] it applied not only to Union Republics but also to Autonomous Republics, and even lower to Autonomous Provinces and Autonomous Districts. By this law the federal authorities retained policy-making authority over economic matters, but the Republics and lesser ethnic regions were to manage the land and natural resources within their boundaries, with one caveat: management had to be in the mutual interest of both the Republic and the USSR.

Probably the most important concession in the two laws was the extension to the republics of the right to tax, to adopt their own budget, to regulate investment even by the federal government, and to share with the federal government in establishing investment policy within the Republic, to regulate Republic banks and currency circulation within the Republic, to conduct foreign economic relations "subject to conformity to international and interrepublic agreements," to register joint ventures and international associations and organizations, to set rules for environmental protection, and to decide matters of social development, including wages and pensions.

These grants of authority created the possibility of establishing budgets at three governmental levels: All-Union, republic, and local, in much the same way as in Western federations. The major difference was expected to be during the transitional period when the National Economic Plan would have remained in force.

Other similarities with Western federations were to be found: the currency based on the ruble was to be regulated by the central bank; no tariffs between Republics were to be allowed since the economy was to be maintained as one market; and discrimination against Republics, their legal entities or citizens was to be forbidden.

Gorbachev Creates a Presidency

Although concessions were being made to the republics in 1990, strife based on nationalist pressure continued, and it seems to have alarmed Gorbachev and his colleagues. He broached the idea of amending the Constitution once again to create an institution previously rejected by his predecessors, namely a USSR Presidency. When the draft amendments appeared, it was evident that the institution emulated the French Presidency created by General De Gaulle and the Presidency of the United States. By the amendment of March 14, 1990[83] a new Article 127 with several subsections was inserted in the 1977 Constitution providing for election of a President by secret ballot.

To avoid influence of minorities the amendment required that not less than 50 percent of qualified voters participate in the voting. Further, more than half of those voting plus a majority of the Union Republics would have to support the candidate. Although the amendment was clear, Gorbachev persuaded the Congress of People's Deputies that on the first occasion the electors should be the deputies to the Congress itself without reference to the nation as a whole.

Nationality policy was affected by creation of the institution of the Presidency since the President was authorized to form an advisory Council of the Federation, whose members were to be the supreme officials of the Union Republics, supplemented by officials of less autonomous formations appearing in a nonvoting capacity. The Council's task was set as assuring conformity to the Treaty of Union, which was still in negotiation. Its second task was to implement policy with regard to ethnic matters.

Gorbachev utilized the Council of the Federation frequently after its institution. The most dramatic moment was in June 1990 at the height of the altercation with Presidents of the Baltic Republics, who were maintaining that their Republics were not a part of the USSR and never had been. The three Presidents heeded his call to a meeting of the Council, suggesting that they recognized the utility of continuing to act within the federal system in seeking a solution to their aspirations.

Soon after election to the Presidency Gorbachev obtained from the Supreme Soviet a law of April 3, 1990[84] prescribing a procedure to be followed by a Republic seeking to exercise its constitutional right of secession. Gorbachev later demanded that the Lithuanian Republic take the steps indicated in the law and rejected the argument that incorporation within the USSR in 1940 had been illegal, thus freeing Lithuania from any obligation to follow USSR law.

Perhaps the most difficult requirement the law placed on an applicant was that minority national formations located geographically within the applicant be satisfied with accompanying the majority nation in secession. The test of satisfaction was conduct of referenda among the minority formations. Further, individuals among the minority formation had to be asked whether they wished to leave both the Union and the minority group of which they were a part. If they wished to separate, they were to be paid resettlement costs.

A referendum was required both at the outset of any secession proceedings and again at the end of a mandatory transition period which might last up to five years. The referenda might be dispensed with if there was no request for it, although provision that not more than one-tenth of the permanent residents might request it suggested that the intermixing of peoples in all Republics would easily provide the requisite number of demanders; the referendum was to be accepted as supporting secession only if two-thirds of the permanent residents supported it.

The wishes of members of minority ethnic groups within Republics to protect their own cultures were recognized by a law of April 2, 1990.[85] Under this law minority groups living outside of a national Republic to which they claimed affinity were to have been accorded the right to form "national settlements, national villages, and national rural settlements." Such communities were to have been assured the use of their language in ethnic schools and the right to establish national cultural centers, ethnic societies, and national groups.

Enforcement of these rights against recalcitrant local officials was to be accorded through suit in court against not only individuals but also local governments that might violate the rights established by law.

Constitutional Supervision

A USSR Committee on Constitutional Supervision was created by one of the amendments of December 1, 1988 to the 1977 Constitution.[86] Members were to be elected by the Congress of People's Deputies for ten-year terms, each Union Republic being guaranteed one seat. By a subsequent amendment, the number of members was increased to 27 so as to permit the Autonomous Republics to have some representation.

Following the naming of the President and Vice President, there was published as a law of April 28, 1990[87] the names of nineteen members. Evidently the three Baltic Republics refused to propose candidates, for they were the only Republics not represented. Also, only one Autonomous Republic member appeared on the list, namely a Tatar. All but two of the listed persons had advanced degrees in law, as Doctors or Candidates. The two exceptions were Doctors of Philosophy and History respectively. One member was from the staff of the Central Committee of the Communist Party and another from the Academy of the Ministry of Internal Affairs. The rest were from the great cities of the Russian Republic.

In conception the Committee was not a constitutional court but advisory to the Congress and the Supreme Soviet. They might call upon it for opinions on drafts of laws. High officials and citizens might ask for opinions on enacted law. If a regulation and not a law were challenged, the opinion on unconstitutionality suspended the regulation until the Congress, the Supreme Soviet, or the administrative agency superior to the issuing authority acted. If a challenge to any legal act, presumably including a Supreme Soviet or Congress law, violated human rights, the Committee's decision was to become effective immediately after issuance. The Committee's competence to review constitutions and laws of republics to determine their conformity to the federal constitution was left in abeyance until the central problem of the relationship between the members of the federation and the center could be resolved.

Resolving the Burning Question

Shortly before termination of the spring 1990 sitting of the Supreme Soviet the deputies turned to the months long-postponed question of demarcation of competence between the federation and its members. When it was settled by law of April 26, 1990,[88] an analyst could conclude that the progression of laws from the Baltic Republic Law of November 27, 1988 through the general law for all Republics of April 10, 1990 marked milestones along the road to resolution of the problem. By the implementing law of the same day,[89] the April 26 law was to become the text of a constitutional amendment to be presented to the Congress of People's Deputies for action.

Most of the general provisions of the April law were carried over from existing law: the right to secession was restated, although the procedure established by the law of April 3, 1990 had to be followed; territorial boundaries of a Union or Autonomous Republic or a lower ranked autonomous formation could not be changed without its consent; federal laws took precedence over Republic laws, so long as the latter had been enacted in accordance with the competence of the federal parliament. Economic autonomy as granted in the Baltic and general laws was reaffirmed, although exercise of this autonomy could not be at variance with the interests of the federation or another Republic.

The federation's competence was listed in thirteen paragraphs, establishing a very comprehensive basis for maintenance of a common policy in the conduct of international relations, the establishment of a uniform monetary system, the management of transport, defense, and long-range prospects for the country's social and economic development, establishment of state banks, a tax system, a federation's budget, regulation of production, storage, and use of fissionable materials, questions of peace and war, protection of the state border, establishment of a single customs territory, formation of federal courts, and a uniform system of procuratorial supervision. None of these powers presumably could be expanded without the consent of all the members of the federation.

The competence reserved to the Republics was not defined, nor did it need to be under the formula adopted for federation. The Republics were deemed to have all the powers not transferred by them to the federation. Nevertheless, these powers were in many cases made subject to the rule that they must be exercised in conformity with fundamental principles established by the federal authority. Comparison of these jointly exercised powers suggested that except for the economic autonomy conferred on the republics by the Baltic and general laws, the federation had retained its dominance in the setting of general policy. Fundamental principles would still be established by the federal Supreme Soviet to be followed by Republics in drafting and enacting codes of law; foreign relations of Republics had to conform to, and be guided by, federal authority; the protection of social order and the fight against crime was guided by federal authority, financial-credit policy and price setting were in federal hands, and laws assuring the functioning of an all-union market and its protection in the interests of all republics were to be federal.

One of the much debated issues, that of the right of Republics to legislate on the status of citizens of other Republics residing within the boundaries of a host Republic, was treated in precise fashion. The federal authority was to protect the rights and freedoms of citizens of the USSR regardless of their place of residence.

A law on language was enacted two days before the law on competence.[90] The Russian language was declared to be the state language and the medium of communication in state organs, but citizens might use their own language with a guarantee of interpretation into the state language. All federal laws were to be published in the languages of the Union Republics. Union and Autonomous Republics' languages were to be set by their legislatures, but their laws also had to be published in Russian. Likewise, business language was that set by the Republic in which it was used, but a Russian translation was to be provided.

So also the names of populated places were to be in the local language but also in Russian. Language in military installations and in the transport and energy systems of national importance was Russian. The media were to use Russian, but might use other languages of the Republics in which they served, but there might be no deprecating of languages of minorities living within the Republic. Violation of the language law was to be punishable in accordance with the general legal principle of prohibiting any disparagement of any language of the peoples of the USSR.

Bicameralism for the Russian Republic

The Russian Republic recognized for the first time in 1989 the desirability of restructuring its Supreme Soviet to reflect the fact that its borders included more autonomous ethnic areas than any other Republic. By amendment of October 27, 1989[91] there was introduced a second chamber, in which the ratio was set at three deputies for each Autonomous Republic, one for each Autonomous Province, and one for each Autonomous District. In departure from the federal model for its Chamber of Nationalities, the deputies from ethnic areas were to sit with a like number (sixty-three) of deputies representing territories, provinces and the cities of Moscow and Leningrad. In this structure the Russian deputies would have balanced the non-Russian peoples.

As in the federal system, the Supreme Soviet deputies were not to be elected directly by the people but by the Congress of People's Deputies of the Russian Republic from their own number. The Congress's 1,068 deputies were to be elected from two groups: (1) 168 ethnically defined districts to which were added Moscow and Leningrad and territories and provinces of the Republic, and (2) also deputies from 900 geographically defined districts. An exact balance was established between deputies chosen from ethnically defined districts plus Moscow and Leningrad and the Russian dominated electoral districts.

A Russian Republic Committee of Constitutional Supervision was to be elected for ten year terms, composed of President, Vice President and thirteen members. As with the federal Committee, competence was limited to advice. The Republic's Congress was to have made the final decision if the issuing authority were subject to its jurisdiction;

otherwise the decision was to be made by the Republic's Supreme Soviet.

A New Tactic to Form a Commonwealth

President Gorbachev's effort to preserve a union seemed doomed to failure until a meeting of representatives of nine Republics on April 23, 1991. Gorbachev and his colleagues of the Republics agreed to a new beginning for these nine who had shown themselves willing to cooperate. The drafts based upon the legislation on competencies enacted on April 26, 1990 were the basis for drafting and the road cleared to a new union treaty draft. On August 15, 1991 it was approved in final form,[92] and a ceremony of signature set for August 20. Gorbachev went on vacation to await the event. For a moment the record suggested that the reconciliation of disputes among the Republics had been achieved, but the expectations proved to be premature. The opponents of the draft staged a coup on August 19.

The dramatic events leading to restoration of Gorbachev in his role as President are known to the world. Less well known are the steps taken to make a new beginning. It became clear that the August draft had already been discarded by several Republics. A demand for a draft taking into consideration the lessons of the coup was expressed in many quarters.

A committee placed the President of the Kazakh Republic in the chair of an extraordinary Congress of People's Deputies called for the occasion. With his first words he explained that "As a result of the coup d'état committed on August 19–21 the process of forming a new relationship between sovereign republics was disrupted. These developments brought the country to the brink of catastrophe."[93]

The chair called for a treaty on a commonwealth of sovereign states between all the Republics that chose to join, with every state being able to define the format of its participation in the commonwealth. He then set forth a state structure recommended for a transition period. The emphasis was to be upon Republic sovereignty. The proposal was a new constitution of a commonwealth of sovereign republics to be drafted by a Council of Representatives of People's Deputies on the principle of equal representation from the Union Republics. There would have been twenty deputies from each Union Republic delegated by their Supreme Soviets to perform legislative functions and to draft a constitution. The executive would have been a State Council to be led with the USSR President and the presidents of the Union Republics, coordinating the economic effort and implementing radical reform. The draft constitution would have been submitted to the Union Republics and finally endorsed at a Congress of representatives of all of the Union Republics.

A *New York Times* correspondent reported that complaints came from the corridors of the Congress, notably on the future of the Autonomous Republics. A representative from the Mari republic was heard to say that Autonomous Republics would be wiped out.[94] His criticism was evidently accepted as valid. It was quite true that in the first treaty of 1922 the national units denied Union Republic status had been led to expect promotion to Union Republic status as they developed economically and politically. Promotion of status was in fact effected in a constitution of 1936, when several republics were elected to union status. There was only one restraint, which has been discussed above. Some politically and economically mature units, notably the Tatars and the Bashkirs had been denied promotion ostensibly because they were not on a frontier with a capitalist country. Stalin said, as has been seen, that they could not have full status because if they exercised the right of a Union Republic to secede, they would have no place to go except to a capitalist world. They would have been capitalist enclaves within a socialist world. With the 1977 revision of the constitution no promotion of Autonomous Republics had occurred, as has been seen.

The complaints from the Autonomous Republics' deputies seem to have been heard, for the structure revised following complaints gave to the Autonomous Republics a measure of legal status, although in a novel form. The deputies from Autonomous Republics or lesser autonomous units were to be placed with deputies of Union Republics among the twenty deputies authorized to the Union Republic, thus augmenting the delegation from the Union Republic within which they were situated. Consequently the Russian Republic would have been granted, in addition to the twenty representatives representing Russians, thirty-two other deputies representing Autonomous Republics and other units. So also the delegations from the Azerbaijani, Georgian, Tajik, and Uzbek Republics would have been augmented to include the lesser ethnic units.

Evidently, to prevent the delegations from the Union Republics, augmented by deputies from the autonomous units, from upsetting a balance based upon twenty representatives from each Union Republic, no group of deputies would have been permitted to cast more than one ballot.[95] Presumably, the deputies within each delegation authorized to cast but one ballot would need to caucus to determine what the single vote would have been.

The State Council, established in accordance with the proposal set before the Congress of People's Deputies of a Council of Presidents, was to coordinate domestic and foreign policies affecting the common interest of republics. Its economic and social activity was to be conducted through an Inter-Republic Economic Committee, chaired by an appointee of the USSR President in agreement with the other members of the State Council. Its competency was set as federal control over questions of defense, security, law and order, and industrial affairs. Decree powers were granted to the State Council to move business within these spheres.

Legislative authority was given, as it had been given in the past to a Supreme Soviet, to form two chambers.[96] It was to have been structured differently from the constitution of 1977, in that the two chambers would not have equal rights. One chamber, the Council of the Republics, would have been the upper house, and the other, the Council of the Union, would have been the lower house. The lower house would have introduced legislation on human rights and any other matters not reserved to the Republics. The upper house would have ratified and denounced international treaties of the USSR and would have adopted decisions on the organization and work of Union Republics. The superior status of the Council of Republics was demonstrated by the requirement that the Council of Republics approve the legislation passed by the lower house. Further emphasis upon republic sovereignty was indicated by the provision that "The supreme organs of state power of the republics have the right to suspend on the territory of the republic the laws adopted by the USSR Supreme Soviet," although only if they had contradicted the Constitution of the Union Republic.

A Declaration of the Congress of People's Deputies was issued on September 5 on Human Rights and Freedoms. It was stated to be in force until a constitution was promulgated. In form it was a declaration of 31 articles declaring that rights and freedoms were inviolable and must correspond to the Universal Declaration of Human Rights, the International Conventions on human rights, and other international norms. These include the right to use the native language, education in the native language and retention and development of ethnic cultures.

The three Baltic Republics of the USSR were recognized by the State Council as its first act. This left only Georgia and Moldavia outside of the new association being formed within the USSR for which a new constitution was to be promulgated.[97] Although seven of the Union Republics were prepared in mid-November to work toward a new "Commonwealth of Sovereign States," Ukraine seemed reluctant to join, saying that it awaited conclusion of a referendum planned for December 1, 1991. The draft was returned on November 25 to the Republic parliaments for reconsideration.

A Surprise at Minsk

Ukraine's hesitancy to commit its legislature evaporated after a strong vote for independence and support for Leonid Kravchuk as President. The road to an accord was cleared, and to the surprise of many both at home and abroad, the leaders of Russia, Ukraine, and Belorussia met in Minsk to form a tripartite agreement. The Kazakh leader was reported as out of his capital for the weekend, but on his return the press carried on December 9, 1991 news of the founding of a Commonwealth of Independent States and the declaration that the USSR "as a subject of international law and geopolitical reality" had ceased to exist.[98]

The text of the agreement was short: declaration of a coordinating center for the Commonwealth in Minsk; establishment of a coordinating institution to apply "principles," confirmation of the goals and principles of the United Nations, the Helsinki Final Act, and the Conference on Security and Cooperation in Europe, and a bill of rights. This bill augmented the document approved by the USSR Congress of People's Deputies to add a guarantee of equal rights of nationality "and of other differences" as well as of civil, political, social, economic, and cultural rights and freedoms "in accordance with common international norms of human rights."

Soon after the agreement was signed, other Islamic Republics followed Kazakhstan in joining the founders. Finally, all but Georgia had joined. This left outside only the three former Baltic Republics, whose governments had been recognized as independent on the final day of the session of the Congress of People's Deputies, held on September 6, 1991.

The agreement of Minsk was followed on December 21 by an agreement of Alma-Ata, signed by eleven states.[99] It augmented the Minsk agreement by outlining the skeleton of an institutional structure. A Council of Heads of State was placed in the policy-making role, while a Council of Heads of Government became the executive body charged with the duty of submitting proposals for installation of coordinating institutions. These coordinating units were to provide the basis for coordination of foreign policy, a common economic space, a common European and Eurasian policy, a customs policy, common transport and communication systems, ecological security, environmental protection, immigration policy, and opposition to organized crime. Disputes over interpretation of the accord were to be resolved under a procedure to be established. Most important, policy on nuclear weapons was to be coordinated by the Council of Heads of State.

Gorbachev signed his last decree on December 25, 1991, after having failed to assemble a quorum of the Supreme Soviet deputies, and the red flag of the USSR that had flown over the Kremlin was lowered.

Searching for a Unifying Cultural Force

The record of over four centuries of Russian history suggests that political leaders, whether Tsars or Communists, have sensed the need when acquiring non-Russian peoples by conquest or diplomacy to forge some common bond likely to keep them within the fold forever. For the Tsars it was "Russification"; for the Communists it was "class" unity. Russification differed in degree in various parts of the Empire, depending upon the form in which the territory was acquired and administered, but one rule was common to all: The Russian language was the official language, and its use was required in state offices and the courts as the official language, subject, of course, to interpretation when necessary to conduct the affairs of the office or court.

For the Communists the tie that was to bind was quite different: it was to be a repudiation of Russification, and the elevation of "class" ties over those of ethnic origin. Lenin held firmly to the doctrine, written into Marx's *Communist Manifesto,* that "workers know no fatherland." He had demonstrated his faith in the *Manifesto*'s credo in criticizing the socialists of Europe for voting for wartime budgets when the First World War broke out. He made his first move toward what eventually became the Communist International when he called socialists of like mind to him at Zimmerwald in 1915. He was determined to establish a new basis for common affinity totally unrelated to ethnicities.

Yet Lenin was a realist, as he proved so often. He could compromise when necessary to preserve power. He did soon on the nationality issue. He preached "self-determination" of peoples because he thought, and rightly so, that if it were to be applied, it would break asunder the Tsarist empire. When his victory was achieved he did not plunge into a unitary class-oriented state. He agreed to let the ethnic groups too large and too powerful to oppose go their own way. One after the other seceded, but events demonstrated that the policy of permitting secession was no more than a tactic. He brought most of the groups, with the glaring exception of Finland, Poland, and the Baltic states, back into his new state structure.

With the hindsight permitted in historical analysis, Lenin's confidence in a future unified state of the working class was probably well founded on two pillars: the Communist Party and objective circumstances. The Party had always been unitary in structure, for Lenin had resisted efforts by the Jewish Bund and the Lithuanian Communists to structure it as a federation. The members of the Party had been chosen to lead—there were no nonprofessional sympathizers permitted among them. They formed a core on which Lenin probably expected to rely to bring the seceding peoples back to the Russians.

The second pillar on which Lenin may well have relied was the objective circumstance of the time, namely the fear of foreign invasion, suggesting the desirability of union to preserve power to resist conquerors, and the economic consequences of separation of regions formerly knit together in economic relationships.

But fears of centuries-old Russification were a counterweight to these centripetal forces. Lenin seems to have had such confidence prior to 1922 in the strength of the centripetal forces that he ignored, as he wrote to Kamenev, the centrifugal force of nationalism. Not until the autumn of 1922 does he seem to have appreciated that he could not expect the Ukrainians and Georgians to enter a union in which they could see no opportunity to escape Stalin's "autonomization."

Lenin's abrupt change in tactics to create a federation of equals came late, yet it was seemingly successful. But within months he could barely attend to work and within a year he was dead. Stalin and his successors transformed Lenin's federal structure into a de facto unitary one, to such an extent that Gorbachev could retort to a complainer against federation, "What do you know of federation; you have never lived in one!"

Communist Party members assembled at the 28th Congress in July 1990 demonstrated that many of them thought that their dream had failed. The "socialist" system, as implemented by Stalin and Brezhnev, had become unacceptable, being inhuman and unproductive. A new course had to be plotted, but which one? Gorbachev offered two slogans: "democratization" and "marketization." He met resistance from those who had been taught, call it "brainwashed" if you will, for more than seventy years that humanity needs vanguard leadership and that merchandising creates no value; indeed, it is the root of the woes of the world. The criminal code since 1932 had punished as crime the buying and selling of goods for a profit. To make the prospects even more unpalatable, they had been accompanied by estimates of widespread unemployment and rising prices.

Such predictions caused both Communist Party members and rank-and-file citizens to question whether the future merited further sacrifices. Many expressed horror at loss of what they associated with the values of socialism: full employment, egalitarian wages, and a workplace without speedups. Gorbachev and his colleagues did not conceal the sacrifices required. They promised a safety-net, but said quite frankly that the competitive world in which the USSR functioned would not permit continuation of the life lived during the decades passed.

By the autumn of 1991 many Soviet citizens seemed to have lost faith in Gorbachev's leadership. The decisive blow was struck in a coup led by Gorbachev's Vice President on August 19. When it failed, thanks to the leadership of Boris Yeltsin as President of the Russian Republic with support of colleagues drawn from intellectuals, democratically inspired youth, and mutineers within the military, Gorbachev was liberated from detention. Significant numbers of persons had refused to be led to what they perceived to be restoration of Stalinism and Russification.

Yeltsin, with his Russian colleagues, supported by Ukrainian and Belorussian leaders, formed a loosely coordinated structure that they called a "Commonwealth of Independent States." Within days of signature in Minsk all but the Georgian leaders had joined the circle. In the words of the Minsk accord, the USSR had ceased its existence.

The founding signatories had seemed to recognize that "sovereignty" had limitations mindful of those Lenin had recognized in 1922 when the union was formed. He and his colleagues had anticipated that the independent Republics formed from the former Russian Empire would have to form an association in the interest of economic and military coordination to stave off economic collapse and hostile neighbors. The Minsk participants evidently felt the same pressures, as stated in their proposals for "coordination," but they would not accept closer "union," lest it lead, as had been the case under Stalin's leadership, to Russification and domination by the strongest members of the "union."

The political accommodations of the Minsk and Alma-Ata accords evidently reflected the maximum compromise acceptable to the leaders of the republics determined to reject Gorbachev and his concept of "union." Consequently, there remained in the formulations in Minsk and Alma-Ata no reference to the "cement" of the Russian language, which had created the formal union of the Tsars and the "class" loyalty relied upon by the communists to overcome the never-ending pressures from the national minorities. For the foreseeable future the slogan would be "sovereignty" and no more. The peoples in the great land mass east of the White Sea, the Bug, and the Danube were determined to work out their own futures within the framework of their various national traditions.

NOTES

1. Report by Nursultan Nazarbayev, September 2, 1991, *New York Times*, September 3, 1991, p. A7.

2. For Eng. trans. of text of RSFSR Constitution of 1918, see A. Unger, *Constitutional Development in the USSR: A Guide to the Soviet Constitutions* (New York: Pica Press, 1982), pp. 24–46.

3. Art. 11.

4. Art. 22.

5. Art. 43. For statute of May 19, 1920, see *Sob. Uzak. RSFSR*, 1920, No. 45, item 202. For statute in amended form of July 27, 1922, see Ibid., 1922, No. 47, item 600. Reprinted in *Istoriia sovetskoi konstitutsii (v dokumentakh)*

1917–1956 (Moscow: Gosudarstvennoe Izdatel'stvo Iuridicheskoi Literatury, 1957). Document No. 158 at p. 366.

6. Basic Law of the Russian Empire. See *Svod Zakonov Rossiiskoi Imperii,* vol. 1, part 1 (1906 edition), Art. 3.

7. Ibid., Art. 1. "Gosudarstvo Rossiiskoe edino i nerazdel'no."

8. N. M. Korkunov, *Russkoe Gosudarstvennoe Pravo* (St. Petersburg, Tip. M. M. Stasiulevicha, 7th ed. 1909). For a brief summary of the status of regions of the Empire inhabited by national minorities, see R. Pipes, *The Formation of the Soviet Union: Communism and Nationalism. 1917–1923* (New York: rev. ed., 1968), pp. 3–7.

9. These highlights of the history of the Baltic Peoples have been drawn from several sources: J. Rutkis, ed., *Latvia: Country and People* (Stockholm: Latvian National Foundation), 1967, pp. 1–10; V. S. Vardys, *Lithuania Under the Soviets: Portrait of a Nation, 1940–1965* (New York: Praeger, 1965), pp. 3–46; A. Bilmanis, *A History of Latvia* (Princeton: Princeton University Press, 1951).

10. For text, see S. Studenikin, compiler, *Istoriia sovetskoi konstitutsii v dekretakh i postanovleniiakh sovetskogo pravitel'stva* (Moscow: Gosudarstvennoe Izdatel'stvo 'Sovetskoe Zakonodatel'stvo', 1917–1936), pp. 31–32.

11. For text of decrees, see Yu. I. Korablev, editor, *Obrazovanie soiuza sovetskikh sotsialisticheskikh respublik. Sbornik dokumentov* (Moscow: Nauka, 1972), pp. 74–77: Latvia, Document No. 25; Lithuania, Document No. 26; Estonia, Lithuania and Latvia, Document No. 27.

12. Vardys, *Lithuania,* note 9, provides a brief account of the events leading to the treaties.

13. Korablev, *Obrazovanie,* note 11 at p. 30. Document No. 9.

14. Ibid., p. 25, Document No. 5.

15. Ibid., p. 30. Document No. 8.

16. Studenikin, *Istoriia,* note 10, pp. 111, 115, 178, 197, 204.

17. Ibid., p. 115. Art 4.

18. Ibid., p. 111. Art 15.

19. Ibid., p. 178. Art. 13.

20. Ibid., p. 197. Art. 2.

21. Ibid., p. 204. Art. 6.

22. For events in Central Asia, see Pipes, *Formation,* note 8, pp. 86–93.

23. The title "Union Republic" may have been short-lived, for a name and status change occurred soon after the declaration as evidenced by the fact that when Turkestan was divided into its ethnic components on October 14, 1924 by the RSFSR central committee, it bore the "Autonomous Republic" and not the "Union Republic" title. Compare documents 131, p. 282 and 205, p. 487 in Studenkin, *Istoriia,* note 5. The index to the *Istoriia,* p. 1020, refers to Document 131 as creating the Autonomous Republic.

24. See discussion *infra* for contrast between Lenin's and Stalin's plans for national minorities.

25. Constitution of April 30, 1920 with amendments of May 20, 1921 and July 1922. See Studenkin, *Istoriia,* note 10, p. 213, Art 6.

26. Ibid., Art. 7.

27. Ibid., Art. 19, paragraph 4.

28. Ibid.

29. Ibid.

30. Constitution of August 18, 1922, See Studeniken, *Istoriia* note 10, p. 219.

31. Ibid., Art. 11.

32. Ibid., Art. 12.

33. Declaration of the Provisional Worker-Peasant Government of the Ukraine. See Studeniken, *Istoriia,* note 10, p. 103.

34. Decree of the Central Executive Committee of Ukrainian SSR, May 20, 1919, Ibid., p. 103.

35. Decree of IV Congress of Soviets of Ukrainian SSR, Ibid., p. 137.

36. These provisions were incorporated in a formal treaty with the RSFSR of 1921. See *Izvestia,* April 6, 1921.

37. Declaration of Temporary Military-Revolutionary Committee of the Azerbaijan Soviet Independent Republic. See *Izvestia,* April 29, 1922.

38. See agreements with Azerbaijan, Ukraine, Belorussia and Transcaucasia. Studeniken, *Istoriia,* note 10, pp. 149, 163, 170 and 176. By a Protocol of February 22, 1922 executed by the RSFSR and all independent republics plenipotentiary powers were transferred to the RSFSR to represent the group at the Genoa Conference of 1922 called by Lloyd George of Great Britain to reestablish a link between West and East Europe. See *Izvestia,* February 22, 1922, and 3 *Sobranie Deistvuiushikh Dogovorov* (1922), pp. 1–3. Also published in Studeniken, *Istoriia,* note 10, p. 202, and L. Shapiro, ed., *Soviet Treaty Series* (Washington D.C.: Georgetown University Press, 1950), 1:163.

39. Constitution of the Transcaucasian Socialist Federated Soviet Republic, Studeniken, *Istoriia,* note 10, p. 223.

40. See Pipes, *Formation,* note 8, p. 193.

41. Stalin's thoughts on nationalities were assembled and published as Joseph Stalin, *Marxism and the National and Colonial Question* (Moscow: Co-operative Publishing Society of Foreign Workers in USSR, 1935). The explanatory notes (p. 289) to the first paper say that it was written at the end of 1912 and the beginning of 1913 in Vienna, and signed by Stalin. Published in *Prosveshchenie,* nos. 3–5 (1913) and again in a pamphlet in 1914 in St. Petersburg, it was republished in 1920 by the People's Commissariat of Nationalities of which Stalin was the People's Commissar.

42. For the Commissariat's Statute, see Studeniken, *Istoriia,* note 5, document No. 158, p. 366.

43. See Constitution, note 40.

44. The Far Eastern Republic was established as a buffer between Soviet Russia and Japan. It had no relationship to the nationality-based origin of other republics. For a brief account of its short life, which ended November 1922, when the Red Army marched into Vladivostok, see Pipes, Formation, note 8, p. 255.

45. See Korablev, Obrazovanie, note 11, Document No. 100, p. 296.

46. Ibid., Document No. 101, dated September 26, 1922, p. 297.

47. V. I. Lenin "Continuation of Diary of 30 December 1922 on the Question of Nationalities or of 'Autonomization.'" See Studeniken, Istoriia, note 5, p. 399.

48. On June 15, 1925 the Kirgiz Autonomous SSR was renamed the Kazakh Autonomous SSR by decree of RSFSR Central Executive Committee. See Ibid., Document No. 222, p. 558.

49. The Tajik Autonomous SSR was transformed into a Union SSR and was incorporated as such into the USSR on December 5, 1929 and the USSR Constitution amended to include it. See Ibid., Document No. 232, p. 610 and constitutional amendment, Document No. 444, p. 659.

50. Decree of RSFSR Central Executive Committee of October 14, 1924 reorganized the Autonomous Turkestan SSR into its several component units. Ibid., Document No. 205, p. 487. The USSR Central Executive Committee then issued a decree of October 27, 1924 authorizing its presidium to form the newly created republics of Central Asia as the Uzbek SSR with its Tajik Autonomous SSR; the Turkmen SSR, the Kara-Kirgiz Autonomous Province within the RSFSR, and authorizing joining the Kirgiz part of Turkestan with the Kirgiz Autonomous SSR within the RSFSR. See Ibid., Document No. 206, p. 489.

51. Declaration of formation of the Uzbek SSR, adopted by First Congress of Soviets of the Uzbek SSR, February 17, 1925. Ibid., Document No. 208, p. 493.

52. Declaration of First Congress of Soviets of the Turkmen SSR of February 20, 1925. Ibid., Document No. 209, p. 495 and Document No. 210, p. 498.

53. Decree of the Third Congress of Soviets of the USSR, May 13, 1925. Ibid., Document, No. 218, p. 547. USSR constitutional amendment of May 20, 1925, Document No. 219, p. 548.

54. For texts of constitutions, see Ibid., pp. 499–546, 573, 589, 635.

55. Decree of Third Congress of Soviets of the USSR, May 20, 1925. Ibid., Document No. 220, p. 551.

56. Decree of Seventh Congress of Soviets of the USSR, February 6, 1935. Ibid., Document No. 261, p. 700. The 1918 RSFSR constitution had weighted representation in the Congress of Soviets in favor of workers over peasants, implementing the Communist Party's position that peasants were less reliable

than workers as constructors of socialism. The 1936 constitutional change gave peasants equal weight with workers.

57. For the draft of a new constitution, see Ibid., Document No. 270, p. 710. It was ordered published on June 12, 1936.

58. By Art. 34 of the 1936 USSR Constitution there would be elected to the Supreme Soviet's Chamber of the Union one deputy for every 300,000 inhabitants. By Art. 35 the seats in the Chamber of Nationalities were to be distributed as follows: Union Republic, 25; Autonomous Republic, 11; Autonomous Province, 5; National District, 1. For text, see Unger, *Constitutional Development*, note 2. The draft of the constitution had not presented such large delegations from each ethnic area, these being respectively, 10, 5, 2 and 0 for national districts.

59. See J. V. Stalin, *Report on the Draft Constitution of the USSR*, November 25, 1936. Part V, section 3, published in Joseph Stalin, *Leninism, Selected Writings* (New York: International Publishers, 1942), pp. 379–399.

60. Law of USSR Supreme Soviet, March 31, 1940. Studeniken, *Istoriia*, note 5, Document No. 290, p. 810.

61. Law of USSR Supreme Soviet, August 2, 1940. Ibid., Document No. 293, p. 813.

62. Law of USSR Supreme Soviet, August 2, 1940. Ibid., Document No. 292, p. 812.

63. Laws of USSR Supreme Soviet: Lithuania, Document No. 294; Latvia, Document No. 295; Estonia, Document No. 296. Ibid., pp. 814–815.

64. Law of USSR Supreme Soviet, February 25, 1947. Ibid., Document No. 311, p. 828.

65. Law of USSR Supreme Soviet, July 16, 1956. Ibid., Document No. 360, p. 934. The USSR Constitution was amended on the same day to reflect the change. See Document No. 361, p. 934.

66. See Laws of the USSR Supreme Soviet, February 1, 1944. These inserted in the USSR Constitution new Arts. 18-A and 18-B. Ibid., Documents Nos. 302–303, pp. 823–824.

67. See E. Matskevich, *Izvestia*, June 23, 1987, p. 3. Eng. trans. in *Current Digest of the Soviet Press* 39(1987):25:21.

68. Amendment of February 11, 1957. Incorporated in Constitution as Art. 14 (u).

69. See Y. V. Andropov, "Sixty Years of the USSR," *Pravda*, December 22, 1983, p. 1. Readers with long memories will recall Stalin's statement on convergence of cultures in his Report to the Sixteenth Congress of the CPSU, June 27, 1930, where he said, "The same must be said of the formula about national culture the flourishing of national cultures (and languages) in the period of the dictatorship of the proletariat in one country, with the object of preparing the conditions for their dying away and fusion into one common socialist culture (and one common language) in the period of the victory of

socialism throughout the world." Eng. trans. in J. Stalin, *Leninism* 2:247 at 343 (Part 3, section 2).

70. For texts of Union Republic Constitutions, as enacted in 1978, see F. J. M. Feldbrugge, ed., *The Constitutions of the USSR and the Union Republics: Analysis, Texts, Reports* Alphen aan den Rijn, The Netherlands: Sijthoff & Noordhoff, 1979.

71. Feldbrugge, *Constitutions*, p. 288. Armenia, Art. 72; Azerbaijan, Art. 73; Georgia, Art. 75.

72. A proposal for a federal code rather than "Fundamentals" was made in the press. See Rynok, "Mnenie iuristov," *Pravda*, June 7, 1990, p. 2. The "Fundamentals" were enacted into law on May 31, 1991. *Vedomosti S'ezda Narodnikh Deputatov*, 1991, No. 26, item 733.

73. For Eng. trans. of text of 1977 Constitution, see Unger, *Constitutional Development*, pp. 232–266.

74. *Vedomosti Verkhovnogo Soveta SSR*, 1988, No. 13, item 195.

75. Ibid., No. 30, item 547.

76. Ibid., 1989, No. 3, item 14. Eng. trans. in *Current Digest of the Soviet Press* 41(2)(1989):5.

77. "Resolution of the 19th Communist Party Conference on relations Between Nationalities," *Izvestia* and *Pravda*, July 5, 1988. Eng. trans. in *Current Digest of the Soviet Press* 40(37)(1988):11.

78. Amendment of December 1, 1988. *Vedomosti Verkhovnogo Soveta SSR*, 1988, No. 49, item 727.

79. By Art. 109 the number of deputies to be seated from ethnic regions was set as follows for the Congress of People's Deputies: Union Republic, 32; Autonomous Republic, 11; Autonomous Province, 5; Autonomous District, 1. From this group, supplemented by deputies named by social organizations dwelling in ethnically organized areas, members were selected by the Congress to sit in the Chamber of Nationalities of the USSR Supreme Soviet. The number seated from each ethnic region is as follows: Union Republic, 11; Autonomous Republic, 4; Autonomous Province, 2; Autonomous District, 1. The procedure to be followed in the conduct of elections was established by law of December 1, 1988. *Vedomosti Verkhovnogo Soveta SSR*, 1988, No. 49, item 730.

80. Report of meeting of Presidium of USSR Supreme Soviet, November 26, 1988. *Vedomosti Verkhovnogo Soveta SSR*, No. 48, pp. 799–801.

81. *Vedomosti S'ezda Narodnikh Deputatov*, 1989, No. 25, item 490.

82. Ibid., 1990, No. 16, item 270.

83. Ibid., 1990, No. 12, item 189.

84. Ibid., 1990, No. 15, item 252.

85. Ibid., 1990, No. 19, item 331.

86. *Vedomosti Verkhovnogo Soveta*, 1988, No. 49, item 727.

87. *Vedomosti S'ezda Narodnikh Deputatov*, 1990, No. 18, item 314.

88. Ibid., 1990, No. 19, item 329.

89. Ibid., item 330.

90. Ibid., item 327.

91. *Vedomosti Verkhovnogo Soveta RSFSR,* 1989, No. 44, item 1303.

92. *Izvestia,* August 15, 1991, p. 1.

93. Nazarbayev, see note 1.

94. Celestine Bohlen, "Soviet Legislators, Pushed Aside, Say They Deserve Better," *New York Times,* September 3, 1991, p. A9.

95. See "Soviet Resolution Approved by Congress of People's Deputies," *New York Times,* September 5, 1991, p. A12.

96. See Resolution of September 5, 1991. *New York Times,* September 6, 1991, p. A12.

97. Serge Schmemann, "New Council Meets," *New York Times,* September 7, 1991, p. 1.

98. For text see *New York Times,* December 10, 1991, p. A19.

99. For text see *New York Times,* December 23, 1991, p. A10.

6. Elites and Ethnic Identities in Soviet and Post-Soviet Politics

Mark R. Beissinger

G IVEN the degree of centralization long characteristic of the Soviet state, it is hardly surprising that models of elite behavior played a central role in scholarly debates over the evolution of the Soviet system in the post-Stalin era. Studies of elites have been among the main instruments used to judge the broader evolution of Soviet politics since the mid-fifties, when Barrington Moore first connected the future of the Soviet system with patterns of elite recruitment and circulation.[1] Looming large among the gaps in this literature, however, was a tendency to oversimplify, and in many cases simply to ignore, the multiethnic dimension of Soviet elite politics. In comparison with the attention lavished on other aspects of elites, Sovietologists devoted relatively little attention to the role of ethnic identities in elite politics.[2]

This lack of attention is all the more puzzling given that one of the crucial elements widely thought to explain the Soviet leadership's ability to contain its nationalities problems in the past was, in one author's words, "the existence and development of indigenous elites in the base ethnic regions."[3] Ironically, under glasnost these very same elites have posed some of the most serious challenges to the existence of the Soviet system. As Joseph Rothschild has pointed out, "the formation, consolidation, and politicization of ethnic groups" is primarily "a mobilization process" that is "always led by elites."[4] Traditional approaches to the study of Soviet elites were not equipped to deal with these seemingly contradictory dimensions of elite behavior. They relied heavily on theories that were devoid of any conception of ethnic politics and on methodologies that utilized formal, descriptive criteria rather than attitudinal or behavioral evidence.

Like all revolutionary change, political change in the former Soviet Union posed the question of "who rules" most sharply. But in an age of heightened mass mobilization, what it means to rule has also changed drastically; certainly, it can no longer be reduced simply to occupying political office. Elites who lack authority in society, who cannot make their decisions stick, or who find themselves the targets of mass protests numbering in the hundreds of thousands can hardly be considered "ruling elites" in the traditional sense in which these words were used. Within this context, ethnicity and elite identity become extremely important, since to a great extent it has been on the basis of ethnicity that new elites have gone about the business of building their followings. The question of "who rules" can now be answered only by understanding how elites rule and why some elites prove capable of ruling and others not.

A full answer to these question cannot be provided within the confines of this essay; on the contrary, a great deal of empirical work on the phenomenon of political leadership will be necessary before they can be answered.[5] Rather, our purpose here is to sketch out some of the parameters that define the ethnic dimension of elite politics. It is the main argument of this essay that, as is the case among those studying elites in other political systems, elite-society linkages, elite attitudes, and elite behavior should be placed at the center of studies of Soviet elites, as opposed to issues of power-building, as has traditionally been the case within Soviet studies.

The Inadequacies of Traditional Approaches

Traditional approaches to the study of Soviet elites suffered from several mutually reinforcing fallacies: a tendency to reduce Soviet politics to a game played out primarily among ethnically Russian elites; an understanding of elites that narrowed the circle of relevant participants to those occupying official posts; and a set of underlying theories of politics that paid little or no attention to issues of ethnicity. What was especially remarkable about these assumptions was that they were made concerning one of the most ethnically complex societies in the world. Certainly, a portion of the blame should be laid at the door of "directed society" models. They gave rise to stereotypes that reduced Soviet politics to a game played out solely among elites. Society, in all its color, was written out of Soviet politics and replaced by issues of power-building. Yet, what is striking is the degree to which nearly all traditional approaches to Soviet politics mirrored these same assumptions.

Patronage models, for instance, explored the ways in which elites built power on the basis of the *nomenklatura* system, focusing in particular on processes of career advancement and elite circulation. Implicit in this agenda was an underlying theory that viewed elite control over society as fundamentally in conflict with the requirements of modernization. And indeed they were. But the way in which patronage politics by and large was conceptualized by Sovietologists was ill-suited for dealing with subsequent developments in Soviet politics.

In contrast to the power-building and modernization focuses taken by Sovietologists studying patronage politics, those who focus on patronage networks in other societies have tended to view patronage as a mechanism of exchange between state and society, examining its place in a broader system of social stratification in which class, ethnicity, and patronage are inevitably linked.[6] For example, the ethnic character of organized crime in the United States has long been noted. Indeed, sociologists ascribed this phenomenon to the particular form of stratification to which immigrant groups were subject—the late entrance of these groups into the economy, their low socioeconomic status, and their cohesive group solidarity. One conclusion reached by such studies is that patronage tends to flourish in situations where the social distance between ethnic groups is great.[7] Yet, with few exceptions,[8] ethnicity was treated in most studies of Soviet patronage politics as a peripheral factor. Indeed, in some cases there was even a conscious effort to wipe ethnicity out of such studies altogether.[9] Moreover, no attempt was made to explore the interaction between such factors as class, ethnicity, and patronage within the Soviet context.

Other traditional approaches fared no better in integrating multiethnicity into their assumptions. Industrial convergence models emphasized the proven connection, found in Western democracies, between education and political participation to argue in favor of an inevitable liberalization in Soviet politics as society (and the elites emerging from society) grew more educated.[10] And to a significant degree such theories were proven true by recent events. Yet, proponents of the industrial convergence approach tended to ignore ethnicity as a factor shaping political behavior. Indeed, they assumed, along with early modernization theorists and Soviet leaders, that nationalities issues in

Soviet politics would diminish under the homogenizing impact of modernization and that Soviet liberalization would be characterized by smooth and continuous evolution.

In actuality, precisely the opposite occurred: the growing educational and technical levels of Soviet elites ultimately helped to bring ethnic issues onto the political agenda, undermining political stability. Considerable comparative research has pointed to the role of the intelligentsia as carriers of nationalist ideologies and as ethnic entrepreneurs.[11] In a survey of former Soviet citizens, Rasma Karklins found that "ethnic privilege is more evident to more educated and politically involved observers."[12] Soviet researchers similarly have reported that higher education and ethnic consciousness appear to be closely related.[13] The implication of such findings is that the cooptation of educated specialists would bring national issues onto the political agenda. Had proponents of industrial convergence theories paid attention to this aspect of Soviet society, they might well have foreseen that the growing educational backgrounds of elites were bound to destabilize the Soviet political system at the same time as liberalizing it.

A similar lacuna could be found in authority-building models. They posited the development of a tacit accord among elites in the Brezhnev era; elite consensus was managed through elite stability and the manipulation of policy platforms.[14] But the extent to which ethnicity played a role in the bargaining over policy (as well as how the shaping of the elite, particularly its ethnic dimension, in turn influenced the political agenda) remained relatively unexplored.[15] Empirical studies demonstrated that Brezhnev's policy of trust-in-cadres was a segmented policy, implemented to various degrees in various parts of Soviet Union; this in turn implied that authority-building had an ethnic component to it that most observers overlooked.[16] Moreover, whenever authority-building strategies were pursued to any degree in a non-Russian context, the inexorable tendency was for specifically national issues to dominate the political agenda.

Toward the end of the Brezhnev era scholars devoted increasing attention to generational models of elite politics, arguing that the younger generation of officials differed significantly in its political attitudes from its elders as a result of early socialization experiences.[17] Yet, little attention was paid to the ethnic dimension of generational change.[18] No one who has witnessed the events of the glasnost period would doubt the importance of generation as a basic division within Soviet politics. But nearly every study of the attitudes of elite generations focused exclusively on Russian and Slavic elites, and somehow generational attitudes toward nationality issues escaped evaluation entirely.

In most Soviet contexts, ethnicity has formed deeper political cleavages than generation. For instance, studies conducted by Soviet sociologists indicate that the reading habits of urban Estonians, regardless of age, are more similar to each other than they are to the reading habits of Russians, Uzbeks, or Moldavians.[19] The one ethnic group that has been most clearly divided in attitudes and behavior along generational lines has been the Russians. Studies in the late 1970s showed that urban Russians aged 18 to 29 were much more interested in science fiction and novels about love and friendship and much less interested in literature on war and politics than were urban Russians between the ages of 30 and 49. And urban Russians under the age of 50 were considerably more interested in literature on the past of their nation than were Russians 50 and over. The extent to which similar generational differences exist within other ethnic groups is unclear.[20] The evidence available suggests that political generations have quite different contours and are associated with quite different political attitudes within different national contexts. No discussion of generational change within the Soviet elite could possibly be lifted out of its specific ethnic context.

A second shortcoming of traditional models has been their heavy reliance on structural approaches to the study of elites. Two approaches stand out within the study of elites: structural and behavioral. The former focuses on the characteristics of eliteness that reinforce or undermine elite cohesion or that might be associated with elite circulation, deriving elite attitudes and behavior from the presence or absence of these characteristics; the latter attempts to deduce the relationships of elites to non-elites and to political leaders by examining empirically elite attitudes, decision-making, and behavior.[21] In general, this latter approach has tended to dominate in studies of American and West European elites. By contrast, the bulk of research on Soviet elites has been structural rather than behavioral, focusing on the questions of elite cohesion and circulation. Moreover, unlike West Europeanists and Americanists, Sovietologists have taken elite attitudes and behavior as assumptions of their studies rather than as objects of research. It is one thing to compare the backgrounds of elite populations that one knows behave differently; it is quite another to assume behavioral differences within a single elite population based on background characteristics. Yet, as Grey Hodnett observed (and not without criticism), the tendency in studies of Soviet elites was "to measure the characteristics of 'the powerful' in a global manner and then draw inferences on the basis of aggregate contours of data."[22]

Of course, there is nothing wrong in making assumptions about elite attitudes, so long as those assumptions are eventually tested against reality through empirical observation. However, for obvious reasons there were no broad empirical studies of the beliefs of Soviet politicians and elites, as have been common in the American and West European fields.[23] The assumptions of existing models, therefore, could never be tested. By contrast, raw biographical data on Soviet officials could be collected with relative ease. The problem was that such data had to be interpreted. As Bert Rockman has noted, "the problems of data gathering in studying elite behavior" have tended to be "less awesome than the problem of theoretical interpretation."[24] Not all research on elite attitudes necessarily required survey techniques, as the occasional use of content analysis to explore the atitudes of Soviet officials demonstrated.[25] Nevertheless, such research techniques were time-consuming and difficult to put into operation, causing researchers to opt for less taxing and challenging approaches.

At times, studies of Soviet elites that relied on a structural approach made assumptions about elite attitudes and behavior that had been proven faulty in other political contexts. It has been shown, for instance, that many beliefs of politicians are entirely unrelated to background characteristics, and that those relationships that do exist between the social profile of an elite and elite attitudes and behavior are often mediated by intervening variables.[26] Moreover, the character of ethnic identities can and do shift over the course of a lifetime. It was often thought in the past that those Russian officials in the non-Russian republics who spent their entire lives in that territory or were born there were likely to defend local interests with greater vigor than those who came to the republic at a later age. However, in a period of increasing division between native and local Russian communities, these same officials became patrons of Russian-nationalist movements within the non-Russian republics, displaying in most cases even more conservative attitudes toward non-Russian nationalisms than Russians in the RSFSR. By relying solely on structural approaches, Sovietologists faced a situation in which the problems of their theories were compounded by research methods that were incapable of raising contrary evidence.

A third shortcoming of traditional approaches was their narrow definition of what constituted "the elite"—their primary object of research. Most studies confined their focus solely to holders of public offices, which in the Soviet context was usually interpreted as personnel on the CPSU's *nomenklatura* lists.[27] Yet, elites contain a greater degree of ambiguity than such an approach admitted. Sovietologists have, wittingly or unwittingly, preferred to operate under the assumptions of Mosca's relatively cohesive ruling class rather than Pareto's looser and broader categories of governing and nongoverning elites.[28] As a result, the crucial area of elite-mass relations was practically ignored.

Some who have examined the history of Central Asia in the twentieth century within the context of broader developments in the Turkic world speak not only of "political elites" in terms of the holders of official offices, but also of "traditional elites," "counter-elites," and "professional elites."[29] No such differentiation found its way into studies of Soviet elites, largely because Sovietologists focused their attentions on official institutions rather than on the relations between these institutions and the society they governed. Obviously, any understanding of the role of elites in Soviet politics under contemporary conditions must include an examination of the leaderships of unofficial movements and organizations. But many of these new elites were active in politics long before the arrival of glasnost, and it is only now, with the help of hindsight, that the inadequacy of traditional definitions of what constituted the elite during the Brezhnev period becomes glaringly clear.

Excessive attention to the center of the political system deflected Sovietologists away from what was probably the most crucial aspect of elites—their roles as mediators between state and society. In the Belgian Congo, for instance, colonial authorities shaped the formation of local elites so as to create "a flexible, and so to speak popular intermediary, which could serve as a connective link between whites and natives, to make them accept the orders of the state."[30] Yet obviously, elites act as much more than mere representatives of state authority. Depending in part on the ways in which the social order is structured, they act to varying degrees as conduits for the expression of societal demands to the state.[31] Elites also act as shapers of societal consciousness. This is no less true for the politics of class, gender, or region than it is for the politics of ethnicity. Like all forms of collective action, ethnic collective action is a mobilization process that requires some degree of leadership.

Nowhere are the dangers of a reductionist approach to elite attitudes and behavior greater than in the area of ethnic identity. It is obvious that the variety and subtleties of ethnic identities cannot be well captured by approaches that deduce attitudes merely from background characteristics. Ethnic background has never been a reliable predictor of attitudes and behaviors, even in the sphere of inter-ethnic relations. To be sure, ethnic identity was perhaps the most important factor shaping political behavior within the Soviet Union. But studies of ethnic identity have pointed to the enormous variations that exist in national consciousness. In turn, the various colors of identity are refracted only indirectly onto elite politics through the prism of state-society relations. Thus, for understanding the ethnic dimension of elite politics, one must first start with an understanding of the basic parameters of ethnic identity, and only then look to the mechanisms by which these identities interact with elite politics.

Contours of Ethnic Identities

A. L. Epstein has distinguished between what he called positive identities, resting on "self-esteem, a sense of the worthiness of one's own groups's ways and values," and negative identities, based on "the internalized evaluation of others," with "much of one's behavior . . . prompted by the desire to avoid their anticipated slights or censure."[32] Most attention by scholars has been devoted to positive ethnic identities. But these also come in a great number of varieties. If Anthony Smith described a type of modern nationalism that sought "the attainment and maintenance of self-government and independence."[33] Elie Kedourie portrayed a type of anomic nationalism that arose in response to the dislocation and anomie produced by modernity.[34] One can also speak of imperial nationalisms that seek to maintain or impose political control over the sovereignty of other societies.[35] All of these forms of positive ethnic identities are easily recognizable within Soviet and post-Soviet politics—from the imperial nationalism of groups like *Soiuz* to the modern nationalism of movements like Sajudis and the anomic nationalism of organizations like *Pamiat'*.

But it is the phenomenon of negative ethnic identities that poses perhaps the most difficult challenge for understanding the contours of ethnic politics. Rejection of one's ethnic background and the adoption of new identities is a widespread reaction within certain social settings.

As Epstein noted, "elements of negative identity are nearly always present where ethnic groups occupy a position of inferiority or marginality within a dominance hierarchy."[36] Negative ethnic identities are characteristic not only of subordinate groups, but of dominant groups as well. If extreme conformity is a typical reaction to domination among coopted elites of subordinate groups, then empathy with the demands of subordinate groups is one form of response to power among dissenting elites of dominant groups. Take, for instance, the following passage from a recent book on Sajudis by the journalist Georgii Yefremov:

> For a long time I went around without an understanding of what national identity was. And even now, when I am asked to identify myself, I call myself a "Muscovite." In kindergarten, on the street, and in school we all considered ourselves Muscovites, though from this small rightless group [bespravnyi sotsium] many of us turned into or returned to being Armenians, Tatars, Germans, Jews, or Latvians. . . . I am, to be sure, a bad Russian. . . . I am tied with Russia only by the language with which I think, speak, and write, only the land where I was born, and only by a feeling of concern for its terrible, monstrous fate.[37]

Approximately 10 percent of the members of the Estonian Popular Front were non-Estonians, while according to public opinion polls about a third of the Russian-speaking community in Estonia supported the major demands of the front.[38] Similarly, an informal poll conducted by Radio Liberty found that about a third of ethnic Russians viewed the ethnic disturbances of recent years as a positive development in Soviet society, seeing them as examples of democracy in action and as channels for airing previously suppressed demands.[39] Yet another poll of 2,000 Muscovites conducted in October 1989 by the unofficial Informal Sociological Service found that 38 percent of those questioned "responded positively" to the idea of political self-determination for the Baltic republics.

The identification of Russians with the aims of self-determination of non-Russians has clear social and ideological bases. The poll conducted by the Informal Sociological Service pointed to sharp divisions among Muscovites over Baltic self-determination along educational, class, and generational lines. While 85 percent of students and 70 percent of the artistic intelligentsia favored Baltic political self-determination, only 25 percent of workers at large industrial enterprises did. And while more than 70 percent of those younger than age 39 responded positively to the prospect of Baltic political independence, almost 70 percent of pensioners responded negatively.[40] Lurking behind these groupings is the deeper division between "democrats" and "patriots." And in this sense, Russian negative identities have constituted not a rejection of Russianness as much as a process of redefinition of a longstanding Russian identity. For young, educated Russians, rejection of official Soviet institutions has been accompanied by the rise of a new post-imperial Russian identity—a modern identity of national self-determination much like that described by Smith. Indeed, the construction of a modern Russian identity could occur only on the basis of the deconstruction of the symbiosis between Russian and Soviet imperial identities.

Mediating Elites, Informal Control, and Ethnic Identity

For non-Russians, the political significance of positive and negative ethnic identities has been much the reverse of that for Russians. Michael Doyle has noted that imperial control almost always "requires a degree of peripheral collaboration," even when policies are largely formulated by metropolitan bureaucrats.[41] Robinson similarly observed concerning classical European colonial empires that imperial politics "was as much a function of its victims' collaboration or non-collaboration—of their indigenous politics, as it was of European expansion." According to Robinson, that collaboration was accomplished primarily through the recruitment of "mediating elites" drawn from the indigenous colonial society. As Robinson asserted, it was "the changing bargains of collaboration or mediation" that "define[d] the actual working of imperialism at the point of impact."[42]

During the period of consolidation of Soviet control over non-Russian areas (1918—1923), Soviet personnel policies bore some resemblance to what Doyle labeled "formal empire,"[43] in which imperial bureaucrats were sent down from the center to administer indigenous society directly. A similar pattern was repeated to some extent in the Stalin period in response to the penetration of nationalism into local elites that occurred in the late twenties and early thirties. During this latter period, and during the post-Stalin period as well, the Soviet system could be characterized by what Doyle called "informal empire" or what John Breuilly labeled the "public colonial state"—that is, imperial polities where the authorities recruited new agents of mediation from indigenous society rather than relying on traditional elites or imperial bureaucrats as agents of control. As Breuilly observed, recruiting new elites from indigenous society was an important precondition for imposing change over the indigenous social structure, since traditional elites could not be expected to support social change that might undermine their authority.[44] Locally recruited nontraditional elites could be expected to exercise greater authority within the population than imperial agents sent down from the center. Thus, the dual goals of modernization and imperial control defined the parameters of Soviet elite recruitment strategies.

The development of loyal non-Russian elites depended on some degree of identity change within local non-Russian societies. In general, for coopted elites from subordinate ethnic groups seeking to prove their loyalty, extreme conformity is a frequent strategy for gaining acceptance. Examples of extreme conformity among non-Russian elites are not difficult to find within the Soviet context. A large proportion of the early Bolshevik leadership was recruited from highly-Russified non-Russians. The non-Russian Bolsheviks were not a uniform group in terms of their attitudes toward their native ethnicities. Nevertheless, a portion of this group (including Stalin and Ordzhonikidze) sought to prove their loyalty by behaving as "super-Russians," earning Lenin's reprimand by their overly conformist behavior in pursuit of the interests of the center. A recent article in the Belorussian press pointed out that the "worst time for the Belorussian language" in terms of pressures for linguistic Russification occurred "when the First Secretary of the Belorussian Communist Party was K. T. Mazurov, when the Chairman of the Presidium of the Belorussian Supreme Soviet was V. I. Kozlov, and when the Chairman of the Belorussian Council of Ministers was T. Ya. Kiselev—all Belorussians by origin."[45]

In another instance, in 1988 the Central Committee of the Kazakh Communist Party began to provide its members with the choice of receiving documents in either the Russian or Kazakh languages; however, only 33 (13 percent) of the 250 members and candidate members requested that documents be given to them in Kazakh, far less than Kazakh representation in the republican Central Committee itself.[46] In all these cases, elites coopted from subordinate nationalities, to one degree or another, shed aspects of their ethnicity in the process of upward mobility, even coming to identify with the culture and language of the domnant group. Indeed, given that under Soviet law formal ethnic reidentification could occur only as a result of ethnic intermarriage, one would expect that overconformity among non-Russian elites would have been a relatively widespread strategy for upward mobility in pre-glasnost Soviet politics.

While cooptation is the product of conscious state policy, those policies always interact with and are aimed at spontaneous and self-interested actors within indigenous society. The recruitment of collaborators from indigenous society usually leads to considerable change in the indigenous social structure. Rene Lemarchand noted that colonial rule in Africa caused enormous ethnic restratification in African societies. In some cases, existing ethnic cleavages were reinforced; in others, whole new ethnicities were brought into being. And depending on colonial policy and local circumstances, "incipient class cleavages associated with various forms of clientage arrangements . . . tended to coincide with, or cut across, ethnic boundaries."[47]

Soviet policies of cooptation similarly involved significant restratification within non-Russian society. Cooptation of non-Russians produced a type of "layering" phenomenon, in which intragroup differences were used to buffer or support a broader system of intergroup stratification. This pattern of stratification, as opposed to the pillarization and segmentation common to consociational politics or the strict horizontal cleavages characteristic of ethnically closed social orders, was long characteristic of Soviet elite recruitment in the non-Russian territories. Its consequences pervaded local political processes in the republics. In the Moldavian national consciousness ethnic Moldavian officials were traditionally divided between so-called "left bank" and "right bank" cadres, the former corresponding to officials originating from the left bank of the Dniestr (the former territory of the Moldavian ASSR of the 1920s and 1930s), the latter corresponding to officials originating from that part of Moldavia that belonged to interwar Romania.[48] In fact, out of 15 ethnic Moldavians who had at one time been department heads in the Moldavian Central Committee Secretariat in the 1970s and 1980s, only 5 (33 percent) were born in the right-bank territories of Moldavia, where more than 90 percent of the Moldavian population of the republic in 1940 was concentrated[49] In Estonia native cadres traditionally were divided between "home communists" (i.e., those who lived their entire lives in Estonia) and "Russian-Estonians" (i.e., Estonians who spent considerable parts of their lives in the RSFSR). In the late 1970s, 9 (82 percent) out of 11 members of the Bureau of the Estonian Communist Party were Estonians, and of these 6 (55 percent) were "Russian-Estonians."[50] Indeed, the changes that occurred in the Estonian Communist Party in the Gorbachev period—ultimately leading to secession from the CPSU— were largely due to a rapid shift that occurred in the character of the Estonian party elite, as "home communists" grew dominant within the party's leading organs.

Indigenization, Patronage, and Populism

The ability of coopted elites to perform their mediating functions depended on two conditions: demobilization of indigenous society; and some degree of hierarchical discipline. It was characteristic of Soviet politics in the past decade that both of these conditions largely disappeared, leading to the nationalization of elite politics.

Much as happened in the case of European imperialisms in the third world, Soviet mechanisms of informal control created the seeds of their own demise. Indigenization of administration made possible the penetration of nationalism into local elites and the cooptation of administration by local social structures. At times, native elites ostensibly recruited to mediate imperial domination over indigenous society instead defended the interests of indigenous society before the center, even seeking to build authority within society on the basis of such an appeal. The first wave of indigenization of elites occurred in the 1920s. It resulted in an enormous penetration of local nationalisms into republican institutions and provided the social base for much of the resistance to Stalin's policies by republican elites. A second wave of indigenization occurred in the 1960s and 1970s. In at least one case— that of Ukraine under Shelest—indigenization was accompanied by attempts at authority-building similar to those that occurred in the 1920s. Shelest typified a style of populist politics that became widespread in the era of perestroika, but which for its own time was premature. Shelest and his followers represented a native elite ostensibly recruited to act as mediators of central control, but who instead chose to build authority within society by bringing national issues onto the political agenda and expanding political participation to sectors of society (in particular, the Ukrainian intelligentsia) formerly excluded from any meaningful role in local politics.

However, the second wave of indigenization in the 1960s and

1970s rarely resulted in the type of local nationalist resistance that similar policies had brought forth in the 1920s. The case of Belorussia is illustrative in this regard. The proportion of Belorussians within the population of the Belorussian SSR steadily declined over the past thirty years, while the proportion of Belorussians within the local party apparatus of the Belorussian Communist Party gradually increased, until by the end of the Brezhnev period it actually exceeded the proportion of Belorussians in the republic's population.[51] Yet, there is little evidence that as a result of indigenization Belorussian nationalism penetrated into the republican party elite to any significant degree; in fact, the Belorussian party apparatus had a reputation as one of the most conservative throughout the country, a reputation it maintained during the Gorbachev period.

Rather than leading to populism, indigenization in the 1960s and 1970s led to corruption and a gradual undermining of organizational discipline from within. Essentially, the center tolerated the flourishing of local patronage networks in exchange for the denationalization of local politics. Clientelism can have a denationalizing effect on politics, for it tends to transform issues of ethicity into issues of personalism and resource distribution. As G. Bingham Powell has noted, "[i]n a social structure in which most citizens are involved in personal patron-client relationships, . . . [i]t will be difficult to mobilize citizens on the basis of national group appeals or organizations, because their orientations will be to the locality and the patron."[52] This is especially true when patron-client relations cross ethnic lines. As one Soviet journalist described the social structure of Tashkent: "People live here in a special kind of micro-climate, within which issues of age, nationality, and occupation do not have a decisive significance. The main thing here is blood ties, personal sympathies, trust, and financial partnership. All of these determine how useful you are to the clan and who will support you."

These "clans" (less criminal organizations than organizations of survival) frequently cut across national lines, in one case including "a police officer (Uzbek), a responsible executive (Jew), an engineer-mechanic (Uzbek), a journalist (Russian), an athletic trainer (Armenian), a cooperative owner (Jew), a local prosecutor (Uzbek), a construction worker (Tatar), and a doctor (Ukrainian)." As the journalist asked, "Is it really possible within such a framework to preach nationalism?"[53]

In other cases, clientelism has been known to reinforce ethnic identities, for ethnicity can provide the grounds for interpersonal trust that lies at the basis of clientelistic networks. As a recent article in the Armenian press noted: "Patronage not only has general features, but also its own national specifics. Thus, for example, in Armenia the local bureaucracy used historically given stereotypes of behavior for patronage purposes, speculating on such traditions as the strength of family ties or love and devotion for one's native district, region, city, or village, often giving patronage and similar phenomena a false sense of national or local patriotism."[54]

Throughout the Soviet Union during the Brezhnev period, a series of clientelistic networks, at times forming along ethnic lines and at times crossing them, blanketed the country at the local level. In those cases when clientelistic ties cut across ethnic lines, this blossoming of patronage allowed the center to denationalize local politics. At the same time it involved a certain loss of organizational control over local affairs and furthered the consolidation of local attention on the resource-distributing functions of the state. This was especially true in Central Asia. There, these mafia-like networks penetrated deeply into the party apparatus, even to the point where the local party elite became the tool of mafia bosses outside the party apparatus.[55]

Detachment and Autonomization of Mediating Elites

It was only in the glasnost period, however, that the real conditions for the demise of mediating elites arose. This involved two separate but related processes: elite detachment and elite autonomization. The former refers to the loosening of the loyalties of mediating elites to the center as a result of attempts to build authority within an ethnically mobilized population. The latter refers to the atrophy of central control mechanisms over mediating elites, transforming mediating elites into autonomous local groupings.

Gorbachev's attacks on bureaucracy and patronage fostered a renationalization of politics by encouraging attacks upon central authority and its local representatives. Precisely because of Russian domination of central institutions, such assaults were generally interpreted within non-Russian society as attacks upon Russian dominance. As a reflection of this identification of central and Russian interests, Givi Gumbaridze, former First Secretary of the Georgian Communist Party, warned his fellow Georgians "not to confuse anger against bureaucratic fiat with anti-Russian sentiment."[56] Nevertheless, among non-Russians the fusion of democratic and national movements (and even the creation of alliances among elites across ethnic boundaries) was the result of the association of bureaucratic centralism with national repression. Any weakening of central institutions provided an occasion for venting anger against local mediating elites, much as a weaking of local institutions provided occasions for attacks upon central authority.

Attacks on bureaucracy also caused a high level of elite circulation within official hierarchies, leading to a debureaucratization of careers and further hastening a renationalization of politics. One such example was that of Anatolii Plugaru, the former Moldavian Central Committee official relieved from office in December 1988 for his vocal advocacy of a dialogue between the CPSU and nationalist informal groups in the republic. Plugaru skipped several layers of hierarchy in his rapid career path to the top, jumping from the head of a raion militia department to deputy head of the administrative organs department of the Moldavian Central Committee Secretariat. Plugaru himself was surprised by his promotion, since he had no patron within the Central Committee and since the act "violated the rules of promotion to the 'higher spheres' of Moldavian politics."[57] It was only natural, then, that Plugaru soon violated the parameters of expected behavior within what was then one of the most conservative party organizations in the country by authoring internal reports calling for the party's cooperation with nationalist groups and, when those reports were rejected by his superiors, publishing summaries of them in the press.[58] In much the same way, massive turnover within the bureaucracy, the introduction of electoral competition, and the entrance of large numbers of relatively inexperienced figures into public office played a key role in flooding the political agenda with nationalist issues.

As ethnic mobilization increased during the Gorbachev period, mediating elites found themselves pulled between irreconcilable demands simultaneously emanating from the mobilized masses and from Moscow. Official elites responded differently to this situation. Some preferred to crack down upon dissent, increasingly isolating themselves from society and at times leading to violent explosions from below. Others chose to seek to build authority within the populace, thereby losing touch with the demands of the center. As Algirdas Brazauskas, First Secretary of the Lithuanian Communist Party, expressed this latter approach at the September 1989 Central Committee

Plenum: "The only way to gain the masses' trust is by becoming deeply imbued with the people's aspirations and interests and by taking radical and resolute political steps. So the familiar slogan 'The party's plans are the people's plan!' now sounds different: 'The people's plans are the party's plans!'"[59]

The detachment of mediating elites occurred unevenly in the USSR, but was particularly evident in areas where mass mobilization was the greatest (the Baltic, Western Ukraine, Moldavia, and the Transcaucasus). Much the same process occurred during decolonization in Africa. As Robinson described it: "when the colonial rulers had run out of indigenous collaborators they either chose to leave or were compelled to go. Their national opponents . . . sooner or later succeeded in detaching the indigenous political elements from the colonial regime until they eventually formed a united front of collaboration against it."[60]

In those areas where ethnic mobilization was relatively low (i.e., Central Asia), patronage remained the basis of authority for mediating elites. However, as the CPSU came undone at the center, the mediating mechanisms of the center over indigenous society collapsed. Local party bosses were able to act autonomously; at the same time, they were limited in their actions by their need to preserve the local patronage networks that underpinned their power. Where ethnic mobilization remained low (or, in the case of Azerbaijan, where demobilization was achieved by force), elite autonomization brought about the consolidation of a "national *nomenklatura*." Commanding their traditional party organizations and supporting demands for greater local autonomy, these bosses acted in a manner that was essentially national in form, but personalistic in content. The uninterrupted power of the national *nomenklatura* depended to a great extent on the continued demobilization of their populations.

Nationalism and the Coalescence of New Elites

The detachment of mediating elites was simultaneously accompanied by the emergence of new political elites. Unlike the communist elite, these new political actors gained power not through control over bureaucracies, but through their ability to mobilize the population. Mass protest and electoral competition were accompanied by the emergence of a completely new type of political figure within the Soviet context—the mass politician—whose task it was to manage elite-mass relations by articulating demands and projecting images to the populace. Chief among those images and among the bonds gluing mass politicians to their followings was national identity.

It is well known that mass mobilization requires leadership and organization. That leadership formed unevenly in various parts of the country, but where it did form, it generally coalesced around three elements: pre-existing counter-elites, including those who had long been involved in dissident activities; a portion of the party *aktiv,* particularly the party intelligentsia, which ultimately defected from the CPSU in large numbers; and those completely new to politics.

The extent to which pre-existing counter-elites played a role in mass mobilization varied across the Soviet Union. In the fall of 1986, political prisoners gradually began to be released from the camps. By the summer of 1987, Baltic nationalists released from incarceration began to organize the first major demonstrations of the glasnost period in the region—on the occasion of the anniversary of the Molotov-Ribbentrop Pact. Former activists of the human-rights movement also played key roles in organizing nationalist movements in Ukraine and the Transcaucasus, as well as among the Crimean Tatars. In Georgia, former political prisoner Zviad Gamsakhurdia became President of the republic. Only in Central Asia—where a dissident movement before glasnost had hardly developed—were Brezhnev-era dissidents largely absent from the leadership of new movements. Indeed, the low level of mass mobilization in Central Asia can partly be explained by the lack of organization of counter-elites in the region, due in part to the absence of dissident tradition.

While already existing opposition groups provided some of the organizational impetus for nationalist movements, there was also a degree of overlap between communist elites and emerging counter-elites in the glasnost period that was extremely important in accelerating the disintegration of official institutions and in organizing new movements. Precisely because the motives for joining the CPSU were almost entirely careerist rather than ideological, the CPSU in the pre-Gorbachev period had become an umbrella organization within which a wide range of perspectives could be found. As the CPSU disintegrated, layer after layer of party members broke off—at first along nationalist lines, and later along ideological lines; those remaining within the confines of the organization polarized into opposing groups.

The examples of Yeltsin, Yakovlev, Shevardnadze, and Aliev—former members of the Politburo all of whom eventually quit the party in order to organize opposition movements—illustrate just how enormous the transformations in elite consciousness were within the course of a very short period of time. At the July 1991 Central Committee Plenum, Gorbachev revealed that over the previous eighteen months 4.2 million Communists left the Party, with especially large defections occurring in those republics where secessionist movements had come to power. According to Gorbachev, of those who quite the CPSU, only 2 to 3 percent joined other political parties or movements.[61] While the vast majority of those who left abandoned political activity altogether, nevertheless somewhere between 80,000 and 120,000 activists of alternative political movements came from the CPSU. As one poster at a mass meeting farcically proclaimed: "Long live the CPSU—the forge of leaders of all opposition movements!"[62]

Finally, a significant number of leaders of alternative political movements and parties were recruited from people who were entirely new to politics. One survey of informal organizations conducted in various parts of the Soviet Union from 1985 to 1987 found that the majority of those involved in such groups were between the ages of 25 and 35.[63] Delegates to the founding congress of Rukh in September 1989 were similarly young, typically "between the ages of twenty-five and forty-five."[64] Most of these young activists had no prior experience in politics, either within the CPSU or outside of it.

The diverse origins of new elites had an important impact on the character of elite politics. The popular fronts that successfully mobilized millions of Soviet citizens, largely on the basis of ethnicity, during the 1988–1990 period essentially constituted broad coalitions of groups, united only by a common enemy—the CPSU. As Romual' sas Razhukas, chairman of the board of the Duma of the Latvian Popular Front, observed, the front "consists of a number of political tendencies which in toto form a center. If the front were to fall apart, then small parties would remain that would have significant differences with one another, and a large number of people would not belong to any party."[65] Indeed, Soviet politics in the era of democratization was distinguished by the extreme fractiousness of elite groupings and the weakness of political organization. One reason for such weakness was the low level of trust that exists among new elites, especially along the lines of non-Communists and former Communists. Within this context, a key factor that was capable of bridging the gap between these two groupings was nationalism. In general, where nationalism was strong, political alliances across the elite groupings of an ethnic group tended to be more stable than in those cases where national identities came under stress and attack.

With the exception of the workers' movement, which was overwhelmingly Russian in character, the leadership of most informal movements and alternative parties came almost exclusively from the intelligentsia, regardless of CPSU membership. An examination of the class and occupational backgrounds of 120 members of the ruling Duma of the Latvian Popular Front, for instance, indicates that more than 90 percent came from the intelligentsia, including large groups from the technical intelligentsia, the scientific intelligentsia, the creative intelligentsia, and the professional intelligentsia. None came from the peasantry, and only 4.2 percent from the working class.[66] Similarly, 965 (87.0 percent) of the delegates to the founding congress of Rukh were members of the intelligentsia—mainly "employees of education and culture, lawyers and engineers, scientific workers, doctors, and journalists." Only 9.8 percent (109) of the delegates were workers, 1.4 percent (16) were peasants, and .5 percent (6) were employees of the party apparatus.[67] Given the role that the intelligentsia has played in most societies as the carriers of nationalist ideologies, as well as the evidence (cited above) that existed long before perestroika concerning the strength of nationalist orientations within the Soviet intelligentsia, it is hardly surprising that the activization of the intelligentsia in Soviet politics was accompanied by a destabilization along nationalist lines.

Elite Identities and the Post-Soviet Future

Democratization in the Soviet Union forces Western scholars to revise old habits of research that were long taken for granted. This is especially clear in the field of elite studies. The assumptions behind structural approaches to the study of elites need to be reexamined and subjected to rigorous empirical research. Narrow definitions of what constitutes the elite can no longer capture the vitality of politics in an age of mass mobilization. The area of elite-mass relations, too easily ignored in the past, has become the critical arena within which the decisive battles of politics are being waged. The need to probe the attitudinal and behavioral dimensions of elites grows ever more important in an age when elites and elite identities have undergone massive change.

If one accepts these criticisms and the general approach to the ethnic dimension of elite politics outlined here, then what issues deserve attention from those studying elite politics in the post-perestroika era? Simple descriptions of elite backgrounds or the pace of elite turnover have obviously outlived their usefulness. In my opinion, several areas of research on elites should prove fruitful for empirical investigation. An ethnic dimension looms large within each each of these areas.

First, there is the continuing issue of formation and character of elite identities—in particular, the degree to which particular types of elite identities are grounded in certain types of social structures or processes of elite recruitment. Elite recruitment is itself in a state of flux. But as new political organizations consolidate their power, more-or-less stable career paths will form—career paths that will differ markedly from those of the past. In the forefront of questions to be answered will be the extent to which the new processes of elite formation in the former USSR will encourage interethnic conflict or interethnic compromise.

Second, there is the issue of the consolidation of power among new elites—i.e., obtaining stable control over the institutions of the state. In most parts of the former Soviet Union, new elites have yet to build stable mass followings within the population on the basis of permanent political organization. This will undoubtedly involve the replacement of popular fronts with political parties (a process that has already occurred in some places) and the development of predictable party loyalties within the population toward particular parties. Ethnic identity will play perhaps the decisive role in the formation of these organizations and loyalties.

A related aspect of elite consolidation concerns control over the bureaucratic institutions of the state and relations between politicians and bureaucrats. And here too, given that in many parts of the former Soviet Union whole branches of the economy are associated with particular ethnic groups, ethnic relations are bound to be a major issue. In Latvia, for instance, 85 percent of all industrial executives speak only Russian.[68] It is difficult to imagine Latvian politicians establishing good working relations with those charged with implementing their policies without taking the ethnic character of the bureaucracy into account.

Third, there is the issue of the formation of new types of elites and their relations with the political system. Privatization is already bringing into being a new business class. That business class is organizing to influence the political system. It also has its own specific ethnic configuration. The establishment of a market economy will bring groups of national business elites into contact with each other, perhaps even in competition with each other. How new business elites will react in this situation is unclear. However, it is difficult to imagine a market economy functioning effectively without some degree of integration within the business elite—i.e., placing class interests above ethnic interests.

Finally, towering over all other questions is the question of the integration of new elites and the extent to which new elites will be able to find a common language across elite boundaries. As Ralf Dahrendorf has pointed out, democratic elites require a degree of confidence and trust, as well as skills of compromise, in order to affect policy.[69] This not only concerns the acceptance of the concept of a "loyal opposition," but also a sense of shared fate or community—i.e., some sense of nationhood. For much of the 1988–1991 period, communication across ethnic boundaries was clearly absent, pushing the country deeper and deeper into crisis. In April 1991 (after almost six months of the so-called "war of the laws," during which newly elected republican elites and all-union authorities wrestled over whose authority was "sovereign," and after the failed efforts of the all-union government to curb by force secessionist strivings in the Baltic, Moldavia, and the Transcaucasus) leaders of nine Soviet republics reached agreement in the Moscow suburb of Novo-Ogarevo over a basic framework for a new union treaty. The Novo-Ogarevo agreement (known euphemistically as the nine-plus-one agreement) represented an accord for social peace and a basis for the ethnic reconstruction of the Soviet state—one reached by elites over the heads of the masses, and in some instances (particularly in the cases of Russia and Ukraine) in the face of considerable opposition.

In the aftermath of the August coup and the centrifugal forces that it set in motion, this accord broke down completely. The creation of the Commonwealth of Independent States was itself the result of the failure of intensive efforts to discover a basis for inter-republican elite accord within the loose confines of a confederal arrangement. Yet, as the conflicts over control of the Crimea and the Black Sea fleet in the months following the Minsk agreement demonstrate, the fate of the commonwealth as a loose community of sovereign states rests decisively on the ability of its governing elites to communicate with one another peacefully across national barriers.

Of course, internally each of the commonwealth republics themselves is in need of elite accord, for each faces quite serious ethnic problems that are unlikely to vanish (and most probably will be exacerbated) under conditions of political independence. In this sense, elite identities are likely to remain a decisive facet of politics in this part of the world for some time to come.

Acknowledgements

The author would like to thank Radio Liberty's *Arkhiv samizdata,* and in particular its director Mario Corti, for access to some of the unofficial Soviet publications used in parts of this essay; Crawford Young, for his guidance with literature on ethnicity and elites in Africa; and Alexander Motyl, for his comments on an earlier draft of this chapter.

NOTES

1. Barrington Moore, Jr., *Terror and Progress—USSR* (Cambridge: Harvard University Press, 1966), pp. 179–231.

2. For a sampling of the literature on ethnicity and elites, see Teresa Rakowska-Harmstone, *Russia and Nationalism in Central Asia: The Case of Tadzhikistan* (Baltimore: Johns Hopkins Press, 1970); J. W. Cleary, "Elite Career Patterns in a Soviet Republic," *British Journal of Political Science* 4(1974):323–344; John H. Miller, "Cadres Policy in Nationality Areas: Recruitment of CPSU First and Second Secretaries in Non-Russian Republics of the USSR," *Soviet Studies* 29(1) (January 1977):3–36; Grey Hodnett, *Leadership in the Soviet National Republics* (Oakville: Mosaic Press, 1978); Jaan Pennar, "Soviet Nationality Policy and the Estonian Communist Elite," in Tonu Parming and Elmar Jarvesoo, eds., *A Case Study of a Soviet Republic: The Estonian SSR* (Boulder, CO: Westview, 1978), pp. 105–127; Bohdan Harasymiw, *Political Elite Recruitment in the Soviet Union* (London: Macmillan Press, 1984), pp. 140–146. None of the major theoretical approaches to Soviet

politics in the 1960s, 1970s, and early 1980s emphasized ethnicity as a central aspect of their theories, nor did existing models even point to ethnicity as a major assumption of their hypotheses. See Alexander J. Motyl, "'Sovietology in One Country' or Comparative National Studies?" *Slavic Review* 48(1) (Spring 1989):83–88; Mark Beissinger and Lubomyr Hajda, "Nationalism and Reform in Soviet Politics," in Lubomyr Hajda and Mark Beissinger, eds., *The Nationalities Factor in Soviet Politics and Society* (Boulder, CO: Westview Press, 1990), pp. 305–306.

3. Seweryn Bialer, *Stalin's Successors: Leadership, Stability, and Change in the Soviet Union* (Cambridge: Cambridge University Press, 1980), p. 213. See also Hodnett, *Leadership in the Soviet National Republics,* p. 3.

4. Joseph Rothschild, *Ethnopolitics: A Conceptual Framework* (New York: Columbia University Press, 1981), p. 30.

5. On the beginnings of such research by Soviet scholars, see Vladimir Amelin, "Politicheskoe liderstvo i politicheskii pliuralizm," *Obshhestvenye nauki,* no. 1 (1990):96–108; Yuri Levada, "Populism in Soviet Politics," *At the Harriman Institute* 3(13) (1990):1–2.

6. For a review of such studies within the African context, see M. Crawford Young, "Nationalism, Ethnicity, and Class in Africa: A Retrospective," *Cahiers d'Etudes africaines* 26(3) (1986):471–473.

7. Ulf Hannerz, "Ethnicity and Opportunity in Urban America," in Abner Cohen, ed., *Urban Ethnicity* (London: Tavistock, 1974) pp. 48–54.

8. For studies that raise aspects of the relationship between clientelism and ethnicity, see Joel C. Moses, "Regional Cohorts and Political Mobility in the USSR: The Case of Dnepropetrovsk," *Soviet Union* 3(part 1) (1976):63–89; J. P. Willerton, Jr., "Clientelism in the Soviet Union: An Initial Examination," *Studies in Comparative Communism* 12 (Summer/Autumn 1979):159–183; Donald Carlysle, "The Uzbek Power Elite: Politburo and Secretariat (1938–1983)," *Central Asian Survey* 5(3/4) (1986):91–132. Most of these studies were actually interested more in the question of power-building than elite-mass relations.

9. Interesting in this regard is Michael Urban's justification for choosing Belorussia, where national consciousness has traditionally been weak, for a recent study of elite recruitment patterns. "I wanted to exclude as much as possible the national factor in order to examine Soviet elite circulation in more general terms." Michael Urban, "Elite Stratification and Mobility in a Soviet Republic," in David Lane, ed., *Elites and Political Power in the USSR* (Hants, England: Edward Elgar, 1988), p. 143. Similarly, Ronald Hill's study of elite recruitment in Tiraspol omits all discussion of the nationality dimension of elite recruitment in a region where ethnicity has played a very important role in elite politics—the left bank territories of Moldavia. See Ronald J. Hill, *Soviet Political Elites: The Case of Tiraspol* (New York: St. Martin's Press, 1977), pp. 35–83.

10. See Frederic J. Fleron, Jr., "Cooptation as a Mechanism of Adaption to Change: The Soviet Political Leadership," in Roger E. Kanet, ed., *The Behavioral Revolution and Communist Studies* (New York: The Free Press, 1971), pp. 125–150.

11. See, for instance, Anthony Smith, *Theories of Nationalism* (New York: Harper, 1971), pp. 230–254.

12. Rasma Karklins, "Nationality Policy and Ethnic Relations in the USSR," in James R. Millar, ed., *Politics, Work, and Daily Life in the USSR: A Survey of Former Soviet Citizens* (Cambridge: Cambrdige University Press, 1987), p. 311.

13. For a discussion of Soviet research on this issue, see Steven L. Burg, "Nationality Elites and Political Change in the Soviet Union," in Hajda and Beissinger, eds., *The Nationalities Factor*, pp. 28–30.

14. See George W. Breslauer, *Khrushchev and Brezhnev as Leaders: Building Authority in Soviet Politics* (London: George Allen and Unwin, 1982).

15. For one attempt to explore this issue, see Burg, "Nationality Elites and Political Change," in Hajda and Beissinger, eds., *The Nationalities Factor*, pp. 24–42.

16. See Mark Beissinger, "Ethnicity, the Personnel Weapon, and Neo-Imperial Integration: Ukrainian and RSFSR Provincial Party Officials Compared," *Studies in Comparative Communism* 21(1) (Spring 1988):71–85.

17. For a sampling of the literature on generational change within the Soviet elite, see Bialer, *Stalin's Successors;* Jerry F. Hough, *Soviet Leadership in Transition* (Washington, D.C.: Brookings Institution, 1980); Myron Rush, "The Future Soviet Leadership," in Richard Melanson, ed., *Neither Cold War Nor Detente?: Soviet-American Relations in the 1980s* (Charlottesville, VA: University of Virginia Press, 1982), pp. 69–82; William E. Odom, "Choice and Change in Soviet Politics," *Problems of Communism* 32 (May-June 1983):1–21; George Breslauer, "Is There a Generation Gap in the Soviet Political Establishment?: Demand Articulation by RSFSR Provincial Party First Secretaries," *Soviet Studies* 36 (January 1984):1–25; Mark R. Beissinger, "In Search of Generations in Soviet Politics," *World Politics* 38(2) (January 1986):288–314.

18. For an exception to this, see Bialer, *Stalin's Successors*.

19. Yu. V. Arutiunian, L. M. Drobizheva, *Mnogoobrazie kul'turnoi zhizni narodov SSSR* (Moscow: Mysl', 1987), p. 294.

20. Ibid. The relationship between generation and ethnicity appears to be extremely complex. For instance, data for urban Moldavians and Uzbeks indicate that there are enormous differences in the literary preferences among older and younger generations of both these groups. But it also appears that these patterns may be due to growing rates of literacy rather than to a generation gap per se. Thus, young urban Moldavians and Uzbeks display markedly greater interest in all kinds of literature than their elders, no matter

what the category of literature—a pattern that is significantly different than that of urban Estonians and Russians. Recent events also confirm differences within the Soviet younger generation along ethnic lines. In Georgia, for instance, young people in their teens and twenties have been in the forefront of the recent national ferment in that republic; by contrast, in Lithuania the younger generation has not exhibited the same degree of activity.

21. Bert A. Rockman, "Conclusion: Elites and Social Inquiry," in Ronald H. Linden and Bert A. Rockman, eds., *Elite Studies and Communist Politics* (Pittsburgh: University of Pittsburgh Press, 1984), p. 326.

22. Hodnett, *Leadership in the Soviet National Republics,* p. 12.

23. See, for instance, Robert D. Putnam, *The Beliefs of Politicians: Ideology, Conflict, and Democracy in Britain and Italy* (New Haven: Yale University Press, 1973); Joel Aberbach, Robert Putnam, Bert Rockman, *Bureaucrats and Politicians in Western Democracies* (Cambridge: Harvard University Press, 1981).

24. Rockman, in Linden and Rockman, eds., *Elite Studies and Communist Politics,* p. 343.

25. For examples of efforts at content-analysis, see Milton Lodge, *Soviet Elite Attitudes Since Stalin* (Columbus, OH: Charles E. Merrill Publishing, 1969); Breslauer, "Is There a Generation Gap in the Soviet Political Establishment?"; Beissinger, "In Search of Generation in Soviet Politics."

26. See, for instance, Lewis J. Edinger and Donald D. Searing, "Social Background in Elite Analysis: A Methodological Inquiry," *American Political Science Review* 61 (1967):428–445; Putnam, *The Beliefs of Politicians.*

27. See, for instance, Bohdan Harasymiw, "Conclusion: Some Theoretical Considerations on Advancement within the Political Elite in Sovie-Type Systems," in T. H. Rigby and Bohdan Harasymiw, eds., *Leadership Selection and Patron-Client Relations in the USSR and Yugoslavia* (Boston: George Allen and Unwin, 1983), p. 236.

28. For an example of one author who was clearly aware of the assumptions lying behind these definitions, see Harasymiw, *Political Elite Recruitment in the Soviet Union.*

29. See Kemal Karpat, "Introduction: Elites and the Transmission of Nationality and Identity," *Central Asian Survey* 5(3/4) (1986):5–24.

30. J. Magotte, quoted in Crawford Young, "The Colonial State and Post-Colonial Crisis," in Prosser Gifford and William Roger Louis, eds., *Decolonization and African Independence: Transfers of Power, 1960–1980* (New Haven: Yale University Press, 1988), p. 10.

31. See in particular Robert Putnam's discussion of elite-mass linkages in Robert D. Putnam, *The Comparative Study of Political Elites* (Englewood Cliffs, NJ: Prentice-Hall, 1976), pp. 133–164.

32. A. L. Epstein, *Ethos and Identity: Three Studies in Ethnicity* (London: Tavistock, 1978), pp. 102–103.

33. Smith, *Theories of Nationalism,* p. 171.

34. Elie Kedourie, *Nationalism* (London: Hutchinson and Company, 1960).

35. For more on these three forms of nationalism within the Soviet context, see Mark Beissinger and Lubomyr Hajda, "Nationalism and Reform in Soviet Politics," in Beissinger and Hajda, ed., *The Nationalities Factor*.

36. Epstein, *Ethos and Identity*, pp. 102–103.

37. Georgii Yefremov, *My liudi drug drugu* (Moscow: Progress, 1990), pp. 5–6.

38. *Radio Liberty Research Report*, no. 461, October 21, 1988, p. 7; Foreign Broadcast Information Service, *Daily Report: Soviet Union*, October 20, 1988, p. 50; *Sovetskaia Estoniia*, May 11, 1989, p. 2.

39. Kathleen Mihalisko, "Poll of Soviet Citizens' Attitudes towards Ethnic Unrest," *Report on the USSR* 1(10) (March 10, 1989):31–42.

40. *Atmoda*, December 4, 1989, pp. 4–5.

41. Michael W. Doyle, *Empires* (Ithaca, NY: Cornell University Press, 1986), p. 38. Eisenstadt referred to such support as "free-floating resources;" he saw it as a crucial condition for the emergence and maintenance of bureaucratic empires. S. N. Eisenstadt, *The Political Systems of Empires* (New York: The Free Press, 1969), pp. 27–28.

42. Ronald Robinson, "Non-European Foundations of European Imperialism: Sketch for a Theory of Collaboration," in William Roger Louis, ed., *Imperialism: The Robinson and Gallagher Controversy* (New York: New Viewpoints, 1976), pp. 129, 133.

43. Doyle, *Empires*.

44. John Breuilly, *Nationalism and the State* (Chicago: University of Chicago Press, 1982), p. 188.

45. *Sovetskaia Belorussiia*, February 15, 1989, p. 4.

46. *Kazakhstanskaia pravda*, March 14, 1989, p. 1.

47. René Lemarchand, "The State and Society in Africa: Ethnic Stratification and Restratification in Historical and Comparative Perspective," in Donald Rothchild and Victor A. Olorunsola, eds., *State Versus Ethnic Claims: African Policy Dilemmas* (Boulder, CO: Westview, 1983), p. 54.

48. See the speech by then Moldavian Communist Party Second Secretary V. I. Smirnov, in *Sovetskaia Moldaviia*, May 31, 1987, p. 2.

49. Biographical information drawn from: *Deputaty Verkhovnogo Soveta Moldavskoi SSR* [9th-11th sessions] (Kishinev: Cartea Moldovenească, 1976–1985), *Enciclopedia Sovietică Moldovenească*, vols 1–7 (Chişinău: Redacţia principală a enciclopediei Sovietice Moldovenesti, 1970–1977). On 1940 population of Moldavia by nationality, see V. S. Zelenchuk, *Naselenie Moldavii* (Kishinev: Ştiinţă, 1973), p. 40.

50. Pennar, "Soviet Nationality Policy and the Estonian Communist Elite," in Parming and Jarvesoo, eds., *A Case Study of a Soviet Republic*, pp. 120–122; Toivo U. Raun, *Estonia and Estonians* (Stanford, CA: Stanford University Press, 1987), pp. 190–193.

51. For instance, in 1959 Belorussians made up 81.1 percent of the population of the Belorussian SSR, but only 69.3 percent of the *obkom, gorkom,* and *raikom* secretaries of the republic. At the same time, Russians comprised only 8.2 percent of the population of the republic, but 26.1 percent of the *obkom, gorkom,* and *raikom* secretaries. By 1989 the Belorussian proportion of the population had dropped to 77.8 percent, while Belorussian representation among *obkom, gorkom,* and *raikom* secretaries had increased to 80.1 percent. Similarly, the Russian proportion of the population had increased to 13.2 percent, but Russian representation among *obkom, gorkom,* and *raikom* secretaries had dropped to 15.7 percent. See *Kommunisticheskaia partiia Belorussii v tsifrakh, 1918–1988* (Minsk: Belarus, 1988), p. 218.

52. G. Bingham Powell, Jr., *Contemporary Democracy: Participation, Stability, and Violence* (Cambridge: Harvard University Press, 1982), pp. 86–87.

53. *Literaturnaia gazeta,* no. 2, January 16, 1991, p. 8. The author, himself a "clan" member, directly ascribes the low level of protest mobilization in Tashkent to the ubiquitous presence of such networks. I am grateful to Vladimir Amelin of the Sociological Faculty of Moscow State University for bringing this article to my attention.

54. *Kommunist* (Yerevan), May 25, 1989, p. 2.

55. The classic case was that of Akhmajan Adilov, a farm boss in Uzbekistan, who controlled local party bosses and terrorized the local population with his own private army. See *Literaturnaia gazeta,* no. 3, January 20, 1988, p. 13.

56. *Zaria vostoka,* June 9, 1989, p. 1.

57. *Kolumna* [Kishinev], no. 1, 1990, p. 54.

58. Ibid., pp. 53–57.

59. Foreign Broadcast Information Service, *Daily Report: Soviet Union,* September 22, 1989, p. 45.

60. Ronald Robinson, "Non-European Foundations of European Imperialism: Sketch for a Theory of Collaboration," in Roger Owen and Bob Sutcliffe. eds., *Studies in the Theory of Imperialism* (London: Longman, 1972), p. 139.

61. *Pravda,* July 26, 1991, p. 2.

62. *Rossiiskaia gazeta,* July 25, 1991, p. 2.

63. *Current Digest of the Soviet Press,* vol. 39, no. 51 (January 20, 1988), p. 7.

64. David Marples, "A Sociological Survey of 'Rukh,'" in *Report on the USSR* 2(2) (January 12, 1990):19.

65. *Baltiiskoe vremia,* no. 36, September 18, 1990, p. 1.

66. *Atmoda,* October 16, 1989, p. 3. Occupations for 15 members of the Duma are missing.

67. *Atmoda,* October 16, 1989, p. 6.

68. On the ethnic breakdown of various sectors of the economy in Latvia, see *Edinstvo* [Latvia], April 26, 1989, p. 1; *Atmoda,* October 2, 1989, p. 6; *Edinstvo* [Latvia], no. 19, November 1989, p. 13.

69. Ralf Dahrendorf, *Society and Democracy in Germany* (New York: Norton, 1967).

7. The Political Police and the National Question in the Soviet Union

Amy Knight

A LT H O U G H the nature and dimension of the national question in the Soviet Union changed considerably during the USSR's existence, the prominent role of the political police in managing the relationship between the Soviet state and its multifarious national groups remained constant. The regime always relied heavily on the political police to implement its nationality policies. While this may seem a fairly obvious point if we view the national problem simply in terms of a coercive state maintaining its dominance over unwilling national groups, the role of the political police has in fact been complicated by the twists and turns of the regime's policies as it grappled with the vexed problem of reconciling centrism with ethnic diversity.

In their quest for legitimacy the Bolsheviks sought to gain the support of national groups by espousing the principle of self-determination. Although they backed down on this guarantee after their power was well established, they created an administrative system that gave symbolic recognition to nationhood, in the form of a federal structure, and allowed the various national groups to preserve their linguistic and cultural identity. This policy of course ran counter to the Bolshevik premise that class rather than nationality should form the foundation for their new state. More important the recognition of national rights conflicted with the development of a highly centralized political and economic system, run by a monopolistic Communist Party. Increasingly the latter priority won out over the interests of non-Russian nationalities, whose rights and prerogatives eroded steadily from the mid-1920s onward.

Nonetheless, the Russian-dominated Soviet regime and Communist party did not obliterate the national identities of its non-Russian minorities and even during the most repressive periods acknowledged, at least superficially, national and ethnic aspirations. Moreover, just as

Soviet history in general has witnessed periods of relaxation and repression, so too have such changes occurred with regard to the national question specifically. Although coercion was the primary instrument through which the regime managed the national question under Stalin, Soviet leaders after 1953 sought to de-emphasize coercion and to rely more on harnessing the support of national groups through persuasion and conciliation. This did not always work of course and they often had to revert back to coercion in some form or another. But the post-Stalin regime, in its quest for legitimacy, showed a strong preference for managing its nationality affairs without the use of force.

This does not necessarily mean that the political police played a lesser role in nationality affairs, however. Its ubiquitous presence served as a constant reminder of the potential coercive powers of the regime if things got out of hand. Moreover, the political police developed new strategies and tactics, relying more on its role as a gatherer of information and on relatively benign "phrophylactic" methods than on force; but it was always actively involved. Before perestroika was introduced, the Soviet regime was successful in keeping a lid on national discontent without resorting to widespread police repression. But Gorbachev's reforms unleashed such national tension and violence that the political police, called since 1954 the KGB, was faced with serious challenges. Indeed, the nationality problem turned out to be the single greatest threat both to the KGB and the regime as a whole. In order to shed light on these developments and assess their implications, this paper will examine the role of the political police in managing nationality problems as it evolved.

The Police and Nationality Policy Under Lenin and Stalin

From the early days of the Soviet regime until the end of the Stalin era repression was the main function of the political police in implementing the regime's nationality policy. Thus, while Lenin was pursuing at one level a policy of appeasement toward national groups, his political police, the Cheka, established by the Bolsheviks in December 1917, was combatting nationalist opposition to the Soviet regime.[1] Initially the Cheka had been occupied primarily with struggling against the Mensheviks and Socialist Revolutionaries, as well as against monarchist groups, but it became increasingly preoccupied with nationalist "counter-revolution" as the Bolsheviks extended their domination over new territories.

During 1920–22 the Cheka applied ruthless measures to suppress nationalist movements in Ukraine, Uzbekistan, and Transcaucasia. Often combining forces with the regular army, the Vecheka and its special troops brutally put down nationalist seccessionist revolts. In the Northern Caucasus, for example, the Vecheka plenipotentiary K. I. Lander distributed an announcement among the population that warned against further insurgency: "In the event of mass insurrection by individual villages, Cossack settlements and towns, we shall be forced to apply mass terror: for every Soviet worker killed, hundreds of inhabitants of such localities will pay with their lives."[2]

By 1922, much of the nationalist opposition to the Soviet regime had been successfully suppressed, but Transcaucasia remained a special problem. Armenia, Azerbaijan and Georgia had only recently been taken over by the Bolsheviks after initially experiencing independence when the Tsarist government collapsed. So nationalist, anti-Bolshevik sentiment ran high, especially in Georgia, which had always been predominately a Menshevik stronghold. In February 1922, as part of a reform of the political police, the Bolsheviks abolished the Cheka in Russia and Ukraine, replacing it with a new, less powerful organization, the State Political Administration, or GPU. But this reform did not take place in Transcaucasia because of the continued political turbulence there and the Chekas were retained until July 1926.[3]

Bolshevik policy toward Transcaucasia is a good example of how the regime used police coercion to suppress nationalist demands. Ironically, the most hard-line policies were advocated by Georgians: Stalin, who was Commissar of Nationalities, and Konstantin (Sergo) Ordzhonikidze, head of the Transcaucasian Regional Party Committee (Zakkraikom). Over the opposition of many leading Georgian Bolsheviks, they launched a drive to unite the Transcaucasian republics economically and politically, with little concern for national sentiment. The efforts of the "centralizers," as Stalin and his supporters were called, culminated in the establishment in December 1922 of a single republic, the Transcaucasian Federated Soviet Socialist Republic (ZSFSR).

Alarmed over the bitter conflict that arose among Georgian Bolsheviks over the issue of the Transcaucasian Republic, Lenin sent a commission led by GPU chief Felix Dzerzhinsky to investigate the matter. Dzerzhinsky, a Pole whose sympathies lay with Stalin and Ordzhonikidze, tried to exonerate them by giving Lenin a favorable report of their activities. But Lenin soon realized that their tactics had been high-handed and insensitive and sided with the Georgians whom Stalin and Ordzhonikidze had accused of nationalism. Noting that Stalin, Ordzhonikidze, and Dzerzhinsky, all non-Russians, were extremely chauvinistic "Russians" who were anxious to force assimilationist policies on national minorities, Lenin made this now well known observation: "That Georgian who is disdainful of this side of the matter, who disdainfully flings accusations of 'social-nationalism' (when he himself is not only a real and true 'social-nationalist' but a crude Great Russian *derzhimorda* [brutal police type]), that Georgian in essence hurts the interests of proletarian class solidarity."[4]

Lavrentii Beria, who became a deputy chairman of the Georgian Cheka in 1922, was the archtypical *derzhimorda* and the ideal person to implement Stalin's and Ordzhonikidze's assimilationist policies. Indeed the success of his career was closely linked to the defeat of the "national communists," who favored some autonomy for Georgia and the consequent victory of the advocates of strong centralized control by Moscow. Beria's tenure in the Georgian Cheka was marked by a bloody vendetta against "counterrevolutionary elements" in Georgia that reached its peak with the brutal suppression of the August 1924 revolt by Menshevik oppositionists. Although the Cheka managed to put down the rebellion quickly and to arrest its leaders, they continued mass arrests and executions for some time. Armed detachments, composed of army and Cheka troops, raided villages and killed entire families. Some estimates on the number of those arrested and executed by the Cheka ranged as high as 4,000.[5]

The Cheka in Georgia and elsewhere was characterized by striking racial heterogenity. Of the twenty top Cheka officials not more than seven were of pure Great Russian origin, and even in the middle and lower strata of the Cheka there was a disproportionately large foreign strain. Poles, Latvians, and Jews predominated, but there were also considerable numbers of Hungarians, Estonians, Armenians, Letts, and Ukranians.[6] Of course the Russian Social Democrats as a whole were ethically diverse. But the war against the Central Powers had shifted to Russia vast numbers of foreign prisoners of war, who were heavily influenced by Bolshevik propaganda, and this may have contributed to the influx of foreigners into the Cheka. Also, the close ties between

Polish and Russian Social Democrats, together with Dzerzhinsky's dominant influence on the police, may account for the large proportion of Poles. Cheka staffing policy in the non-Russian areas discriminated strongly against the indigenous ethnic groups. Native Ukrainians were in a minority in the Ukrainian Cheka as were native Georgians in the Georgian Cheka. Apparently this policy sprang from the idea that alien Chekists would be less likely to recoil from the unpleasant task of indiscriminate terror. But if men like Beria and his close comrade D. M. Bagirov, chief of the Azerbaijan political police, were an example, natives could be more ruthless against their countrymen than could non-natives.

After a period of considerable relaxation of political repression during the mid twenties, the political police were again enlisted by the leadership to enforce central authority in the non-Russian areas. As part of a campaign against so-called "national chauvinism," the police arrested during 1929 many prominent intellectuals in Ukraine and Belorussia. In the next few years the purge of intellectuals was extended to such areas as Armenia, the Crimea, and Turkestan. Forced collectivization and de-kulakization brought more police repression. Of course this was carried out in the Russian republic as well, but in the non-Russian areas such as Ukraine, Transcaucasia, and Central Asia, this process had clear antinationalist overtones. Indeed, as Robert Conquest demonstrated in his study of collectivization and the ensuing famine, Stalin viewed the nationality problem largely as a peasant problem and took the view that national resistance was responsible for peasant opposition to collectivization. Considering the example of Ukraine in particular, Conquest goes on to point out that one of the aims of collectivization there was stated officially as "the destruction of Ukrainian nationalism's social base—the individual land-holdings."[7]

From the point of view of the native population, collectivization was seen largely as a repressive measure imposed by the Russian-dominated Soviet regime and in some areas gave rise to a resurgence of national unrest. The Basmachi in Central Asia, for example, who had been successfully subdued for several years, formed armed bands to move against the authorities who were forcing peasants into collective farms. In Kazakhstan, roving groups of rebels attacked kolkhozes and killed livestock. The OGPU, as the political police was called at this time, was in the forefront of Stalin's war against the kulaks and his drive to collectivize the countryside, particularly when these efforts met with resistance from recalcitrant peasants and force had to be applied, which was often the case. Throughout the countryside troikas, consisting of the secretary of the party, a member of the local Soviet, and the responsible OGPU officer, made lists of those peasants to be labeled as kulaks and deported. OGPU troops then moved in to carry out the process, as well as to force peasant households into collectives and later to requisition grain from the peasants. The British journalist Malcolm Muggeridge, who traveled through parts of the North Caucasus and Ukraine in 1933, described the situation: "On the one side, millions of starving peasants, their bodies often swollen from lack of food; on the other soldier members of the GPU carrying out the instructions of the dictatorship of the proletariat."[8]

In suppressing nationalist unrest and in imposing forced collectivization the OGPU usually worked together with the native party elite, which was largely committed to centrist antinationalist policies from the mid-twenties onward. With the onset of the purges, however, which culminated in the widespread terror of 1936–38, the police apparatus [renamed the NKVD in 1934] moved against the indigenous party elite in the non-Russian areas. Indeed "national deviationism" was a common accusation against non-Russian party and state cadres. Although this in itself was not a crime, usually it was mentioned as motivating some specific form of "counterrevolutionary activity." The purges literally decimated the native elites in Ukraine, Transcaucasia, and Central Asia, bringing in a new generation of young, inexperienced, and less-educated cadres to fill the ranks of the party and state bureaucracies and impose unquestioningly Moscow's domination.[9] Of course, Russians suffered just as much as non-Russians. But the purges gave Stalin, who had always been suspicious of any manifestations of national identity on the part of non-Russians, an opportunity to get rid of many prominent national figures, both political and cultural. Indeed, the purges virtually decimated the native elites in non-Russian areas.

In most cases the victims included the top party leaders in the non-Russian areas, but the first secretaries of Georgia and Azerbaijan, Beria and Bagirov, survived, although both were natives of the republics they headed. Most probably their long-time connections with the police apparatus contributed to their good fortune. Both Beria and Bagirov had stacked the police apparatus with their own supporters before moving to their party posts. As a result, contrary to the situation in other non-Russian republics, where NKVD chairmen and their deputies were sent in from the center and were therefore rarely members of the indigenous nationality, Georgian and Azerbaijan NKVD officials were often natives, who were more loyal to the republic party chief than to the police leadership in Moscow. According to one source, in late 1937 NKVD Chief Nikolai Ezhov sent a telegram to the head of the Georgian NKVD, S. A. Goglidze, ordering Beria's arrest. Goglidze, a long-time Beria ally, warned him. Beria then flew immediately to Moscow and successfully pleaded his case with Stalin.[10] Within a year Beria occupied Ezhov's post as USSR NKVD chief and the latter was in prison.

Ironically Beria's leadership of the NKVD was accompanied by a winding down of the purges and a period of relative calm within the Soviet Union for both the Russian and the non-Russian nationalities. Repressions continued, but on a much smaller scale, as concerns about nationality problems gave way to the larger preoccupation with events in Europe and the threat of war. After the Soviets annexed Poland and the Baltic states, however, the NKVD, in addition to murdering thousands of Polish officers at Katyn and elsewhere, carried out mass deportations. These operations, lasting from the autumn of 1939 through the spring of 1941, involved the deportation of about 400,000 Poles and about 140,000 Latvians, Lithuanians, and Estonians to the interior of the Soviet Union.[11] Once the war began the NKVD unleashed itself upon national minorities anew, this time in the form of mass deportations of ethnic groups that had fallen under the shadow of Stalin's suspicion for disloyalty to the Soviet regime. Beginning in August 1941 NKVD border, interior, convoy, and special purpose troops deported hundreds of thousands of Volga Germans from their homeland to remote areas of Siberia and Kazakhstan.

In 1943–44, the NKVD deported the entire population of Crimean Tatars, Kalmyks, Meskhetians, Chechens, Ingushi, Karachai, and Balkars to these inhospitable, far-off regions. Tens of thousands died during transport, while many more died of famine and disease once they reached their destination. Although estimates on the total number of victims are uncertain, Roy Medvedev assumes that between four and five million were deported on the basis of their nationality and that no less than one third died in transit or exile.[12] NKVD coercion was also called into play when the Red Army moved westward in 1944, "liberating" German occupied territory. Its troops were charged with conducting operations against rebellious nationalist groups and subsequently were responsible for the deportation of large numbers of Balts and Ukrainians.

After Stalin

Somewhat surprisingly, it was Beria who became the strongest advocate within the leadership of making concessions to national minorities after Stalin's death. In March 1953 Beria became head of the MVD, an organization encompassing both the regular and the political police in one vastly powerful body, and took it upon himself to repudiate those who advocated strong Russification policies.[13] He urged that cadres policy in the national republics focus on greater use of members of the indigenous nationality and seemingly was behind a Soviet press campaign against Great Russian chauvinism.[14] Beria was no doubt appealing to non-Russian nationalities as a means of increasing his political stature and not out of any conviction about national rights. Nonetheless, his policies might have had a significant impact if he had not been ousted from the leadership and arrested in June 1953.

Although the Krushchev leadership criticized Beria for stirring up nationalist sentiments and sowing discord among Soviet peoples, it did not return to the harsh anti-nationalist stance of the Stalin regime. Indeed Khrushchev's political and legal reforms, which included efforts to place some permanent restrictions on the powers of the political police (established as the KGB in March 1954), assured national minorities some measure of protection against police coercion. The Khrushchev era marked the beginning of an effort, which continued under Brezhnev, to substitute persuasion, prophylaxis, and less overt forms of coercion for police violence as a means of suppressing nationalist dissent, and all political dissent for that matter. The KGB of course still arrested and persecuted those who criticized the regime's nationality policies and demanded more recognition of national rights, but violence on a broad scale was avoided and increasingly these cases were handled in such a way as to give the impression to the outside world that the KGB was observing socialist legality.

One question that arises in considering the KGB's role in nationality policy as it developed after Stalin is whether or not its strategy toward non-Russian dissenters differed from that employed toward Russians. Several Western scholars have noted that in fact the KGB has been harder on the non-Russian dissenters than on their Russian counterparts. As Alexander Motyl has pointed out, the constraints upon the KGB in dealing with with the former have generally been much less. Far away from the center of events in Moscow, where Western journalists and diplomats learned quickly about the treatment of political dissenters, the KGB had a freer rein to deal with non-Russians who spoke out against the regime.[15]

Indeed there is much evidence to show that during the period from the mid-1960s to the early 1980s the KGB was especially harsh in its treatment of dissenters among non-Russian ethnic groups. We need only to consider the waves of arrests and repressions among Ukrainian political activists, who often received draconian sentences for what Frederick Barghoorn has termed "within-system" dissent—relatively modest demands for greater cultural autonomy and an end to violations of "Leninist nationality policy."[16] After the severe crackdown that occurred from 1980 to 1983, during which members of the Ukrainian Helsinki Group received prison camp terms of up to fifteen years, Ukrainian dissenters were driven almost completely underground.[17]

Other ethnic groups that were subjected to such treatment are the Crimean Tatars residing in Uzbekistan, hundreds of whom were arrested in the late 1960s and early 1970s for demanding a return to their homeland in the Crimea. General Petro Grigorenko, who became an outspoken defender of the Crimean Tartars, although he himself was Ukrainian, was victimized by the KGB for several years. The authorities no doubt wanted to avoid a trial of Grigorenko, who was a prominent Soviet general with an outstanding war record. So they enlisted the KGB to harass him with threats and continuous surveillance. When these tactics did not silence Grigorenko, the KGB declared him insane and incarcerated him in a psychiatric hospital, where he remained until his release in 1974.[18] The Lithuanians, who according to Motyl constituted (until recently) the largest group proportionately in labor camps, have also been subjected to especially harsh reprisals for dissent.[19]

Another reason for the KGB's special severity toward non-Russian dissent is that the authorities probably perceived a greater threat from these groups than they did from Russian political activists. They had traditionally been concerned about political activism that might threaten Moscow's domination over the republics, particularly since they constitute strategically sensitive borderlands. Even those non-Russian dissidents with broad human rights concerns, such as the Helsinki Monitoring groups from Lithuania, Georgia, Armenia, and Ukraine were viewed by Soviet authorities as spokesmen for their nationalities. The KGB and the party leadership was especially wary of the potential for mass action on the part of national groups based on a strong religious foundation, like the Muslims in Central Asia and the Catholics in Lithuania and the Western Ukraine. Furthermore, the KGB often took the xenophobic stance that domestic discontent was foreign-inspired and that nationalist groups were especially vulnerable to the subversive efforts of anti-Soviet organizations abroad.[20]

It is important to note that, although the KGB enjoyed considerable discretion in dealing with dissent in the non-Russian areas, its overall strategy during the Khrushchev and Brezhnev eras was established by the party leadership in accordance with broad policy goals. Thus, in the mid-to-late 1970s, when the Soviet Union was anxious to improve relations with the West, KGB officials had to be careful about their image abroad and thus avoid highly publicized arrests and trials of non-Russian dissenters, just as they did with Russians. The KGB focused instead on more indirect methods, such as forced confinement in psychiatric hospitals and harassment (dismissal from employment, surveillance, illegal searches and periodic interrogations or "chats," as KGB officials euphemistically call them). In some more sinister cases the KGB used covert violence. In addition to numerous cases of random beatings of dissidents by "hooligans," there were several unsolved, highly suspicious murders of religious and nationalist activists in Ukraine, Latvia, and elsewhere toward the end of the seventies.[21]

In the case of certain national groups the authorities were wary about arousing nationalist feelings by overt persecution of dissidents even during periods of strong repression toward other nationalities. Thus, for example, as Peter Reddaway pointed out, officials fears of provoking nationalism inhibited the KGB from carrying out widespread arrests of political activists in Georgia during the late 1970s and early 1980s. He notes that a street demonstration by several thousand Georgians in 1978 to protest a clause in the new Georgian Constitution that downgraded the status of the Georgian language had caused the authorities to immediately rescind the objectionable clause and had made them more aware of the dangers of offending national sensitivities.[22]

What role did the ethnic background of the KGB leadership play in influencing policy? At the national level, in Moscow, the KGB was staffed primarily by Russians after 1954. All USSR KGB chairmen with the exception of Vitalii Fedorchuk, who served briefly in 1982, were Russians. And Russians, along with a few Ukrainians, predominated in other leading posts at the center. This marks a sharp contrast to the ethnic diversity of the Cheka-OGPU-NKVD-MGB leadership, which was dominated by Poles, Jews, and Georgians. The Russian orientation of the KGB leadership did not necessarily translate into harsher policies toward non-Russians, however. We need only to recall the cruelties inflicted under Stalin by non-Russian police leaders, particularly on their native countrymen, to realize that national sentiments have had little influence on KGB policy in either direction. In short, the KGB has been no more "Russian" in focus than the leadership as a whole.

What about the ethnic composition of the KGB in the republics? Here differences in strategy toward the various national groups were also reflected in the pattern of appointments to top KGB posts in the national republics. In some republics, such as Georgia, Lithuania, and Ukraine, the KGB chairman was always a native of the republic. Armenia and Estonia had native KGB chairmen for all but a few years. Yet five republics have not (with one recent exception) had a representative of the indigenous nationality as KGB chairman: Belorussia, Tajikistan, Turkmenistan, Uzbekistan and Moldavia. And in the remaining four republics ethnic occupancy patterns for the top KGB post varied over time.[23] It might be added that, although Gorbachev made numerous changes in the republic KGB leadership, ethnic patterns remained pretty much the same.[24]

The fact that, contrary to what Western scholars had often assumed, Moscow by no means appointed only Russians to the highly sensitive job of republic KGB chairman suggests that several considerations were involved when these appointments were made. Some republics, such as those in Central Asia, where the rise of Islamic fundamentalism made Soviet authorities nervous, were probably seen to require tighter Russian control than others. They may also have lacked qualified indigenous cadres to choose from, as may be the case in Moldavia, which has low rates of native occupancy for many leading republic posts.

There was of course an obvious advantage to having a member of the dominant ethnic group in the post of KGB chairman, or a deputy KGB chairman: a native-born KGB official aroused less resentment on the part of the local population, which was understandably sensitive about the imposition of centrist cultural, political, and economic policies by Moscow. This was especially true in view of the increasingly visible public role that KGB officials assumed in the USSR's final decade, a trend that became even stronger under Gorbachev.[25] The KGB devoted considerable effort to propaganda as a means of persuading national minorities to see things through the eyes of the Moscow regime. Its officials regularly attended party meetings and visited factories, schools, and collective farms to warn the public about subversive measures to arouse unhealthy nationalist sentiments.

Developments Under Gorbachev

Not surprisingly, the KGB's role in implementing Kremlin policies toward non-Russian national groups changed significantly under Gorbachev. First, the KGB's overtly coercive functions all but ceased, in the sense that after late 1986 there was a virtual moratorium on political arrests. This did not mean that nationalists could express dissident views and instigate demonstrations and protests with total impunity. Several of the most outspoken and troublesome dissident nationalists were arrested on trumped-up charges of hooliganism and other lesser crimes (which were not, strictly speaking, under the purview of the KGB) and on occasion were subjected to more severe reprisals. In July 1988, for example, Armenian activist Paruir Hairikian was stripped of his Soviet citizenship, at the instigation of the KGB, and expelled from the Soviet Union without a trial. But in general official tolerance for the expression of nationalist demands tied the KGB's hands, depriving it of the ability to contain nationalist inspired dissent within safe limits.

Before Gorbachev came to power the KGB's potential for coercion served as a substantial deterrent against nationalist dissent, but this was no longer so by the late 1980s. The fact that non-Russian nationalists had little fear of reprisals, together with the general atmosphere of raised expectations created by glasnost, contributed to the astoundingly rapid growth of nationalist movements in the Soviet Union after 1987. The political upheavals in Eastern Europe fueled the mounting nationalist sentiments in the non-Russian republics.

Most nationalist groups striving for some form of independence from Moscow saw the KGB as the ultimate symbol of Russian domination and their angry protests, frequently resulting in violence, were often directed against the KGB. The Lithuanian independence movement imposed a blockade of KGB headquarters in Vilnius in January 1990, to prevent the removal of documents incriminating the KGB and their shipment to safekeeping in Moscow. In April 1990 members of the Armenian Pan-National movement gathered outside KGB headquarters in Erevan and threw stones and torches at the windows. And Georgian protesters stormed the KGB building in Tbilisi in October 1990. The Soviet media did not refrain from reporting these dramatic confrontations to the general public, which saw the KGB as an institution under siege, rather than the invincible police apparatus it was before perestroika.

The reduction in the level of repression and the decline of the Communist Party's power changed the dynamics of the relationship between Moscow and the republic elites in the sense that the latter could no longer be relied upon to do Moscow's bidding. In order to gain legitimacy in the eyes of their own ethnic groups, members of these elites joined in the chorus of those expressing nationalist demands and venting their grievances against Moscow. The KGB, as an arm of the Communist Party, had in the past acted on behalf of and in concert with the non-Russian elites, since both shared the goal of preserving the party's monopoly and keeping a lid on nationalist sentiments.[26] When the Communist Party began to decline in power and lose its political monopoly, that relationship changed, and the KGB no longer had a common cause with much of the republic leadership.

For all their declared support for perestroika and reform, KGB officials, Russian and non-Russians alike, still saw their primary task as protecting the interests of Moscow and defending the political supremacy of the Soviet regime. The growing democratic movements in the non-Russian republics and the assertiveness of those defending the interests of their national groups made the KGB's job increasingly difficult, particularly since many nationalist organizations saw reform of the KGB as a major goal. Some nationalist leaders called for the subordination of the security apparatus to republic governments, rather than to the central authorities, and for the transformation of the KGB into a straightforward intelligence organization, without investigative and punitive powers.

What was the response of KGB officials to the growing tension between Moscow and the non-Russian republics? Publicly KGB representatives voiced their support for perestroika, welcoming the changes introduced by the Gorbachev leadership. Indeed, they acclaimed the new era of glasnost as an opportunity for them to convey their views to the Soviet people and used the media to launch a full-scale public relations campaign on their own behalf. Clearly KGB representatives were trying to offset the increasing public criticism of their organization by projecting a new, progressive image and attempting to persuade Soviet citizens that they were following the dictates of perestroika.

It is evident from their statements, however, that KGB officials at both the republic and the national level viewed ethnic discontent as a serious threat to their institution and to the stability of the Soviet regime. Interestingly they continued to adhere to the standard KGB line that much of the ferment was foreign inspired, thereby casting aspersions on legitimate demands by national groups and justifying possible KGB interference. In late 1989 the Lithuanian KGB Chairman Eduardas Eismuntas stated that "foreigners are rendering extremist forces in the republic not only moral, but also material assistance," noting that such interference was fraught with grave consequences.[27] Subsequently, the first deputy chairman of the Ukrainian KGB, Col. E. Marchuk, observed that western "special services" had a keen interest in "everything that may lead to the emergence of hostilities between national groups, everything that may result in illegal actions . . . everything that leads to bloodshed and to fraternal conflicts."[28] Similar claims about foreign subversion have been made by KGB officials in other republics.

Although the KGB had to be more circumspect in applying repression, its officials had no intention of standing by while the Soviet Union unraveled. Having seen how the security services in Eastern Europe were dismantled, they were all too aware of what fate had in store for them if the Soviet regime collapsed. Faced with the job of stemming the tide of nationalist unrest on behalf of the Gorbachev leadership, the KGB came up with some resourceful strategies. In addition to a wide-ranging publicity campaign to warn the non-Russian population of the dangers of excessive nationalism, the KGB took an active role in dealing with a whole gambit of nationality-related problems. The KGB was in the forefront, for example, of a new campaign against official corruption, instigated by Gorbachev. Because much of this type of crime stemmed from party-based mafias in the non-Russian republics this campaign had important implications for the nationality question and not surprisingly was resisted by republic party elites. The most sensational such mafia in recent years was that exposed by the KGB and the procuracy in Uzbekistan. The Uzbek case was the subject of intense controversy in the national press particularly because it implicated certain Moscow-based leaders.[29]

From September 1988 to September 1989 the KGB's involvement

in nationality issues was overseen by Viktor Chebrikov, who, after resigning from his position as KGB Chairman, served during this period as Central Committee secretary for the Legal Affairs Commission, the party body responsible for the KGB (and the military). Chebrikov's views on the nationality question were much more akin to those of Stalin that those of Gorbachev and he encouraged the KGB to take a strong stance against manifestations of national discontent.[30] Chebrikov stressed the importance of formulating a broad program for dealing with ethnic problems, establishing a special subcommittee for this purpose within the Legal Affairs Commission. According to reports in the Soviet media, Chebrikov was responsible for the decision to call in troops to break up the Tbilisi demonstration in early April 1989. Chebrikov was also credited with the authorship of amendments to the Law on State Crimes, issued immediately after the Tbilisi affair, that broadened the interpretation of criminal liability for various forms of public expression.[31] He apparently was anxious to provide the KGB with a stronger legal framework for suppressing nationalist dissent and the amendments did just that. In addition to making the infamous Article 7 of the Law on State Crimes (Article 70 of the RSFSR Criminal Code, prohibiting anti-Soviet agitation and propaganda) open to looser interpretation, the changes also broadened the scope of Article 11 (Infringement of National or Racial Equality) and made the criminal sanctions more severe. Also, a new Article, 11–1, was added, making it a crime to insult state organizations or officials.

The pubic outcry was such that the USSR Congress of People's Deputies voted to repeal Article 11–1 in June 1989 and the next month the Supreme Soviet pushed through a revision to the law that eliminated some of the most egregious features of Article 7. But KGB officials remained undaunted, making it clear that they considered the criminal legislation sufficiently to justify moves against nationalist unrest. Tajik KGB officials, for example, made the following declaration:

> When democracy and pluralism are seen as total license and a legal opportunity to combat the Soviet system and are used to encroach on the friendship of the peoples and the country's territorial integrity, no one should be in any doubt with regard to the KGB's stance. Strictly guided by existing legislation, security officers have upheld and will firmly uphold the position of defending the gains of socialism, the constitutional rights and interests of Soviet people.[32]

And Gorbachev himself, once he assumed the awesome powers of Soviet President in March 1990, enacted a sweeping "USSR Law on Enhanced Responsibility for the Encroachment of the National Equality of Citizens and the Forcible Violation of the Integrity of USSR Territory," which added a new clause, on "the violent disruption of the unity enshrined in the USSR Constitution," to Article 7.[33]

In a resourceful effort to portray themselves as legitimate defenders of the Soviet state, KGB officials, in the final months of the USSR, placed increasing stress on their role in upholding the Soviet Constitution. USSR KGB Chairman Vladimir Kriuchkov, who demonstrated considerable adeptness at public relations in his numerous media appearances, announced in the summer of 1989 that the KGB's Fifth Chief Directorate, formerly charged, among other things, with suppressing national and religious dissent, had been abolished. It was replaced, curiously enough, by a new directorate, which was given the task of "protecting the Soviet Constitution."[34] Kriuchkov himself was vague on the precise functions of this new directorate, but according to *Pravda,* its work included opposing "encroachments on the constitutional foundations of the USSR," attempts to "forcibly overthrow or change the Soviet state and social system" and "anti-Socialist manifestations of a violent character, including those aimed at fomenting interethnic discord."[35]

The KGB was, at the end, restrained in making arrests among political activists in the national republics, limiting its focus to the most outspoken dissenters and to areas where widespread violence occurred.[36] Increasingly the KGB was called upon to help restore order when civil strife erupted to a dangerous level. The KGB did not have a large paramilitary force specifically designated for quelling outbursts of violence, a task that was left mainly to the MVD's internal troops and the regular army, but its elite body of Special Troops, numbering some 40,000, often assisted these forces. Also, the KGB was charged by law with investigating the causes of ethnic violence and arresting those responsible.

Impact of the August 1991 Upheaval

By August 1991 the mechanisms for increased KGB suppression of nationalist unrest were in place, in the event that the Gorbachev leadership would deem it necessary to resort to stronger methods to protect the Soviet regime. There was every indication that Gorbachev wanted to avoid such an eventuality, but he was hoping to depend on the KGB if things got out of hand. This may be why Gorbachev had been careful not to offend the KGB's vested interests and had sought to contain the demands for substantial reforms of the KGB and the Soviet legal system within tolerable limits. The fact that he did not institute widespread personnel changes within the KGB and apparently sanctioned the appointment of a long-time KGB official, Kriuchkov, as USSR KGB Chairman, promoting him to full membership on the Politburo, indicated an awareness on Gorbachev's part that he could ill afford to lose the KGB's support. On the other hand, the KGB's fate as a political institution depended to a great extent on its ability to work together successfully with the Soviet leadership to hold the Soviet state together. A fragmentation of the Soviet Union into separate republics represented a grave threat to the KGB, a highly centralized bureaucracy that served the interests of Moscow.

Given the KGB's stance on the question of independence for the republics, it is not surprising that Kriuchkov was one of those who attempted to institute a State of Emergency on August 19. Boris Yeltsin, a leading proponent of national rights, was becoming more powerful with each day. And a union treaty, offering substantial concessions to the republics, was about to be signed. What was surprising, however, was that Kriuchkov and his colleagues acted without the collaboration of Gorbachev. It was he, after all, who had pushed through the Law on a State of Emergency back in March 1990, and apparently he had considered invoking it on several previous occasions. In all likelihood, Gorbachev led his hard-line colleagues to believe that he would go along with their plans and then backed out at the very last minute. This would explain the lack of organization, planning, and resolve that went into the attempted coup.[37]

Whatever the case, the KGB was singled out as the main culprit in the plot and became the focal point for reform by the post-coup leadership. The new KGB chairman, Vadim Bakatin, announced sweeping personnel and organizational changes in the KGB, including cuts in manpower and transfers of some KGB troops to the regular army. The most far-reaching effect of the August episode for the KGB, however, was the impetus that it gave to independence movements in the republics and the resultant breakup of the USSR.

NOTES

1. For a comprehensive, scholarly study of the Cheka, see George Leggett, *The Cheka. Lenin's Political Police* (Oxford: Clarendon Press, 1986).

2. *Ibid.,* p. 335.

3. E. A. Skripilev, ed., *Sovetskoe gosudarstvo i pravo v periode stroitel'stva sotsializma (1921–1935 gg.)* (Moscow, 1968), p. 402.

4. As quoted in Ronald Grigor Suny, *The Making of the Georgian Nation* (Bloomington: Indiana University Press, 1988), p. 217.

5. See D. Charachidze, *H. Barbusse, Les Soviets et la Georgie* (Paris: Editions Pascal, 1930), pp. 14–151. For an excellent overview of Bolshevik nationality policy in Transcaucasia at this time, see Stephen Jones. "The Establishment of Soviet Power in Transcaucasia: The Case of Georgia, 1921–1928," *Soviet Studies* 40(4) (October 1988):9.

6. See Leggett, *The Cheka,* pp. 260–263.

7, Robert Conquest, *Harvest of Sorrow. Soviet Collectivization and the Terror-Famine* (New York and Oxford: Oxford University Press, 1986), p. 219.

8 As quoted in Conquest, *Harvest of Sorrow,* p. 260.

9. The most comprehensive studies of the purges are Robert Conquest, *The Great Terror. Stalin's Purge of the Thirties,* Revised edition. (New York: Collier Books, 1973); and Roy Medvedev, *Let History Judge, The Origins and Consequences of Stalinism.* Revised and Expanded Edition. Edited and Translated by George Shriver. (New York: Columbia University Press, 1989)

10. Suren Gazarian, "O Berii i sude nad berievtsami v Gruzii," *SSSR: vnutrennie protivorechiia,* New York, 1982, pp. 119–120.

11. See S. Swianiewicz, *Forced Labour and Economic Development. An Inquiry into the Experience of Soviet Industrialization* (London: Oxford University Press, 1965), pp. 41–42, and Jan T. Gross, *Revolution From Abroad. The Soviet Conquest of Poland's Western Ukraine and West Belorussia* (Princeton, N.J.: Princeton University Press).

12. Medvedev, *Let History Judge,* p. 775. Also see Robert Conquest, *The Nation Killers. The Soviet Deportation of Nationalities* (London: Macmillan, 1970); and *Argumenty i fakty,* September 30–October 6, 1989, p. 6.

13. Conquest, *The Nation Killers,* pp. 134–135.

14. On this point see Charles H. Fairbanks, Jr., "National Cadres as a Force in the Soviet System: The Evidence of Beria's Career, 1949–53," in Jermey R. Azrael, ed., *Soviet Nationality Policies and Practices* (New York: Praeger, 1976).

15. Alexander J. Motyl, *Will the Non-Russians Rebel? State, Ethnicity and Stability in the USSR* (Ithaca and London: Cornell University Press, 1987), p. 127.

16. Frederick C. Barghoorn, "The Post-Khrushchev Campaign to Suppress

Dissent: Perspectives, Strategies and Techniques of Repression," *Dissent in the USSR. Politics, Ideology and People.* ed. Rudolph L. Tokes (Baltimore: The John Hopkins University Press, 1975), pp. 76–83.

17. See Peter Reddaway, "Dissent in the Soviet Union," *Problems of Communism,* November–December 1983, pp. 1–14.

18. See Petro G. Grigorenko, *Memoirs,* trans. Thomas P. Whitney (New York: Norton, 1982).

19. Motyl, *Will the Non-Russians Rebel?,* p. 129.

20. On this subject see L. Alekseeva and V. Chalidze, *Mass Rioting in the USSR* (Silver Spring: Foundation for Soviet Studies, 1985), Report No. 19.

21. See Amy Knight, *The KGB: Police and Politics in the Soviet Union* (Boston: Unwin/Hyman, 1988), p. 199.

22. Reddaway, "Dissent in the Soviet Union," p. 3.

23. See Knight, *The KGB,* pp. 167–169. Often when a native was KGB chairman a Russian would serve as his first deputy.

24. As of September 1990, Kirgizia and Moldavia had native KGB chairmen; they had Russians before Gorbachev came to power. Kazakhstan, where a Kazakh was KGB chairman until 1986, had a Russian in that post.

25. Judging from the example of Vitalii Fedorchuk, KGB Chairman in Ukraine from 1970 to 1982, having a representative of the indigenous nationality serve as KGB chairman did not result in more tolerance towards dissent, but the fact that he was a Ukrainian may have made his draconian policies more palatable to outsiders.

26. An example would be the close working relationship that existed between KGB Chairman Fedorchuk and Party Chief Shcherbyts'kyi in Ukraine from 1972 to 1982.

27. Moscow, TASS in English, December 6, 1989, as reported in *FBIS, Soviet Union,* December 7, 1989, p. 63. Eismuntas was replaced as KGB chairman by R. Marcinkus in March 1990.

28. *FBIS-SOV,* August 28, 1990, p. 69.

29. KGB involvement in anticorruption campaigns in the national republics had a long history. In the 1960s the KGB helped the MVD rout out the corruption ridden regime of Georgian party chief Mzhavanadze.

30. See, for example, a speech he delivered in Kazakhstan in June 1989, where he warned that "unless the situation is taken in hand, elements with extremist and nationalist leanings could gain the upper hand." *Kazakhstanskaia pravda,* June 24, 1989; In a speech shortly before Chebrikov was unceremoniously ousted, he noted that it was "necessary to cut short instigatory actions of those who, speculating on national sentiments, try to achieve not brotherhood and good neighborliness but inter-ethnic strife and hatred." He also said that a number of additional measures would be taken to strengthen law-enforcement bodies. See *FBIS, Soviet Union Daily Report,* September 5, 1989, citing TASS, September 1, 1989. No doubt to the satisfaction of the

more reformist elements in the leadership, this speech was Chebrikov's swan song.

31. See *Izvestiia*, April 11, 1989, for the text of the amendments. Additionally, Chebrikov may well have been behind the issuance in August 1989 of the harsh Central Committee statement on the Baltic Republics, which appeared in *Pravda*, August 27, 1989. It is important to note, however, that Gorbachev must have gone along with these moves. Chebrikov was not powerful enough to have taken these steps without Gorbachev's assent.

32. *Kommunist Tadzhikistana*, September 8, 1989. Former Lithuanian KGB chief Eismontas said in an interview that "we will combat those who incite interethnic discord with the greatest determination." *Sovetskaia Litva*, August 17, 1989.

33. For the text of the law, see *Pravda*, April 6, 1990.

34. See an interview with Kriuchkov in *New Times*, 8–14 August, 1989.

35. *Pravda*, November 2, 1989.

36. In some cases the KGB would issue warnings instead of arresting individuals. See, for example, *Krasnaia zvezda*, September 17, 1989, where it was announced that the Tajik KGB had issued a formal warning to Mirbob Mirrakhimov, a Tajik academician, for inciting ethnic hatred.

37. For a further discussion of this point, see Amy Knight, "The Coup that Never Was: Gorbachev and the Forces of Reaction," *Problems of Communism*, November–December, 1991.

8. Nations of the USSR: From Mobilized Participation to Autonomous Diversity

Theodore H. Friedgut

E VEN before the advent of Marxism, socialist thinking allotted little importance to nations in the development of society. They were considered a passing phenomenon, perhaps of some use in the struggles of current politics, but essentially irrelevant to the ultimate form of human society. Great as was its emphasis on the community and on society as a whole, the socialist movement focused essentially on the needs of the individual and on his right to an equal share in social goods. His societal connections were looked at only from a class viewpoint. The solutions to the ills of mankind were considered universalist in application, disregarding national and other particularities. This approach became doctrine in the *Communist Manifesto,* with its concept of global capitalism and global class struggle. The slogan "Workers of all lands, unite!" was the ultimate expression of Marx's class approach, belittling the vertical divisions of humanity into ethnic, cultural, and religious groups, and asserting that only the horizontal, socioeconomic divisions were of political importance.[1] Marx was not alone in this, for even Renan's description of the nation as "a daily plebiscite" ascribes to national groups a fluidity and fragility that are belied at almost every turn of history.

Yet as the European socialist movement developed, the appeal to national sentiment proved to have great power, for the political and social context of Europe, even after 1848, remained that of the multinational empires with their metropolitan and colonial holdings that involved power over diverse national groups. These preceded by centuries the multinational corporations analyzed by Marx. National minorities, with their sense of discrimination and powerlessness, were fertile soil for all the revolutionary movements, and it is in this social structure that we may find the roots of the phenomenon existing even today, that communist parties and other movements of dissent and protest in almost all countries are made up largely of minority nationalities.

There were two models offered by the European socialist movement with regard to the national question. The Second International adopted as its formal position the concept of self-determination, informed by the experience of Western Europe with the emergence of comparatively homogeneous nation-states. In this approach, the right of the national group to its own independent political expression was central. There had come into being a realization that a dialectical process of national development would precede the emergence of socialist society. Each national group would have to come to grips with its own identity before embracing a universal human identity. The Austrian Social Democrats, influenced by the particularly complex ethnic relations existing within the Austro-Hungarian Empire, formulated a supplementary proposal. Their theory of "national-cultural autonomy" was seen as a solution to satisfy the hunger for national identity among minorities residing in areas in which no claim to political independence could be substantiated. Here the cultural side of nationality was foremost—in particular the use of language as a carrier of national consciousness. Whichever of the two models was favored, the idea of national autonomy and national distinctiveness for their own sake was belittled. Nationality was perceived in instrumental terms as a phenomenon to be overcome, or at best as something that could facilitate the mobilization of the national minorities in support of the anticipated revolution. It is to the development of this mobilization, and to the position of Soviet nationalities under perestroika, that our discussion is devoted.

Among the central problems in this discussion is that of the development of institutions appropriate to participation of national minorities in a supranational framework—particularly one that is ideologically opposed to national individualism. All political participation must take place within appropriate institutions if it is not to undermine the stability of the political system involved. In a multinational system, the creation of institutions that will be considered authentic and authoritative by the various minorities, while balancing the general good against particularism, is a first-degree exercise in statecraft. The problem is only compounded when a numerically dominant majority inherits previously existing patterns of political domination despite a purported revolution in the values of the system. There exists an extensive literature dealing with the development of the nationalities question in prerevolutionary Russia, and, in addition, the question is reviewed elsewhere in this volume.[2] There are, however, a few salient points to be touched upon that highlight the continuity of certain problems of national relations. One such is the mobilization of majority nationalism against minorities as an instrument of antiestablishment agitation. In pre-revolutionary Russia this was exemplified by the debate among the populists as to taking part in anti-Jewish pogroms in order to mobilize Russian peasant support for the revolution and turn the disorders against the autocracy. A second such problem is the inherent contradiction between support of full national self-determination and the unitary structure of the Communist Party. Lenin's adamant stand against federalism in the party created a dilemma for Gorbachev in an era of restructured national relations. A third problem, persisting to this day is that of the nature of the supranational culture that was to replace those of the national groups. In Lenin's time this debate was exemplified by a letter to *Iskra* complaining that Lenin's support of assimilation resulted in all minorities giving up their own cultures in favor of the majority Russian culture. In the latter years of the Soviet Union this phenomenon took the form of an asymmetry of language knowledge in the USSR, with growing numbers of non-Russians learning the Russian language, but few Russians knowing the language of another Soviet nationality. Only in the 1989–1991 discussions of a radical change in the values and structure of the Soviet federation did this assymetry receive public attention.

When Imperial Russia finally collapsed there was already a gap between theory and practice that presaged future complications. The promise of equality and independence excited great expectations among the national minorities. These were to remain largely unfulfilled by both the February and October revolutions. Yet neither were the assimilationist and centralist aspirations of Lenin and Stalin to be realized. Bolshevik capabilities were never sufficient for the implementation of their intentions. In the revolutionary period and the Civil War that followed, the support of the national minorities weighed too crucially in Bolshevik prospects for success for it to be neglected or defied.

National Participation in the Revolution and Civil War

Even before the February 1917 revolution the Russian government had eased its attitude to national minorities in the face of the wartime difficulties, though it had by no means eliminated their main civic disabilities. For instance, the Pale of Settlement restricting Jewish residence was relaxed in August 1915 because of the growing mass of Jewish refugees fleeing the advance of the Central Powers' armies.[3] At the same time other restrictions on Jews remained in force.

It was, however, the first Provisional Government, headed by Prince Lvov, and with the parties of the "Progressive Bloc" as its main support, that removed all national and religious restrictions within the Russian Empire. Sukhanov records hearing a Petrograd worker define the aims of the February Revolution as "Bread, peace with the Germans, and equality for the Yids," a formulation which he thought brilliantly succinct and comprehensive.[4] Certainly in the ultimate political context of the revolution, the national question was no less important than the war or the food shortage.

The result of the revolution, with its appeal to liberal civic values of universal democratic enfranchisement, was an outburst of expectations among the nationalities. This was perhaps less so in the central institutions of the new Russian Republic, in which there was a strong strand of continuity, than in the alternative structure of the soviets, in which both individuals from the national minorities, and national parties were prominent. Perhaps even more important in this context was the growth of autonomous national political organization away from Petrograd. Once the limitations imposed by the autocracy were removed, the national minorities acted swiftly to create their own institutions within which they could participate in the liberated politics of revolutionary Russia. The limited capacities of the Provisional Government, and the staggering overload of urgent problems with which it was forced to grapple, created a golden opportunity for the national minorities. The social revolution preached in the soviets became inextricably interwoven with national aspirations of the long-suppressed minorities at the same time that social struggles were taking place within these minorities.

All of these processes served to draw the entire population of the empire, and with it the national minorities into intensive participation in determining their own political future. At the same time, the institutions within which these political battles raged were new, unproven, and fragile, creating the perilous instability that is the hallmark of revolution. The bloody revolution and counter-revolution in Finland, the many-sided struggle for control of Ukraine, the fragmentation of the Caucasus, all were decided by force for lack of legitimate, recognized political institutions to mediate the multiple conflicts that had been let loose with the collapse of the *ancien regime*. The first lesson learned by the national minorities from the experience of revolution and civil war was that whatever the rhetoric of liberal, participatory democracy, *raison d'état* imposed by force of arms was still the ultimate arbiter of politics.

This lesson, however, was to be learned only after the civil war. The first and most prominent alternative offered was between the promise of minority equality raised by the revolution, and the insistence on "One Russia, Great and Indivisible," supported not only by arch-reactionaries, but also by comparatively moderate conservatives and liberals. The Russian Civil War was not simply Red against White, but also involved any number of national governments that fought with the intervention against Bolshevik control as well as with the Bolsheviks against White reassertion of imperial prerogatives. In this way, Poland, the Baltic republics, Finland, and the three Caucasus republics were able to proclaim independence from the Russian Empire. Once free of Russian political dominion, these republics were able to elaborate a political system with the common base of national identity, with differences of social and political orientation creating a demarcation between the various parties, cultural groupings, and social movements that arose.

In the violent and uncertain context of civil war, the Bolsheviks had an advantage in gaining the support, or at least the neutrality, of large sectors of the national minorities. This phenomenon, paralleled in the peasant sector, was crucial to Bolshevik survival. The enrollment of large numbers of national minority persons in the Bolshevik Party, and consequently in the Red Army, and their active participation in both these institutions was a central phenomenon in the early development of the Soviet regime. While national minorities also joined in political coalitions against the Bolsheviks, the social character of the White movement and its great instability rendered such alliances short-lived and relatively ineffective. In Ukraine, the coopting of national minorities into the successive independent national regimes was a central characteristic, but the rapid displacement of these regimes by stronger forces prevented such interethnic cooperation from developing to a point of institutionalization.

The participation of national minorities in the Soviet regime was, however, not without its own complications. Just as there was friction between the Bolsheviks and other groups regarding nationality policies, so was there friction within the Communist regime. The rivalry between the Kiev and Kharkiv Bolsheviks in Ukraine, and the suppression of the indigenous Georgian Bolshevik leadership by Stalin and the "Muscovite" Georgians are only two examples. While nationality questions played a prominent part in these antagonisms, the issue was essentially one of centralism versus local autonomy in all fields of life. It should be remembered that the early 1920s, the last years of Lenin's life, were the years in which the trade union controversy was settled in favor of central control, and in which the Democratic Centralists and the Workers' Opposition were defeated in their bid to maintain some vestige of local workers' control over their own fate.

A sense of weakness and imminent peril to their regime, the trauma of the civil war, reliance on the tested and proved structure of the centralized party run by a professional *apparat,* and the underlying sense that class interests were the only truly general interests to be considered, all weighed in the choices that pushed Soviet Russia toward a centralized partocratic state whose content stood in essential contradiction to its federal form. Along with the other central elements in the Soviet state, the national minorities were being forced into a mold in which their national consciousness was manipulated from the center rather than growing from its own roots. Consistent with their policy choices in the early years of the Bolshevik movement, the Soviet leaders now opted for a course of supranational uniformity, essentially assimilation of the nationalities into an as-yet undefined Soviet socialist identity, fated ultimately to come under the decisive influence of the Russian majority.

The Consolidation and Expansion of the Soviet Union

The sixty years that passed between Lenin's death and the beginnings of perestroika were not woven from any single strand. The entire period presents a series of complex economic, social, political, and military upheavals, all of a massive character, and mostly accompanied by violence that left virtually no corner of the society untouched. In much of this period the question of nationality played a minor role, subordinated to the massive social and economic transformations that were expected to create a "new historic human community—the Soviet people." Nevertheless, national factors remained present and at several stages assumed importance in Soviet policy-making. At times the consequences in the sphere of nationality might have been totally unintended when a policy decision was taken, yet these consequences still affected future developments. When, after Lenin's death, a "Lenninist Draft" was declared, the intention was to broaden the party's base in the proletariat. Among the numerous ancillary results was the changing of the national composition of the Soviet Communist Party, with the Russian presence undergoing considerable dilution.[5] The annexations of territory that took place in 1939 and 1940 were motivated by strategic and historical considerations, but brought into the Soviet Union nationally conscious minorities that remained resentful of the Russification practiced by the Soviet regime and became increasingly active in demanding radical change in these policies.[6]

The early years of this period, coinciding with the period of the New Economic Policy, were a time of hope for the nationalities. The entire period was one in which development, experimentation, and diversity were prominent in Soviet life as the society recovered from the tragedies of revolution and civil war, and sought its way over the uncharted ground of building a socialist polity and society. In the national sphere, this was a period of flowering. Political control had been established by the party, the army, and the police. Now this control had to be translated into a functioning society.

The most prominent national phenomenon of the 1920s was the movement of *korenizatsiia,* the rooting of society in national forms. This involved the encouragement of the use of national languages, not only in newspapers, literature, and schools, but also in courts, soviets, and in the entire gamut of the citizen's intercourse with the regime. The aim of this promotion of language was to bring the regime closer to those masses of people who had been subjected to the revolution, but not active in it, remaining cocooned in their traditional social environment, alien and often hostile to the values of secular, revolutionary socialism. Indeed, the participation of so many national groups in centripetal independence movements, or their collaboration with non-Bolshevik and anti-Bolshevik movements in the course of the Civil War, made the Communist regime sensitive to the need to open avenues of communication in order to remold the attitudes of these minorities. To this end, in addition to all the institutions of daily life mentioned above, the most familiar and powerful of national institutions, language, folklore, art, music, and literature, were mobilized into the effort of political socialization. This was a period in which for the less developed nationalities, such institutions were formalized. Written alphabets, national musical forms, and national literature were systematically spread, opening the way for the regime to influence the sympathies of various minorities.

As a revolutionary regime dedicated to bringing new values and habits to the population, the Bolsheviks faced the problem, common to all radically new regimes, of penetrating the grass roots of society. Participation of the national minorities in the programs of the regime, and in the administration of society through the use of national language and symbols, was to be the first step in coopting each minority into active participation in the building of socialism. In particular, the *korenizatsiia* program was important in mobilizing representatives of the minorities who could become authentic, authoritative leaders in their communities. Though minority representatives were prominent and numerous among the Bolsheviks, such people were a relatively small part of their communities, and those who joined the Bolsheviks were generally estranged from their own people and from their traditions, tending toward Russification. The slogan of the times was "National in Form and Socialist in Content," a formulation maintained in programmatic documents almost to this day.[7]

This slogan appeared to meet the needs both of the nationalities and of the regime. On the one hand it would preserve at least the outward forms of national cultures, thus attracting the participation of the members of the national group. On the other, it would ease the socialization of the national minorities to the new values embraced by the regime. The difficulty lay in the disadvantages embedded in both halves of the formula. For those members of a minority inclined toward accepting modernization and new social values, the use of national forms was a hindrance, and the education of a child in the national language might limit his social and economic mobility, particularly if the person were a member of one of the smaller minorities. If a Tatar, a Jew, or a German child really aspired to a career in the USSR, education in Russian was necessary, and experience in contact with Russians an advantage.[8] While this did not necessarily preclude the learning of the national language as a second language, it lessened the attractiveness of the national schools with their emphasis on the ethnic group and its outlook. At the same time, for those parents steeped in the tradition of their national group, particularly if this tradition was bound up with religion, the teaching of Marxism-Leninism and of atheism in the national tongue was abhorrent. The parents often tried to separate tradition and revolution by giving their children a traditional education at home, leaving it to the general school to "render unto Caesar those things which are Caesar's."

The period of the 1920s saw an apparent success of *korenizatsiia* and of the mobilizing of national cadres into the CPSU, particularly among Ukrainians and the Central Asian nationalities where the party had previously aroused little participation. The federalism of the Soviet Union was fleshed out with the creation of numerous national units— Autonomous Republics, national regions, and national districts. National forms of literature, music, and art were given vigorous organizational and financial support, with nonnational specialists designated to create such forms where native cadres were lacking. Even when the emphasis on experimentation and innovation of national forms dwindled in the face of the massive unity imposed on Soviet society as part of Stalin's "Revolution from Above," and the purges that made any possible deviation dangerous, the development of the national republics was accompanied by a growing prominence of indigenous activists. The educational advances accompanying industrialization drew wider and wider groups of the national minorities into positions of activity and prominence. The educational revolution, professional advancement, and growing urbanization that characterized, albeit unequally, all sectors of the Soviet population, meant a greater proclivity for joining the Party, and the growing numbers of people involved in the soviets, the trade unions, and all the other mass public organizations in which Soviet society abounded, included by plan a quota of representatives of the national minorities. The varying degrees of representation of various nationalities in three different systems indicates the problematics of national representation in the USSR in the 1970s. Representation in the party, in the soviets, both local and the Supreme Soviets of the Union Republics, and in the cadre of scientific workers is presented in Table 8.1 (see p. 219). The index of party representation is the relation of the number of communists per thousand in any given nationality, divided by the same ratio in the entire population. The remaining indices compare the percentage of a given nationality in each category to the percentage of that nationality in the Soviet population. An index of 100 indicates that the number of nationals in any category is commensurate with its weight in the general population, an index above 100 indicates overrepresentation, and an index under 100 indicates underrepresentation.

At first these figures appear consistent only in their inconsistency, but by drawing on supplementary knowledge we may make some sense of them. It has been suggested that there is a correlation between urban residence, higher education, and Party membership, and this is borne out by the findings in the table, with the exception of the disparities appearing in the case of Latvians and Estonians, explained by nationalist resentments of the Communist Party. The reader will immediately discern the glaring discrepancy between over-representation of Jews in the Communist Party and in science and their underrepresentation in all levels of the soviets. The prominence of Jews in the two former institutions should, on the face of it, have induced a similar level of presence among the elected representatives. The seeming contradiction may be resolved by reference to the growing Jewish emigration of the early to mid-1970s, and the knowledge that candidates for the soviets were selected to give a public image that may be held up for emulation before the Soviet people.[9] By emigrating, Jews disqualified themselves as role models for the Soviet public.

The Central Asian nationalities, lagging in urbanization, are underrepresented in the party as well as among scientific workers, but have high overrepresentation among members of the republic supreme soviets. This may be understood as reflecting the cooptation of the indigenous intelligentsia of Central Asian nationalities into the prominent positions from which the deputies of the supreme soviets were drawn before perestroika. Their representation in local soviets is, however, uneven, but closer to normal, ranging from an index of 70 for Uzbeks, up to 114 for Kirgiz.

The Tatars, as a rural population lacking a Union Republic, emerge as the most underrepresented of all the national groups investigated. Their closest approach to normality is in the local soviets where, nevertheless, they reach an index of only 88. An additional caution must be introduced here. The roles represented in the table are open only to adults, but the age structures of the various nationalities differ greatly. The Jews of the Soviet Union, for instance, were an aged population, while the Tajiks, and other Central Asian nationalities, had a large cohort of under-eighteen. These age structure differences worked to moderate the disproportion of representation.[10] At the same time, when we are discussing phenomena of subjective consciousness such as the perception of representation in any sphere of public prominence, subtleties of national age structure may be assumed to play a minimal role.

If we take the proportions of national representation among scientific workers in 1970 as a product of historical development, then an interesting facet of Soviet nationality policy is revealed by comparing this structure to the national structure of the student body in institutions of higher education in the same year—a structure that may serve as an adumbration of the future body of scientific workers.[11] During this period a program of "affirmative action" had been instituted in higher education to raise the representation of local nationalities in their own republics. This was also a period of considerable growth of the Soviet system of higher education. As a result there was a sharp general movement toward a more proportional representation of the nationalities, with the sole exception of the Latvians, whose index retreated from 100 to 83 in this comparison. The Moldavians, whose index of 27 put them at the bottom of the scale of scientific workers, achieved an index of 64 among students, while two of the Central Asian nationalities emerged with an index of 100 or more, while the other three advanced considerably, and the Tatars rose from 52 to 76. Jews plummeted from 767 among scientists to 256 among students, while Russians dropped more moderately from 124 to 111, Georgians to 146, and Armenians to 120. With the exception of the Jews, where dwindling university age cohorts, emigration, and the imposition of national quotas had a cumulative effect, the losses of the overrepresented nationalities were generally less dramatic than the gains of the underrepresented. It is clear that the regime policy of drawing national minorities into higher education was effective and may be expected to have an impact on the urbanization of the various nationalities. While cultural differentials among the nationalities and the hereditary impact of historical trends in educational advancement will still be felt into the future, it is clear that the regime's policy of drawing national minorities into higher education was effective and may be expected to have an impact on the urbanization of the various nationalities. This, in turn, may be expected to influence the level and forms of political participation of the various national groups.

At the end of the Brezhnev period there were, however, many additional questions to be asked. The most prominent was in the field of language policy, as a test of general nationality policy. The pressure for Russification was clear, and aroused resistance from some sectors of the population. Language controversy was sharpened by the dispute as to whether scientists in the national republics should publish their research in their national languages, or whether all should share Russian as the language of Soviet science. The demands of modernity and the urges of national pride conflicted openly here. In addition, in the political sphere, the Communist Party institution of appointing a Slavic Second Secretary in the national republics became a virtually inviolable rule once more, after having been in sometime abeyance under Khrushchev. This, of course, could not but be a gall to the sensitivities of the native leadership and intelligentsia of the republics. Finally, as the economy slowed down and the sensitivity to ecological problems grew, there was a growing awareness among the national minorities of the contradiction between national self-determination on the economic plane, and the bureaucratic, planned, and centralized character of the Soviet economy. Two conflicting tendencies came into play at this time. The demands of modernization were for freer communication, greater physical mobility, and free social mobility on the basis of talent. All of these weakened the boundaries of national communities, creating not only greater contact, but also, as a result, mutual influence and interculturation. At the same time, such a free and fluid social structure, whether in science, culture, or industry, contradicts a centrally instituted determination of resource allocation and use, let alone ideological content. This is particularly true when the center is dominated by the majority nationality, creating "internationalism" in its own image.

The Nationalities Question Under Perestroika.

At the end of the Brezhnev period there were already numerous warning signs of national tensions in the USSR. A number of patterns may be discerned. The first is the pressure for emigration. This affected primarily the Jews and the Germans, two nonterritorial minorities ostensibly leaving the USSR for their historic homelands, as well as Armenians who were leaving the Armenian Republic for a diaspora.[12] Whatever their other reasons for leaving the USSR, disappointment with national and cultural conditions was prominent in the expressions of the emigrants. A different pattern may be discerned in the behavior of Estonians and Georgians who expressed their protest by withdrawal. It may be seen in the diminution in the percentage of Estonians admitting a knowledge of the Russian language, and in the Georgian demand for retention of official status for the Georgian language in the new constitution of 1977, and the subsequent dialogue between the Georgian intelligentsia and the then-First Secretary of the Party in Georgia, Eduard Shevardnadze, as to the advantages of knowing and using Russian as well as Georgian.[13]

A third pattern was the growth of corruption on the basis of local, nationality-based cliques, as was the case in Azerbaijan, in the multimillion ruble cotton scam in Uzbekistan, and traditionally in the entire economy of Georgia. A different, and more ominous, pattern was to be found in the nationalist overtones accompanying disorders and demonstrations over sports events in Lithuania, presaging the open violence that was to break out in numerous national areas once police control was loosened. In addition, the same prominence that had once marked the participation of national minorities in the revolutionary movement now marked their participation (as well as that of religious minorities) in the dissident movement from the late 1960s on. Dissatisfied with the establishment version of mobilized participation, and encouraged by the relaxation of terror that accompanied the aging of the Soviet regime in the post-Stalin years, all types of minorities pressed to widen the limits of autonomous political participation, creating their own particularist institutional frameworks and increasingly shunning the regime-sponsored institutions that had served to mobilize them in service of an all-Union Soviet goal.

Faced with mounting difficulties in every sphere of life, the Brezhnev regime reacted with a mixture of concessions and attempted repression. Party leaderships were shaken up and new leaders with police backgrounds were brought in to cut down corruption.[14] Emigration was stopped, and would-be emigres were exhorted to lead normal Soviet lives, while Brezhnev warned that the regime would tolerate "neither nationalism nor chauvinism, for example, neither Zionism nor anti-Semitism."[15] At the same time, much of the discrimination against Jews in employment and education began to be eased. While Georgia and the two other Caucasus republics had their national languages retained as official languages, none of the other republics enjoyed this privilege at the time. Perhaps most significant for the authorities was the fact that except for the Georgian protest on language, channeled through the Georgian Supreme Soviet thanks to the political skills of Shevardnadze, all the patterns of behavior that we have mentioned were a denial or an evasion of the legitimacy and authority of the state institutions. In the great majority of cases, the citizens did not seek redress from the state, but ignored, subverted, or abandoned it. For an observer with historical sensitivity, the public attitude was strongly reminiscent of that which prevailed in the period of the civil war.

With the advent of perestroika the form of expression of national discontents changed sharply. The change began gradually as Gorbachev's slogans of glasnost and democratization took on flesh and blood in the press, in party and government debates, and most of all, in the encouragement of the "informal organizations" (in fact, incipient political parties in many cases) that sprang up in all areas of life. In one republic after another, discussion groups and cultural movements coalesced into popular national fronts. The multitude of discontents that had been repressed burst forth. The form of demands and protests varied from mob violence in Alma-Ata in December 1986, and murder (as in the Azerbaijani pogroms against Armenians in Sumgait and Baku, those of the Uzbeks against the Meskhetian Turks in the Fergana Valley, or the clashes between Georgians and Abkhazians), to a sophisticated coopting of the local Communist Party leadership into the national cause (as in all three Baltic republics and Ukraine). The forms were as varied as are the cultures of the Soviet multinational state.

The Armenian demand for the incorporation of Nagorno-Karabakh was the first national demand addressed to state institutions. The mass demonstrations in Erevan at the beginning of 1988 were addressed to the Armenian Supreme Soviet as a *nakaz*—a public mandate to which the legislators are formally obliged to respond. The resolution of the Armenian Supreme Soviet supporting the demands to bring Nagorno-Karabakh into the Armenian Republic was contrary to the expressed decision of the Politburo and of the presidium of the Supreme Soviet. This was the first time in Soviet history that a republic legislature had upheld its constituents' demands against the wishes of Moscow, a precedent soon to be followed by a number of other national republics. One must go back to the much more discreet bargainings between Moscow and the Ukrainian leadership during the formation of the USSR to find anything remotely resembling such defiance.

The demonstrations in Erevan served as an example of legitimate, autonomous political participation by national minorities for the advancement of particularist interests, even when those interests had been opposed by the authorities in Moscow. Despite the harsh denunciations of particularism and nationalism by Gorbachev and the rest of the Soviet leadership, and the eventual banning of the Karabakh Front, this example spread widely. The most outstanding examples were the demands of the Popular Fronts formed in the Baltic republics that led to independence. The popular fronts established in the majority of the former Soviet republics became to all intents and purposes independent national political parties. Their representatives succeeded in the elections to the republics' Supreme Soviets, taking advantage of the possibility of multicandidate elections offered by the Gorbachev reforms, and evoking high public interest, particularly in the second round of elections, when it had been proven that independent candidates stood a fair chance of election.

The interest of the Soviet public in the nominations, and in the election campaigns, going far beyond the specific national questions that arise in the various republics, was a participatory revolution unrivaled since 1917. So great was the public popularity of these organizations that the local Communist Party leadership was coopted into supporting their demands. The most striking example of this is the Ukrainian Supreme Soviet's declaration of Ukrainian sovereignty, adopted under the aegis of a leadership of Communist Party functionaries. For the local leadership the only alternative has been to be swept aside and to lose all influence. The result was that the Supreme Soviets of the Baltic Republics became an example to other republics in legislating autonomy in both the cultural and economic spheres.

This movement took on various forms as it spread across the Soviet Union. In Ukraine, in September 1989, a three-day conference of 1,700 elected delegates marked the founding of a Ukrainian Popular Front, *Rukh* (Movement), which claimed at that time 280,000 members but grew steadily until independence.[16] Open organization of the movement had started at the beginning of 1989 under the stimulus of the impending multicandidate elections to the new Congress of People's Deputies. In addition to providing stimulus and organizational models, the "more advanced" national minorities provided political support to their weaker brothers. When the nascent Popular Front of Belorussia was denied access to any public meeting place by the conservatively inclined authorities of its own republic, Lithuania provided a meeting place and permission to hold the gathering. In March 1989, when no hall in Moscow could be found to hold a meeting of representatives of fifty newly organized Jewish cultural centers from across the Soviet Union, the Latvian Republic hosted the meeting in Riga.

Language has been one focus of national attention in many of the republics. In the Caucasus, of course, the official status of the national language was retained in the 1977 constitutional revisions, and there was no reason to raise the subject. In Estonia, then the most radical of the Baltic republics, the demand was raised that the national language should be recognized not only as the official language, but also as the sole public language of daily intercourse.[17] In Moldavia the demand was for institutionalization of the Moldavian dialect and use of the Latin, rather than the Cyrillic, alphabet. Both of these republics' demands had a clear anti-Russian bias, and evoked reactions from the large Russian minorities in the republics, who, as we have noted, often do not know the local language even after decades of residence in the republic. Not all the republics have been so open in their resentments. Ukraine included official status for its own language in its draft constitution, but hedged this with a clause guaranteeing the free use of Russian "as the language of interethnic discourse in the USSR," as well as charging the state to enact appropriate legislation for the free use and teaching of all national languages of the population of the Ukrainian Republic.[18]

The stimulating of public participation in the elections and legislation in the various republics must be counted as one of the great successes of perestroika. If Gorbachev's reform program were to be summed up in one sentence, it would have to be defined as the re-energizing of the Soviet system by engaging the citizen's attentive participation in public and governmental institutions in all fields of life. It may be understood from the context of Gorbachev's speeches that his original intent was to focus citizens' activities in the institutions of production, administration, and distribution, improving their performance, and thus raising the standard of living. But the perhaps unintended result of the policy of democratization is that his policies left the citizens autonomous in the creation and choice of participatory institutions, and as a result the price paid by the Soviet state and in particular by the Communist Party was high.

The example of successful mass national organization for a particular interest stimulated emulation in other sectors. The coal miners' strike of July 1989 was not uninfluenced by the scenes of crowds in Tallin, Erevan, or Baku shown on Soviet television. The miners' strike was, in turn, followed by the organizing of strike committees in the metallurgical industry, on the railroads, and even by Moscow subway workers.[19] Once again this was a mixed blessing for the leaders of perestroika. Though the strike communities were central to the ousting of petty bureaucrats and conservatives in the coal fields, and their replacement by democratically elected officials and administrators who enjoyed the confidence of the workers, the threat of a transportation strike in Moscow, or a general railway strike, must have been insufferable to the regime.

Through 1989 and 1990, ethnic unrest often found expression in strike action. The Russian backlash against Estonian and Moldavian nationalism affected dozens of enterprises and tens of thousands of workers. The general strike in Azerbaijan in the summer of 1989 effectively paralyzed all local transport as well as the oil production of the republic. The easing of national grievances thus became intertwined with the central effort of perestroika for a revival of the Soviet economy. Moreover, the existence of national independence movements was used by the miners in their bargaining with federal Moscow. Both in the Donbass and in the Kuzbass the miners supported sovereignty and then independence, in hopes that a strengthened republic authority would grant greater satisfaction to their demands.

The Regime's Responses to the National Challenge

The response of the Soviet regime to the new urgency of the nationalities question was mixed and tentative. Clearly there was little agreement in the leadership as to how this problem might best be solved. Harsh as the leadership's denunciation of particularism and separatist demands was, action against the organizers of such demands was strikingly limited.

Where public order was violated and lives or property threatened, the army and militia were called in and restored order using violence with firmness but generally with restraint.[20] In Armenia this was accompanied by the administrative dispersal of the Karabakh Front that had led the Ereven protests. The glaring exceptions to restraint were the massacre of demonstrators in Tbilisi in April 1989, and the January 1991 killings in Vilnius. Despite the report of a governmental commission of inquiry, and the resignation of the First Secretary of the Communist Party in Georgia, Patiashvili, who took responsibility for ordering in the troops who killed the demonstrators, the incident remains insufficiently explained.[21] The killing by soldiers of civilians in Lithuania appears to have had similar dark origins.

In other cases, senior officials were sent to persuade local nationalists of the dangers of extremism. Where such quiet diplomacy proved inadequate it was bolstered by personal and collective declarations against extremism by both party and governmental leaders. When the Estonian Supreme Soviet limited the franchise of new immigrants into the republic by setting a residence qualification of two years for voting and five years for candidates, Gorbachev, in his capacity as Chairman of the Presidium of the Supreme Soviet of the USSR signed an *ukaz* declaring the action of the Estonian legislature *ultra vires,* and setting a deadline for the Estonians to remove the offending clauses from the law.[22] These latter actions showed a refreshing commitment to the principles of political negotiation in Soviet life that counterbalanced the persistence of old patterns of coercion displayed in the Tbilisi and Vilnius massacres. Persuasion was preferred to coercion, and there was respect shown for the demands of legality and for noninterference in the workings of local institutions.

The pressure of the Moscow authorities against Lithuania's secession was more questionable, for the constitutional position of the Lithuanians appeared unassailable, Moscow's claims to the contrary notwithstanding. Nonetheless, even the then leader of the conservative faction of the CPSU, Egor Ligachev, was cited as acknowledging that tanks could not solve this dispute. Resort to naked force, however disguised or embellished, as a sole line of action, was clearly rejected. To do otherwise would have been to discredit and disable the entire program of perestroika on the political plane. Yet these statements and actions were only reactions to situations. Their principal value was that they maintained an overall framework of legality within which new nationally-based participatory institutions could crystallize and gain experience, authority, and stability. They were not in themselves a policy for the restructuring of national relations.

As late as November 1987, in his speech on the seventieth anniversary of the Bolshevik assumption of power, Gorbachev repeated the claim that the nationalities question had been solved, and that the peoples of the Soviet Union were filled with respect and gratitude to the Great Russian people "for its selflessness, its genuine internationalism, and invaluable contribution to the creation, development, and consolidation of the socialist Union of free, and equal republics."[23] Nevertheless, he did couple these bombastic phrases with the announcement that nationality questions would be reviewed in depth in the nearest future. At that time it was already clear that the national question was a volcano that might erupt at any time. In the intervening years, the situation became steadily more complex, with the regime attaining very limited success in containing and moderating nationalist pressures. Only in mid-August 1989 did preliminary discussions end. With the publication of the Communist Party platform on national relations, an intensive public debate opened. This led to a plenary session of the Central Committee of the Communist Party in late September which amended the draft into a statement of principles to be presented to the Supreme Soviet of the USSR for legislation. This was the customary route of policy-making. Yet the Communist Party platform was clearly unacceptable to the various national popular fronts. These organizations were successful in taking legislative initiative away from the party, particularly since the elections for the republic Supreme Soviets in early 1990, and had much success in taking their politics directly to the public in extra-parliamentary demonstrations.

The nationalities platform published in the press was the fruit of active consideration by ethnograhers and other academic specialists over a long period. Reflections of this can be found in the academic journals throughout 1989. Within the Soviet Sociological Association a new section was set up in October 1988 to study "national-political relations" in the USSR. Its first session, on October 25, was attended by eighty sociologists and ethnographers, and was devoted to an examination of the Nagorno-Karabakh problem.[24] Among those participating were representatives of the Armenian Academy of Sciences. Representatives of the Azerbaijani Academy of Sciences had also been invited to participate, but had not responded. The discussion was sharp, frank, and far-reaching. It used both theoretical constructs and empirical observation, and drew on historical (the American South in the period of reconstruction) and contemporary (New Caledonia and the Iran-Iraq conflict) world experiences in the search for a model for settlement. Perhaps most important was the active participation of a representative of the Presidium of the Supreme Soviet who promised that the deliberations of the meeting would get the attention of the policymakers in Moscow.

Some of the considerations of the academics who discussed the problems of national relations over the past several years did indeed find reflection in the nationality platform of the party.[25] First of all was the care and the sobriety with which the document was formulated. The extravagant claims of having solved the nationalities problem and created a new and more perfect union of peoples in the Soviet Union were not only avoided, but also such an approach was specifically charged with having caused a blindness to the festering conflicts that led to the end of the USSR. The tone of the platform reflected a consciousness of the complexity and seriousness of the problem. Despite these qualities, this, like so many documents of the Gorbachev period, appears also to have been a "committee document," expressing at once all the opposing positions that coexisted uneasily in the Soviet leadership. Along with a declaration of the civic equality and equal value of each Soviet nation, there remained a special recognition of the Russian people. While far from the near apotheosis granted them in 1945 by Stalin, and something less than the "elder brother" status common in the Brezhnev period, and, as we have shown, used by Gorbachev in his seventieth anniversary speech, the Russians were cited as "having been and continuing to be the consolidating factor of our entire Union, having contributed decisively to overcoming the backwardness of the national areas." There was, however, no more of the nonsense of "the language of Lenin" that found such common expression in linguistic writings through the 1970s and early 1980s, and the section on language ended with a call for the creation of conditions for development of "Russian-national and national-Russian" language communication, a first recognition of the asymmetry of attitude that reflected Russian dominance.

In the discussion of Nagorno-Karabakh cited above, one of the participants suggested that the bad press the Armenians were receiving in Moscow was a result of a widespread feeling among Russians that Russia had been plundered by the peripheral republics. This feeling, not unique to Russians, found expression in several of the republics, and served as a foundation for demands to gain full economic independence from the center that was said to batten parasitically on the national wealth of the disaffected republic.[26] No less than the actual economic damage done by strikes and disorders on a background of nationality conflicts, this feeling created difficulties in securing the participation of the various nationalities in improving the overall economy of the Soviet Union. The dilemma remained unresolved in the draft platform, with the proposal that the republics must own and control the disposition of all natural resources while the federal government must have the determining voice in their use not only for defense and for internal security, but also for general economic development and inter-republic interests.

This ambivalence of phraseology existed in other areas as well. The uniqueness of each national culture and its right to preservation were recognized, yet further on there was mention of "preservation of *progressive* traditions," (emphasis added—T.F.) leaving open the question of what is progressive, and who is to decide.[27] These ambiguities, clear to readers in the Party's rank and file, were an expression of the Party's confusion as to its role in Soviet society in general. The institution that had been central to every development in the history of the Soviet Union proved incapable of the adaptation needed for continued influence in today's conditions. This inadequacy, carried through stubbornly in all spheres, is what brought Gorbachev to abandon, however reluctantly, the Communist Party as the sole vehicle of power, and acquiescence to a pluralism of power that legitimized the existence of institutions based on an autonomously defined national and social identity. In essence, by its refusal to adapt, the CPSU not only committed suicide, but also caused the demise of the USSR. In 1917, Professor Miliukov urged retention of the monarchy as the sole institution capable of maintaining the unity of Russia's society. It may yet prove that a flexible and adaptive CPSU, capable of maintaining a modicum of authority in Soviet society, might have been the one institution that could have countered the centrifugal nationalisms that tore apart the Soviet Union.

The elements of conflict within the party become apparent when the draft of the nationalities platform is compared to the final document approved by the CPSU Central Committee in September 1989.[28] It is a conflict caused by the rise of Russian nationalism, and by fear from the integrity of the Soviet federation in its configuration of Russian dominance. Most prominent among these was the call for legislation to make the Russian language the official state language of the Soviet Union, with equality to each national language in the republics. It will be recalled that it was the attempt to eliminate the national language as official state language, making all languages equal, that spurred the Georgian protests of 1977–78. In addition, the central control of the economy was tightened by stipulating joint ownership of all resources by the republic and federation, rather than republic ownership as proposed in the draft. With the handwriting already on the wall in the Baltic republics and the Caucasus, the party nevertheless unequivocally rejected any consideration of federalism in its structure. This caused a crisis by putting before the CPSU the choice of giving up any effective presence in those republics where communist parties independent of the CPSU had already formed, and in other republics where this appeared imminent, or of totally burying the Leninist party structure by accepting federalism in addition to renouncing the party's monopoly on political power and accepting factions with different platforms within the party.[29]

This Hobson's choice was compounded by a general loss of legitimacy by the party and by the regime. The January 1990 riots in Dushanbe included demonstrators calling for the resignation of the Tajik Party First Secretary as a "traitor." In Azerbaijan and Moldavia, demonstrations of the Popular Front turned into attacks on Communist Party buildings. The "perestroika from below" that accompanied the July 1989 mine strike included expressions of no confidence in a number of local party officials. This was accompanied in the spring 1990 election campaign to the local soviets by demands "that all of them be removed."[30] The source of this loss of legitimacy was the persistence (and temporary success) of a large part of the *apparat* in resisting the Gorbachev reforms, and continuing with the coercive monopoly of power to which they had accustomed themselves over the years. As group after group in Soviet society found an autonomous organizational base for the representation of its interests, the party bosses at the middle and local levels were more and more threatened, and felt the need to redouble their self-assertion. It was, if you will, a sort of ironic caricature of Stalin's theory that the closer the USSR comes to achieving socialism, the fiercer the class struggle will be.

In the meantime, Gorbachev, frustrated by the party's refusal to reform itself, reinforced the power and autonomy of the soviets, both local and central, anchoring that autonomy in a free election system and the beginnings of budgetary autonomy. This attracted the energies and loyalty of Soviet citizens, and the result was the support of autonomous national groupings, and an abandonment of the party-dominated institutions.

The most hopeful characteristic displayed in the party's platform of nationality policy was the turn toward establishing an operative framework of law in which nationality questions were to be anchored. The attempt to make the Soviet Union a state based on law was one of the cornerstones of perestroika, engaging the active and enthusiastic attention of jurists, academics, and legislators. From matters of daily life and civil rights, to the workings of a Constitutional Supervisory Commission that was to have acted as a Supreme Court in matters of dispute between the republics and the federal government, and a proposal that the USSR Congress of People's Deputies should have the final word in disputes between republics, proposals for the rule of law figured prominently and repeatedly in the nationalities platform.

At the same time there evolved a new institution, the Council of the Federation, which, after drafting new principles on which a revamped treaty between the republics was to be negotiated, was transformed by Gorbachev into a federal advisory body for the Executive Presidency. Essentially, this body grew out of a special committee of the Supreme Soviet, formed in 1988 and active for only a few months. It became a council made up of delegates of all the republics willing to remain part of a federal Soviet Union. As a basis for its treaty-drafting activity it adopted the principle of "polyphony," explained as a spectrum of status ranging from agreed federation to confederation and applying to inter-republic relations as well as republic-federal relations.[31] As examples of this we might take the RSFSR or Ukrainian declarations of sovereignty, which while providing for superiority of republic law over federal, explicitly retained the concept of the federation.[32]

After two preliminary drafts that failed to gain wide acceptance in the republics, a turning point was reached in April 1991, when the so-called "nine plus one" agreement was signed, anticipating a new Soviet Union of nine republics, and implicitly recognizing the right of the other six to secede by stating that those republics refusing to endorse a new Union Treaty would be regarded as foreign countries by the USSR. The "polyphony principle" elaborated earlier then found enunciation in the suggestion of Lithuania's secessionist President, Landsbergis. Replying to a suggestion of Kazakhstan's President Nazarbaev that a meeting of all fifteen "Soviet Republics" be convened to coordinate positions regarding the new treaty of federation, without participation of the federal authorities, Landsbergis spoke of a "nine plus three plus three" relationship that might be evolved, with each component relating differently to the whole. He thus defended the Baltic republics' claim that they were not Soviet, while acknowledging the desirability of an institutionalized relationship with the Soviet Republics.[33]

This proposed conference, initiative for which was taken autonomously from below, without any overt initiative from the federal government, was a long overdue expression of the type of confidence-building relationship that might have eventually attenuated the fears of Leninist centralization and the weight and tradition of Russian dominance that crippled Gorbachev's efforts to find a successful federal formula for the continued survival of the USSR. The draft of the new Union Treaty was approved by the USSR Supreme Soviet on July 23, 1991, and was to be signed on August 20 by the nine republics and the federal authorities. The abortive August coup attempt frustrated the signing and resulted in the reopening of the whole question, with the various republics vying with one another in posing new demands. Despite intensive efforts by Gorbachev, the republics chose independence, with the Commonwealth of Independent States (*Sodruzhestvo nezavisimykh gosudarstv*) as their form of association. Explicitly not a state, it has chosen to shun all symbols of political community such as a flag, an anthem, and a capital. However, in putting an end to the USSR the new commonwealth has not put an end to its interethnic problems. Both within the various republics, and between them, the heritage of past conflict remains to be overcome.

In the tendency toward balance through law on which perestroika was based, we may see the first expressions of a consciousness that no legislative provisions can be fully or permanently satisfactory in a society as complex as that which made up the former USSR. A dynamic of optimalization and continuous adjustment will be the key to success. If the leaders of the Commonwealth of Independent States have anything to learn from the experience of other countries regarding interethnic relations, it will not be the copying of this or that piece of legislation, but the realization that political stability rests in the creation and maintaining of an institutional framework that protects the existence of minorities, prevents, or at least mitigates, majority tyranny, and gives the minorities both a measure of satisfaction and autonomy in their own corporate life and access to the centers of judicial or legislative power for protection of their status and for a fair hearing for grievances, real or imagined. The changing social and national relations that result from the modernization of the commonwealth societies will demand a flexibility of institutions, a mechanism for the ongoing redistribution of power that is perhaps the most difficult for any ruling political elite to create. Yet such a mechanism is necessary if all the particular demands of national (or any other) groups are to be drawn into and processed by the political system. If mass participation, generated by social and economic development, is not to be a destabilizing factor, it must be contained within institutions accorded legitimacy and accepted as authoritative by the overwhelming majority of the public.

Today this is only doubtfully the situation. The CIS leaders are therefore under considerable pressure to create, in a relatively short period and without the luxury of further leisurely experimentation, their own unique "machine that will go of itself," a structure of institutions that will answer the needs of a freely associating multinational commonwealth. The alternatives are a return to an authoritarian centralized regime, or chronic civil strife within and between the former components of the Soviet Union.[34]

Unlike the United States, where a voluntary federal association was based on divergent economic interests but a largely homogeneous ethnic and cultural basis that grew gradually, the Soviet federal system had overlapping ethnic and administrative divisions that were inherent in its very inception, and were, indeed, the *raison d'être* of the federal structure. The Soviet federation was, throughout its existence, plagued by both divergent and unequal national and cultural traditions as well as by a growing perception of compulsory rather than voluntary association. The nation-building practiced by the Soviet authorities created civic expectations that were in large measure frustrated, since neither the small nor the large republics, nor any of the other national institutions, enjoyed an autonomous political, territorial, or cultural existence. Neither can it be claimed that the former Soviet nationalities had transcended their primary ethnic identities, grafting these onto any supranational Soviet citizenship. A long period of economic wellbeing, accompanied by a greater equalization of living standards and cultural levels, would have been one necessary component of such a development. Yet the economic development of the USSR was thrown into reverse by the attempts to stimulate faster growth. When the economy of the CIS eventually resumes some measure of growth, this will have to be accompanied by full equalization of opportunities for education and employment, stimulating greater mobility and mutual acceptance, both within each independent republic, and between republics.

At the level of the citizen, the form and extent of the individual's participation in his community and in the state will have to be determined on the basis of civic conscience and interest, rather than administratively determined mobilization. Patience and belief in the efficacy of the mobility and the enhanced opportunity that are the citizen's lot in modern society will have to replace Bolshevik activism in making the Russian language, or any other single tongue, the actual *lingua franca* of the CIS. All these characteristics are negations of deeply entrenched political and social values that are a heritage of both the Soviet and pre-Soviet eras. They are in many ways based on values foreign to Russia and to many of the other formerly Soviet republics. As is the case with the economy, a long process of convergence will be necessary before the political institutions in the various republics come to resemble each other, and form a common root. This convergence will most likely be preceded by a period of divergence in which each different society attempts to determine its own identity and create appropriate institutions.

As we have commented, even many of the best examples of liberal, participatory democracies, comparatively homogeneous ethnically, and enjoying a relatively high general standard of living, are woefully incomplete, abounding in injustice and social tensions that demand constant reform efforts.[35] It is not to be wondered, therefore, that the most reliable forecast for the future of the newly independent nationalities is one of prolonged dangerous unrest, and that the political and social restructuring of what was once the USSR, its conversion into co-existing political cultures based on equal and free ethnic diversity, if attainable at all, will be, as Gorbachev said of perestroika in his June 1986 meeting with Soviet writers, "a task for generations."

NOTES

1. An explicit presentation of the difference between the vertical and the horizontal perceptions of social structure together with an exhaustive but clear discussion of theory of the nation as formulated by Marx and his followers will be found in Walker Connor, *The National Question in Marxist-Leninist Theory and Strategy* (Princeton: Princeton University Press, 1984), ch. 1.

2. For details see ibid. In addition, Solomon Bloom, *The World of Nations: A Study of the National Implications in the Work of Karl Marx* (New York: Columbia University Press, 1946); Richard Pipes, *The Formation of the Soviet Union: Communism and Nationalism, 1917–1923* (rev. ed.), Cambridge: Harvard University Press, 1964); Samad Shaheen, *The Communist (Bolshevik) Theory of National Self-Determination: Its Historical Evolution up to the October Revolution* (The Hague: W. Van Hoeve, 1956). Stalin's essay, *Marxism on the National and Colonial Question,* should be read closely for an understanding of the Bolshevik outlook on the question.

3. See Salo W. Baron, *The Russian Jew Under Tsars and Soviets* (2d ed., revised and enlarged, New York: Schocken, 1987), p. 163. Restrictions on publications in national languages in the military zone were not relaxed.

4. N. N. Sukhanov, *The Russian Revolution, 1917* (New York: Harper, 1962), 1:17.

5. T. H. Rigby, *Communist Party Membership 1917–1967* (Princeton: Princeton University Press, 1968), p. 396, writes that Russians dropped from 72 percent to 65 percent of the party between 1924 and 1927. In the same period the Ukrainian percentage nearly doubled, from 5.9 to 11.7. It should, however, be noted that Russians were still overrepresented in the party, and Ukrainians underrepresented. The Russian percentage in the party continued to drop until World War II, after which it rose back to the 1927 level, and then diminished gradually to 60 percent in 1976, leaving the Russians still overrepresented in comparison to their percentage in the population, but less so than Jews and Georgians. The determining factors in party membership today appear to be urbanization and education rather than national origin, though other criteria[,] such as a proletarian occupation[,] have determined recruitment at various times.

6. Consider, for instance the radically anti-Russian nationalism in Estonia and Moldavia and that the radical wing of Rukh, the Ukrainian Popular Front, is based in the Western Ukraine, the area taken from Poland in 1939, and historically the home of Ukrainian nationalist fervor.

7. *Trud,* October 25, 1985 carries the draft of the new edition of the party program. In the section on nationality we read as one of the fundamental tasks of the CPSU: "To develop a unified culture of the Soviet people, socialist in content, and heterogeneous in its national forms." No form of this slogan appears in the draft platform of the CPSU on nationalities policy published in *Pravda,* August 17, 1989.

8. For a description of a Ukrainian *Komsomol* activist's unsuccessful efforts to enlist Jewish children in a national-language vocational school, because of parents' objections on career grounds, see Petro Grigorenko, *V podpol'e mozhno vstretit' tol'ko krys* (New York: Detinets, 1981), p. 93.

9. For discussion and statistics on this question see Theodore H. Friedgut, *Political Participation in the USSR* (Princeton: Princeton University Press, 1979), p. 90.

10. I am indebted to the anonymous referee of this paper for raising the problem of differentiated age structures. Lacking comprehensive age statistics from the 1970s on a nationality basis we were unable to calculate representation indices for the adult population only.

11. The national composition of the body of students in higher education is to be found in *Narkhoz 1970* p. 651. For data on nationalities representation in higher education today, see Theodore H. Friedgut, "Erosion of the Jewish Presence in the USSR: Some Recent Statistics," *Jews and Jewish Topics in the Soviet Union and East Europe,* no. 1(14)(Spring 1991):5–13.

12. Although a nominal Jewish Autonomous Region existed in the USSR, it never attracted a significant percentage of Soviet Jews, and today Jews make up less than 5 percent of its population. The level of Jewish culture in the Jewish Autonomous Region was no more intense than elsewhere in the USSR.

The Armenian emigration began after World War II, and in the 1980s Armenians sought repatriation to America with their children and relatives. The desire to emigrate appears to have spread far beyond this group. In 1989, emigration on Israeli visas included nearly 14,000 non-Jews, mostly Russians and Ukrainians who were members of various religious sects, who left the USSR evidently feeling that emigration would give them the freedom of conscience and security that was lacking for them in the USSR.

13. The percentage of Estonians stating that they know the Russian language dropped from 29 in 1970 to 24.2 in 1979. Curiously enough, in the 1989 census, the percentage of Estonians with knowledge of Russian as a second language grew to 33.8. For a presentation of the knowledge of language by various nationalities see T. H. Friedgut "The Unity of Language and the Language of Unity," *International Journal of the Sociology of Language,* no. 33 (the Hague: Mouton, 1982), p. 85. A discussion of the language issue in Georgia in 1977 will be found in ibid., pp. 82–84.

14. Gaidar Aliev in Azerbaijan and Shevardnadze in Georgia became first secretaries in their republics in this way, both having previous police backgrounds. Similarly, G. G. Gumbaridze, previously Chairman of the KGB in Georgia, was appointed First Secretary of the party in the republic following the April 1989 Tbilisi massacre.

15. See Brezhnev's speech to the 26th Party Congress, *Pravda,* February 24, 1981.

16. *Haaretz* (Tel Aviv), September 11, 1989, p. 8. The movement was headed by Ivan Drach, a poet, and Professor Myroslav Popovych, a philosopher. In the spring of 1990, Rukh claimed a membership of one million.

17. The Estonian initiative resembled the controversial "Bill 101," passed in the province of Quebec during the heyday of French-Canadian separatism, which limited commercial signs to the French language, and imposed stringent conditions limiting education in any language other than French.

18. See the proposed constitutional amendments as published in *Sotsialisticheskii Donbass,* August 5, 1989, Article 73.

19. See Theodore H. Friedgut and Lewis Seigelbaum, "The Soviet Miners' Strike, July 1989: Perestroika From Below," *The Carl Beck Papers* no. 804, (Pittsburgh: University of Pittsburgh Center for Russian and East European Studies,1990), pp. 32–33.

20. The intensity of these clashes should not be minimized. In the Fergana Valley, arms were obtained by attacks on local militia stations, and in the Sukhumi riots 5,500 firearms and a ton and a half of explosives were seized from rioters by the authorities. See *Moscow News,* no. 31, July 31, 1989.

21. A report of the investigatory commission's conclusions is in *Moscow News,* no. 33, August 13, 1989. The report limits responsibility for the massacre to local governmental and military officials, explicitly declaring that no clearance was received from the Ministry of Internal Affairs in Moscow.

The commission calls for "calling to account" those guilty of giving the illegal order to disperse the demonstrators by force. The massacre took place in the night of April 8–9, and the order to bring MVD troops from the Russian Republic to Tbilisi would have to have been given earlier. Gorbachev had returned from a visit to Cuba and Great Britain only in the afternoon of April 7. Many blank spots remain to be filled in.

22. *Pravda,* August 18, 1989. The decree bases itself on international human rights agreements as well as on the Soviet Constitution. Though residence qualifications for the franchise are common in many countries, they have never been in use in the Soviet Union, where an organized effort has been made to attain not only a universal adult franchise, but also its universal use. The Estonian Supreme Soviet met this deadline, suspending, though not abrogating, the offending clause.

23. M. Gorbachev, *October and Perestroika: the Revolution Continues* (Moscow: Novosti, 1987), p. 48.

24. This account is based on a twenty-five page typescript report of the meeting, dated November 5, 1988.

25. See the draft text of the document "National Policy of the Party in Contemporary Conditions," *Pravda,* August 17, 1989. A detailed comparison of the draft program with the final document published in *Pravda,* September 24, 1989 will be found in Theodore H. Friedgut, "Perestroika and the Nationalities," *Soviet Jewish Affairs,* forthcoming.

26. A similar complaint was included in the coal miners' strike demand for economic autonomy of the mines. They complained that under central control 70 percent of their product was taken by the center, and only 30 percent remained for local needs. The miners were demanding a reversal of the proportions. To resort once more to the Canadian parallel, Quebec's renewed demand for independence has been ridiculed on the grounds that the bulk of the province's welfare payments and social services are funded by federal transfers, and that Quebec has been a deficit province for the past generation or more.

27. In drawing up the 1961 Party Program, the drafters had called for the extirpation of "obsolete" customs. The adjective was deleted from the program as adopted. See Jan F. Triska, ed., *Soviet Communism, Programs and Rules* (San Francisco: Chandler, 1962), p. 109.

28. The proceedings of the plenum and its resolutions may be read in *Pravda,* September 20–24, 1989.

29. Both of these latter changes were accepted by the CPSU at its February 1990 plenum after a campaign by Gorbachev that lasted three years.

30. For a detailed analysis of the political processes accompanying the mine strike see Theodore H. Friedgut and Lewis H. Seigelbaum, "The Soviet Miners' Strike, July 1989" (Pittsburgh: University of Pittsburgh Center for Russian and East European Studies, 1990), Carl Beck Papers, no. 804. The

point of our repeated references to the miners' strike is to emphasize the common roots and differing outward forms of reaction to the immense social tension released by the policies of perestroika. For the demand that the whole *apparat* be ousted from their positions see the report of the women's committee demonstration in *Vechernyi Donetsk*, February 12, 1990, p. 1.

31. Radio Moscow in English, 18:00 hours GMT, June 21, 1990.

32. See the closing sentence of the "Declaration of State Sovereignty of the Ukraine" adopted by the Supreme Soviet of the republic on July 16,. 1990.

33. *Nezavisimaia gazeta*, no. 72, June 20, 1991, p. 1.

34. A Soviet journalist visiting Jerusalem in June 1989, shockingly predicted that the non-Slavic republics would all secede within the next two years, and that the Russian public would respond with "good riddance!" He had no clear answer as to what would happen to the large Russian minorities in the Baltics, Moldavia, or Kazakhstan.

35. Until 1962, a Catholic presidential candidate was considered unelectable, and in 1988, a black candidate was considered merely interesting.

Table 8.1 **Representation in the Party, the Soviets, and Science (mid-1970s)**

Nationality	Party	Supreme Soviets	Local Soviets	Science
	(1976)	(1971)	(1975)	(1970)
Russians	108	52	87	124
Ukrainians	94	59	139	64
Belorussians	95	168	103	55
Georgians	123	423	121	154
Armenians	101	380	93	147
Azerbaijanis	82	300	100	78
Kazakhs	82	190	112	43
Uzbeks	54	171	70	34
Turkmens	49	600	100	33
Kirgiz	52	567	114	33
Tajiks	46	444	73	33
Latvians	71	633	160	100
Lithuanians	62	373	100	81
Estonians	75	650	125	125
Moldavians	38	318	109	27
Jews	211	34	28	767
Tatars	78	20	88	52

Sources:
Party membership: "KPSS v tsifrakh," *Partiinaia zhizn'*, no. 10 (1976): 16.
Supreme soviets: *Itogi vyborov i sostav deputatov verkhovnykh sovetov soiuznykh i avtonomnykh respublik, 1971 g.* (Moscow: Izvestiia, 1971), pp. 18–20.
Local soviets: *Itogi vyborov i sostav deputatov mestnykh sovetov deputatov trudiashchiksia, 1975 g.* (Moscow: Izvestiia, 1971), pp. 24–26.

9. Development and Ethnicity in the Soviet Union

Zvi Gitelman

T H E dramatic outburst of ethnic violence and tensions in the USSR since 1988 shocked Soviet citizens and foreigners alike. Many assumed that the USSR was immune to such conflicts, some because they believed in Marxist-Leninist myths about the progressive diminution of nationality tensions in socialist societies; others because they were persuaded by Western theories about the decline of ethnicity and religion in developed or advanced societies; and still others because they assumed that the USSR was a highly centralized state that could resort to a great deal of coercive power to prevent such outbursts. By 1990, more than 500 people had died in ethnic clashes in the Soviet Union, the Communist Party of Lithuania had declared itself independent of the All-Union Party, and the republic itself declared itself independent, as did the Armenian Republic, while almost all of the other republics declared sovereignty, meaning generally that their laws would take precedence over laws passed by the federal authorities in Moscow.

The central authorities seemed unable either to repress or to accommodate the ethnic pressures. Both domestic and foreign observers often regarded the Soviet Union as one of the few multiethnic states that had found the means to solve, or at least control, the problems of interethnic relations which bedevil so many other countries. Whatever one may have thought of the means used to obtain the seeming tranquillity that prevailed in Soviet society, the stability they had brought about could not be denied. It seemed to Leninists, on one hand, and to some Western social scientists, on the other, to prove the validity of their theories of the evolution of social relations in a developing society. Now both Leninists and social scientists are forced by recent events to re-examine their theories and the premises on which they rest.

When the Soviet Union began to evolve away from what was described as a totalitarian system, social scientists began to search for concepts that would help them understand a system which was no longer viewed as completely *sui generis*. Moreover, it was argued, unless this vast and important state, along with its East European and Asian allies, were integrated into the study of comparative politics, the latter would be seriously deficient. One characteristic of nearly every socialist state was that at the time it became a Leninist system it had been a largely agrarian society, often with low levels of literacy and health, politically parochial populations, and technologically primitive. In short, with the exception of Czechoslovakia, the socialist countries were more or less underdeveloped. Furthermore, authentic rather than imposed Communist revolutions had taken place in some of the least developed countries—the USSR, China, Yugoslavia, Vietnam, and Albania. Thus, the relationship between development or modernization and Communist systems intrigued analysts. Some suggested that it would illuminate our understanding of those systems as well as of development if the concepts evolved in the study of development were to be deployed in analyzing Communist systems.

Development or modernization—the two are sometimes differentiated but more often are used synonymously—has been defined as the "process by which historically evolved institutions are adapted to rapidly changing functions that reflect the unprecedented increase in man's knowledge, permitting control over his environment, that accompanied the scientific revolution."[1] Development is seen as economic, political, cultural, and social. It entails the growth of the per capita gross domestic product; the expansion of political consciousness and participation to individuals and groups hitherto outside the political arena; an enlarged capacity of the state to affect society and the economy and to develop stable political institutions; the growth of literacy and exposure to mass media; and the proliferation and integration of functional roles in a society.[2] Most analysts conceive of modernization as entailing urbanization, mass education, industrialization, the expansion of communications, improvements in health and material well being, bureaucratization, functional differentiation, and secularization. These processes must be accompanied by the acceptance of new values, beliefs, attitudes, and patterns of behavior on the part of most members of the societies in which they take place. While once it was believed that these processes occur simultaneously, more recent analyses find that they may more often occur sequentially.[3]

Even the casual observer of Communist systems would be struck by how well the characteristics of modernization seemed to apply to them. More dramatically and perhaps violently than other systems that were described as modernizing or developing, the USSR, China, and other countries attempted to lift themselves by the bootstraps economically, expand the scope of the political more ambitiously than perhaps any other systems had done, increase literacy rapidly and universally, alter the social structure more radically than any other societies, and force reluctant societies to abandon traditions and adopt new modes of thinking, believing, and behaving.

Indeed, Marxism-Leninism itself can be regarded as both a theory and ideology of development. In its original Marxian version, the theory posited certain ineluctable, spontaneously generated social and economic forces that would propel societies from one stage of development to another. Unlike most of the modern Western theories, Marxism explicitly posited a final stage of development, communism. But like those theories, it assumed that societies moved to ever higher stages, at each of which was an identifiable syndrome of economic, political, cultural, and social characteristics.

Lenin modified the original scheme by introducing a more voluntaristic element. Development could be pushed along or retarded, depending on people's choices. It would be politically naïve to sit back and wait for forces of history to move humanity from one stage to the next, though human volition alone would not suffice. Stalin infused even more subjective and voluntaristic elements, as exemplified in the battle cry, "Bolshevik tempos decide everything." Rather than relying on the impersonal forces of history, he insisted that heroic efforts had to be made to develop the country as quickly as possible in order to avoid the defeats that had plagued Russia in the past. In a famous address in 1931, Stalin argued that "Science, technical experience, knowledge are all things that can be acquired. We may not have them today, but tomorrow we shall. The main thing is to have the passionate Bolshevik desire to master technique, to master the science of production. Everything can be achieved, everything can be overcome, if there is a passionate desire for it." He then detailed "the continual beatings [Russia] suffered because of her backwardness" and asked, "Do you want our socialist fatherland to be beaten. . . . ? If you do not want this, you must put an end to its backwardness in the shortest possible time and develop a genuine Bolshevik tempo in building up its socialist economy. There is no other way."[4] Development was necessary for survival, and it could be willed, even against formidable objective obstacles.

What is the Marxist-Leninist-Stalinist scheme of development? In 1920 Lenin defined communism as "Soviet power plus the electrification of the entire country." This pithy phrase captures the essence of the Leninist developmental strategy: using state power to modernize the country through industrialization. Stalin specified how that industrialization was to be carried out. The two Marxist leaders assumed that using the political superstructure to transform the economic base would, in turn, create irreversible social changes and react upon the polity to further transform it as well. Their strategy of development rested upon the following assumptions: 1) industrialization is the key to economic and social progress; 2) industrialization goes hand in hand with urbanization; 3) science and technology are the keys to general progress and to industrial success; 4) religion is the antithesis of science and is, hence, anti-progressive; 5) universal literacy and education will combat ignorance and superstition, of which religion is a manifestation, and will promote scientific, technological and political knowledge; 6) class is the most important social cleavage, and development means moving toward the abolition of classes; 7) all inequalities—between the city and the countryside, between men and women, among races and ethnic groups—will be abolished; 8) hence, ethnicity, as an epiphenomenon of the capitalist era, will disappear as socialism replaces capitalism. Eventually, there would be a "world without nations."

The Evolution of Soviet Nationality Policy

Over the decades, successive Soviet leaders have had to modify the original vision of a world without ethnicity. Lenin began with an orthodox Marxist expectation that ethnicity would take second place to class in the transformation of society and that as soon as the socialist revolution was achieved, it would fall away together with capitalism. The more he became involved in the practical tasks of making a revolution in the Russian Empire, the more Lenin came to appreciate the importance of ethnic grievances and their potential for mobilizing large numbers of people to overthrow tsarism. By 1913 Lenin had dropped his original hostility to national autonomy for groups even within a new socialist structure, though he limited his autonomy to compact territorial ethnic groups. He even adopted the popular slogan of the time, "self-determination of nations." However, as the recent struggle to define that right in the USSR shows, this concept was never spelled out and was vitiated in practice by the establishment of a unitary Communist Party to counterbalance the federal state.

During the revolution and civil war, some nations broke away from the former Empire and succeeded in remaining outside the evolving Soviet state; others tried to break away but failed; and still others remained in the Russian-dominated state. However, tsarist discrimination in favor of Russians was abandoned and for the first time in history all peoples of the country enjoyed equal opportunities and rights, though social attitudes changed less rapidly. Undoubtedly, this change of status helped the Soviet state win the loyalty of at least some of the non-Russians, along with that of Russians who had been in the "have-not" classes. In order to strengthen the adherence of the non-Russian masses to Bolshevism, in the 1920s a policy of korenizatsiia was adopted. This meant "rooting" the ideology in the peoples by bringing them the message of Bolshevism in their own languages. In practice, this became a "nativization" of cadres and even of elites in the non-Russian areas, where feasible, and the construction of an impressive panoply of institutions—schools, newspapers and journals, trade unions, Party cells, courts, theaters, research institutes—operating in the native languages. This strengthening of ethnic cultures, and hence of identities, seemed to run counter to the goal of eroding ethnicity and amalgamating the peoples into one ethnically unidentifiable unity. The ideological rationale for the policy was the rather mechanistic formula that those nations who had been denied their national rights had to experience them before they could realize that this would not be the ultimate solution of their problems. That solution could be found only in the universalist class-based solution of socialism, but in order to convince themselves of that the non-Russians would first have to have their fill of ethnic expression. Thus, the great danger, as it was defined in this period, was "great power chauvinism," i.e., Russian nationalism, and not the nationalism of the other peoples.

The flourishing of nationality cultures and even the development of various "national Bolshevisms" was ended almost as soon as Stalin came to power. Stalin was not comfortable with the development of authority structures other than the political center. The cultural and political leaders of the nationalities posed a threat to his monopoly of power and fealty on the part of the Soviet peoples, or at least that is the way he probably perceived it, judging by the purges of the national elites in Belorussia, Ukraine, and elsewhere. Moreover, once Stalin launched his plan for the rapid and intensive modernization of the country, he demanded that all energies be channeled into that plan. Just as before the Revolution Lenin had seen the Bund's demand for national-cultural autonomy as a diversion of energy and resources from the main task, the making of the revolution, so did Stalin see attention to national concerns as diversions and even deviations from the overall national goal. At best, Soviet cultures could be "national in form" but they had to be "socialist in content." The main danger now became not Russian chauvinism, but "petit bourgeois nationalism," that is, non-Russian nationalism. As time went on, even the mildest expression of interest in national cultures could provoke the accusation of "nationalism" or "nationalist deviation."

Simultaneously, two forces other than coercion were at work which weakened ethnic attachments. One was the idea, apparently believed in by many, that ethnicity was outmoded and irrelevant at a time of the literal coming together of the peoples in the constructions sites, cities, and amalgamated collective farms then being constructed. "Proletarian internationalism" was seen not as an empty phrase but as a reality. It rendered ethnicity archaic. Secondly, as we shall argue in greater detail, the first stages of modernization did loosen old ties, shake up primordial loyalties, literally cut people off from their places and hence cultures of birth, and revolutionized their beliefs, attitudes, and patterns of behavior. As people streamed out of the villages and into the cities, they changed not only their residences and occupations, but often their dress, culinary habits, languages, friends, holiday celebrations and avocations as well. In most cases, the particularistic features of their ethnic cultures were blurred or erased.

In later stages of his life, Stalin became more explicit about the primacy of the Russians. His well known toast in the Kremlin at the end of World War II singled them out as the most heroic of the Soviet peoples. The "anti-cosmopolitan" and anti-Western campaigns of the 1940s, along with absurd claims of Russian superiority, flowed from this commitment to elevate the Russians above all others.

As in so many other ways, Khrushchev modified the most irrational features of Stalin but failed to change the situation fundamentally. Believing that he could push Soviet society further along the developmental path, Khrushchev optimistically outlined economic and political goals designed to advance the USSR from socialism to Communism. As part of this effort, he envisioned a process of *sblizhenie,* or the rapprochement of nations, which would be followed by *sliianie,* their complete assimilation and amalgamation. Though it was not explicitly stated, the idea was apparently that assimilation would take place into the Russian people and culture.

Khrushchev's successors were more conservative and less sanguine, on the nationality issue as well. *Sliianie* was gradually deferred into an ever receding future. While it was asserted that the nationality question was solved fundamentally, it was admitted that ethnic identity and tensions among the nationalities persisted longer than had been expected. In practice, Brezhnev cut a deal with the republic elites which allowed them considerable autonomy, especially in personal matters, in their republics, but kept them out of federal decision-making, where Russians continued to dominate. A kind of "affirmative action" policy in the republics resulted in large numbers of non-Russians entering higher education and taking important positions in the republics, to the point that Russians and other nonindigenous peoples complained that they were being discriminated against. Thus, ethnicity had not faded into irrelevance. Indeed, at the end of Leonid Brezhnev's tenure it had reemerged as a sensitive political issue. There was no clear and consistent correlation between modernization and the decline of ethnicity.

Theories of Development and Ethnicity

Like Marxist-Leninist conceptions, Western theories of modernization or development also foresaw the demise of ethnic identities. It was generally assumed that industrialization and urbanization, the spread of mass communications and mass education, and the emergence of large masses of people from geographically limited and culturally circumscribed environments into broader arenas would loosen ties with local communities. "Tribal" affiliations would yield to attachments to larger communities. Assimilation was seen as the consequence of urbanization. People of different cultures would come together in the cities and abandon the parochialism of the village for the cosmopolitan international culture, while technology would make production and consumption patterns more similar around the world, reducing the distinctiveness of parochial cultures.

At it turns out, both Western and Soviet conceptions of development have serious defects and make assumptions that turn out to be false. Both suffer from economic determinism. Social, psychological, and cultural factors turn out to operate quite independently of economic ones. In the third world, the growth of ethnic politics and the rise of political movements around religion and ethnicity rather than class confounded both Marxist and Western expectations.[5] Not only in Iran, but also in the Soviet Baltic, Caucasus, Ukraine, Central Asia, and Russia itself religion proved to be a powerful force in the eighties. Not only among Kurds, Tamils, and Palestinians, but also among the peoples of the USSR ethnicity proved to be a more powerful force than class.

Traditionalists have sometimes turned out to be skillful politicians, as for example when ayatollahs outfox American presidents or Popes triumph over socialist politicians. Traditionalist ideologies have appealed not only to society's marginal, "backward" elements but even to those seemingly well integrated into modern society. Revivalist movements have emerged in modernizing societies because they are ways of dealing with the pressures of modernization, perhaps rejecting them, or because new ideologies often cloak themselves in traditionalist mantles. In the former USSR and other formerly socialist societies, these movements may be the first to form because they require little planning and construction. We shall return to this idea.

Both Western and Marxist analysts thought of modern societies as more rational than traditional ones. Achievement, rather than ascription, would define status and identity. Modern societies would operate "much less on the basis of affective responses and more on rational judgments and choices. Since (it was assumed) a rational basis of self-interest was associated with class affiliations, whereas ethnic and religious ties were affective and nonrational, the latter would prove increasingly nonfunctional."[6]

Samuel Huntington had defined "locomotive" theories as those which posit that one change pulls along many others in its wake. Western analysts assumed that the components of modernization were associated with each other, so that changes from tradition to modernity in one sector would cause changes in others. In the case of Marxists, the "locomotive" is the revolution that, it was assumed, would inevitably lead to economic growth, cultural development, and the disappearance of both religion and ethnicity.[7] Needless to say, things have not fallen into place quite so neatly.

Walker Connor has listed more than a dozen reasons why ethnicity has been underrated in studies of modernization. Aside from those already mentioned, there are several that seem especially relevant to the Soviet Union, though Connor writes with the third world in mind. For example, the assumption that "greater contacts among groups lead to greater awareness of what groups have in common, rather than of what makes them distinct"; that assimilation is irreversible; overemphasis on the importance of the national center rather than the provincial peripheries; too much concentration on the dominant group.[8] Connor points out that scholars have been reluctant to deal with subjective feelings of kinship perhaps because they are uncomfortable with the nonrational and also because they look for quantifiable and tangible explanations.[9]

Modernization and Ethnicity in the Soviet Union

The Soviet Union modernized rapidly during its existence. From a largely rural society it became at the end a largely urban one. From a country in which four of every five inhabitants could neither read nor write, it became a country whose literacy levels were high by world standards and where many citizens could read more than one language. Soviet industry, though problematic, developed on an enormous scale. To be sure, the USSR was an unevenly developed country, and some areas resembled the third world more than they did the West in their standards of living and health. Nevertheless, by most conventional measures the USSR ranked as a developed country.

Yet, development did not have quite the impact on ethnicity that Marxist-Leninists or some Western analysts had expected. Some of the Soviet nationalities listed in the 1926 census disappeared from subsequent ones, presumably because the peoples themselves died out or amalgamated with larger groups. Yet, the overwhelming majority of the nationalities remained. Even those who were highly acculturated—Jews, Poles, other small peoples—never assimilated to the degree one would have expected. That is, while they might have lost their cultural trappings—language, ethnic foods and dress, religion—they did not lose their identities. In large part this was because the state insisted that people retain an officially determined ethnic identity, one reinforced in daily life by the registration of that identity in the course of numerous official transactions. Clearly, a succession of Soviet elites put a higher priority on retaining control of the ethnic composition of education, employment, and politics than on the assimilation of people, many of whom would have been glad to change their ethnic affiliations or have no affiliation at all.

According to Soviet doctrine, assimilation of nationalities (*sliianie*) would have taken place later than their drawing closer together (*sblizhenie*). But even the latter seems to be a very gradual process. In 1979, only 14.9 percent of Soviet families were considered ethnically mixed. True, this was a significant increase from the figure of 10.2 percent twenty years before, but it means that more than sixty years after the October Revolution more than four out of five Soviet families were ethnically homogeneous. Even in Latvia, the republic with the highest proportion of ethnically mixed families, three-quarters were homogeneous.[10] Similarly, the "mutual enrichment of languages," considered the main feature of *sblizhenie,* turned out to be a slow and uneven process. It really means the spread of Russian as the language of ever more Soviet people. Yet, a leading Soviet ethnographer observed that "In some republics the older generation knows Russian better than the young people."[11] A manual for propagandists and students in Party educational institutions, published in 1988, hedged a bit when it said that there had been both progress and stagnation in ethnic relations in recent years. *Sblizhenie,* it suggested, "has to be seen as dynamic and contradictory, and not as uninterrupted progress and endless triumphs." *Sliianie* is a long way off, and when the Party program spoke of "unity of nations" it meant not ethnic but socioeconomic unity.[12]

When we examine some of the processes that are part of modernization, we find that in the USSR—and, no doubt, elsewhere—their outcomes were not unidirectional. Thus, education does broaden people's horizons and makes them aware of alternatives to their own cultures and values, but, especially in Soviet Central Asia, it also gave people a literate culture that is perceived as national and that buttresses the sense of ethnic distinctiveness. Culture is no longer only visual, as in art, nor aural, as in orally transmitted epics, but also written and hence more easily spread and preserved. No doubt, the literacy conferred by the Soviets upon Central Asians and promoted among other peoples enabled the authorities to spread the messages of internationalism and even Russification, but it also simultaneously strengthened non-Russian cultures and identities. In those cases where the national language was suppressed or indirectly eroded (Belorussians, Poles, Jews, Germans), the overall tendency of literacy was to diminish national culture and perhaps even identity, but in those cases where native languages were invented or promoted, distinctive identity and culture may well have been strengthened even while a broader culture was introduced.

This illustrates an important point: the impact of modernization on ethnicity is not undirectional or undimensional, especially in the Soviet Union. Modernization strengthened ethnicity among some peoples, and weakened it among others. Within the very same nationality, modernization led some people to identify more closely with their co-ethnics (and co-religionists), and some to move away from them. Some chose to use modern technology to promote tradition and "parochial" values, while others used them as gateways to the cultures of other peoples.

A second process that is part of development Soviet style is the acquisition of Russian language facility. Again, some nationalities became thoroughly familiar with Russian—and a few even substituted it for their own languages—but others did not. In 1979, 93 percent of the Soviet population listed their national language as their mother tongue, down only 1 percent from 1959. However, only 14 percent of the Jews, 29 percent of the Poles, and 57 percent of the Germans did so. Even within their own republics or autonomous republics only small proportions of some nationalities claimed their national language as their mother tongue. Thus, only 74 percent of the Belorussians and 67 percent of the Bashkirs did so in 1979. On the other hand, 99.9 percent of the Russians, 83 percent of the Ukrainians, and more than 95 percent of each of the Central Asian nationalities with republics claimed their national languages as their mother tongues.

But even when a national language is no longer used or understood, it can be a symbol of ethnic identification and is fought for. The struggles over the use of Russian and other languages is less a matter of practicality than of pride and patriotism. Especially in the eighties, language became an important ethnic symbol, and hence a matter of contention, for many Soviet peoples—Moldavians, Estonians, Lithuanians, Latvians, Ukrainians, Jews, Georgians, and even some Belorussians, who were assumed to have the weakest language loyalty of the major nationalities.[13]

A third concomitant of modernization is the transformation of some traditional roles, the disappearance of others, and the introduction of new ones. While medicine men may disappear and clergyman become fewer in number and less sought out, engineers and managers come on the scene. No doubt, this weakens traditional social relations and forms of culture. Again, however, we see that modernization may strengthen ethnicity by the very same means by which it weakens it. Members of a nationality who assume the new, "modern" roles often become a source of pride to their co-ethnics ("one of our people made it"), and may themselves see their attainments as rebounding to the credit of their group. Others may see their new roles as an escape from their "backward" original cultures and may use them to dissociate themselves from the ethnic group. On the whole, the elites of the ethnic group do tend to change and are populated increasingly by people whose occupations are associated with modernity more than with tradition.

Secularization, a process hoped for by Marxists and assumed by some Western social scientists, also cuts two ways. The loss of theological belief may well erode ethnic identity, especially among peoples who have a distinctive or unique religion or religious organization associated with them (Georgians, Jews, Armenians, Azerbaijanis, and Lithuanians in the Soviet context where there are few other Catholics). On the other hand, people with strong emotional attachments to the group may transfer the lost religious fervor or allegiance to the ethnos. Thus, generations who regarded themselves primarily as Muslims are succeeded by those who regard themselves primarily as Uzbeks. Jews who once defined themselves by religion come to define themselves by nationality. Religious authority figures are replaced by national leaders, though religious leaders may act as national leaders.

In the Soviet pattern of modernization, industrialization held pride of place—a pattern that, to be sure, introduced many occupations which are ethnically neutral and nondistinctive. Only a minority sticks to traditional vocations associated with particular ethnic groups. Many Central Asians apparently preferred to remain in the countryside, where ethnic solidarity and culture were less threatened, than to move to the cities, and they thereby resisted the occupational transformations associated with industry and urban life. Yet, even in the cities there is some congruence between ethnic and occupational stratification. Certain ethnic groups, though perhaps not many, are associated with particular occupations. Georgians, Jews, and Armenians are thought to be "overrepresented" in the arts, sciences, and commerce. Germans are thought of as skilled workers and farmers, and occupational data support this image. Ukrainians are thought to dominate the noncommissioned officer ranks in the military, and so on.

Sometimes, modern societies create such superficial sameness that people look for ways to differentiate themselves from others. When clothing, child-rearing practices, music, art, language, leisure entertainments, and cultural pursuits become more and more the same for large numbers of people, some try to differentiate themselves by dressing or acting differently from the "mainstream." One way of asserting distinctive identity is to make ethnicity distinctive and visible. As products become standardized, some go back to native crafts. There is a protest against industrialization through a return to pre-industrial ways of production. Clearly, in the former USSR and elsewhere, this is done only by a few. Industrialism remains king.

In the Soviet case, as in most others, industrialization implies urbanization. This is thought of as an aspect of modernization that weakens ethnicity. As Blair Ruble notes, "Soviet observers have long contended that urbanization would lead to the integration of society around a set of homogeneous socialist values. Nationalities and classes would come to share common, urban-oriented educational experiences, professional aspirations, cultural tastes and family relations. . . . Observable differences in attitudes and behavior would fade away as the professional culture of the city replaced the folk culture of the countryside." While this "remained one of the central legitimation myths of the Soviet regime" it has not happened.[14] Ruble acknowledges that in the cities of the European USSR, people, especially the more educated, had larger "international" identifications, though he asserts that ethnicity mattered more than it did in a predominantly rural USSR. It is in the Asian areas that "confessional and ethnic boundaries run deeper . . . limiting ethnic interaction."[15] Seweryn Bialer asserts that "to the extent that ethnically non-Russian regions were swept by the tide of modernization, they have developed a new type of intensive, urban-centered ethnic identity."[16]

Western scholars may be tempted to go too far in negating the Soviet premise that urbanity erodes ethnicity. True, cities may heighten the sense of ethnicity in several ways. Ernest Gellner describes "Ruritanians" who when leaving their family, and village or valley, which had defined their group and religion, seek out other exploited and impoverished individuals speaking dialects "recognizably similar."[17]

The city may heighten ethnic consciousness because one becomes more aware of one's ethnicity by encounters with "the other," people who are different in language, dress, appearance, religion. In the countryside, ethnicity was more "primordial," assumed and unquestioned. In the city one's ethnicity is challenged. It is more threatened than in the more ethnically homogeneous countryside, and while some may choose to yield to the threats and abandon ethnicity, others may opt to defend it.

On the other hand, we should not forget that in the great rush to industrialization and urbanization in the 1920s and 1930s, many people did indeed abandon their ethnicity along with their villages. They changed their languages, styles of life, friendship patterns, family patterns, clothes, foods, and religious beliefs. We know that interethnic marriages rose precipitously among some groups. If ever there was true assimilation among large numbers of Soviet people it is likely to have been in the 1930s. It is not clear whether this was the result simply of very rapid industrialization and urbanization, or whether it was more directly due to the genuine enthusiasm for "proletarian internationalism" which gripped many at the time. They were building a new physical world and it seemed quite plausible that a new spiritual world was also being constructed, one in which ethnicity did not matter, and, indeed, could only get in the way of the mutual understanding needed to have everyone pulling together in the heroic and costly effort to modernize backward Russia as quickly as possible. No doubt, a third stimulus to assimilation was the terror of the period and the campaigns against "bourgeois nationalism," which made most people hesitate to display even a mild interest in non-Russian cultures and ethnicity.

Whatever the case, the urban experience no doubt has resulted in both the erosion as well as the preservation and promotion of ethnic allegiances. Perhaps there is a curvilinear relationship between urbanization and ethnicity, at least in the USSR: in earlier periods, the urban experience weakened ethnic belonging, while more recently it has worked in the opposite direction. Joseph Rothschild believes this is more generally true of the influence of modernization on ethnicity. ". . . Some local identities and loyalties are dissolved and fused into larger ones in the early stages of modernization, with its revolutionary productive, scientific, technological, cultural, psychological, and political impacts. But in subsequent stages, middle-level ethnic groups in all types of societies become increasingly resistant to further assimilative pressures, suspecting that the modernist, scientific, cosmopolitan images in which such pressures are garbed often really veil the interests and norms of the dominant ethnic groups." This resistance is usually successful because "the very same modern state that is the vehicle for pressure also supplies the instruments for resisting it."[18]

Modernization, then, does not have a unidirectional impact on ethnicity, nor does it affect all groups or individuals in the same way. Its impact on ethnicity is complex and varied. Subjective choices play a crucial role in whether modernity will be used to "liberate" people from their ethnic identities and cultures, or whether it will be harnessed to the purposes of preserving, protecting, and promoting ethnicity. Alexander Motyl invokes the image of an "ethnic ladder," with the rungs representing different levels of ethnic consciousness and assertiveness. He notes that modernization by itself does not move a group up or down a ladder.[19] It takes subjective choices to do so.

The End of Innocence

Just as Western scholars have had to revise their ideas about the relationship between development and ethnicity, so did Soviet scholars implicitly and explicitly challenge the ideological assumptions of Marxism-Leninism regarding ethnicity and development. Recently, three important myths were shattered in the Soviet Union: 1) national or ethnic consciousness fades as society moves closer to "mature" socialism; 2) Soviet society is characterized by "druzhba narodov," or friendship of the peoples; 3) the USSR is, in the words of the national anthem, an "unshakable union of free republics."

Already in the late 1970s Soviet scholars were pointing out that national consciousness was growing and not diminishing among many Soviet peoples. The head of the Institute of Ethnography of the Academy of Sciences noted that "In our country there has actually been a headlong growth of national self-consciousness" and that this is part of a world-wide "ethnic renaissance."[20] Mikhail Gorbachev was the first politician to admit that "The development of our multinational state is naturally [sic] accompanied by a growth in national consciousness. This is a positive phenomenon. . . ."[21] Recent events make that abundantly clear. Sovietologists are arguing over whether this is to be welcomed or not, but the facts cannot be denied.

The deaths of more than a thousand people in ethnic clashes from February 1988 through the breakup of the USSR, the plight of nearly 400,000 refugees who fled Armenia and Azerbaijan, the emigration of Jews, Germans, and Armenians, and the rise of extremist forms of various nationalisms, including Russian, make the claims of "friendship of the peoples" sound hollow indeed. They demonstrate that the socialization and modernization of decades did not suffice to eradicate national hatreds, and they may have even exacerbated them. Many Soviet commentators finally admitted that ethnic tensions were ignored or papered over for years. "We are past masters at ignoring difficulties in the national question," observed Yuri Poliakov.[22] A Soviet study of 240 works published between 1977 and 1982 on theoretical problems of nationality relations in the USSR condemned the authors of almost two-thirds of the works because they "barely mentioned the survivals of nationalism and chauvinism in the consciousness of people under socialism. An overwhelming majority of the authors did not even consider the possibility of the development in current conditions of any negative phenomena, including . . . in the sphere of national relations."[23]

Soviet nationalisms have become so visible owing to four reasons: First, the visibility of nationalism was a direct result of glasnost, which allowed old grievances to be aired. Freedom of expression made it possible for Balts to claim that their annexation to the USSR was illegal and coerced, for Jews to learn about the "Doctors' Plot" and other manifestations of anti-Semitism, for Belorussians to learn of the horrors of Kuropaty and Poles of Katyn, for Ukrainians to demand a full accounting of the famine of the 1930s, and so on. Glasnost also exposed the economic, social, and political shortcomings of the system. Naturally, many look for someone to blame for these shortcomings. The nationalities who felt oppressed by the Russians pointed a finger at the dominant nationality, in effect saying, "You were running the show and look what a mess you've made of it." In turn, the Russians felt put upon and unfairly blamed by the others. Many Russians were taught to believe that, as "elder brothers," they helped the other nationalities, who turned around and blamed the Russians for all the ills of the system. Russian nationalism was excited by anti-Russian accusations. Some Russians, in turn, looked for someone else to blame and found the victims in the unlikely "Judaeo-Masonic conspiracy." A third consequence of glasnost was that communications became more open and so knowledge of ethnic assertiveness spread quickly from one region and people to another. The "demonstration effect" in mass behavior is well known and was made possible by glasnost.

Perestroika is the second reason for the emergence of ethnic assertiveness. The aim of perestroika is to liberate individual and group initiative, not evoked by the state, in the economic and political spheres. Ernest Gellner suggests that "seven decades of resolute centralism" have "all but destroyed" Soviet citizens' abilities to form associations in a pluralist setting. "Modern ethnic feeling, on the other hand, does not require for its emergence and political manifestation any pre-existing institutions. It has no roots in social structure. . . . It wells up in otherwise anonymous, atomised populations, and it is evidently capable of producing its own organisations, almost effortlessly."[24]

The third short-term stimulant to ethnic assertiveness is what has happened in Eastern Europe. The rejection of Communism is not an internal matter alone; it is a declaration of independence from the Soviet Union. Those Soviet peoples who see themselves as having once been part of Eastern Europe are quick to draw the analogy between the East European states, whose formal sovereignty is now being infused with meaning, and themselves.

Finally, religion in the USSR was revived, ethnicized, and politicized. Gorbachev admitted that the traditional Soviet hostility to religion was mistaken. He met with the Pope, permitted more religious freedom than any of his predecessors, and took part in the celebration of the millennium of Christianity in Russia. The Soviet media opened themselves not only to local clergy but even to American evangelists. When Belorussian Communist Kirill Mazurov was buried, Soviet television showed a priest in full regalia approach the coffin, lay a rose on it, and make the sign of the cross over the partisan and Party hero. Thus, religion was made respectable. Insofar as it is linked to the ethnicity of many Soviet peoples—Jews, Christians and Muslims—it reinforces and legitimates that ethnicity. As in Poland and elsewhere, the line between ethnicity and religion cannot be sharply drawn.

Development has not eradicated ethnicity, neither in the former USSR nor elsewhere. Its effects on ethnicity are varied, multiple, and complex. They vary with the time period and the people affected. A single aspect of development may have contradictory effects on the ethnicity of one people, or contrary effects on the ethnicity of several peoples. Situational and historical variables must be taken into account when trying to measure the impact of development on ethnicity. For example, while urbanization in the 1930s led Jews to acculturate into Russian culture and even assimilate into the Russian people, the same process probably strengthened the ethnic identities of most Central Asians who moved to the cities in the 1950s and 1960s. Industrialization may have led Ukrainians to become more like Russians in their styles of life and language, but it seems to have heightened Baltic sensitivities and stimulated them to differentiate themselves from Slavs to a greater degree. Contemporary events make it dramatically clear that neither the traditional Marxist-Leninist nor some Western views of development and ethnicity have taken into account the richness, complexity, and diversity of both.

If the post-Soviet states continue to modernize, ethnic self-consciousness may be even more stimulated because modernization will force people to change their ways of working and living, thereby engendering the search for identity, security, a sense of belonging to a stable, defined community. That, in turn, is likely to lead back to the ethnic community as a "primordial" one. Moreover, the general pluralization and differentiation of post-Soviet societies, in economic, political and cultural life, will render the assimilationist myth, which entails homogenization rather than differentiation, even more quaint. The real prospect of multiparty systems in societies that have not developed institutionalized forms for the expression of differing political ideas means that, at least initially, the first non-Communist parties to form may be ethnic parties or have social bases which are closely associated with particular ethnic groups. A multiparty system would strengthen the multiethnic character of post-Soviet society. Again, we see that situational variables influence the relative strength and salience of ethnicity.

In the longer run, however, for the same economic and pragmatic reasons that West European states have found it attractive to develop closer relations, parts of the former Soviet empire may choose to re-associate in relationships which will be defined not by the *diktat* of an imperial center but by mutual agreements arrived at by sovereign, independent entities. Lenin over-simplified when he argued that assimilation is the inevitable next step after national assertiveness has run its course. Neither Leninism nor developmental theory is convincing on the inevitability of "stages." But it could be that, at least for some areas of the present USSR, voluntary association, not coerced assimilation, will follow a period of conflict and secession. The former

Soviet Union is too fragile and the pace of change too rapid to allow any predictions. But at least, for the first time in decades, the peoples of the USSR can shape their own collective and individual futures. Not "stages of history" or of "development" but human thought and action hold the keys to the future of the peoples of the USSR.

NOTES

1. C. E. Black, *The Dynamics of Modernization* (New York: Harper and Row, 1966), p. 7.

2. The literature on modernization and development is huge. Some works are: Jason Finkle and Richard Gable, eds., *Political Development and Social Change* (New York: Wiley, 1966); David Apter, *The Politics of Modernization* (Chicago: University of Chicago Press, 1965); Samuel Huntington, *Political Order in Changing Societies* (New Haven: Yale University Press, 1968); Lucian Pye, *Aspects of Political Development* (Boston: Little, Brown, 1966); and Gabriel Almond, *Political Development: Essays in Heuristic Theory* (Boston: Little, Brown, 1970).

3. Myron Weiner and Samuel Huntington, eds., *Understanding Political Development* (Boston: Little, Brown, 1987), pp. 6–19.

4. Joseph Stalin, "The Tasks of Business Executives," *Works* (Moscow, 1955),13:40–41.

5. Myron Weiner, "Political Change: Asia, Africa, and the Middle East," in Weiner and Huntington, *Understanding Political Development,* p. 33.

6. Joan Nelson, "Political Participation," in ibid., p. 112.

7. Samuel Huntington, "The Goals of Development," in ibid., pp. 7, 10.

8. Walker Connor, "Ethnonationalism," in ibid., pp. 197–199.

9. Ibid., p. 205.

10. A. Orlov, *Protsessy internatsionalizatsii sovetskogo obraza zhizni* (Kiev, 1986), pp. 133 and 149. See also A. A. Susokolov, *Mezhnatsional'nye braki v SSSR* (Moscow, 1987).

11. Iu. V. Brolei, "Natsional'nye problemy v usloviakh perestroiki," *Voprosy istorii,* no. 1, 1989, p. 35.

12. *Aktual'nye problemy razvitiia natsional'nykh otnoshenii, internatsional' nogo i patrioticheskogo otnoshenii* (Moscow, 1988), pp. 69, 72.

13. See Roman Solchanyk, "What's in a Language," *Soviet Analyst* 19(10), May 17, 1989.

14. Blair Ruble, "Ethnicity and Soviet Cities," *Soviet Studies* 41(3)(July 1989):405.

15. Ibid., p. 406.

16. Seweryn Bialer, *Stalin's Successors: Leadership, Stability and Change in the Soviet Union* (New York: Cambridge University Press, 1980), p. 200.

17. Ernest Gellner, *Nations and Nationalism* (Ithaca, N.Y.: Cornell University Press, 1983), p. 62.

18. Joseph Rothschild, *Ethnopolitics: A Conceptual Framework* (New York: Columbia University Press, 1981), p. 255.

19. Alexander Motyl, *Will the Non-Russians Rebel?* (Ithaca, N.Y.: Cornell University Press, 1987), p. 26.

20. V. Tishkov, "Narody i gosudarstvo," *Kommunist,* no. 1, 1989, p. 51.

21. "On Progress in the Implementation of Decisions of the 27th CPSU Congress and the Tasks of Deepening Reconstruction," *Pravda,* June 29, 1988, translation in *Current Digest of the Soviet Press* 40(26)(1988):16.

22. "Ne bylo gotovykh obraztsov v razvitii natsional'nykh otnoshenii," *Izvestiia,* March 22, 1989, p. 5.

23. V. I. Glotov and L. V. Yakusheva, "National'nye otnosheniia v SSSR: Nekotorye voprosy issledovaniia," *Voprosy Istorii KPSS,* no. 5 (May) 1987. Cited in Teresa Rakowska-Harmstone, "Gorbachev's Nationality Policy," paper presented at the Twentieth Annual Convention, American Association for the Advancement of Slavic Studies, Honolulu, November 1988, p. 7.

24. Ernest Gellner, "Nationalism in the Vacuum," in Alexander J. Motyl, *Thinking Theoretically about Soviet Nationalities* (New York: Columbia University Press, 1992), pp. 249–250.

10. Soviet Economic Structure and the National Question

Richard E. Ericson

THE "national question" was always an important political issue in the Soviet Union—one that, because of the nature of the Soviet political and economic system, became inexorably intertwined with economic issues and decisions. The ideologically necessitated drive to resolve this question had a noticeable impact on economic policies and the process of their formulation. This can be seen with regard to issues of investment, subsidy, and distribution, and regional development and specialization. Thus there was an impact on the industrial, physical capital, and administrative structure of the economy. But the structure of the *economic system,* of the "house that Stalin built," was only superficially influenced by nationality/ethnic considerations. It rather developed largely according to its own iron laws: those of the "command economy." We might say that its "form" was influenced by the national question but that its "content" was socialist, planned, centralized, and command-administered according to its own logic.[1]

The economic structure, however, had a strong and lasting impact on the national question, an impact that has become all too obvious in the last several years. Far from ameliorating ethnic and national tensions, the structure and logic of the economy, at least since the 1930s, has systematically distorted interethnic relations, aggravating old animosities and creating new grievances. This led to a festering of nationality problems under the veil of "proletarian internationalism" and "friendship of peoples" supported by the rigidly imposed tranquility and uniformity of the Stalinist-Brezhnevite political and economic system. Under Gorbachev's troika of perestroika, glasnost, and *demokratizatsiia,* the accumulated grievances burst forth as the pressure of the Stalinist system was reduced and the possibility of diversity, pluralism, and initiative opened up. The preceding destruction of civil society and the withering away of Marxist/Soviet ideology have left nationalism as a primary inspiring idea, one that has found its voice and muscle under the emerging conditions of decentralization and growing local responsibility and control, culminating in a collapse of the center in September–December 1991. Economic reform opened the possibility of material empowerment of competing nationalisms as it attempted to harness national initiative in the drive to modernize the Soviet economy. Yet the material empowerment of national passion became increasingly disruptive of regular economic activity as well as of economic development and modernization.[2]

Thus the attempt to radically change the existing economic system and structure stirred up winds of passion, yielding national ethnic squalls that grew into a major storm. Indeed, it became a hurricane, sweeping away Gorbachev's perestroika along with the old Soviet Union, and opening the way to political revolution and truly radical economic reform.

The Soviet "National Question"

The Soviet Union, as its Russian predecessor, was a multinational empire, encompassing more than 100 ethnic groups.[3] Its Communist leadership long sought to maintain Russian preeminence and legitimate their unitary state by addressing the perceived causes (material bases) of ethnic animosity and conflict: discrimination and deprivation. Following Lenin, they believed national animosity to have been an epiphenomenon, i.e., the consequence of an outdated, exploitative socioeconomic system and an oppressive Russian chauvinist imperial regime ("the prison of nations"). Thus the "national question," the demands for national autonomy and even dissolution of the empire, should fade away as society develops and "class" replaces "nation" as a central element of individual and group identity. Eliminating inequities—cultural, political, and economic—became therefore an ideological imperative, indeed an inevitability, informing policy choices in the development through socialism to communism.

While that was expected to be a long process, it was to be facilitated by allowing equal expression of national identity (cultural equality), some forms of limited autonomy with a strict prohibition against ethnic discrimination (political equality), and by aiding those relatively deprived groups (nationalities) to develop more rapidly to the socioeconomic level of their more advanced brethren (economic equality). Indeed, the policy of socioeconomic equalization among regions and peoples increasingly came to be the key operational principle behind the Leninist solution, as it lends itself to quantifiable policy measures and observable implementation.[4] This Leninist formula of "national equality" allows for a "flowering of nations" within the single socialist polity until both the material basis and social consciousness have evolved to the higher stage at which national distinctions would have lost meaning and withered away. It provides the transitional solution to the "national question," one which the arrival of Communism will ultimately resolve.

This "Leninist" solution to the national question was formally embodied in the major political, economic, and social institutions of the Soviet Union.[5] Fifteen peoples of the Soviet Union, the major titular nationalities, were important enough for each to have had its own Soviet Socialist Republic (SSR)—the highest administrative unit—which, all together, formed the USSR. Other nationalities were recognized in less important administrative units, including 20 Autonomous SSR's, 8 Autonomous Regions (*Oblasti*), and 10 Autonomous Areas (*Okrugi*). Each of these structures had important economic and cultural rights as well as functions, directly affecting life, and lending a "national" coloration to central policies pursued or implemented in these regions. This can be seen in the "dual [branch-territorial] subordination" of most forms of economic activity. In particular, the structure (institutions) and process of economic planning and of the allocation of produced and natural resources were shaped by this subdivision of economic administration. The pursuit of economic equality as a step toward eliminating national distinctions also had a distinct, differential impact on these regions, in particular with respect to productive and infrastructure investment.[6]

However, the permissible "national" diversity has never been much more than a surface phenomenon, relating more to appearances and procedure (ritual) than to the essence of economic or political policy and structure. Both political and economic policies and processes were highly centralized and hierarchically administered, with Republic and local (national) administrators/politicians largely implementing decisions reached at higher levels. True to the Stalinist version of the Leninist formula, both structure and policy were "national in form and socialist in content." The national question had a clear and continuing influence on the structure of the economy and its development, a legacy of its Leninist "solution." But the structure of the Stalinist economic system had a deeper, if not so visible, counter-influence. That influence did much to negate Lenin's solution, counteracting policies of equalization and generating new grievances between national groups within the Soviet Union.

The Evolution of National Policy: An Economic Perspective

Lenin's Bolshevik Russia (RSFSR) emerged from the civil war (1921) shorn of many of the nationalities of the Russian Empire and struggling to retain the rest, though closely allied with the formally independent Soviet Socialist Repubilcs of Ukraine, Belorussia, Azerbaijan, Georgia, and Armenia. In Central Asia there was a closely related Turkestan SSR, and the independent Soviet People's Republics of Khiva and Bukhara. All the Soviet republics proclaimed a Leninist policy of national political, cultural, and economic equality in their constitutions. After flirting with a more centralized solution to multi-nationalism through "autonomization" within the RSFSR, the Bolshevik leadership adopted a "federal solution," proclaimed Leninist, of "equal and independent republics" within the USSR (December 30, 1922). In May 1925 two more Central Asian SSR's (Turkmen, Uzbek) were admitted bringing the total to nine. Stalin's Constitution of 1935 provided a geographic criterion (a republic had to be on a border to be able to secede) that allowed the Transcaucasian Federation to split into three Republics (Georgia, Armenia, Azerbaijan) yielding eleven Soviet Socialist Repubilcs in the Union.[7] By this time, the basic structure and principles of the Soviet (Leninist) solution to the national question were fully in place.

These principles, however, were sufficiently dialectic and vague to have been subject to wide interpretation and variation in implementation over the succeeding periods. The idea of assimilation/fusion through national equality and self-expression allowed varying interpretations of pace and emphasis.[8] These variations can also be seen in the development of economic structure and the evolution of economic policy. The period of the New Economic Policy saw the only true period of strict national equality as Lenin, and then Stalin, drew the nationalities back into the empire, reconstituted as the USSR. This was the period of the "flourishing of nations" where pluralism was to lead to gradual assimilation without coercion. The economy was largely operationally decentralized, with regional economic councils (*Sovnarkhozy*) responsible for most economic activity, including price control, most wholesale trade, and the coordination of the activities of nationalized firms, the syndicates, and newly formed trusts (most of the "commanding heights"). Only macroeconomic planning, state finance, industry of strategic (military) importance, transportation, and communications were directly run from the center, leaving most economic activity in the hands of local activists and national cadre. The overwhelmingly private agricultural sector was also naturally in the hands of the local ethnic group. As a period of recovery, with most effort directed toward the restoration of previous economic activity, this decentralization and local economic empowerment defused much of the economic input into ethnic tensions; each group could pursue its own economic advancement with visible success.

This decentralization gradually faded in the second half of the 1920s as the Supreme Council of the National Economy (*VSNKh*) assumed more control over the increasingly monopolized industrial sector. Then it rather abruptly ended with Stalin's "Great Socialist Offensive" of collectivization and the First Five Year Plan (FYP), which overshadowed all nationality considerations. This involved "industrialization" of the workers, "proletarianization" of the peasantry, and massive construction and production solely for the sake of industrialization, regardless of the consequences for individuals or groups. Together with a dramatic increase in the centralization of economic authority, depriving national groups of any independent economic base, Stalin engaged in a war against the nationalities, as against all other autonomous (of the state) socioeconomic-political institutions, as part of the collectivization drive and struggle with "class enemies" and "foreign agents." The Ukrainian and Central Asian Republics were particularly affected. Accompanying and following this "restructuring" through the use of arbitrary force, famine, and terror, the "high Stalinist period" (1935–53) was marked by accelerated acculturation and assimilation, the "denationalization of cadre," and a policy of ethnic dilution aimed at creating new socialist supranationals.

This was also the dramatic period in which the Soviet economic system as we know it was formed, its basic structure and principles of functioning worked out. This "command-administered" economic system preserved the forms of the Leninist solution to the national question in its hierarchical structure, while depriving them of most economic influence or meaning. All real economic decision-making became focused in the branch and functional ministries (until 1946, People's Commissariats—*Narkomy*) in Moscow, with the ministers directly and personally subordinate to Stalin. Along with the destruction of civil society, all autonomous economic regulators and all intermediating horizontal structures were supplanted or destroyed.

Regional (national/ethnic) economic units were held responsible for territorial planning and coordination and for the implementation of all plans and directives from above, but were not granted any independent control over resource flows or uses. Indeed, territorial planning became largely a formality, an ex-post rationalization, of decisions made on other grounds. Though local and regional authorities could lobby for resources or changes in decisions, and could represent their regions in the negotiations involved in all planning and plan implementation, they were forced to accept central (ministerial) decisions and implement them as if their own, justifying them to their own populations as both necessary and desirable. Thus, while economic equality remained an official goal, it became one to be pursued only when and how the center saw fit; the limited economic autonomy, in terms of decision-making and control over economic activity, that the national groups had previously enjoyed was now reduced to a fiction. The goal of economic equality could still be appealed to, and was, in arguing for or against policies that affected the national regions, but the central authorities made the final decisions regarding the formulation and implementation of those policies.

After Stalin's death, the collective leadership moved to reverse the "excesses" of Stalin's assimilation policy, allowing greater pluralism in the cultural sphere. However, Khrushchev soon returned to a somewhat milder version, consonant with his major modernization and expansion drives in construction, heavy industry (e.g., "chemicalization"), and agriculture. These policies were carried out through massive central campaigns, with local initiative relegated to implementation and the generation of enthusiasm. These also fostered "russification" by bringing large numbers of Russian "specialists" and "mature cadre" into national regions.[9] Further, an education reform in 1957 began a long period of the systematic russification of education. This coincided with the beginning of growing pressure for the "drawing together" (*sblizhenie*) and "merging" (*sliianie*) of nationalities, culminating in the claim in the 1961 Party Program that the "national question" had been resolved according to the Leninist formula. The remaining superficial manifestations of nationalism, it was believed, would surely fade with the coming of communism shortly after overtaking the advanced capitalist states in the 1980s.

However, in the economic sphere a step was taken that increased the importance of many national regions, and the leadership of some nationality groups. This was the decentralizing, *Sovnarkhoz,* economic reform of 1957 that abolished most economic ministries and placed most operational economic decisions, in particular those affecting standards of living, in the hands of 105 Regional Economic Councils *(Sovnarkhozy).* These economic regions fell within Republic boundaries, though the large Republics had more than one economic region, somewhat dissipating the influence of the national republic leadership. Thus the role of the Republics was somewhat degraded, particularly in planning, although more local political units, indeed often more dominated by the local national group, attained greater economic power— a clearly unintended consequence of the reform.

From an economic perspective, this radical reform addressed a severe, inevitable tension that arises in any centralized, hierarchically administered economic structure or system—it must choose between conflicting principles of organization of centralized planning and control through the necessary hierarchy. Two primary competing principles, each with its own logic and shortcomings, have clashed throughout Soviet economic history: branch/functional and territorial.[10] The first has predominated as more consistent with thorough central control. Branch organization of planning and administration facilitates control over production activities, over the creation of physical product, and over wealth. It simplifies both planning and administration by providing for a simple clearcut interface between organizations and activities, clarifying the central tasks of coordination of the interaction among subordinates. This principle leads to a focus on gross physical indicators of performance as necessary to central coordination and allows some decentralization in secondary, functionally dependent, areas that depend on the outputs of centrally controlled production. This focus, however, naturally leads to the distortions of "departmentalism" *(vedomstvennost')*—empire building and organizational aggrandizement with insufficient attention paid to the needs of the rest of the system; the center alone is responsible for those consequences and for interbranch coordination.

The second, territorial, principle was fully implemented for the first time in these reforms.[11] While better addressing many, in particular local, economic objectives and needs, this organizational principle renders the overall economy, and particularly its production structure, much more difficult to control. Territorial regions are vastly more complex as objects of planning and have many more significant objectives than production branches, with their relatively homogeneous technologies, processes, and products. They have a natural tendency to focus on production for local needs at the expense of central development projects and interregional resource needs. Thus this organizational principle is supportive of local industry and agriculture rather than functional integration of the system. Adopting the terrritorial principle moves critical decisions closer to consumers and thus provides a focus on consumption and standard-of-living issues. This leads inexorably to the (centrally defined) sin of "localism" (*mestnichestvo*) which, in the absence of automatic autonomous integrators, i.e., the market, is destructive of the system's cohesion and the maintenance of central power. The logic of the "Soviet economic model" thus militates against this principle, despite some of its natural attractions, rendering it increasingly nonviable in that environment.

The disadvantages and dysfunctions, from the central perspective, of this radical decentralization soon led to a gradual recentralization. In 1960, those Republics with multiple economic regions regained some influence with the establishment of a Republic Economic Council (*Sovnarkhoz*) to coordinate the planning and activities of intrarepublic *Sovnarkhozy*. This power, however, was soon attenuated in the reorganization and recentralization that transferred more economic authority to existing and reconstituted central organs and amalgamated the over 100 *Sovnarkhozy* into 47 in 1963, under a new central Supreme Council (*VSNKh*).[12] This again brought the national component of, and influence on, economic structure close to a mere formality, though it was still greater than under the Stalinist ministerial system.

It took the overthrow of Khrushchev to fully re-create the structure and functioning of the Stalinist economic system, although this time without the driving and motivating force of terror. Brezhnev reunited the Party and oversaw a reform that both centralized and decentralized control over economic activity. The Stalinist ministerial system was re-created, with most ministries becoming All-Union rather than Union-Republic, and economic planning was recentralized under a reconstituted State Planning Committee (*GOSPLAN*), while the territorial organization of the *Sovnarkhozy* supply system was retained but centralized under a new State Committee, *GOSSNAB*. On the other hand, more input into planning and greater latitude in the implementation of plans were granted to enterprises. Although dual subordination was maintained in the Union-Republic structures of much industry, intermediate territorial organs were thus effectively cut out, and input of the national groups effectively reduced to a minimum.

The reform was accompanied by much exhortation to undertake territorial planning and to integrate it with sectoral/branch plans, and for the comprehensive and integrated development of the regions, but local units were given no real decision-making autonomy or control over resources.[13] In addition, territorial planning was divorced from the nationalities by the creation of nineteen economic regions, amalgamating national units along lines of "economic rationality" rather than traditional ethnic ties. The influence of the Republics and regions was further undercut in the 1971 reorganization, introducing industrial and production associations (*ob'edinenie*) as intermediate administrative levels in the economic hierarchy, frequently cutting across both regional and national lines. Brezhnev thus finished building the massive economic structure of Stalin, one antithetical to nationality, and ultimately to any local, interests. Thus the nationalities were almost completely cut off from formal influence over the structure of the economy and of economic activity.

On the other hand, the Brezhnev era took a step back from accelerated cultural assimilation and struck a more equitable balance between "drawing together" and "flourishing," with an increase in the number of showcase national cadre. There was a greater devolution of responsibility in the political, social, and cultural spheres to local and regional Party organizations, allowing virtual satrapies to arise. The "national question" was rediscovered, but elided with stability, patronage, corruption, and the dissipation of true central control. Operative "national interests" came to be determined by national elites more interested in themselves than the nationality, but protected by their national identity. These national Party organizations further garnered some, unofficial but real, economic influence through corruption and the rise of locally based "shadow" economies, necessary and natural lubricants for the hypertrophied economic structure, thus counteracting some of the nationality impact of the reformed economic system. These "shadow economies" grew particularly strong on the fringes of the empire, far from the attention, or indeed interest, of the central authorities, and frequently under the protection of the local national apparatus. Hence they carried a strong national coloration, frequently with "nationalist" overtones, generating noticeable regional diversity particularly with regard to the consumer economy.[14] They also led to certain ethnic frictions as some groups, particularly Caucasians, came to be associated with officially proscribed and more generally censured activities. Thus corruption, the shadow economy, and "national tradition" arose as autonomous economic regulators modifying the impact of the recentralized system, though ones easily turned to the particular (private) interests of the national elites.

Consequently, despite the purported resolution of "the national question," new national questions were soon discovered under "mature socialism," requiring a renewed push toward assimilation. Investment and subsidization were specifically targeted toward economic equalization, and interrepublic migration was encouraged and indeed sometimes financially rewarded with higher income scales.[15] Steps were taken to continue the Khrushchevian Russification of education and of political and economic life, as can be seen in the language provisions of the 1977 constitution. Finally, on reaching "developed Socialism," the goal of economic equality among regions was apparently dropped in favor of "the need to insure the utmost efficiency of the whole economy," reflecting a growing recognition of increasing economic difficulties. Indeed, by the end of the 1970s, the whole question of regional economic development had been eclipsed by the need to maintain any economic forward momentum. Thus the period was characterized by a fading of the role of the Republics and national units in the economy, coupled with a growing economic gridlock: production was increasingly undertaken solely for its own sake without real final use value for the output.[16] As now recognized, economic stagnation set in, making overall economic growth a much higher priority than regional development, never mind equalization.

An interregnum then began around 1979–80, spanning the regimes of the largely incapacitated Brezhnev, the ailing Andropov, and the fading Chernenko and ending only in 1985 with the accession of Mikhail Gorbachev. This period saw a continuation of the preceding policies in most spheres, including national relations, together with some economic experimentation to address growing economic problems and an anti-corruption drive largely aimed at national "mafias." Gorbachev, however, inaugurated a qualitatively new period. He wrought radical changes in the social, political, and even (though to a lesser degree) economic spheres, with a resulting dramatic impact on the "national question" and issues of ethnic status and relations in the Soviet Union. It is an impact that he failed to fully appreciate, at least before mid-1989. Indeed, by the beginning of 1991 the possibility of national disintegration had become a real issue, leading to the abortive coup of August and the consequent collapse of the preceding Union and the following December.

The National Question and Economic Structure

This longstanding historical interaction between the national question and the economy had a deep impact on both. Most directly, nationalities have had an influence on economic structure through policies pursued to ameliorate, and eventually eliminate, the "national question." The "Leninist" policy of "equalization" in order to remove the material basis for national animosity and distrust had an impact on investment and regional development projects, particularly in the 1950s, 1960s, and early 1970s. Less developed regions, e.g., Central Asia, received a larger than proportional share of investment resources and were systematically subsidized in terms of the allocation of other central resources.[17] Direct subsidization of incomes in underdeveloped and climatically harsh regions was also a part of the policy mix influenced by considerations of the national question. Finally, a number of these regions were favored with comprehensive regional development projects, although ones largely based on a focused demand for resources by the rest of the economy.[18] However, the results of these equalization efforts were mixed, particularly with regard to the titular nationalities in each national territory. Much effort has gone into the development of the backward regions of the RSFSR, often aiding Slavs as well as the other nationalities there, and most of it has yielded highly unbalanced, even destructive, industrial expansion—for reasons to be discussed below. Thus the transfer of resources was less than fully effective, while penalizing, at least on paper, some Republic titular nationalities that were above average in terms of economic welfare.

The policy emphasis on equalizing development, together with that on rapid industrialization, also had a direct impact on the national composition of the regions. In 1991, in two of the fourteen non-Russian SSRs, the titular nationality formed less than 50 percent of the population, in no SSR was it greater than 90 percent, and on average less than two-thirds of the population was of the titular nationality, while in 12 of 16 ASSRs of the RSFSR the titular nationality was less than 50 percent of the population. Industrialization, and the shifting of industry eastward, largely for strategic reasons before and during the war, brought massive Russian in-migration to national territories, while native out-migration was encouraged to meet growing labor needs in other parts of the country, especially the eastern RSFSR (Siberia).[19]

Kazakhstan was similarly affected by an influx of Russians and Ukrainians during the "Virgin Lands" agricultural expansion. Further, collectivization had a role in crushing Ukrainian and Central Asian national resistance, and hence was partly derived from Stalinist national policy. Thus this policy, which had such a great impact on the structure and performance of the economy, was in part a response to nationalisms perceived to be a threat to the unitary socialist state. Finally, massive national (e.g., Baltic, German, Crimean Tatar) deportations, particularly from western portions of the USSR, left a natural impact on the structure of the labor force, and hence on the economic development, of those regions as well as the Siberian, Far Eastern, and Central Asian destinations.

The national question also had an impact on the structure of the economy through the practice of regional economic planning, partly a derivative of the Leninist nationality policy. During the period of their greatest impact the *Sovnarkhozy* actively planned and implemented the allocation of resources, to the great advantage of the local and consumer economies, if frequently contrary to central desires and even economic rationality (the sin of *mestnichestvo*). At other times, regional planning was largely subsequent, and subservient, to sectoral planning, and hence generally lacked the ability to command resources for the pursuit of regional interests; territorial leaders could only argue as supplicants, and only in terms of higher central objectives, e.g., Leninist equalization. At all times, however, regional and local (national) Party organs have coopted and/or extorted resources, especially labor, from centrally run industry on their territory, to meet immediate economic needs, such as for roads, sewage and other construction, and seasonal agricultural input. Finally, at the central level at least some attention was given to regional economic planning, with Republic *GOSPLANs* playing an important role, in deference to considerations of national policy and the growing together of the Soviet peoples.[20] This provided a major channel for the articulation of the needs and desires of at least the titular national groups. Their expressed preferences were, at least to some degree, reflected in the economic plans and programs pursued by the Ministerial hierarchy, and thus had some impact on the resulting economic structure.

The influence of the national question on economic structure, while clearly recognizable, seems far less than the opposite impact of the economic structure on the national question. By the nature of the economic system, that structure imposed severe requirements on the policies pursued to ameliorate nationality problems. They had to be consistent with All-Union development plans, and, more importantly, consistent with and indeed derivative of branch (ministerial) production and development plans. This implies a conceptual uniformity, allowing only weak regional/national differentiation, imposed through uniform central planning guidelines and norms. Further, the policies had to be hierarchically structured and simple enough in detail to be plannable and implementable. The logic of the system all but ensured that they would be implemented on a massive scale, exploiting all perceived (and frequently imagined) economies of scale, and economically rational only according to the peculiar logic of Soviet-type socialism.[21] Finally, they had to be quantity, rather than quality, oriented; outcomes had to be physically observable and measurable, so that inputs were frequently measured in their place. These characteristics were the natural consequences of the complexity and uncertainty of the tasks facing the Soviet leadership and their planners, and the inherent bounded rationality of any and all decisionmakers in tackling those tasks.

Centralized directive planning and command administration of plans posed a well nigh impossible decision and coordination problem, one that required hierarchical subdivision and severe compartmentalization even to approximately formulate and begin to solve. In the attempt to resolve complexity at the center, artificial uniformities were imposed, for example in planning norms, that ignored all differences but those few that could be centrally managed. Further, the issue of choice of principle of organization—branch vs. territorial—inevitably arose, and was, for the reasons discussed above, ultimately resolved in favor of the branch principle. Such planning was also incompatible with any decentralized measure of equivalent value or "bearer of options"; all options had to be reserved to the central authorities and their hierarchical subordinates. Thus there could be no real money—no generalized anonymous command over goods, services, and re-sources—and prices became largely irrelevant to resource allocation and production decisions. Based on information about feasibility re-ported from below, objectives were chosen above, suballocated through the hierarchy, and implemented by subordinates to the best of their ability, subject to the closest possible monitoring by agents of the central authorities. To maintain even a semblance of coordination and aggregate balance it was necessary that unauthorized initiative be excluded (*initsiativa nakazuema!*); unplanned (uncommanded) initia-tive is merely disruptive of the planned order. The problem was further aggravated by the fact that subordinates, both functional and regional, had interests often widely divergent from those of the central authorities, whose objectives drove the system. Thus self-interested behavior further distorted both the information provided by subordi-nates in the economic and territorial hierarchy and their actions taken in order to implement central policies, plans, and programs.

However, only a small portion of economic activity could be ac-tually planned; the detail and complexity of the real economy was just too vast. Thus only "important," priority matters were properly taken care of, while most economic activity was left to make do with re-sources left as a residual from priority activities. Similarly, many of the details of implementation, even in priority spheres, were left to self-interested agents, acting beyond the ken of the central authorities. For technical reasons, closely related to the perceived advantages of branch over territorial organizational principles, this "residual principle" most directly affected those parts of the economy that did not have a direct technological feedback into the production cycle: foods, consumer goods and services. These sectors involving, as they did, an interface with the non-state agents were also the most structurally complex and subject to random disturbances and uncertainty. Thus they remained an afterthought to the seriously overburdened bureaucracy of the economic hierarchy, and the most fertile ground for the flourishing of "national" second economies.

The functioning and structure of this system had a major impact on the implementation of nationality policy and the well-being of the various Soviet nationalities. While input flows (e.g., industrial invest-ment, infrastructure construction, income and consumption subsidies) were generally greater into the less developed national regions, they generated highly uneven development within those regions despite some leveling of interregional disparities.[22] Production sectors, related to the resource needs of the whole economy, grew rapidly, expanding industrial labor and raising incomes. Though this exerted some pull on infrastructure development, the latter lagged far behind, as did all areas of consumer goods and services. Even areas with a specialization in consumer goods production, such as Estonia, found the development of those sectors isolated from the general development of their economies and tightly integrated with upstream suppliers and downstream distributors outside the region.[23]

Indeed, the nature of the system and the structure of the economy at best fostered branch/sectoral integration of economic activity, and seriously impeded regional integration, despite the best of intentions. This resulted in massive loss in transportation, massive waste of resources, the replication of an unbalanced structure of production throughout the country, and the growth of corruption and shadow economies to smooth over consequent dislocations and disruption. It also had the natural consequence of regional/local autarky with respect to the supply of food and primary consumer goods, as its central coordination involved more detail than the system could handle. The logic of the system was one of branch/ministerial aggrandizement, where development was largely driven by resource availability and abstract, planned All-Union demand, without consideration of opportunity costs or real demand, or indeed the interests of impacted national or ethnic groups.

The problem was aggravated by the inherent, to the economic structure, absence of real money (generalized anonymous command over goods and services) and real prices (marginal valuations). A natural consequence of that lack of proper valuation is ubiquitous unbalanced exchange; implicit, unmeasured subsidization and confiscation necessarily takes place, generating the perception of intentional national exploitation. A further consequence is the opening of vast opportunities for corruption, speculation, and black market exchange. That absence also hides the true economic situation from decision makers in the economic hierarchy, distorting the information on which decisions must be based and obscuring the consequences of those decisions, even beyond the distortions introduced by the self-interested behavior of hierarchical subordinates. Thus decisions were naturally taken without consideration of most essential details of the local situation, often with tragic consequences for the local population.[24]

The consequences were ubiquitous imbalances, irrationalities, and lack of complementarities in the economic activity of all regions, both generating and aggravating ethnic national animosities. Massive projects, undertaken without local consultation or consent, resulted in the uprooting of native groups and ways of life. This is seen most clearly in major water projects (dams and irrigation systems, e.g., Nurek and Aral areas) and the building of major industrial complexes around some natural resource (mineral or fuel, e.g., Karaganda and Tyumen regions). It can also be seen in those massive projects, such as Siberian river diversion, desired by some local national leaderships as supposedly benefiting them, while the costs were to be borne elsewhere. A typical major imbalance that the structure of the economy generated was that between production activity and the social infrastructure necessary to support the work force. This led to serious imbalances in the quasi-markets that the Soviet economic structure allowed: labor, and consumers' goods and services. Indeed, wages were growing rapidly while desirable consumers' goods and almost all consumers' services were conspicuous by their absence. This lack of attention to consumers' goods and services, in a system where only central attention generated real results, led to an only slowly growing, and ultimately—stagnant, standard of living and a rising level of frustration among all Soviet peoples with their situation. By 1990 stagnation had turned into an accelerating decline and the frustration burst into the open, as central economic authority and effectiveness crumbled under a perestroika that failed to provide new economic mechanisms to replace them.

That frustration was only aggravated by the unbalanced, industrial-production nature of the economic growth generated by the Soviet economic structure. In addition, this industrial orientation meant the importation of "qualified" outside cadre to run technology, particularly, though not exclusively, in the less developed regions. Both the stagnant or falling standard of living and the introduction of an alien work force in national regions, natural consequences of the logic and structure of the traditional Soviet economic system, were quite conducive to ethnic hostility. Finally, the logic of the economic system generated massive external environmental, as well as population and infrastructure, impacts on the regions affected by development decisions. As they were blinkered by the hierarchical structure and blinded by distorted valuations, as well as distorted information supplied by self-interested subordinates, economic decisionmakers necessarily ignored all impacts but those considered and desired by central superiors. The consequences were tragic for the environment, and were perceived as intentional by nationalistic local groups, thereby seriously complicating the formulation and implementation of any national policy. Thus the structure of the Soviet economy had a major, and overwhelmingly negative, impact on the "national question," one that swamped the Leninist policy solution to that problem. The difficult national situation that brought an end to the Soviet Union was to a significant extent the fruit of this economic implementation of Soviet Socialism.

Gorbachev's National Problem and Policy Response

Under Gorbachev the national question burst forth with a vengeance. Beginning with the Alma-Ata riots in December 1986, Gorbachev faced a crescendo of national unrest, from ever more strident complaints of discrimination and assertions of national identity, to demands for true national autonomy and independence from the USSR, to bloody ethnic pogroms. The Crimean Tatars protested their expulsion from the Crimea, the Baltic republics protested their annexation in 1940 and demanded full independence, the Armenians protested Azerbaijani control over their nationals in Nagorno-Karabakh, Azerbaijanis slaughtered Armenians in Sumgait, and both killed each other in ongoing violence only weakly contained by the presence of military forces. Uzbeks slaughtered and forced evacuation of Meskhetians, Uzbeks and Tajiks fought over land and housing around Osh, the Abkhazians demanded autonomy from Georgia, as did Gagauz from Moldova, while Georgians and Moldovans jointed Armenia in demanding greater Republic autonomy, and even independence. Troops gassed demonstrators in Tbilisi, and national fronts, formed to maintain political force and momentum in each of the western Republics, were then emulated in the southern tier of Republics, and countered by the formation of opposing, largely Russian, "international" movements.

By the end of July 1989, Gorbachev was pleading for calm and warning of the dangers to perestroika, and indeed to the existence of the Soviet Union, from national unrest, and the Supreme Soviet approved sweeping plans for economic autonomy in the Baltic republics, though some enabling legislation stalled in part due to Baltic intransigence.[25] Meanwhile the Baltic republics forged ahead with the "desocialization" of the local and agricultural economies, and the imposition of language and residency requirements for full citizenship in the Republic, generating strikes by Russian workers and a legal impasse with the central authorities over the constitutionality of such requirements.

By 1990, the situation had apparently moved beyond any control, with national conflict and ethnic strife evident in virtually every part of the Union. In March 1990, as Gorbachev moved to acquire sweeping new powers as President of the USSR, Lithuania declared independence and began passing laws to implement that decision. Local elections began to empower national fronts and parties in legislatures, Gorbachev tried to force Lithuania back into the fold with an economic, in particular energy, embargo, and Boris Yeltsin led the Russian Republic (RSFSR) in breaking that blockade. Nationalism had suddenly reappeared as a strong political force, driven by, yet also driving, the vast changes associated with perestroika, glasnost, and *demokratizatsiia*. By mid-1990 nationalism had acquired a sweeping force and logic of its own, pushing each group in the direction of independence from the Soviet Union and rejection of everything Soviet, including perestroika. The process was most advanced in the Baltic Republics, although all of the other Union Republics including the RSFSR had already declared their sovereignty and autonomy, if still within the Union, by early 1991. Even the RSFSR was subject to pressures of disintegration, and there appeared the real possibility of the Union degenerating into a loose confederation, or even dissolving altogether, as proved to be the case.

The reason seems to lie in a number of factors, including the rise of nationalism and dearth of alternative ideologies, the opportunities presented by the loosening of central political and social controls, and the growing hardships and accumulated grievances associated with an increasingly difficult economic situation. Marxism-Leninism died intellectually and spiritually, national identity was enshrined in the administrative and economic structure, the Leninist-Stalinist policies of equalization and assimilation failed to achieve their ambitious goals, and the economy was a conspicuous failure in generating the "material basis for communism," succeeding only in despoiling regions and localities in the pursuit of industrial and military prowess. And even that prowess crumbled in the accelerating collapse of the economy in

1991. Further, the pursuit of material wellbeing was politicized and centralized by the economic structure, rendering all outcomes "their" responsibility and all problems and slights "someone's" fault. The "nation" thus became the prime source of support and identity, a rallying point and source of strength for the defense of one's interests. National traditions and "otherness," in particular the differences from other nationalities and the wrongs suffered, or perceived to be, at their hands, became major factors of local cohesion, and provided orientation for political demands and action. Economic outcomes adverse to ethnic interests, and particularly those outcomes caused by others, became an important part of national identity and a strong unifying factor.

In such an environment, the economic, environmental, and social distortions that are inherent to centralized planning and command administration of an economy have a particularly strong and dangerous impact. Each national group feels itself helpless and exploited in the interests of others, often with justification, and none more so than those initially more economically developed. Each finds its resources, including human, and ecology misused in the pursuit of distant or worthless goals, and its identity trampled, indeed imperiled, by economic integration and decisions taken in all-Union interest. That is particularly the case within the economic structure, where the nature of the system imposes a disregard for local and regional factors, an emphasis on functional and branch requirements, a priority on massive indiscriminate projects, and a concentration on inputs rather than final economic results. As a consequence, investment aimed at equalizing levels of development is largely unrelated to true local needs, frequently abusive of resources and the natural environment, and destructive of local culture and traditions. The structure of the Soviet economy thus led even well intentioned policies to further aggravate national tensions.

The rebirth of national passion, inflamed if not solely generated by Soviet economic structure, initially raised two major sets of economic issues, both related to a perception of economic discrimination and exploitation. The first related to the continuing regional and ethnic disparities in income level and standard of living.[26] While a natural situation throughout the world, it is politically explosive in a system where the central political authorities have declared its elimination a major objective, presumably have the authority and power to implement that objective, yet are backing away from the objective after very little progress toward its achievement. Further it raises a host of issues under the rubric of "equivalent exchange." Someone must be paying for the "equalizing" transfers of resources and hence is, arguably, being exploited, as can be seen in the incessant Soviet national polemics around "who is subsidizing whom."[27]

The economic system, by systematically distorting valuations (prices), allowed a plausible argument to be made by each and every national group; even Uzbeks and Yakuts were subsidizing others by providing their products (cotton and oil) at prices well below their true value. The problem was aggravated by the inherently unbalanced development fostered by the branch/functional economic structure of the Soviet Union, and even more so by planners' adoption of an arbitrary "standard of comparative return" when they had virtually no way of comparing the real returns from alternative development projects. It was further aggravated by economic stringency, by the lack of additional real output to distribute among the nationalities, which undermined the modest degree of achieved equalization and created an impression of regression.

The second set of issues was that of territorial, and hence (in the Soviet structure) national/ethnic, economic rights. Discussion of these issues revolves around the concept of regional and/or Republic autonomy, self-financing, and full cost-accounting (*khozraschet*). At stake was the right to effectively control the Republic/regional economy and its natural and human resources, and to have at least a significant influence over central planning, investment, and development decisions as they related to the region. Claims, however, evolved rapidly throughout 1989, as central political authority and economic performance both deteriorated, becoming extremely radical. Indeed, by late 1990 the moderate nationalist goal became the virtual elimination of central planning and allocation, devolving all property and decision-making power to the Republic and local levels, while more radical nationalist elements aspired to, and ultimately succeeded in achieving, full national independence.

The demand for enhanced territorial economic rights addressed at least three longstanding economic grievances. The first is that central controls and sectoral plans distorted the quality of life and destroyed the environment, as they were largely carried out independently of local conditions and local needs. Indeed, environmental issues became a ubiquitous political mobilization source, for Russians in the RSFSR as well as other nationalities in their Republics. Second, they involved a massive misuse of local resources, most particularly in irrational and costly crop priorities, such as the substitution of cotton for fruit and vegetables in Central Asia. This is particularly important in view of the role that land and the traditional peasantry play in determining national identity. Finally, the territorial planning that was done, often in an attempt to ameliorate the negative consequences of central development plans, was unsupported by resources (even local resources were largely centrally controlled) or even timely and accurate information on central intentions and changes in central plans. These led to nationalist calls for radical decentralization of economic authority and control, giving the nationalities control over their own economic destinies, and ultimately independence.

These issues, of course, did not arise entirely spontaneously. Though the problems were real, they had long festered in silence, and might have continued to do so still longer, were it not for the dramatic changes introduced by Gorbachev in almost all spheres of Soviet life. Glasnost threw open the door to virtually any criticism and permitted the discussion of virtually any problem, allowing repressed national discontent to burst forth. *Demokratizatsiia* permitted and even (indirectly) encouraged the formation of national interest and political pressure groups, and indeed began to politically empower them at the local and Republic levels. And *ekonomicheskaia perestroika* legitimized radical decentralization, self-financing, local economic control, "socialist markets," alternative (largely cooperative) property forms, and limited private initiative and economic activity. Further, the increasingly evident failure of this economic perestroika spawned still further radicalization, delegitimizing most central economic control and action, and further legitimizing local and private forms of property, enterprise, and initiative. All of these fit nicely with, and indeed supported, the reborn nationalist agenda of the more active groups.

Gorbachev had been attempting to use this apparent coincidence of interests in order to restructure and modernize the overall Soviet economy, but evidently lost control of the process. He had admitted, initially only indirectly, the failure of the economic system and its justifying ideology: traditional Soviet socialism is bankrupt in deed, and is now overwhelmingly recognized to be so in word. Thus he legitimized the search for alternative economic structures, while removing the main ideological alternative to nationalism. Radical nationalist forces in the most advanced regions seized upon this, first declaring their wholehearted support for perestroika and striving to redefine it in ever more radical, and increasingly less socialist, terms, and finally moved beyond it altogether. Gorbachev, on the other hand, had attempted to channel, to redirect and focus, this nationalism to the end of rapid, yet still socialist, economic reform. He had hoped that it would provide a potentially useful and inspiring ideology for the revival of the economy, for the resuscitation of a moribund economic structure and system. Yet national sentiments developed their own logic and dynamic, bursting through the bounds of perestroika and destroying the system rather than reviving it.

One relevant aspect of Gorbachev's program, at least initially, was the apparent policy of using national regions, in particular the small Baltic Republics, as "'laboratories of perestroika." Thus territorial decentralization was at the heart of his economic reform, establishing regional economic rights and responsibilities, thereby "harmonizing" interethnic relations. This involved acceding to many of the nationalist demands for economic autonomy within an all-Union economic structure, while insisting that the Republics and local governments must accept much greater responsibility for final results not only in the economic but in the social sphere as well. Some steps were taken to place certain national regions, starting with the Baltic Republics, on *khozraschet* and full self-financing. This was to have involved dramatically reduced central planning and direction, greater freedom to introduce markets and to rely on market interactions to generate and guide economic activity, and new latitude to encourage private and cooperative initiative. On the other hand, all regions would have to rely more on their own resources to meet social and economic needs as the center cut back on its role in investment and subsidization under that stage of perestroika. Thus Gorbachev's program in that period involved shifting the burden of responsibility for meeting the needs of society to the Republic and local level, together with some devolution of authority to manage the regional economy to those levels.

That policy has, of course, now totally collapsed. Yet even in the best of circumstances it could have gone only part of the way toward alleviating those nationality problems aggravated by the traditional Soviet economic structure. Greater local control associated with even limited economic autonomy and self-financing might have helped to reduce national feelings of alienation and exploitation had it been consistently pursued early enough. The dominance of industrial branch interests could have been reduced, if not eliminated, and significantly greater consideration of regional differences and local conditions should have entered production and development decisions. Thus there might have been fewer negative externalities induced by the hierarchical structure, particularly with respect to environmental issues. Even central policies and projects, to the extent that they were to be subject to Republic/local approval, might have been subject to more sophisticated, detailed implementation by local authorities.

Further, this limited decentralization could have helped counter the "residual principle" in planning and providing consumer goods and services. Local and regional governments (Soviets) subject to direct popular influence, if not control, should have become much more responsive to the needs of their populations. And local initiative could have taken the reform much further, even within an all-Union framework. The emphasis on fostering real markets in, for example, the Estonian proposals for Republic *khozraschet* could have gone a long way toward ending gross disproportions, particularly in consumer markets, and toward ensuring that improvement in quality became a real objective. Indeed, by allowing further economic decentralization and experimentation through markets, Gorbachev's policy hoped to allow the more progressive Republics to become true laboratories of perestroika, searching for the elusive "socialist market."[28]

However, in other respects, Gorbachev's policies only amounted to throwing fuel on smoldering embers. Republic/regional *khozraschet,* even when relations with the center were governed by stable normatives, gives a clearer idea of the costs and benefits deriving from central decisions, aggravating inter-Republic tensions. Indeed, as Republics and national groups began contemplating the prospect in late 1989, the debate over who is subsidizing/exploiting whom grew quite heated. It was further aggravated by the prospect of an intensified struggle over resources, and growing regional inequities, as the center cut its investment and subsidies.

In 1990, beginning with the Lithuanian declaration of independence, Republics and localities, such as Leningrad and Moscow, began to take protectionist measures in order to avoid losses to other regions. By mid-year it was clear that Gorbachev's policy was crumbling; economic deterioration accelerated rapidly, the central authorities and administrative organs were being regularly if not uniformly ignored, and the blockade of Lithuania was on the verge of being destroyed by independent action (special trade deals) of Yeltsin's Russian Republic. The Baltics, Ukraine, Russia, and even some Central Asian republics were demanding that reforms go much farther than Gorbachev's perestroika theretofore had envisioned. The idea of an acceptable reform had moved well beyond economic decentralization to full Republic economic autonomy and potentially thorough marketization of economic interaction, at least between Republics, with the center retaining only limited delegated powers. This was the vision of Yeltsin's dramatic "500-day" plan for transition to a market economy that in late summer 1990 had captured the imagination of radical reformers and non-independence minded nationalists across the Soviet Union.

That Gorbachev's vision of moderate decentralization within a centrally directed union should have failed is hardly surprising from an economic perspective. Local responsibility without sufficient command over resources naturally led, in the absence of constraining political pressure, to local protectionism and hence threatened any gains made toward regional equalization. Decentralization, particularly with respect to the allocation of consumer goods, in an environment of general imbalance and deficit, only aggravated availability problems of areas not directly controlling production, and hence fostered even greater local protectionism. Thus a "dual economy" began to form, with a privileged dominant ethnic group and regional residents isolated by a complex supply interface from the rest of the Soviet economy. Apparent ethnic exclusivity with respect to desired consumables generated even greater ethnic conflict and demands for still greater subdivision of autonomy, as more ethnic groups asserted their right to exclusive control over desirable economic activity and output. Thus, for example, Russian districts demanded autonomy within Estonia and Moldova, Tyumen claimed mineral and energy resources in the RSFSR and the Tatar ASSR proclaimed sovereignty and economic autonomy within the RSFSR. As Donna Bahry has noted, "more radical territorial decentralization raises the prospect of a society in which ethnic/linguistic cleavages and economic inequalities coincide ever more closely—making both more difficult to manage in a new and more open political environment."[29] Indeed, 1991 saw the breakdown of the ability to manage either.

These problems were accentuated by the fact that, in Gorbachev's vision, decentralization was intended to hold only with respect to implementation; regions were still to be held responsible for centrally desired outcomes. As the decentralization of control was not to be complete, the responsibility of the central authorities and their implementing hierarchy for the regional economy's problems only became clearer; the economic structure still highlighted national regions and their subservience to the whole. The greater economic responsibility placed on Republics and national regions, together with increasingly limited central resources allocated to them, only increased demands for regional authority to deal with their increased responsibilities. That demand for economic power carried inevitable political consequences, particularly in the existing environment of heightened national consciousness. Economic responsibility implied a push for political responsibility—for autonomy, which, coupled with strong nationalist and irredentist feelings, proved explosive. There was also an economic danger that such decentralization would merely trade one set of bureaucratic masters, the central Russian authorities, for another, the regional dominant ethnic group authorities, eliminating many of the advantages of true economic decentralization. Territorial autonomy and self-sufficiency without true markets and prices only fostered the misuse of scarce resources.

This type of moderate economic reform also vastly complicates, as well as expands, local tasks, particularly during its formative period. There was natural confusion over relative planning roles and the formulation of guiding normatives, reflected in the economic problems of 1990–91. The center lost much control over state revenues, yet the income sources of the Republics and regions were only vaguely defined, and were still subject to manipulation by enterprises outside of local control. Further, all-Union enterprises and their central superiors failed to cooperate in providing necessary information for local planning and for implementing local plans. This generated ever more insistent demands for greater, even full, local control over all industry, challenging control by the center over general economic development and culminating in the Baltic drive to full independence, the RSFSR's conclusion of bilateral economic agreements with most other Republics, and the takeover of all central economic activities by the Republics in the wake of the failure of the August coup.

In addition, attempting territorial decentralization within a centrally directed all-Union framework implied a less rigid, but also less manageable, system of local–center relations. It also implied more wrangling over "rules of the game" and other issues of economic interaction, such as industrial location, environmental protection, and trade flows. The onset of such wrangling became a major contributor to the gridlock in economic reform and the decay in economic performance in 1990–91. It also left the Republics in an inferior position, with the center attempting to play off one against the other. Hence they soon began looking for a way out, for true autonomy on the basis of equal negotiated exchange. When the failure of the coup presented such an opportunity, they all seized it.

Finally, the overall failure of the economy meant that there was less to go around, a lack of surplus to reallocate, while demands were strongly rising. That only accentuated regional/ethnic disparities, and led to claims that regional surpluses were "stolen," when in fact none had been created. Thus the impression was fostered that the center and its economic structure had pushed the economy into a deep hole, and were now demanding that the economically decentralized national regions pull the Soviet Union out. Leaving the Union thus increasingly appeared to be a more viable alternative, as even Russia, Kazakhstan, and Ukraine looked to break the power of the central authorities. Only after the total collapse of the center and the Union did economic considerations force the former Soviet Republics into a search for a looser economic union under the Commonwealth of Independent States (CIS).

Gorbachev's policies may also have been ethnically explosive since they seemed to contain, at least initially, clear ethnic biases. The Baltic Republics were allowed to go much further than others in taking control over their regional economies, though that could be because only they had asked so much, or perhaps in the hope that they would have failed for going too far. However, there also seemed to be greater acceptance of separatist feeling in the Baltic than in other regions, cadre changes there had favored Baltic nationalism, and religious tolerance seemed to be greater for the Baltic religions. Initial leadership changes in Central Asia, on the other hand, seemed to punish the titular nationalities, while religious policy no longer remained repressive of the Uniate Church and Islam.

The same dichotomy seemed to hold with respect to glasnost in national culture and revisionism in history, though everywhere there was much greater freedom. Baltic and Russian nationalisms seemed favored, as Gorbachev seemed to make concessions to nationalisms that improved the prospect of economic reforms, while remaining cool to the nationalism of others, such as Armenians, Abkhazians, Crimean Tatars, and the Central Asian peoples. Thus the rather dramatic changes in economic structure that Gorbachev proposed, while in many ways promising some improvement, were fraught with ethnic dangers. Indeed, this last aspect of Gorbachev's policies seems to have backfired. Gorbachev felt the need to crack down in the Baltic Republics, but then was forced to let them leave the union; Nagorno-Karabakh was first returned to Azerbaijan, and then again made autonomous; religious, cultural, and political freedoms developed an apparently unstoppable momentum of their own; and full economic independence had come to be expected by all.

The inconsistencies and contradictions in Gorbachev's policies outlined above only accelerated the largely autonomous national and political dynamic that drove the Soviet Union to destruction. In the wake of the August coup all pretense of central policy control collapsed. In every area of endeavor, including the "commanding heights" of the economy, former Republics (now new independent states), local governments, and newly unleashed autonomous social and political forces have taken the initiative and are determining the direction and pace of change. The greatest restraint on change now seems to be national political leaderships, particularly in the less economically developed former Republics, as they scramble to avoid the debris of the collapsing center and struggle to retain political control. Yet that leadership is under increasing attack from popular national forces unleashed by the policies of Gorbachev and the former central leadership, and arising in the chaos and violence facilitated by the collapse of effective central controls. Thus the national question is as great as it has ever been, and is indeed multiplied by the creation of new multinational states in the CIS. The economic policy response to it is now differentiated by states, complicated by new interstate relations, and still largely halting and uncertain, even if more radical in the increasingly extreme circumstances.

A Conclusion

Economic grievances of national minorities were not peculiar to the former Soviet Union. There exist natural conflicts between the center and the periphery due to the inherent externalities of many actions in, and the complexity of, any advanced social economy. In any economic system, central decisions can injure particular national and ethnic interests. However, the great ethnic complexity of the Soviet Union, the close relationship between economic and national regions in the economic structure, and the politicization and personalization of all economic activity in, and the peculiar nature of, the command-administrative economic system all implied typically adverse economic outcomes and a particularly strong inflammation of national passions as a result of economic grievances.

In general, the sources of nationalism and the principles of national justification are largely orthogonal to economic issues. However, economic grievances can stimulate an appeal to nationalist principles and passions, an appeal all the more strengthened by economic failures, shortages, and ecological concerns. This is particularly true when the state presumes to be all-knowing and all-powerful, yet fails to deal with, and even exacerbates, these problems. Economic difficulties and hardship, particularly when coincident with ethnic boundaries, can turn normal nationalist feelings into dangerous actions.[30] On the other hand the "good life," particularly when it is largely the result of individual effort in a decentralized, impersonal system, can deprive nationalist agitation of an audience. "Making a good living" becomes more important than abstract nationalist principles—arguably a reason for the mellowing of nationalist passions in Western Europe after World War II.

Despite policies toward "equalization," Soviet economic structure did nothing to ameliorate national passion. Soviet socialism provided neither "plenty" to distract from the national question, nor "virtue" to compensate for its absence. Truly fundamental economic reform, had it been pursued soon enough and with sufficient determination and persistence, might have offered some hope. Economic decentralization through real markets with real competition and real prices—implying local and sublocal autonomy, economic liberation of the individual and private groups, and removing the State, the central authorities, and the Russians (except in the RSFSR) from the direct management of economic activity—might have helped defuse the situation. It could have removed one aspect of the "us against them" confrontation by diffusing both sides of the dichotomy. "They" could have become an impersonal market and "we" might have fractured along lines of economic interests. It would not have eliminated the problem of national and ethnic conflict—undoubtedly nothing can. Any final solution, Leninist or otherwise, is a fantasy. But truly radical economic decentralization through markets could have removed the peculiarly Soviet economic stimuli to national passion and hostility. A liberal economic reform, vigorously pursued at an early enough stage, might have removed the festering irritant of the Stalinist economic structure, reducing levels of tension to those more normal for a multinational state.

It is now, however, too late for the Soviet Union to follow such a path. The failure of the August 1991 coup brought an end to the last vestiges of central control. The close of 1991 then brought a formal end to the Soviet Union as a state, and its powers and functions devolved into the former Republics, in particular to Russia. There are now fifteen more or less multinational states, each burdened with the legacy of the economic structure of the Soviet Union. It is a structure with a unifying, centralizing logic, now broken into pieces with little economic coherence. In recognition of this Russia, Ukraine, Belarus, Kazakhstan, and six other new states (former Republics) began 1992 with efforts to mold a loose economic and military confederation (CIS), while struggling to stabilize and reform their internal economies. But again national passion and fear of domination by others, in particular by Russia, are posing major obstacles, and the question of reforming the smaller, but no more rational, economic systems looms just as forbiddingly as it did for the Soviet Union. And still the "national question" festers within each former Republic, exacerbated by the inherited economic structure and deteriorating economic conditions.

Russia, as the largest multinational and largest successor state, faces perhaps the greatest problems of national tensions and economic reform. It, and the other new post-Soviet states, must now make the effort where the Soviet Union failed—undertake true decentralizing reform both to save the economy and to remove the peculiarly "Soviet" economic stimuli to national passion and hostility. However any reform, even the most radical and ultimately correct, must make things worse before they get better; the structure of the economy, its patterns of production, consumption, and interaction, are far too distorted for any quick or easy transition. For seventy years Soviet socialism systematically and perversely warped all economic activity and relations, leaving a crushing legacy in both the physical structure of the economy and the psychology and knowledge of its people. It will take years, and may take generations, of pain and deprivation for that legacy to be overcome. But decentralizing through markets and allowing the full pursuit of individual well-being can remove the ethnic edge from economic hardship, placing the blame on impersonal economic/market forces rather than the ill will of others' controlling the nation's destiny. Russia began 1992 with the apparent intention of pursuing such a reform. How consistently, and with what consequences, we can only wait and see.

NOTES

1. This essay addresses the issue only with respect to the traditional "command-administrative" Soviet economic system, rather than whatever is now replacing it. Thus the Soviet Union of this paper is that which existed prior to the abortive reactionary coup of August 19–21, 1991. The logic and structure of the new economic system coalescing in its aftermath will surely be quite different from, if inevitably affected by, the old system discussed here.

2. Clear indications of this can be seen in the mid-year and final 1990, and mid-year 1991, economic performance reports. *Ekonomika i zhizn:* no. 32, August, 1990; no. 5, January 1991; No. 32, August, 1991.

3. The census data include 125 indigenous groups. See *Journal of Soviet Nationalities* 1(1) (Spring 1990):150–54.

4. See, for example, S. Gililov, "The Worldwide Significance of the Soviet Experience in Solving the Nationalities Question," *International Affairs* (July 1972):56–69.

5. See note 2 above.

6. See A. Nove, *The Soviet Economic System* (London: Allen & Unwin, 1986), Chapter 3. Also see the discussion of relative living standards and investment in NATO Colloquium, *Regional Development in the U.S.S.R.* (Newtonville, MA: ORP, 1979), in J. F. Schiffer, *Soviet Regional Economic Policy* (New York: St. Martin's Press, 1989), and the discussion of investment policy in D. A. Dyker, *The Process of Investment in the Soviet Union* (Cambridge: Cambridge University Press, 1983).

7. The remaining SSR's—Estonia, Latvia, Lithuania, and Moldavia—were added after 1940 as the territories were annexed. A sixteenth republic, the Karelo-Finnish, was temporarily created at the end of the war in anticipation of the annexation of Finland. It was made an ASSR in 1958. For a fuller discussion, see John Hazard's essay in this volume.

8. For a survey of this, see Walker Conner's essay in this volume.

9. See the discussion of population movements in chs. 4 and 6 of R. A. Lewis, R. H. Rowland, R. S. Clem, *Nationality and Population Change in Russia and the USSR* (New York: Praeger, 1976).

10. For a clear exposition and introductory analysis of this issue see R. W. Campbell, "On the Theory of Economic Administration" in H. Rosovsky, ed., *Industrialization in Two Systems* (New York: John Wiley & Sons, 1966), pp. 186–204.

11. While the territorial principle was important during the NEP period, the economy itself was far more decentralized and undeveloped, and there was not yet the pretense and striving for central direction and control of all economic development.

12. For example, the small Republics of Central Asia were placed under one *Sovnarkhoz*, with a Russian at its head. See A. Nove, *The Soviet Economic System*, p. 360.

13. See. G. V. Mil'ner, A. V. Topilin "The Standard of Living and Migration," in *The Problems of Migration and Labor Resources* (Moscow: Statistika, 1970), pp. 44–48, on the lack of any real regional economic plans for social infrastructure or income development.

14. The literature on the regional, and hence national, distribution of "second economy" activity is summarized in the Berkeley-Duke Occasional Paper no. 21, July 1990, by G. Grossman. It is a rather understudied aspect of the Soviet second economy.

15. The latter involve regional coefficients and income supplements (*nadbavki*). See N. P. Kuznetsova, L. N. Shirokova, "*Raionnoe regulirovanie zarabotnoi platy* (Moscow: Ekonomika, 1987). Also see I. S. Koropeckyi, G. E. Schroeder, eds., *Economics of Soviet Regions* (New York: Praeger, 1981), and J. F. Schiffer, *Soviet Regional Economic Policy* for a more nearly complete discussion of both investment and standard of living issues.

16. This is clear from the discussion of the roots of *Perestroika* in A. G. Aganbegyan, *The Economic Challenge of Perestroika* (Bloomington: Indiana University Press, 1988), and in N. Shmelev, V. Popov, *The Turning Point* (New York: Doubleday, 1989).

17. This can be seen in the papers in Koropeckyj and Schroeder, *Economics of Soviet Regions,* and in J. R. Schiffer, *Soviet Regional Economic Policy* with regard to the eastern regions.

18. See again Schiffer, ibid., and David Dyker, *The Process of Investment.*

19. Lewis, Rowland, and Clem, *Nationality and Population Change,* provide statistics on the degree and nature of the shifts.

20. For a concise discussion of the role of Republics, regions and localities in planning see Denis J. B. Shaw, "Spatial Dimensions in Soviet Central Planning," *Transactions (Institute of British Geographers)*, ns, 10 (1985):401–12.

21. On "rationality" in a Soviet-type system, see J. Winiecki, *The Distorted World of Soviet Type Economies* (Pittsburgh: Pittsburgh University Press, 1988).

22. For a balanced discussion see D. Bahry, C. Nechemias, "Half Full or Half Empty?: The Debate over Soviet Regional Equality," *Slavic Review* 40(3) (1981):366–83.

23. The point is made, for example, in O. I. Shkaratan, L. S. Perepelkin, "Ekonomicheskii rost i natsional'noe razvitiie," *EKO,* no. 10, 1988, pp. 3–20. It also became clear in Soviet discussions of Republic self-financing, for example in, "Respublika na khozraschete? Estoniia predlagaet eksperiment," *EKO,* no. 12, 1988, pp. 88–105.

24. A now classic example of this is the "Aral catastrophe" discussed in *Novy mir,* no. 5, 1989.

25. The Baltic Republics received formal authority for broad experimentation with economic independence in the Fall session of the Supreme Soviet. See *Pravda,* December 2, 1989. Implementation stalled right up to the August coup largely because of central foot-dragging in negotiations. The issue became moot with the disappearance of the Soviet Union.

26. For example, G. Schroeder, "Regional Living Standards," in Koropeckyj and Schroeder, *Economics of Soviet Regions,* and Shkaratan and Perepelkin, *"Ekonomicheskii."*

27. This is a recurrent theme in *Ekonomicheskaia gazeta* and its successor *Ekonomika i zhizn* throughout 1989 and 1990.

28. A summary of the Estonian proposals and their spirited defense can be found in "Respublika na khozraschete? . . . Estonia predlagaet eksperiment," *EKO,* no, 12, 1988, pp. 88–104.

29. Donna Bahry, *"Perestroika* and the Debate over Economic Territorial Decentralization," *The Harriman Institute Forum* 2(5) (May 1989). This is an excellent, early analysis of the whole issue of territorial decentralization.

30. Walker Connor, "Eco- or Ethno-nationalism," *Ethnic and Race Studies* 7(3) (1984):342–59, argues against economic problems as a prime causal factor in nationalist conflict, but does argue that economic factors "are very apt to serve as catalytic agent, exacerbator, or choice of battleground" (at p. 356).

11. Class, Social Structure, Nationality

Walter D. Connor

> It is becoming ever plainer that Marx would have been closer to the truth had he described nationalism, not class, as the force that moves history.
>
> *The Economist*, July 8, 1989

Foreword: Spring 1992

The Economist had it right in 1989, as subsequent events have more than amply demonstrated. The USSR is no more, done in by tensions long-suppressed then released in the post-1985 period. It received its effective death warrant in the botched August 1991 coup that, in its attempt to restore something of the old order, accomplished the opposite. Yeltsin's preemptive Russian politics, and the Ukrainian independence vote, amounted to the execution; Gorbachev's December 25 resignation was the State funeral. But in the current and future context, class, while secondary, is not irrelevant—it will, it *must* as the move toward the market accelerates under harsh economic conditions, assume an important place in the still-nascent arena and structure of post-Soviet politics.

This chapter offers come selective explorations of that class component, in a general sense: that of group economic resentments, conflict of interest, perceptions of justice violated, interacting with or exacerbating ethnic tensions. Realities, or perceptions, of group advantage or disadvantage along economic/welfare dimensions—the groups typically the ethnic groups that gave their names to the fifteen Soviet republics and to lesser territorial subdivisions—obviously add to the stakes in the fragmented politics of an empire dying, and new states just emerging.

My brief, then, in this volume of contributions on (post-) Soviet nationality issues by Soviet specialists who have generally *not* focused in the past on ethnic problems, is "class and social structure." My approach is eclectic rather than systematic. The four sections that follow—on what official statistics tell us, and do not, about living standards in various republics; on aspects of social mobility and occupational attainment in highly-developed Estonia; on peculiarities of "segmentation" of the labor force in less-developed Uzbekistan and other parts of Central Asia, and "concluding-thoughts" as of late 1990—reflect issues I have found interesting as one whose work draws on both the concerns of political science and sociology. Others might have made other choices. The pressures of time, other projects, and the sheer onrush of events have persuaded me to leave essentially unaltered those four sections, last updated in late 1990 after their initial drafting in 1989: the problems with which they deal have not gone away. A postscript of Spring 1992 offers some reflections and reconsiderations based on the events of that tumultuous year.

Within the USSR, the long prevalence of totalitarian, then post-totalitarian politics, blunted expressions of class *or* nationality in any recognizable political sphere: the public "realm" of more fortunate countries, wherein the state is one, but not the only, actor, was abolished by a *state* realm that expanded to monopolize politics. State dominated society. In more recent years, as the grip of the state on spontaneous social processes weakened in the later Brezhnev time, the issues of class identity, of the salience of national/ethnic affiliation, assumed greater "life"—for analysts if not for a Brezhnev regime that never really came to grips with those social changes. Were ethnic tensions mainly of a center-periphery, "Moscow vs. minority" sort, wherein economic/class distinctions within the various non-Russian groups were irrelevant? Or, were the peoples of fourteen SSRs divided between an "elite" promoted and developed to a large degree by Moscow's policies, and a mass of ethnics, the elite essentially operating as the *agents* of Moscow—and "Russia"? Or, finally, was the issue of political, economic, cultural "clout" increasingly a matter—outside the RSFSR—of contention *between* Russian/Slav components of the local political/occupational elites, and indigenous members of those elites in Vilnius, Kishinev, Tashkent?[1] If so, what sort of class concerns might affect relations between those national elites and "their" masses?

These were not the only questions, of course. They derive from a core question, framed broadly as "is class, or nationality, the more important factor in determining. . . ?" a myriad of things: individual expectations, levels of satisfaction, loyalty to the Soviet system; group perceptions of, and aspirations about, the outputs of that political system, among them. The broad question was hard to answer: for one thing, class—as shorthand for socio-economic/occupational status, or as a matter of felt, conscious membership in a group—was harder to define than nationality. Assumptions that class would be dominant over nationality overlooked the general historical lesson that educated, high-status groups are, at least initially, the major carriers of new or "rediscovered" nationhood. Assumptions that nationality would count for more ran afoul of evidence that, it is a thing felt differently at different times, at differing levels of intensity, by many people. One could, in the past, suspect, surmise, pose questions, but hardly reach solid conclusions—in the pre-1985 USSR, the state dominated the society to a degree great enough to contain, suppress, hide evidence of the sort that might yield answers. Since then, even prior to the death of that old, unitary state in 1991, enough has happened to demonstrate how important nationality is, without in any sense rendering the question of class—by itself or in interaction with nationality—irrelevant.

Social Structure and Living Standards: Impressions from Goskomstat

What do official Soviet data tell us about variations in social structure across the republics, about those things that might bear on class and other structured aspects of social inequality and diversity? The answer, thus far, is "not very much," if we limit ourselves (as, in general, this author must in the context of the chapter) to national statistical data purporting to describe whole populations.

The 1987 estimate for the "social composition" of the population of the USSR gives the following breakdown:[2]

(white collar) employees	workers	collective farmers cooperative craftsmen
26.2%	61.8%	12.0%

These figures indicate a moderate "advance" on the 1979 census figures—the last available with the appropriate breakdowns—which recorded the following respective shares of the same groups.

25.1%   60.0%   14.9%

"Modern" sector—white-collar employees encompassing routine clerical work and intelligentsia professions, and workers—occupations grew moderately, the collective farm sector declined moderately. Of more interest for our purposes, are public variations in these social-structural characteristics. The 1979 census data, shown in table 11.1, for a selection of republics give us some sense of the range of variation.

Table 11.1. **1979 Census Data**

	employees	workers	coll. farmers
RSFSR	26.9	63.0	10.0
UK SSR	22.2	54.8	23.0
Estonian SSR	28.8	60.9	10.2
Latvian SSR	27.8	58.6	13.5
Uzbek SSR	22.3	52.9	24.7
Turkmen SSR	22.2	44.2	33.4

Differences here are largely in the direction one would expect on the basis of general impressions of Soviet internal diversity. In the two advanced Baltic republics of Estonia and Latvia, the farm share is small—though not the smallest for 1979 among all republics. Both Kazakhstan (at 6.5%) and Armenia (at 9.7) reported smaller shares—but this does not mean the total farm sector was smaller in these, since the "worker" category in all cases includes state farm workers (*sovkhozniki*).

Treating "employees" as an indicator, roughly, of the tertiary sector, the Baltic republics beat the Slavic RSFSR and Ukraine, and by a wider margin the two Central Asian SSRs. But the *Kazakh* republic employee figure was hardly behind Latvia's at 27.5%. All in all, the "employee" variation in these figures is not great—the variation on worker percentages in the republics recorded in tabular form above is more striking—from the RSFSR's 63.0 to the Turkmen 44.2—and obviously affected mainly by the varying size of collective farm populations.

Figures such as these seem dim reflections of what is "known" in a deeper, if looser and more impressionistic, sense. Estonia, on the whole, surely has a feel we would characterize as more advanced, more upscale in social structure, than the RSFSR; yet the figures seem not all that different—and our impressions of the RSFSR are likely to have been gathered from visiting its better-developed parts, not the backward ones averaged into these figures as well. There is, also, precious little difference between the indicators for Ukraine and Uzbekistan. Yet do these seem to us similar places, similar societies, in development, and deployment of the labor force?

Part of the problem is likely to involve precisely the "farm" component in the worker category. More Uzbek workers, proportionately, work on farms, especially on cotton farms, in the state sector, than do Latvian or Estonian "workers" in state farming. Central Asia is more agrarian; we know this. Beyond this, the composition of "workers," by branch of industry, skill profile, etc. may greatly distinguish the Slav republics from the Baltic, *both* from Central Asia and the Caucasus, even setting aside state farm "workers." Nothing in these figures tells us that the Baltic republics, at least Estonia and Latvia, are not more advanced, in addition to their more Western look, than Russia and the Ukraine—in point of fact, they tell us nothing about this.

Social structure data do not, necessarily, tell us who is "rich," who "poor." Figures on *per capita* income by republic, and on republic GNP per capita, do indicate large differences. Such figures have been discussed at length elsewhere,[3] and may, in any case, capture less of core economic realities than we think. Misreporting, lack of data on "second economy" earnings etc., may all be sources of confusion. Instead, we may take a brief look at the possession of big ticket durables as a more effective way to approach the matter; the figures in table 11.2, on facing page, for the same republics, derive from a September 1984 nationwide sample survey of 310,000 Soviet families (households), and indicate, by republic, the number of the relevant items per 100 households; households are divided into "worker and employee," and collective farmer, families.

The impressions one can gather from data such as these are diverse. There are, certainly, differences in material life reflected here, but in most cases they are not particularly striking.

Looking only at "workers and employees," and hence at the urban sector (plus, presumably, rural intelligentsia and state farmers that fell into the sample), deviations among republics in different regions, and from the USSR mean (heavily influenced, in any case, by the RSFSR and Ukrainian figures) are small with respect to color TVs, refrigera-

Table 11.2. **Durables per 100 Families, Worker/Employee and Collective Farm, Selected Republics (September 1984)**

	workers/employees				collective farmers			
	color TV	refrig.	wash. mach.	auto	color TV	refrig.	wash. mach.	auto
USSR	24	93	76	16	4	69	63	12
RSFSR	24	96	79	15	4	77	77	1
UkSSR	27	92	74	16	3	61	58	9
Estonian SSR	29	94	77	32	22	83	85	40
Latvian SSR	32	91	76	2	14	83	81	25
Turkmen SSR	22	101	6	22	3	94	50	20
Uzbek SSR	19	85	62	20	4	61	41	22

tors and washing machines. There is no real "Baltic" advantage save in color TVs, while the Central Asian disadvantage in these and in washing machines is not immense. The refrigerator figures do not confirm a notion of "traditional" lifestyles wherein Central Asian "ethnics" do without—although these are republican, not ethnic group figures. Turkmenia records 101 per 100 households, the highest of all SSRs—while the Tajik republic, not listed here, had the lowest rank at 74/100. It is in automobiles that the differences are marked—the Baltics are ahead of the natural average, but so are Uzbekistan and Turkmenia, and the other (unlisted) Central Asian republics save Kirgizia at 15/100.

In the rural areas, differences among collective farmer families in possession of durables are more marked. Across the board, Estonia and Latvia are well ahead of RSFSR and Ukraine, with washing machine and auto ownership higher in the Baltic countryside than among the workers and employees. But rural Central Asia does not seem especially disadvantaged—far from it. Auto ownership well exceeds the national average (the range for the four republics plus Kazakhstan is 13/22/100); refrigerators, by these data, are not particularly rare items in the Central Asian farm sector. Though the Turkmen figures (94/100, and 101/100 among workers and employees!) seems suspiciously high, and the Tajik SSR figure is a low 38/100, the range across Kazakhstan and the four Central Asian republics proper is 77/-38/100, disallowing the Turkmen anomaly.

All in all, one can make several points—or suggestions—on the basis of these data.

- there is evidence of a general "Baltic" living-standard advantage; modest in some items, greater in others
- in the Baltic, urban-rural differences as reflected here are not large (though unlisted Lithuania is well behind Estonia and Latvia, its collective farm rates of durable ownership are generally well above USSR national averages for this category)
- given this, there is no reason to assume that Estonians, Latvians, Lithuanians are to any degree "excluded" from the relative affluence of their republics; certainly, the collective farm sectors here are not likely to be dominated by Russian immigrants
- Central Asia "lags" behind Baltic and Slavic levels, but the lags in many cases are not overly large; the lag of rural Central Asia behind urban areas is large on some items, small on others

To be sure, such data do not directly address a number of questions of social inequality, of class. None of these data preclude substantial economic inequality within republics, class tensions over the distribution of scarce goods and opportunities that could develop within ethnic groups, or be exacerbated by perceptions that the disadvantaged population overrepresents one ethnic group, underrepresents another. There may be many problems with the sample, beyond definitional ones (variations in the state-farmer component in the "workers and employees" category, for example, may badly compromise even the rough image of urban vs. rural living standards we can adduce from such data). The gross differences by and large run in the expected direction—a relatively affluent Baltic, including an affluent countryside, a poorer Central Asia—but the differences are not so gross as we might have expected. The lesson most readily drawn here—and worth emphasizing, however simple it may be—is that Soviet data, at this level of aggregation, may not yield terribly interesting insights into republican (or, indirectly, ethnic/national) variations in social structure, nor in living standards as measured by household disposition of consumer durables.

Social Structure and Mobility: Estonian Anomalies, Baltic Implications

Nationwide social mobility data, available for some time and in a relatively complex form for some East European states, have been regrettably absent for the USSR. While this situation began to change in the 1980s,[4] and we may see the publication of already-collected data in more complete form, we are bereft, in general, of the sort of data that might illuminate many matters of interest in the dynamics of class, social structure, and nationality.

Data on intergenerational social mobility, depending on what sorts are collected, can tell us, simply, the rates at which offspring of a certain socio-occupation origin category (defined, typically, by the status of the father) remain in, or leave, that category, reproducing, rising above, or falling below, parental status. They will tell us, thus, the chances that a farm son will become a blue-collar worker, or a white-collar employee or professional; that offspring of blue-collar workers will move to white collar, or remain in what Soviet ideology has referred to as the leading class, that children of the diploma-bearing intelligentsia will retain this status or fall to less rarefied levels.

Social mobility studies, then, inform us about the dynamic aspect of social stratification. The experience of any single generation (or cohort), as it moves from childhood social identity determined by household of origin, to its own destinations in early-mid work life, will be compounded of many elements, most measurable, but some more so than others. Economic development, first of all, drives mobility: a shrinking farm sector, growing industrial employment, expansion in routine and professional-level white-collar nonmanual jobs, require that mobility from field to factory, peasant to worker, and across the manual-nonmanual divide, occur; just as an absence of development cancels such demand. Within this limit of structural mobility, more or fewer people will be intergenerationally mobile depending on equality or inequality in access to education and other certification, access to particular areas of the labor market, personal capacities, etc. Some fall, even though the occupational structure itself moves upward; others stay in their origin categories. Parental education, income, occupational levels, urban vs. rural residence, and other elements—accessible in more complex research programs—all contribute to offspring's educational and occupational outcomes (mobile or immobile).

Among the interesting variables in any USSR-wide studies would be ethnicity and area of residence. Would/does research give evidence of significantly different rates/patterns of mobility, overall, in one republic vs. another? What are the differences, and to what degree are they explicable by structural factors—i.e., the boundaries set by the different occupational structures of SSRs and their rates of change? (For example, from 1959 to 1979, judging by census data, the kolkhoz population share in Latvia fell from 26.1 to 13.5 percent, while the (white-collar) employee share grew from 19.5 to 27.8; over the same years in Turkmenia, the kolkhoz component fell from 42.1 to 33.4 percent, while white-collar shares grew from 19.5 to a still modest 22.2. Such data tell us something about the possibilities of different magnitudes of mobility, even in the absence of direct data.)[5]

More critically, to what degree might mobility data indicate that, in a republic, the indigenous nationality enjoys substantially greater opportunities—or lesser—than other groups, most notably the Russian/Slavic immigrant population, independent of social structure limits?

Or, to what degree might a nationwide study show patterns linking success/failure in the mobility sweepstakes to ethnicity as an individual variable, a factor operating in the same fashion as parental education, income, occupation, etc.?

These would have been, and obviously were, very sensitive issues within the generally sensitive arena of Soviet social research. Against the odds, such research expanded greatly during the Brezhnev years, but a great deal of controversy threatened the search for data on certain indicators, to say nothing of the publication of data that might reflect poorly on Soviet reality. In the area of nationality/ethnic relations and fair shares, any finding that nationalities varied radically in their mobility experience would require explanation. If Russians, for instance, were well behind native attainments in the Baltic, was this a matter of Baltic nationalism, exclusivism? If they were ahead of native attainments in Central Asia, was this simply a "legacy of the past," to be eliminated slowly, but surely by beneficent development? If they were behind, was this Turkic nationalism again, or merely evidence of a (natural and defensible?) "nativization" of intellectual, scientific, industrial cadres in the less-developed but advancing parts of the USSR?

All these questions, in a sense, are posed too broadly. As we shall see, it is difficult—especially in Central Asia—to connect a specific economic payoff to a particular occupational destination. That one group seems to dominate certain areas of state administration, and technical/scientific cadres, and at the same time is overrepresented in blue-collar jobs in traditionally favored heavy and extractive industry, does not necessarily mean it enjoys overall economic advantage, or feels that it does.

For all the qualifiers, it is worth examining some data bearing—even if indirectly—on some of these matters. They derive from Estonia—where the Russian "immigrant" reaction to post-1985 manifestations of "native" nationalism, expressed in language and electoral laws as well as historical rhetoric, political and economic reform blueprints, took on a blue-collar, "worker" cast.

Research initiated at Tartu State University and the Estonian SSR Academy of Sciences in 1966 tracked a 2,260 person sample of secondary school graduates of that year. Born mostly in 1948, these represented a large cut of the ca. 7,000 who graduated from (11-year) secondary schools in that year. Re-surveys of essentially the same group in 1969, 1976, and 1979 completed a program whose aim was more the study of career or intragenerational mobility, but yielded results of some interest, for reasons to be made clear below, on intergenerational mobility as well.[6]

In a summary form, the results of the 1966–79 research, presented as a standard mobility table wherein sons disperse across the rows from the fathers who define sons' social origin,[7] finding their own niches in a range of destination categories, look as in table 11.3.

Any student of social mobility, confronted with this set of outcomes, would likely be perplexed. We have here a massive predominance of winners over losers, an extraordinary amount of intergenerational upward mobility. Note that intelligentsia sons maintain fathers' status in a quite clear (72 percent) majority of cases; that different levels of attainment of intelligentsia status for lesser origin groups vary, essentially, little (the total range of variation is only a very modest 5 percent); and that the majority destination of all sons regardless of social origin is the intelligentsia.

What is happening here—what happened in Estonia to the 1948 birth cohort? First of all, let us note that the people whose careers are involved here are, to all indications, overwhelmingly Estonian. The sample of 2,260 in all represented about half of the 4,440 graduates of Estonian language secondary schools in 1966. (Overall, about 7,000 graduated republic-wide in that year, leaving a residual of some 3,500 who probably were in Russian-language schools—or around 37 percent of the total.) These, then, are Estonian life trajectories, within their own republic.

Second, they are atypical. A partial key to the extraordinary success story is that these are all, by the definition of the sample, secondary-

Table 11.3. **Father-to-Son Intergenerational Mobility, Estonian SSR (in percent)**

Father	son in 1979				
	1	2	3	4	5
1. intelligentsia	72	10	9	8	1
2. routine white-collar	59	12	11	15	3
3. skilled worker	54	10	18	11	7
4. semi/unskilled worker	57	17	14	7	5
5. farm (coll/state)	54	12	11	14	9

Source: adapted from A. V. Kirkh, "Opyt izmereniia mezhgeneratsionnoi mobil nosti molodezhi," *Sotsiologicheskie issledovaniia*, no. 4, 1984, p. 109.

school graduates, a level of attainment not typical in 1966 for members of the 1948 birth cohort who entered first grade in 1955. (Republic-wide, about 18,500 entered first grade in 1955; while 7,000 graduated on schedule, eleven years later in 1966). We do not have the differential completion rates as between Estonians and (immigrant) Russians, but the general indication is that only a minority of either element of the cohort finished academic secondary schooling.

Third, for a group atypical by definition as completers of academic secondary school, they are also quite successful; a reported 60 percent acquired a higher, or specialized secondary education. This is the key to the majority which, in each origin group, gains intelligentsia status.

But unless the experience of this cohort is totally atypical, given its parameters, this evidence suggests that Estonians are likely to be anything but socio-occupational orphans in their own republic. While there are many technical pitfalls in interpretation[8] and data we should like arranged in different ways for our purposes, secondary education, once achieved, leads on, for the Estonians, to quite upscale occupational outcomes, independent of origin. True, children of the highly educated were probably greatly overrepresented among those who completed secondary school, and even more so among those who then completed higher education—but secondary education, and hence inclusion in this sample, was a prelude to remarkable upward mobility for worker and peasant sons as well. If we assume that the Estonian drop-out rate between grades 1 and 11 was at the average level of the whole cohort—wherein 18,500 started and 7,000 finished—we get 37.9 percent completion rate for Estonians completing the 11 years. The majority of these, something on the order of 19 percent of the whole cohort achieve intelligentsia status (assuming that none of the 62.1 percent dropouts later achieve it). This is no mean performance.

Nationwide data indicate that it was easier to continue from secondary school to higher education in 1966 than it was two decades later; higher education did not expand as did the number/share of 17–18 year olds completing secondary education. Still, processes like the ones detailed here worked to produce a sizable Estonian elite/professional class: one that emerged as a carrier of suppressed national identity in the late 1980s in that republic, as in others.

Was it the same for the Russians in Estonia? The study, unfortunately, does not track the graduates of the Russian-language schools of 1966. Assuming they were mainly Russians, few were native to the republic, in the sense of having been born there in 1948; the big immigrations came later. Relying on hunches as much as anything else, it would seem likely that:

♦ Russian drop-out rates prior to the 11th grade would have been, and likely continued to be, somewhat higher than Estonian: a matter of culture and practice back in the RSFSR influencing behavior in Estonia.

♦ Russian access to higher education in Estonia would have been reduced by this fact, and perhaps as well by limited opportunities for Russian-language higher education in Estonia.[9]

♦ Exit from the republic to the RSFSR for higher education for graduates of Russian language schools would have been more normal, and there would be some devaluation of higher education among others who remained in the republic.

In all, a reasonable guess would be that parallel data for Russians would show a less upscale outcome—or if it were similar, one wherein the career trajectories had taken Russians out of Estonia.

It is a long way from this, however, to offering hard data to support another argument. Much of the Russian population of Estonia in the late 1980s saw itself besieged by locals laying exclusive claim to goods—essentially political goods—Russians felt equally entitled to, anywhere in "their" USSR. But did Russians also see themselves as a mainly blue-collar population, looked down upon by Estonians who seem relatively few in many of the large factories, but only too present in professional and public capacities that signify intelligentsia status? Did a class component add itself to the national resentment of the Russians who responded with strikes and stoppages to separatist politics and nationalist legislation? We cannot confirm this from the data at hand, but nothing we have seen in this section would be inconsistent with such feelings.

Class in this case would be nested in a set of national issues of extraordinary depth and bitterness, driven by the sharpness of Baltic memory, the fuzziness of the Russian. Invaded as World War II began, Estonia, Latvia and Lithuania lost status as independent European nation-states: no other SSR can make so clear a claim to this status. Nordic Protestant culture in Estonia and Latvia, Polish influence and Catholicism in Lithuania, both made for a poor fit with Russia—and the rest of the USSR.

The military invasion and forced annexations, at war's beginning and again at the end, exposed Baltic peoples to what they took as an overwhelming, Eastern force, backward, alien, culturally inferior. (If Soviet power brought electricity and irrigation to Central Asia, to the Baltic, in the eyes of the natives, it brought troops who had never seen wristwatches or flush toilets.[10]) The demographic invasions (marked in Estonia and Latvia, less in Lithuania) followed—largely workers of Russian/Slav background, to staff new, large-scale industry geared to all-Union economic purposes. Some stayed, some were transient— perhaps 50 left the Baltic for every 100 who arrived[11]—but, for the Balts, too many stayed. That few immigrants learned the local language, of course, was something that exacerbated local reactions to the invasions. As Karklins put it in 1986 (and as subsequent events have shown), in the Baltic and elsewhere in the non-Russian SSRs, there are mutually irreconcilable notions about proprietorship, and about the appropriateness of language use.

> While even those nationals who accept the basic union with the USSR perceive their titular republic as being uniquely "theirs," the Russian population appears to hold a notion of historically given entitlement to these areas as a "natural" extension of their own homeland.[12]
>
> The republic nationals feel that they have a right to have their native languages dominate all spheres of communication within "their republic" and that everybody living there should learn and use them. There are numerous reports of locals refusing to reply to strangers in the street or to customers in a shop or restaurant, if addressed in Russian. Russians for their part feel insulted by such behavior and often respond with a hostile remark of their own since, in their perception, Russian should be accepted as the dominant means of communication unionwide.[13]

Beyond language, there exists a generally constrained framework within which Russians can develop their perceptions of Baltic relations with the rest of the USSR. The tendentious "canned" history learned by working-class Russians has told them little of what the "world" knows; their responses to assertions of Baltic national pride and consciousness are constricted by ignorance, defensiveness, and surprise that Balts see things differently. A 1986 declaration by the "Helsinki 86" organization, founded by three Latvian workers, makes the point nicely.

> Russians simply laugh at us when we point out that in Latvia they should learn Latvian; they call us nationalists and fascists and [insist] that they

should not have to learn the language of dogs, [because] their language is the principal and international [language].[14]

Much then is national, involves communal separation, distance, resentment: but there is also, one suspects, a felt consciousness among Russians of contempt for them by Estonians and Latvians, a barely-hidden conviction that their guests from the leading nation of the USSR are, somewhat like their counterparts of the invasion a half-century ago, rubes, drunks, lazy—as long as the majority do not learn the local languages.

It is true, as well, that Soviet sociologists—later major backers of perestroika—have recognized a work ethic and culture that distinguishes the natives from their guests. As two of these observed in 1980, citing the well-above-average labor productivity in Latvia and Estonia

> the energy supply per worker, the level of equipment, education, and vocational knowledge of the workers of Latvia and Estonia do not differ fundamentally from the corresponding indices in the other republics. One may conclude that it is *precisely the habituation of personnel of this region, due to a number of concrete historical circumstances, to high accuracy and care in their work* that is the principal reason for the high efficiency of their labor.[15] (emphasis added)

It is unlikely that many Russian—or Latvian or Estonian—workers were readers of *Voprosy filosofii,* the journal in which these words were published. But had they been, they would not have missed the cultural implication, even if the remarks might include the Russian workers in these republics as well. For Estonian sociologists, such as those who produced the research discussed earlier, the implications would have been clear indeed.[16]

There is, then, the possibility that the point where many Baltic Russians experience maximum discomfort is that where their feelings of USSR-wide dominance are met not only by Estonian-Latvian linguistic exclusivism, but by this contempt, based on class and culture. For the native intelligentsia of the Baltic, whose visibility is surely great to the whole population, there was obviously, under phase-one glasnost, little evidence of gratitude that entrance into the USSR gave them, as small peoples, access to world culture, exit from provincialism. The Russian language is not the mode of access; the English language is. Whether Baltic intellectuals take as reference groups the intelligentsia of Finland and Scandinavia, or of Poland and Hungary, this fact is brought home to them. More recently, the rejection of Soviet symbols, of Russian examples, of the idea of association with even a reformed, confederal USSR, has become more pronounced. It is precisely this wholesale rejection of the Russian big brother/liberator that blue-collar Russians may find most galling.

It is, surely, too early to try to unravel class and nationality among Russian worker protests in Latvia and Estonia in 1989. Russian dock workers struck in late April one of Riga's port facilities, under the aegis of the (Russian-dominated) Interfront organization, citing discrimination against parts of Latvia's population, especially in language law proposals.[17] In August, 1989, Russian workers in Tallin, and Kohtla-Jarve, struck in large numbers, in response to new language and, more critically, electoral laws that could disenfranchise many immigrants in elections that were now real and competitive. Interests and symbols were both at stake here. (In the elections earlier that year to the new USSR Congress of People's Deputies, predominantly Russian districts in Estonia and to a degree Latvia selected candidates from the Russian-dominated organizations opposed to the two Popular Fronts representing the local ethnics.[18])

These were not labor-management conflicts. The directorships of many of the enterprises struck were largely Russian, they were often tolerant—or more—of the strikes (and there is evidence of Russian directors locking out what may be Estonian workers in similar protest against the drift of Estonian legislation[19]). Partially spontaneous, they also reflected organized attempts to mobilize working-class resentment in general against certain aspects of economic reform policies and intelligentsia dominance in reform political thinking. Those forces emerged clearly—if with indifferent success—in the wave of Congress and Supreme Soviet elections, and deliberations, in the spring of 1989,[20] and later found organizational expression in the "United Front of Workers of Russia" (OFTR), which includes the Baltic Interfronts: an attempt to link "populist" concerns of class with Russian nationalism.[21]

Since 1988, those who "know" the Baltic as Russian immigrants have witnessed attempts, effectively led by the national political leaderships, and backed by the Popular Fronts in Estonia and Latvia, by Sajudis in Lithuania, to distance themselves politically and economically from the rest of the USSR. Even short of open secessionism, these moves generated resentment on many grounds. Would the Baltic republics, with their traditions of "enterprise," become, by holding their corporate rates low, tax havens for the cooperatives whose practices have made them unpopular in so many areas?[22] How, as one discussant asked on a Moscow TV talk show in March, could the Lithuanian SSR establish higher annual motherhood benefits, and authorize mothers to stay home with children for eight years and still enjoy an uninterrupted job record, when the rest of the USSR had a 1.5 year limit—were they better than workers in the Donbass, in Tyumen oblast?[23]

Stark indeed—and from a Baltic viewpoint, no doubt accurate—was the comment from a reformist (Russian) Supreme Soviet deputy in the July 1989 debate that eventuated in giving the green light to an unprecedented amount of economic autonomy for Estonia and Lithuania (in which Latvia later joined)—and which seemed radical at the time. Criticisms of the move expressed fears that the Baltic would overcharge for its consumer goods going to the rest of the USSR, leaving Russia behind. As the deputy put it:

"I haven't heard . . . concern that Lithuania and Estonia, in going over to economic independence, would fall apart and become poor. . . . On the contrary, the undertone of the speeches was the envious fear that they would grow richer. . . . This comes from slavery. After all, a slave cannot stand that another slave become free."[24]

It will not be so easy, of course, for the Baltic to be rich, to distance itself from a Russia that will be poor—for three republics to gain a clear class advantage over the others. The general Soviet economic chaos as of early autumn 1990 affects all the republics. Baltic exit is, eventually, a near certainty. But any rapid inclusion of independent Estonia, Latvia, and Lithuania in the new Europe will be difficult indeed: the queue heading toward 1992 includes many EFTA members as well as Poland, Hungary, and Czechoslovakia. Rich by Soviet standards, Estonians, Latvians, Lithuanians will find their poverty, contrasted even with Europe's weakest economies, sharply underlined when they cut loose. Economic issues and ethnic resentment have far from exhausted their potential in intergroup relations in the Baltic, and nothing on the horizon indicates any likely resolution of these soon; the best one can say, perhaps, is that Yeltsin's assertion of RSFSR sovereignty, and symbolic recognition in presidential-level negotiations of Baltic sovereignty, is a better political footing on which to address grievances and search for compromise than any established before 1990.

Employment, Income, Social Structure: Appearance and Reality in Central Asia

In September 1984, a survey of Soviet families found that, in the Karakalpak ASSR—the autonomous republic bordering the Aral Sea and occupying westernmost Uzbekistan—there were 90 black and white TV's, 8 color sets, 88 refrigerators, 45 washing machines, and 16 autos; collective farm families had no color TVs, (but 101 black and white), 88 refrigerators, 43 washers, and 25 autos. Not much of an urban-rural gap, and on the whole a record not bad by Uzbek or USSR standards—as consultation of the data arrayed earlier will indicate. If not rich by Soviet standards, Karakalpakia did not seem brutally poor. Indicators such as these do not seem overly third-worldish.

But, in fact, Karakalpakia is a wasteland, a sink of pollution and environmental damage wherein the daily drink is industrial waste, the combined effect of cotton-industry pesticides and river diversion befouling the environment and a hair-raising rate of sickness and infant mortality; a region whose under-service with simple medical care could hardly be predicted, in a socialist society, from the data on dispersion of consumer durables.[25]

It may also be a lesson in how far general data on Central Asia, of the sort we find in Soviet statistical publications, from the TsSU to Goskomstat, will take us. Central Asia has suffered various kinds of massive damage from the policies that have brought development, of a sort, in the Soviet period.[26] Until recently, it would have been hard to tell this from Soviet sources.

The picture with respect to class and nationality, as opposed to general welfare issues, is also complicated and confused. This section can only touch upon some major aspects. Clearly, throughout Central Asia, any general notions of a daily life where a Russian minority and a Muslim ethnic majority interact in terms of superordination/subordination—Slav bureaucrat to Muslim clerk, Slav foreman to Muslim worker—is wrong. This is not, in any case, the sort of colonial stereotype most readily entertained about the region.

More typical is an impression with more to back it up—a high degree of regional and economic segregation between Russian/Slavic and indigenous populations. The "big" cities tend to be Slavic, the countryside and small cities Muslim; the industrial sectors, especially heavy industry, Slavic in their management and worker (especially skilled) cadres, the agricultural sector and services Muslim. By the numbers typically ascribed to salary and wage levels, and to the urban-rural differences in amenities, durables, etc., the Slavs would seem to have the advantage—an economic class advantage—moderated how-ever to a degree by the fact that, linguistically and contextually, Slavs and Muslim do not live next door to one another, and the possibility that, given their reluctance to move not only to labor-short areas outside their own republics for good wages, but even to move to the large cities of their own republics, Muslims simply prefer another way of life, whatever its material costs.

While to some degree accurate, this image missed a good deal—of Central Asian reality, a reality before the economic collapse outlined, for the Uzbek SSR, by Lubin's *Labour and Nationality in Soviet Central Asia*.[27] What she reveals about the Uzbek situation, allowing for some republican variations, is likely to be roughly true of the other three Central Asian republics proper.

- Slavs do dominate heavy industry, both in manual and technical positions, and are overrepresented in productive sector engineer-ing-technical intelligentsia jobs in general: these are jobs whose stated wage/salary levels are rather high.
- Uzbeks in turn supply light, food-processing, and local industry with workers, and in general occupy the highest and lowest skilled jobs in services, retail trade, etc. as well as in agriculture—all areas where official salaries and wages tend to be lower.
- On the whole, Uzbeks are underrepresented in the socialized sector (state enterprise and collective farming) for their share of the working-age population (in 1970, 68% of the republic's working-age population, but only 57.5% of those in social pro-duction; of the urban population, 41% and 30% respectively) while in the same years Russians who made up 12.5 percent of the work-age population contributed 18% of those employed in social production.[28]

Why—when it is also clear that government administration and economic-management cadres in Uzbekistan are heavily indige-nized—should Uzbeks be in this situation of apparent disadvantage? It is not a matter of signs (in Russian) indicating that "no Uzbeks need apply." Higher education in the republic is largely in native hands, and indeed Uzbek applicants evidently pay small to no bribes (!) for admission, while Russians and others are required to pay.[29]

The point, as Lubin puts it, is that there is really "no sign that Central Asians in fact desire those jobs which Europeans hold."[30] The reasons are manifold.

- while cultural preferences play some role, the economics of Uzbek enterprise and employment, not picked up in general state statistics, are of a sort that tend to reverse official patterns of class/socio-occupational advantage
- access to food and consumer goods comes not via the wages of heavy industry but in those branches of industry, in trade and other services, where Uzbeks dominate
- earnings opportunities (semilegal to illegal) from control of such goods are great, as are those in the ostensibly low-paid nonproductive spheres, such as medicine
- absence from the sector of "social production," in favor of private agriculture, could generate (1) a high income from sale of deficit food items and (2) a lower cost of living in the household
- much of the economic rationality of Uzbek choices is indicated by bribes typically paid to secure jobs: *no* bribe for a well-paid (ca. 200 rubles per month in the early 1980s) job in heavy industry, perhaps thousands of rubles for a low-paid job in retail trade, warehousing, etc., where the opportunity to divert goods to private-profit channels existed[31]

Uzbek economic advantage—only partially perceived as such by the urban Russians—is also cloaked by consumption patterns not manifestly affluent.[32] Adobe homes make more sense than apartment blocks; propensities are to save currency in cash hoards or valuables rather than bank in the *sberkassa;* to consume expensive meat rather than buy household appliances. (Even so, while Lubin sees Uzbek women unconvinced of the merits of modern refrigerators, one notes from earlier data that 61 of 100 Uzbek collective farm families had them in 1984—only 8/100 less than the USSR average for that year.)

Patterns such as these suggest a well-developed alternative economy, to a degree culturally/ethnically based, and within its context, economically quite rational. For a time, at least, the adaptive capacity of this economy proved great, even in the face of a high indigenous fertility rapidly outpacing Slavic birth rates, and increasing vastly Central Asia's weight in the total population. Centralized investment policy might dictate that increments to Uzbek republic industrial infrastructure go to already-developed areas and emphasize the heavy industry likely to be manned by Russians, while ignoring the small towns and rural areas where an ostensible labor surplus, heavily Uzbek, existed.[33] Still, the native economy somehow absorbed the consequences: the number of working-age, able-bodied not employed in the socialist/collective sector grew by a modest 3,000 per year in Uzbekistan between the 1959 and 1970 censuses; and then, more ominously, by 38,000 per year between the 1970 and 1979 accountings,[34] without massive disruptions.

But these, and similar processes in other Central Asian republics, would finally overrun the adaptive capacities of the Central Asian economies, threatening to link (economic) class and nationality issues. The job preferences of Central Asians, the economic and cultural attractions of such jobs, might remain constant; but, given population pressures, there was no reason to think that the supply of such jobs could continually rise to met the demand. Even though the demand did not include Russians, segregated in heavy industry jobs, there was no guarantee that Central Asians facing increased economic pressure would not blame the "aliens" among them—especially when glasnost and increased room for independent political expression lowered the costs of open complaint. Writing in the interim of the early 1980s—after Brezhnev, before Gorbachev—Lubin put it well.

> Thus, however unjustified their feeling may be, indigenous Central Asians have begun to hold "the Russians" responsible for everything, from long lines at stores, to shortages in consumer goods, to the rise in crime and "hippy culture" infecting their republic. It makes little difference that the Russians who came to Uzbekistan during the past fifteen years had little impact on meat availability in most government stores—or that the decline in most per capita indicators in Uzbekistan has been due to rapid indigenous, rather than Slavic, population growth. For the indigenous nationalities, a perceived worsening quality of life has already become linked with the presence of "outsiders" in their republic. The possibility of a more extreme economic slowdown in Uzbekistan, therefore—or the disappearance of many basic goods, services and job opportunities altogether—would hold immense ethnic implications which go beyond purely economic considerations alone. It could spark deep-seated nationalist hostilities and resentments which would be difficult to contain.[35]

The extreme economic slowdown came in 1988–89. The results have been turbulent, violent: outbursts of an anomic to quasi-organized sort, but often with an economic as well as a nationality component, and certainly not always aimed against Russians per se. Shortages are rampant; new cooperatives charge high prices while state stores seem poorer than ever in what they offer. Unemployment is admitted to exist, and to be growing, among young Central Asians whom neither the "first" nor the "second" economy seems now able to absorb. There is, surely, no socio-occupational, class disadvantage more burdensome than this, when superimposed on long-term ethnic resentment in the context of a Soviet economy now in deep crisis.

1989 was a bad year. In the riots in Novyi Uzen, on the oil-exploiting Caspian coast of the Kazakh SSR, evidently Kazakh youth rioted in June against mainly Armenian, Azerbaijani, and other Caucasian oil workers, demanding their expulsion, the closing of the cooperatives at which they bought, and which seem to have been run by their co-nationals, and jobs for the unemployed local Kazakhs, numbering perhaps 1,500 to 2,000 in a city of about 50,000 people.[36]

In Uzbekistan's Fergana valley (where industrial development in an overwhelmingly Uzbek area favored industries that drew non-Central Asian personnel[37]), at the beginning of June 1989, locals rioted against the Meskhetian Turk minority in a context where the available cadres included "tens of thousands of youth" who, "for years," in the words of a local party chief, "were unable to find work and lacked normal housing."[38] In Ashkhabad on May Day, Turkmen youth rioted, evidently "set off" by a combination of perceived high prices in cooperative stores and enterprises,[39] and the evidence that these were disproportionately operated (or so perceived to be) by the largish Armenian population in the city.[40] In mid-July, at the borders of Tajikistan and Kirgizia, "thousands" of village people clashed over land and water rights[41]—issues fundamental to populations whose growth places immense pressure on natural resources.

Later 1989, and 1990, saw little abatement of the climate of conflict and violence. Intercommunal, ethnic violence between Central Asian nationalities erupted over scarce goods (housing, land, water). Perceptions of long-term deprivation in Central Asia, combined with suspicions that recent Armenian refugees from Armenian-Azerbaijani violence would be given preference in housing, etc., led to riots in Central Asian receiving areas.

If the economic component of Baltic conflict has been rooted in a feeling of relative deprivation among the natives (the widespread conviction that, had history worked differently, the Baltic would be part of a Western, Nordic world) as well as, perhaps, class resentment among many Russians, in Central Asia the issue is more likely to be one of more absolute deprivation. There is too little of everything to go around. Food, housing, clean air, and water are all in short supply, and competition can easily take on a violent aspect. More broadly, there is little reason not to anticipate further rejection of Russian/Slav European hegemony on national/religious grounds in Central Asia— something that can quite well co-exist with inter-communal rivalry among the indigenous nationalities. If rejectionism is based on a feeling of Westernness, as well as earlier independent existence, the rise of national movements in the various Central Asian republics affirm Muslim/Turkic cultural and historical identity at least as distant from East Slav culture. The occupational/economic segregation between Slav and Muslim noted earlier reflected this cultural split, to a degree. The collapse of the economic base that allowed this, at the same time as the possibilities of expression of political grievance and separatism have increased, is likely to increase Slav/Muslim tensions. Conditions in the RSFSR economy are not such as to encourage re-migration of Slavs out of Central Asia, but conditions may give them little choice. If conflict and violence in Central Asia had been, as of late 1990, mainly intra-Muslim, there was no guarantee that this would remain the case.

Concluding Thoughts

It is not, of course, only the Baltic and Central Asia where nationalism/separation are on the rise, and where national and economic tensions combine in various ways. Politics and economics have greatly increased the force of fissiparous tendencies: there is separatism in every republic, including the RSFSR.

What we are witnessing is the political dissolution of the USSR as we have known it—what we await, against a background of an economic near-meltdown, is the outcome. Several sovereign states? Fifteen? Or a new confederation, a new treaty which will legally repose sovereignty in republics which have already, in many cases, claimed it? Class issues in the future, will more likely be fought out within whatever sort of (semi-) sovereign states develop out of the current political confusion. Within the RSFSR especially, class politics have emerged with the economic tensions of decline and projected reform that will abandon a social contract no longer workable nor affordable (just as in Estonia, where early price reforms have already generated social tension). What began in the miners' strikes of July 1989 has, in the context of a new (if unconvincing) populism on the part of the official trade union organization, the foundation of the United Front of Workers of Russia, drawing on both worker confusion and resentment of the threatening market and its disciplines and national/ethnic pride (as well as resistance to the new politics by a rearguard of anti-reform political figures), and increasing levels of authentic independent organization by workers, made progress toward the solution of economic problems all the more urgent, and difficult.

Russian nationalism comes in several varieties—some clearly anti-reform, anti-perestroika,[42] others not so, but driven by the logic, economic and political, of RSFSR sovereignty in the framework of near-universal claims for such by the other republics. The politics of 1990, which saw the constitutional disestablishment of the CPSU's leading role followed by its political debilitation at the 28th party congress, witnessed also the establishment of Yeltsin's RSFSR government, and with it the distancing of Russia—its political identity, its economic resources—from the USSR. If Yeltsin's program for economic reform, privatization and marketization in Russia goes forward, the consequences for the other republics must be profound. In varying ways, the tensions—however moderated by Yeltsin's popularity and relative authenticity as leader—of what may finally be radical reform in the RSFSR will be passed on to other SSRs. The stage may be set, however incompletely, for an exacerbation of class and economic justice issues just as the way opens in 1991 for a resolution of some national issues via the effective end of the USSR as a centrally-governed political entity. This, however, may be greater optimism than the situation warrants.

The peoples of the USSR have travelled a long way since 1985. A year earlier, Mary McAuley, in an overview of theorizing and analyzing Soviet nationality problems, noted that the sorts of factors working to cause and perpetuate nationalism seemed present to such a degree in the USSR that it should seem "a veritable nationalist's paradise"; but the rampant nationalism that might be predicted was not there.

> A simple but unsatisfactory explanation of its absence might be that state's ability and willingness to crush any manifestations of nationalism. Now, this might explain the inability of a nationalist group to consolidate itself,

it may be (and, we would argue, surely is) one factor that can help explain parts of the picture, but it cannot account for the very different manifestations of nationalist attitudes, or their absence, that we observe. It does not, for example, help us to explain why some sections of the Ukrainian or Russian intelligentsia should adopt national positions-and at particular times-while their counterparts in Kirgizia, Armenia or Moldavia show no signs of doing so.[43]

One might have taken issue—Russian nationalism was a sort that in the eyes of many, from foreign observers to non-Russians, the state had always, to a degree, encouraged and protected. (Though many Russians, by the end of the 1980s, were hardly inclined to agree.) Since McAuley wrote, nationalist manifestations have broken out everywhere. In the same essay, she laid out some keys to a nationalist resurgence she—and so many others—found it impossible to predict at the time.

> If the central authority in a multi-ethnic state rests on a territorial and cultural community that distinguishes it from the rest, or if a period of repressive rule is followed by liberalization, or if the central power is unable to offer protective benefits to the minorities, then all these are conducive to minority nationalism.[44]

Amen. What ethnic (other than Russians) would claim that central authority did not rest on a Russian territorial/cultural community— what was more Russian than Gorbachev's Politburo? What liberalization ever, in Soviet history, matched that which came after 1985? What benefits, in the parlous state of the Soviet economy in 1989–90, had minorities received to compensate for their subjection?

Perestroika, allowing for the fact it never assumed real programmatic coherence, aimed at dealing with economic and political-structural problems in general. It was, as Shanin observed, "radical with regard to the social economy," but ethnic/national issues were "essentially deferred."[45] Gorbachev and his advisers at least anticipated confronting certain class-type issues in working out the logic of reform.[46] The growing public anger at the cooperatives, at increasing inequality and violations of social justice, showed that class issues would be hard to resolve under any circumstances. The question was how hard. One condition that might have helped—the deferrability of ethnic/national issues—proved to be an illusion. They have not been deferred, they could not be. Both national and class issues will thus be dealt with, well or poorly, in a different political/territorial context than the one which has framed the work of students of Soviet affairs for the past 40 years.[47]

Postscript: Spring 1992

The post-Soviet era is upon us. The USSR is gone, the "Commonwealth of Independent States" is not its successor—it is not, according to its eleven signatories, a state at all. The deals being cut between successor states—on matters economic, political, military—do not really depend on the existence of the paper Commonwealth at all. Within the successor states, issues of class and social justice are sharpened by the continuing economic free-fall, the reality of hyperinflation; price rises that affect all the former Soviet republics' peoples in different ways. The picture is complicated, and on the whole more grim than not.

In Estonia and the other Baltic states, the native intelligentsia/professionals written of earlier seem well able to take in hand the political-diplomatic aspects of their new independence. Economic issues are a different, more complicated matter. Many Russian/Slav immigrants in Estonia and Latvia took the side of independence in the plebiscites. This bodes well for interethnic relations. But the marketization of the Baltic economies, occurring as the price of Russian fuel imports rises, may well involve economic moves that threaten some of the industrial sectors, the plants in which the Russians bulk so large as the work force. It is too early to tell, but possibilities of unemployment hitting Russians particularly hard as Estonian and Latvian economies try to move Westward and upward, reducing their reliance on the industry now so dependent on Russian energy resources toward more appropriate, less material-intensive sectors, may exacerbate a class divide between Balts and Russians suggested earlier. It is still early going here, but to limit anticipations of interethnic tensions to the issues of language/citizenship/voting rights, without taking into account the potential economic dimensions in these two countries, might well be an overly simple view of the future. (Lithuania's different demography, with a much smaller nonindigenous share of the population, is quite different and on the whole less problematic in this regard.)

Central Asia—its peoples, its native leaders on the whole much more enmeshed in the party mafia political style of the past—also seems less ready for the market. But its economies are as badly affected as any others of the old components of the USSR; their absorptive capacities low vs. the supply of native hands to be employed; their Russian/Slav populations thus potential targets of economic resentment and scapegoating beyond that alluded to earlier. How might these tensions play out? Within the Commonwealth structure, political Russia will be sensitive to any targeting of co-ethnics in the Central Asian states, whether as aliens, colonists, or simply people occupying jobs now more attractive—as an alternative to unemployment—to natives than they were when the alternative economy could still absorb them. Class resentments in addition to ethnic-national ones could thus arise among both Russian and native, each seeing deprivation imposed at least partly by the other. Kazakhstan and, perhaps, Kirgizia seem to be moving forward on realistic, if painful, economic policies. Tensions in Uzbekistan, Turkmenia, and Tajikistan seem more likely to arise from attempts, under old-style rule, to retain a number of old command-administrative economic practices that cannot be afforded.

If the curtain, then, has fallen on the seventy-four year Soviet drama, it is now rising on many new ones, wherein under a Commonwealth mantle that may soon be discarded, post-Soviet governments will have to deal, among other problems foreign and domestic, with tensions of class and economic inequality for which they are ill-prepared.

NOTES

1. For some thought-provoking observations on some of these issues before Gorbachev's USSR went into its crisis phase, see Paul Goble, "Gorbachev and the Soviet Nationality Problem," in M. Friedberg and H. Isham, eds., *Soviet Society Under Gorbachev* (Armonk, N.Y.: M. E. Sharpe, 1987), pp. 76–100.

2. Figures are derived from Goskomstat SSSR, *Sotisial'noe razvitie SSSR* (Moscow: "Finansy i statistka," 1988), pp. 107–108.

3. See, e.g., the discussion in Robert Lewis et al., *Nationality and Population Change in Russia and the USSR* (New York: Praeger, 1976), pp. 116 ff; also Ralph Clem, "The Ethnic Dimension of the Soviet Union," in Michael P. Sacks and Jerry G. Pankhurst, eds., *Contemporary Soviet Society: Sociological Perspectives* (New York: Praeger, 1980), pp. 11ff.

4. See L. A. Gordon and V. V. Komarovskii, "Dinamika sotsial'no–professional'nogo sostava pokolenii," *Sotsiologicheskie issledovaniia*, no. 3, 1986; also F. R. Filippov et al., "Trudovye biografii pokolenii," *Sotsiologicheskie issledovaniia*, no. 4, 1986.

5. Source noted in Table 1.

6. See the major report, P. O. Kenkman, E. A. Saar, M. Kh. Titma, "Sotsial'noe samoopredelenie pokolenii (issledovanie kogorty s 1948 po 1979 g., Estonskaia SSR)," in AN SSSR, ISI, *Sovetskaia sotsiologiia*, vol. 2 (Moscow: Nauka, 1982), pp. 82–110; a summary of path analysis of the intergenerational mobility component, A. V. Kirkh and E. A. Saar, "Prichinaia model' mobil'-nosti molodezhi," *Sotsiologicheskie issledovaniia*, no. 1, 1984, pp. 70–73, both translated in *Soviet Sociology* 14(1–3) (1985–1986):180–214 and 173–179, and A. V. Kirkh, "Opyt izmereniia mezhgeneratsionnoi mobil'nosti molodezhi," *Sotsiologicheskie issledovaniia*, no. 4, 1984, pp. 108–113.

7. We use only the male component of the study in this section, because of the readier alignments of socio-occupational categories of fathers–sons than mothers–daughters—the differences (see Kirkh, "Opyt izmereniia," p. 109) are not great.

8. The table lacks the marginals, in either numerical or percentage form that would allow us to calculate cell frequencies, "inflow" as opposed to outflow consequences of the changes over the generations.

9. See Rasma Karklins, *Ethnic Relations in the USSR: The Perspective from Below* (Boston: Allen and Unwin, 1986), p. 108. for some discussion of this likelihood.

10. Some of the feeling likely in this regard, and the brutality and "exoticism" of Soviet invaders can be gathered from Jan Gross's excellent account of the USSR's 1939 invasion of eastern Poland; see *Revolution from Abroad: The Soviet Conquest of Poland's Western Ukraine and Western Belorussia* (Princeton: Princeton University Press, 1988), esp. pp. 225–240; see also Romuald J. Misiunas and Rein Taagepera, *The Baltic States; Years of Dependence, 1940–1980* (Berkeley: University of California Press, 1983), pp. 15–125.

11. Karklins, *Ethnic Relations*, pp. 55, citing Rein Taagepera, "Baltic Population Changes, 1950–1980," *Journal of Baltic Studies*, 22(1) (Spring 1981):45.

12. Karklins, ibid., p. 53.

13. Ibid., p. 57.

14. See Radio Free Europe Research, *Situation Report/Baltic Area*, no. 2. (March 20, 1987), p. 19.

15. L. A. Gordon, A. K. Nazimova, "Proizvodstvennyi potentsial sovetskogo rabochego klassa: tendentsii i problemy razvitiia," *Voprosy filosofii*, no. 10, 1980, pp. 26–70 (trans. in *Soviet Sociology* 19(4) (Spring 1981):50.

16. The sociologist M. Kh. Titma, who directed the 1966–79 study, under the impetus of the Estonian reforming thrust, occupied in 1989 the secretaryship for ideology in the Estonian CP Central Committee—in effect, the

no. 2 slot. Some of his views are available in *Sovetskaia Estoniia,* Feb 22, 1989; more strongly, the *Financial Times* (July 25, 1989, p. 2) reports his words in an interview with *Sovetskaia Rossiia.* "Forty-nine years ago against the people's will Stalin's regime set up a Soviet republic in Estonia. Fifty years of Soviet power have not given any victory to Estonians. On the contrary, the nation has been suppressed. The desire of the absolute majority of Estonians to leave the Soviet Union is absolutely normal."

17. See *Izvestiia,* April 29, 1987, p. 7; *Sovetskaia Latviia,* April 27, 1989, p. 1. (FBIS, May 10, 1989, pp. 60–61); *Sovetskaia Latviia,* April 29, 1989, p. 3 (FBIS, May 11, 1987, p. 66).

18. See Dzintra Bungs, "A Victory for Reformers in Estonia and Latvia," RL, *Report on the USSR,* April 28, 1989, pp. 15–17.

19. RL, *Report on the USSR,* August 4, 1989, pp. 35–36.

20. See the following for some aspects of the development of a "worker" based, essentially conservative political force: *Leningradskaia pravda,* April 25, 1989, pp. 1–2 (*FBIS,* May 5, 1989, p. 46); *Pravda,* April 27, 1989, p. 4; *Sovetskaia Rossiia,* May 7, 1989, p. 1. (*FBIS,* May 15, 1989, p. 65); *Pravda,* April 27, 1989, p. 6; *Pravda,* April 27, 1989, p. 7; *Trud,* April 7, 1989, pp. 1–2; *Sotsialisticheskaia industriia,* May 1, 1989, p. 1.

21. The present author addresses some of the general class implications in *The Accidental Proletariat: Workers, Politics, and Crisis in Gorbachev's Russia* (Princeton: Princeton University Press, 1991).

22. *Moscow News,* no. 10, 1989, p. 4 (*FBIS,* March 16, 1989, pp. 85–86).

23. Moscow TV, 1500 GMT, March 29, 1989, (*FBIS,* April 3, 1989, p. 63).

24. As reported by Bill Keller, *New York Times,* July 27, 1989, p. 10.

25. See Annette Bohr, "Health Catastrophe in Karakalpakistan," *Report on the USSR,* July 21, 1989, pp. 37–38; also see Esther Fein in *New York Times,* August 14, 1989, p. 1.

26. See Boris Rumer, *Soviet Central Asia: "A Tragic Experiment"* (Boston: Unwin Hyman, 1989).

27. Nancy Lubin, *Labor and Nationality in Soviet Central Asia: An Uneasy Compromise* (Princeton: Princeton University Press, 1984).

28. Ibid., p. 64.

29. Ibid., pp. 160–162.

30. Ibid., p. 153.

31. Ibid., p. 169.

32. Ibid., pp. 197–199.

33. Ibid., p. 138.

34. Ibid., pp. 58–59.

35. Ibid., p. 234.

36. See *Izvestiia,* June 20, 1989, p. 6; *Izvestiia,* June 21, 1989, p. 3.

37. Lubin, *Labor and Nationality,* pp. 138–39.

38. *Pravda*, June 24, 1989, p. 6.

39. *Pravda*, May 3, 1989, p. 6 (*FBIS*, May 3, 1989, p. 42).

40. *Turkmenskaia iskra*, May 7, 1989, p. 1 (*CDSP*, July 18, 1989, p. 23).

41. *Pravda*, July 16, 1989, cited in RL *Report on the USSR*, July 28, 1989, p. 44.

42. See Ytizhak Brudny, "The Heralds of Opposition to *Perestroyka*," *Soviet Economy* 5 (2) (1989).

43. Mary McAuley, "Nationalism and the Soviet Multi-ethnic State," in Neil Harding, ed., *The State in Socialist Society* (Albany: SUNY Press, 1984), pp. 187–188.

44. Ibid., p. 188.

45. Teodor Shanin, "Ethnicity in the Soviet Union: Analytic Perceptions and Political Strategies," *Comparative Studies in Society and History* (1989), p. 422.

46. See Peter Hauslohner, "Gorbachev's Social Contract," *Soviet Economy* 1(3) (1987): and Walter D. Connor, *Socialism's Dilemmas: State and Society in the Soviet Bloc* (New York: Columbia University Press, 1988), ch. 6.

12. The End of Sovietology: From Soviet Studies to Post-Soviet Studies

Alexander J. Motyl

For better or for worse, Mikhail Gorbachev revolutionized the Soviet Union *and* the study of the Soviet Union. After the haphazard collection of half-reforms known as perestroika brought about the end of the Soviet "internal" empire, the end of Sovietology became inevitable. And just as such developments may lead to the reintegration of Eastern Europe into Europe, so, too, they may herald the integration of Sovietology into political science.

Regardless of how one views Gorbachev—as devilishly clever, supremely inept, or simply overwhelmed by unanticipated events—one thing is quite clear: after perestroika, the former Soviet Union will never be the same. Regardless of what the future holds for the Commonwealth of Independent States, the hypercentralized nature of the Soviet state is a "relic of the past," the formerly Sovietized republics will emerge as full-fledged international actors, and the idea of a European "common home" will move several steps closer to reality.[1]

The implications of such developments for Sovietology are obvious. If the Commonwealth comes to be dominated by Russia, contemporary "Soviet" studies will become little more than an offshoot of Russian studies. Although Russia will remain an important country—something in the nature of a Third World great power—it will be only one of many, equally interesting, independent East European states. Sooner or later, therefore, scholars with an interest in the dramatic changes taking place in all of Eastern Europe will turn inevitably to *post-Soviet* studies—or the comparative study of the post-totalitarian countries of Eastern Europe and the formerly Sovietized republics.

Similar conclusions present themselves if the Commonwealth of Independent States remains just that. Under such conditions, it will be even less possible to privilege Russia over the republics, as the intellectual justification for "Russian studies" will be quite slim in a context of state equality. Soviet area studies will necessarily be the study of independent republics, of which Russia will be but one.[2] Whatever the future of the Commonwealth, therefore, the future of Sovietology is clear. Post-Soviet studies will be comparative nationality studies, with the difference, of course, that the nationalities will be called nations and their republics will be designated states.

Such a fate bodes well for Sovietology, as it means that Soviet studies will become, *volens nolens,* a form of comparative politics. After several decades of discussing the desirability or possibility of such a transformation,[3] Sovietologists will be faced with a *fait accompli* brought about by Gorbachev. Two sea changes are thus in the offing for Sovietologists. First, they will have to acknowledge the importance of the Sovietized nations and, second, they will have to begin thinking as comparativists, as genuine political scientists.[4] There are enormous obstacles to such a perestroika of the field. Institutional interests, professional inertia, personality conflicts, and other, strictly speaking nonintellectual, factors are sure to get in the way. Only "life itself," as the Russians like to say, can resolve these problems. More important for my purposes is that transforming Sovietology into a form of comparative politics will also require a complete rethinking of the conceptual and theoretical apparatus that guided the profession in the 1970s and 1980s.[5] It is this fundamentally intellectual barrier that will, I submit, have to be overcome for post-Soviet studies to be able to emerge as a branch of comparative politics.

In his perceptive survey of theoretical approaches to the study of the USSR, Ronald Amman distinguishes between what he calls "Group A" and "Group B" theories. The former "place a heavy stress on the maximization of power and privilege of the elite," while according to the latter, the "elite constantly looks beyond its own narrow interests and preoccupations to the systematic promotion of mass consumption, security and welfare." Naturally, as Amman notes quite rightly, "these two approaches are not absolutely distinct because there will always be some trade-off between elite self-interest and public welfare in any set of policy options."[6]

Although Amman's distinctions are valid, their analytical utility would be greatly enhanced by means of two emendations. First, his suggestion that both groups of theories enjoy more or less equal status is unpersuasive. Surely, just as Group A theories—which I shall term "social control" approaches—were most prominent in the 1950s and early 1960s, so, too, Group B theories—which I shall call "social contract" approaches—have dominated the field since then. As a result, Group B theories may legitimately be said to have defined the Sovietological mainstream in the 1970s and 1980s.

Second, and no less important, Amman's treatment of both groups of theories is, ironically, curiously atheoretical, in that he by and large fails to explore the conceptual underpinnings of the two approaches. Correcting Amman's oversight, we may conclude that the mainstream paradigm rests on the interaction of at least three central concepts—consensus, political culture, and social contract—and on one theoretical pillar, the priority of the "base." According to this paradigm, relations between Soviet society and the state are essentially harmonious. Obviously, this approach recognized the existence of alcoholism, racism, deviance, blackmarketeering, and other dysfunctional *social* phenomena, but they did not detract from the view of Soviet *politics* as being, despite its profoundly nondemocratic character, fundamentally responsive to the needs of society. Part of the reason for so large a degree of cohesiveness between the social and political spheres was political culture, which was supposed to be nonparticipatory, conformist, even authoritarian. The Soviet population was claimed to be relatively quiescent, not too demanding, and fundamentally satisfied with restrictions on what we, and not they, would consider to be freedoms. No wonder, then, that dissent generally was deemed "marginal" and a "social contract" was said to exist between society and the state: the passive masses required only certain social amenities to continue in their self-satisfaction and consensus. Naturally, a framework such as this had to rest on a reductionist view of politics. The "state," in the Weberian sense of the term, largely was removed from analysis, the Communist Party was transformed into an aggregator of social interests, and society—especially its craving for consensus, passivity, iron rule, and social guarantees—was assigned priority over both.

The obverse of this conceptual and theoretical apparatus, the social control theories that defined the mainstream of the 1950s and early 1960s, was relegated to the margins of the profession in the 1970s and 1980s. This "marginal" framework consisted of its own set of conceptual and theoretical priorities: dissensus, coercion, and opposition were the key concepts, while the superstructure, in particular the "state," was given priority over society. Supporters of this view "saw" what mainstream Sovietologists claimed was not there: extensive disharmony and conflict between society and the state, the importance of state coercion in maintaining the outward stability of an inherently repressive system, the centrality of opposition—and not of social contracts—to state-society relations, and the priority of the directive and manipulative state over society. Unlike their mainstream colleagues, supporters of this framework often appreciated that the key manifestation of Soviet societal dissensus was the nationality question, that the manner in which social dissatisfaction was repressed and the state's policy preferences were imposed involved the exercise of coercion by the secret police, and that the inevitable outgrowth of such fundamentally disharmonious relations between society and the state was opposition of the former, or of significant elements thereof, to the latter. From this perspective it was the state that ruthlessly pursued its preferences and imposed its priorities on society and the Party that, rather than being an aggregator of societal interests, was a parasite at best and a tyrant at worst.[7]

Clearly, the events of the last few years have undermined the mainstream social-contract view, while legitimizing the formerly marginal social-control position. There can surely be no question—as even Soviet officials have admitted by explicitly rejecting Brezhnevite ideology, which Amman, with unintentional irony, also subsumes under the Group B category[8]—that there was far less consensus than imagined, that societal quiescence was as much imposed as chosen, that social contract was a euphemism for social resignation, and that the actions of the state did matter. Just as surely, there can be no question that nationality tensions and class conflict were and are rampant, that coercion was immense in the Brezhnev era, that opposition was far more widespread than believed, and that systemic reform is impossible without reform of the state.

But it is not just that the mainstream approach failed to see the "reality" under Brezhnev. Far more serious, it also failed to come to grips with developments under Gorbachev. By focusing on consensus, political culture, social contract, and society, the mainstream could not account for the disharmony, participation, turmoil, and reforms from above of the Gorbachev period. Worse still, the social contract paradigm led us to expect a continuation of the social passivity, nondemandingness, consensus, and Party legitimacy of the past, especially if social controls were lifted and coercion was reduced, as they were under perestroika. In contrast, the "marginal" approach to Soviet

reality fares much better. By emphasizing the state, coercion, disharmony, and opposition, it led us to expect just what happened in
1985–1991: the explosion of popular activity that followed the removal of coercive controls and the manifest recognition by the Soviet
leadership that the state was as responsible for the "deformations" of
the past as it must be responsible for the reforms of the present and
future.

Naturally, neither of these two approaches should be taken for the
last word on Soviet studies. Just as it was excessive for the marginal
approach to have been banned from Sovietological discourse—to such
a degree that graduate students were unwilling to utilize it lest they be
tarred as reactionary[9]—so, too, *and I stress this point most emphatically,*
it would be incorrect to enthrone it permanently. Rather, Sovietologists should recognize the current utility of this approach while remaining sensitive to the importance of the insights provided by the
social contract paradigm. John A. Armstrong's advice remains as wise
today as it was in 1973:

> The conception of Sovietology as a technology implies that it should use
> not a *single* paradigm derived from the generalizing social sciences, but a
> variety of models relevant to its particular concerns. . . . What I am advo-
> cating, therefore, is that Sovietologists draw freely on what appear to be
> the best and most relevant social science conceptualizations, while keeping
> in mind that these frameworks are expendable *if* they are transcended by
> the parent social sciences *or if* they prove to be useless for specifically
> Soviet problems.[10]

Coming to terms with the social control paradigm would be far easier
for Sovietologists were it not for the awkward fact that it closely
resembles the so-called "totalitarian model"—a point Amman under-
lines.[11] And it was, of course, the full-scale rejection of the totalitarian
model in the 1960s that impelled scholars to search out and adopt its
polar opposite. I have discussed elsewhere why scholarly dislike of the
totalitarian model should be so intense, and the reasons for such
passionate attitudes need not concern us here.[12] Precisely because
opposition to it is so impassioned, however, it is imperative that a
balanced reevaluation of totalitarianism—a term I shall use inter-
changeably with "totalitarian model"—be attempted.

As developed by Hannah Arendt, Carl Friedrich, Zbigniew Brzezinski, and other scholars, the totalitarian model was an apt enough

description of the Soviet Union under Stalin and Nazi Germany under Hitler.[13] Its empirical adequacy notwithstanding, totalitarianism suffered from two failings that contributed greatly to its eventual demise. On the one hand, totalitarianism was said to be a "model." As Frederic J. Fleron, Jr. persuasively argued, however, bona fide models are not just collections of descriptive statements.[14] Rather, models are inextricably connected to theoretical perspectives, or "axiom systems," and thus are "drastically simplified representation[s] of the real world endowed with strong explanatory power."[15] Genuine models, in other words, are not "snapshots," but theoretically grounded attempts at explanation. From this perspective, the totalitarian model clearly was no such thing, as it was unconnected to any larger theory. Fleron's criticism did not exclude the theoretical possibility of such a grounding, but his remarks remained a fair indictment of the totalitarian model's exaggerated theoretical airs.

Few Soviet specialists pursued Fleron's line of argument, perhaps because it was based on an unusually sophisticated reading of the philosophical literature on the nature of scientific enquiry. Instead, the line of attack adopted by most Sovietologists in the 1960s—and continued more or less unchanged to the present—was much more down to earth: that the totalitarian model's descriptive statements were inaccurate.[16] Once again, the charge was not unfounded. What originally passed for the totalitarian model was mostly a set of observation statements—propositions ostensibly derived from observable empirical data.[17] These observation statements might have been appropriate for certain periods of the Soviet and Nazi experiences, but they were, by their very nature as empirical observations, incapable of accurately describing other periods. Quite rightly, as the model's critics pointed out, Friedrich and Brzezinski's list of totalitarianism's characteristics was inadequate as an overall description of the Khrushchev or Brezhnev periods.

With respect both to totalitarianism's inadequacies as a model and as a collection of observation statements, the popularizers of the term had mostly themselves to blame for the confusion that followed. Their casual use of the word "model" led critics such as Fleron to attack totalitarianism's explanatory pretensions, while their failure to distinguish sufficiently between observation statements and analytical typologies led their more vociferous, more numerous, and frequently indiscriminating critics to reject totalitarianism's claim to be an analytically valuable tool. The first problem is insurmountable because totalitarianism cannot, and therefore should not, be developed into a full-blown theory; the second problem can be corrected by recognizing that totalitarianism is not a description but a particular kind of concept.

It is hard to imagine what a specifically totalitarian theory would be like, as the elements that comprise the totalitarian model can be fitted to any theoretical framework—be it that of collective choice, political culture, political economy, class conflict, or some other perspective. But such malleability only underscores the fact that, while many theories *of* totalitarianism are possible, totalitarianism itself cannot be a theory. Once this deceptively simple point is recognized, totalitarianism's analytical utility becomes obvious. Because it is not a theory, then it is not a "body of systematically related generalizations of explanatory value."[18] As it is not a set of observation statements, then it makes little sense to counter its claim to utility by arguing that other observation statements are at variance with those of totalitarianism.

What, then, *is* totalitarianism? Quite simply, it is a *typological construct*. As such, it enables scholars with comparative and theoretical inclinations to differentiate among types of states, political systems, regimes, or other entities to which the construct might be affixed. As will shortly be evident, my own preference is to apply totalitarianism to states, but there is no reason, other than utility and persuasiveness, why scholars should not choose a different unit of analysis. If totalitarianism is to be useful, therefore, its aspirations must be modest: merely to provide scholars with one element of a possible typology that facilitates the ordering of observation statements and the comparison of political units in a theoretically consistent manner.[19]

Typologies are, quite rightly, of little interest to idiographically inclined scholars, but they are the lifeblood of those who desire to engage in nomothetic work.[20] Only typologies can group likes and sort out unlikes, thus enabling scholars to draw relevant comparisons and search for common explanations. Just as comparative politics is impossible without explicit or implicit typologies, so, too, I suggest that the study of the USSR cannot be integrated into comparative politics without the resurrection, if only briefly, of a totalitarian type.

There are many reasons for Sovietology's inability to join comparative politics—some of them are pedagogical, others are historical, still others relate to its policy orientations.[21] Perhaps most important of those reasons that involve its methodological inclinations, however, is the profession's abandonment of the totalitarian concept. In so doing, Sovietologists attained the exact opposite of what they claimed they were after: they not only cut themselves off from typological inquiries altogether, but they also effectively undermined comparison of the Soviet Union with other countries. In a word, *volens nolens* they made the USSR unique. After all, sophisticated adherents of the totalitarian model never insisted on the Soviet Union's uniqueness, as even during the model's heyday totalitarianism was presumed to be the state or system type of which Nazi Germany, the USSR, and a host of other Communist polities were referents. Quite the contrary, rejection of totalitarianism effectively precluded comparison of the USSR with other systems. On the one hand, the USSR's natural points of reference, other totalitarian states, were definitionally excluded from the pool of comparables, while, on the other hand, comparisons with nontotalitarian systems inevitably broke down, so that comparison itself appeared futile. The short-lived utility of pluralist approaches to the USSR is testimony to the fact that typology conflation goes hand in hand with concept stretching and that both are ultimately counterproductive.[22]

Notwithstanding revisionist attempts to think away the Soviet state, the fact is that the pre-perestroika Soviet Union, as well as Nazi Germany, the People's Republic of China, North Korea, Albania, and other pre-1989 Communist states, *were* different, and radically so, from run-of-the-mill dictatorial states, such as Franco Spain. This point, which Juan Linz made some two decades ago and which Phillipe Schmitter restated in somewhat different fashion in 1973, needs no repeating here.[23] Clearly, the most important distinguishing characteristic of totalitarian states is their remarkable *comprehensiveness,* a property with two dimensions: extensiveness and intensiveness, with the former denoting the horizontal *breadth* of a state's involvement with social institutions and the latter the vertical *depth* of a state's penetration of these institutions. Unlike other types of states, ideal-type totalitarian states not only extend into virtually all of a society's nooks and crannies; they also penetrate its institutions "totally," they manage them "completely." The result is that, where totalitarian states exist, *civil* society, as a bounded collection of autonomous public institutions, is always absent, although *some* social institutions may of course be present.[24]

The polar opposite of the totalitarian state may therefore be termed the "laissez-faire" state, which extends into society and penetrates its institutions *minimally,* if at all. Where laissez-faire states exist, we also expect civil society to be "strong." Positioned mid-way between these polar opposites are various states we may designate as "regulative," involving different combinations of extensiveness and intensiveness. Anarchy is, of course, the polar opposite of the state as such.

Naturally, the supervision of social institutions by a totalitarian state may or may not be fully effective—which is simply to say that totalitarian states can be ineffective—but it remains comprehensive nonetheless. This distinction, which lies at the heart of much of the confusion surrounding totalitarianism, is grounded in the difference among states, regimes, and rule. Totalitarianism, at least according to my usage, is a feature only of states, referring specifically to their structural involvement in and penetration of society. Democracy, oligarchy, monarchy, and other such terms refer to types of regime, more precisely, to the manner in which governments are formed and to the rules according to which they function. Finally, the expansion or contraction of the field of permissible behavior, the involvement or noninvolvement of the police, the use or nonuse of terror—all of these are examples of rule and, as such, do not belong to the defining characteristics of totalitarianism. It may very well be the case that totalitarian states incline toward certain regimes and policies—surely, we would not be remiss in expecting them to be repressive and dictatorial—but it is nevertheless critically important not to confuse central characteristics with defining ones and, thus, to produce a catch-all notion that verges on description and eschews conceptualization.[25]

An immediate benefit of defining totalitarianism in this manner is that an unambitious version of the concept permits Sovietologists to get a handle on the enormous changes that swept the Soviet Union since 1985. Indeed, one of the major theoretical lessons of the Gorbachev era is that something like totalitarianism is necessary to explain the former USSR's current transitional stage, a point made persuasively by Geoffrey Hosking.[26] If we acknowledge only regulative and laissez-faire states, or some variants thereof, as valid state types, then we are forced to adopt one of two counter-intuitive positions in light of the vast political changes that have already occurred: either that the former USSR is not engaged in a major transition and that it will stay within the general category of a regulative state, or that it has already made a full-scale transition to a laissez-faire state and that further typological change is impossible. By adding a third category, totalitarianism, we can better appreciate the magnitude both of the change that has already transpired—from totalitarianism to regulativeness—and of the change that must still occur for laissez-faire status to be achieved.

Another major lesson is that the emergence of Soviet civil society cannot be understood without equal attention to the withering away of the totalitarian state, the former comprehensiveness of which was the primary obstacle to civil society's emergence. However true it may be that pre-perestroika Soviet society was neither monolithic nor fully regimented, no amount of pointing to variety, diversity, and textual richness can negate the obvious—that the autonomous public institutions characteristic of civil society were absent. The social historians and their supporters in political science and sociology thus had the logic wrong: although a variety of social processes may be the necessary conditions of the emergence of civil society, they are never sufficient.[27] Rather, it is the totalitarian state—more precisely, the *detotalization* of the totalitarian state—that is the sufficient condition of such an emergence. As Hosking notes quite rightly, "There is no straightforward transition from social to political change. A sophisticated society is a necessary condition for sophisticated politics, but it is by no means a sufficient one. So what stands in the way? The obstacle, as I see it, is the political system handed down from Stalin."[28]

Although resurrecting something like a totalitarian type seems indispensable both to integrating Sovietology into comparative politics and to understanding the former Soviet Union, the methodological utility of totalitarianism may not suffice to overcome a seemingly insurmountable obstacle within the mainstream of the Sovietological profession—the view that totalitarianism is so politically and ideologically slanted as to be useless.[29] There are several responses to this objection.

Even if we accept the implicit endorsement of a hard and fast distinction between facts and values, one may suggest that, in the final analysis, it is immaterial what the term is as long as the concept is retained. If scholars could agree—an unlikely prospect if there ever was one!—on some other term, that would be fine. Despite the connotational richness of totalitarianism, the term is secondary to the concept that it connotes and to the empirical referents that it denotes. Of course, the fact that scholars may not agree on the meaning of totalitarianism is as little a strike against the concept as their inability to reach a consensus on state, nation, ethnicity, class, and revolution is a blow against the utility of these "essentially contested concepts."[30]

There are, however, at least three good reasons—Giovanni Sartori provides many more—for retaining totalitarianism as a term.[31] The first is that its suggestion of totality, of total control, is useful in distinguishing certain types of states that aspire to, if not quite achieve, such control, from others that do not. As noted above, there is something approaching totality about the comprehensiveness of political power and the absence of civil society in the pre-perestroika USSR, other Communist states, and Nazi Germany.

The second argument is that the term is favored by important constituencies in the countries concerned. East European and Soviet dissidents utilized the concept because it seemed to capture a reality they believed was fundamentally different from the experience of most interwar East European states. Soviet scholars and officials also resurrected the concept with regard both to the Stalinist system and to the "period of stagnation" under Brezhnev.[32] The All-Union Association of Young Philosophers and Historians, for example, even held a conference on totalitarianism and published the proceedings as a book entitled *Totalitarianism as a Historical Phenomenon*.[33] There is, of course, no reason for Western scholars to adopt uncritically what East European dissidents and scholars—or, most recently, presidents, such as Vaclav Havel and Gorbachev—suggest, but, surely, their endorsement cannot reflect negatively on totalitarian terminology, if only because it removes the label of "hysterical anti-Communism" that was attached to the term. No less important, Western scholars desirous of engaging their East European colleagues in dialogue will have no alternative but to come to grips with the concepts that make up their particular discourse, however alienating they may at first seem.

Finally, it is not unimportant that totalitarianism does, as its critics contend, have moral overtones. Indeed, to label a system as totalitarian is to brand it as highly obnoxious. Students of other parts of the world—such as the dependencia theorists—do not refrain from making moral judgements about the systems they study. Indeed, students of Nazi Germany are virtually obligated to condemn the entire period. And the truth is that the pre-perestroika Soviet states *were* stifling. As Czeslaw Milosz, surely no hysterical reactionary, cogently put it: "A truth, banal today, deserves to be repeated: The Soviet Union was created by a totalitarian party responsible for unspeakable crimes against humanity."[34] The so-called Gorbachev experiment promised an improvement in human rights, a lessening of repression, and greater democracy, and, quite naturally, most scholars welcomed these trends. Why? Surely not only because such developments are of intellectual interest only, but also because scholars support, or claim to support, human rights. There is, I suggest, nothing wrong or "unobjective" about joining the rising chorus of Russians and non-Russians who denounce the political system inherited from Stalin, Brezhnev, and Gorbachev. Indeed, if anything, silence in the face of such obvious injustice may be more worthy of condemnation.

Will these arguments persuade hardened opponents of the totalitarian model? Probably not. There is little that can—or should—be done about the nonintellectual bases of such opposition. But because those scholars who, like Hosking, reevaluate the concept and come to recognize its utility will be ideally positioned to come to grips with the rapidly changing USSR, we may expect "life itself" to ensure that a kind of bandwagoning will eventually take place.[35] After all, not only will such scholars be able to comprehend both the profound nature of the USSR's transformation *and* the resilience of reactionary forces, but they will also be able to view the dynamics of that transition comparatively, both in relation to the totalitarian states the USSR used to resemble and the laissez-faire or regulative states that its successor states may come to resemble. No less important, such scholars will be able to embark on their own transition to appreciating, and perhaps modifying, the unjustly neglected Group A framework that accounts so well for the magnitude of the USSR's turmoil and the importance of the nationality question.

Ironically, audacious scholars will resurrect the totalitarian concept only to abandon it—a prospect that may soften the opposition of intransigent opponents of the word. Its utility, after all, will be limited to the present period of turmoil. Although a reversion to a thoroughly inefficient form of totalitarianism in some of the USSR's successor states is not a completely preposterous notion, they are far more likely to be, at most, highly regulative. To be sure, post-Soviet studies will make broad use of *post-totalitarianism* as a designation for the state, system, or regime that succeeds totalitarianism, but few opponents of the latter notion will object to a term that represents its demise. However transient its usefulness to scholars, therefore, totalitarianism will have served its purpose—of sensitizing Sovietology to the usefulness and transience of all paradigms, of transforming Soviet studies into post-Soviet studies, and of accelerating the integration of post-Soviet studies into political science. Gorbachev could be envious of that much glasnost, perestroika, and *uskorenie*.

NOTES

I thank Gregory Gleason, Frederic Fleron, Giovanni Sartori, and Edward Walker for their comments on earlier drafts of this essay.

1. For an elaboration of these arguments, see Alexander J. Motyl, "Empire or Stability? The Case for Soviet Dissolution," *World Policy Journal* 8(3) (Summer 1991):499–524; "Totalitarian Collapse, Imperial Disintegration, and the Rise of the Soviet West," in Michael Mandelbaum, ed., *The Rise of Nations in the Soviet Union* (New York: Council on Foreign Relations, 1991), pp. 44–63.

2. For a criticism of these tendencies, see Alexander J. Motyl, " 'Sovietology in One Country' or Comparative Nationality Studies?" *Slavic Review* 48(1) (Spring 1989): 83–88.

3. A comprehensive overview of Sovietology's flirtations with comparative politics is available in Gabriel A. Almond, *A Discipline Divided: Schools and Sects in Political Science* (Newbury Park, Cal.: Sage, 1990), pp. 66–116.

4. An attempt to integrate Sovietology with political science is made in Alexander J. Motyl, ed., *Thinking Theoretically about Soviet Nationalities: History and Comparison in the Study of the USSR* (New York: Columbia University Press, 1992).

5. For a discussion of some of these issues, see Alexander J. Motyl, *Sovietology, Rationality, Nationality: Coming to Grips with Nationalism in the USSR* (New York: Columbia University Press, 1990), pp. 1–13.

6. Ronald Amman, "Searching for an Appropriate Concept of Soviet Politics: The Politics of Hesitant Modernisation?," *The British Journal of Political Science* 16(4):477–478.

7. See Kenneth Jowitt, "Soviet Neo-Traditionalism: The Political Corruption of a Leninist Regime," *Soviet Studies* 35(3) (July 1983):275–297.

8. Amman, "Searching," p. 479.

9. I base this statement on my own personal experience with graduate student advisees at Columbia University. Despite the profession's self-perception as a liberal enterprise, students are extremely sensitive to the politically correct boundaries that may be crossed only at one's risk.

10. John A. Armstrong, "Comments on Professor Dallin's 'Bias and Blunders in American Studies on the USSR'," *Slavic Review* 32(3) (September 1973):585–586.

11. Amman, pp. 478–480.

12. See Alexander J. Motyl, "Building Bridges and Changing Landmarks: Theory and Concepts in the Study of Soviet Nationalities," in *Thinking Theoretically about Soviet Nationalities*, pp. 255–270.

13. The classic statements of the totalitarian model are Hannah Arendt, *The Origins of Totalitarianism* (New York: Harcourt Brace, 1951) and Carl J. Friedrich and Zbigniew Brzezinski, *Totalitarian Dictatorship and Autocracy* (Cambridge: Harvard University Press, 1956).

14. Frederic J. Fleron, Jr., "Soviet Area Studies and the Social Sciences: Some Methodological Problems in Communist Studies," *Soviet Studies* 19(3) (January 1968):313–39.

15. On axiom systems, see A. R. Lacey, *A Dictionary of Philosophy* (New York: Scribner's, 1976), pp. 12–13. The definition of model is from Giovanni Sartori, "Guidelines for Concept Analysis," in Giovanni Sartori, ed., *Social Science Concepts* (Beverly Hills, CA: Sage, 1984), p. 79.

16. See Abbott Gleason, " 'Totalitarianism' in 1984," *The Russian Review* 43 (1984):145–59; Jerry F. Hough and Merle Fainsod, *How the Soviet Union Is Governed* (Cambridge: Harvard University Press, 1979), pp. 518–22.

17. Regarding "observables," see Ernst Nagel, *The Structure of Science* (Indianapolis: Hackett, 1979), 2nd ed., pp. 79–90.

18. Sartori, "Guidelines for Concept Analysis," p. 84.

19. On totalitarianism as one element of a different typology, see Edward W. Walker, "Totalitarianism, Comparative Politics, and Sovietology," Unpublished paper, March 1988; Jim Seroka, "Typologies of Socialist Systems," in Anton Bebler and Jim Seroka, eds., *Contemporary Political Systems* (Boulder, Col.: Lynne Rienner, 1990), pp. 141–152.

20. For a discussion of the conceptual issues involved in typologizing and classifying, see Alberto Marradi, "On Classification," in Bebler and Seroka, eds., *Contemporary Political Systems*, pp. 11–43.

21. See Joseph LaPalombara, "Monoliths or Plural Systems: Through Conceptual Lens Darkly," *Studies in Comparative Communism* 8(3) (Autumn 1975):305–332; Frederic J. Fleron, Jr. and Erik P. Hoffmann, "Sovietology and Perestroika: Methodology, Madness, and Lessons from the Past," September 26, 1990, Unpublished manuscript.

22. The notion of concept stretching is discussed in Giovanni Sartori, "Concept Misformation in Comparative Politics," *American Political Science Review*, no. 4 (December 1970):1033–53.

23. See Juan Linz, "Totalitarian and Authoritarian Regimes," in Fred Greenstein and Nelson Polsby, eds., *Handbook of Political Science*, III (Reading, Mass.: Addison-Wesley, 1975), pp. 175–411; Philippe Schmitter, "Still the Century of Corporatism?," *Review of Politics*, no. 36 (January 1974). Schmitter's monist state is for all practical purposes totalitarian.

24. On civil society, see John Keane, ed., *Civil Society and the State* (London: Verso, 1988).

25. Sartori, "Guidelines for Concept Analysis," pp. 28–35.

26. Geoffrey Hosking, *The Awakening of the Soviet Union* (Cambridge: Harvard University Press, 1990), pp. 1–18.

27. For example, see S. Frederick Starr, "Soviet Union: A Civil Society," *Foreign Affairs,* vol. 70 (Spring 1988).

28. Hosking, *Awakening,* p. 5,

29. For example, see Alfred G. Meyer, "Coming to Terms with the Past ... And with One's Older Colleagues," *The Russian Review* 45(1986):402–403.

30. William Connoly, *The Terms of Political Discourse* (Lexington, MA: D. C. Heath, 1974). Consider the confusion surrounding the concept of the "state," as discussed by James N. Rosenau, "The State in an Era of Cascading Politics: Wavering Concept, Widening Competence, Withering Colossus, or Weathering Change?," in James A. Caporaso, ed., *The Elusive State* (Newbury Park, CA: Sage, 1989), pp. 17–48.

31. Giovanni Sartori, "Totalitarianism: An Exercise in Conceptual Analysis," Unpublished manuscript, 1991.

32. See, especially, A. M. Migranian, "Vzaimootnoshenie individa, obshchestva i gosudarstva v politicheskoi teorii marksizma i problemy demokratizatsii sotsialisticheskogo obshchestva," *Voprosy folozofii,* no. 8 (1987), pp. 75–91.

33. A. A Kara-Murza et al., eds., *Totalitarizm kak istoricheskii fenomen* (Moscow: Filosofskoe obshchestvo SSSR, 1989).

34. Czeslaw Milosz, "Some Call It Freedom," *New York Times,* August 8, 1991.

35. Hosking's willingness to change his mind about a concept is as commendable as it is unusual in Sovietology. Contrast his current views on totalitarianism with those expounded in *The First Socialist Society* (Cambridge: Harvard University Press, 1985).

36. See Juan Linz, "Some Thoughts toward a Characterization of Post-Totalitarian Authoritarian Regimes," Unpublished paper.

About the Contributors

Wakter Connor. John R. Reitemeyer Professor of Political Science, Trinity College.

Ronald Hill. Professor of Soviet Government, University of Dublin.

Neil Harding. Professor of Politics, University College of Swansea.

John Hazard. Nash Professor Emeritus of Law, Columbia University.

Mark Beissinger. Professor of Political Science, University of Wisconsin-Madison.

Amy Knight. Researcher, Federal Research Division, Library of Congress.

Theodore Friedgut. Professor of Russian Studies, Hebrew University.

Zvi Gitelman. Professor of Political Science, University of Michigan.

Walter Connor. Professor of Political Science, Boston University.

Richard Ericson. Professor of Economics and Director of The Harriman Institute, Columbia University.

Gregory Gleason. Professor of Political Science, University of New Mexico.

Alexander J. Motyl. Associate Director of The Harriman Institute, Columbia University.

Index